England and Wales Described. In a Series of Letters

The South West Pros.

hect of Salisbury Cathedral.

ENGLAND and WALES

DESCRIBED.

IN A

SERIES of LETTERS:

EXHIBITING

Whatever is worthy the Obſervation of the Curious Traveller, as well as all others, who wiſh to be made acquainted with the Beauties of this happy Country.

Lately written from different Parts of the Kingdom, And principally to a Gentleman in the Iſle of Wight.

TO WHICH ARE ADDED,

Hiſtorical, Critical, and Explanatory Notes.

By WILLIAM TOLDERVY,

Editor of a COLLECTION of EPITAPHS, &c.

VOL. I.

LONDON:

Printed for L. DAVIS and C. REYMERS, and W. FLEX-NEY, in Holborn; W. OWEN, near Temple-Bar; and J. FLETCHER and Co. in St. Paul's Church-Yard.
MDCCLXII.

PREFACE.

NUMEROUS have been the Writers upon the following Subject; which, after all, has been treated perhaps worfe than any other. This Circumftance, true as it is, muft appear fingular to Foreigners; who may fairly conclude us unequal to the Tafk of defcribing diftant Countries, when few or none have been found able to write a good and perfect Defcription of our own. The Author of the prefent Undertaking would not be underftood in a *particular Senfe*; nor be thought to fpill a Drop of Ink as a Blot on the great Merits of *Bede, Giraldus Cambrenfis, Leland, Camden*, or his right reverend and learned Editor. To thefe, and alfo to that moft excellent Difcoverer of Errors regarding Antiquities, Dr. *William Stukeley*, he acknowledges himfelf to

be

be greatly indebted : But as all thefe (excepting Bifhop *Gibfon)* have wrote of *England* as it appeared formerly, or regarding fome particular Antiquities, it has been thought necef-fary to attempt fomething that may at once pleafe the Antiquarian and the modern Archi-tect, the Hiftorian and Politician, the Admirer of Cities, and the Lover of rural Plea-fures.

A Work of this Denomination, written without Regard to *Antiquities,* and without applying them to Story, muft be flat and infipid. *Hiftory* without *Geography,* is but half under-ftood. Were *Architecture* omitted, the Fault would be unpardonable. And above all, were the lavifh *Beauties* of *Nature,* fo abundant in *England* and *Wales,* to be in any Sort neglect-ed, the Intent and Defign of the Work muft be fruftrated.

There have not indeed been wanting thofe, who, in their Chambers, have defcribed Hills, Rocks, Woods, Caves, Meads, Rivers, and gently purling Rills in *England,* which never had Exiftence. In the Courfe of this Work, fome of thefe Accounts will be tenderly exploded ; not out of a Difpofition to Petulancy, but a neceffary Regard to common Juftice : For though a Writer may, in fome Works, find Advantage accruing from Invention, this Subject requires ftrict Adherence to Truth. It is impoffible to learn practical *Geography* at Home, and 'tis a dangerous Matter to take De-fcripscriptions upon the Credit of the Unskilful. Even *Camden*, whose early Taste for the Study of *English* Antiquities was extraordinary, found himself far from being qualified for the arduous Task of writing his *Britannia*, before he had personally visited the greatest Part of the Kingdom : And it was owing to some late Excursions, which he thought necessary to make, even after the sixth Impression, that he was enabled to complete a Work, which, in the Writings of the learned, gained him the Titles of the *Varro*, the *Strabo*, and the *Pausanias* of *Britain*. Certainly Study is a solid Nourishment of the Mind, and the Spring of its most noble Qualities ; but 'tis looking into, conversing with the World, and seeing the Beauties of Nature, that can make the Scholar a compleat Gentleman. It has been thought a Matter of Concern, to see our young Gentlemen of Fortune and Distinction so entirely bent upon trifling Pleasures and airy Diversions, as unpardonably to neglect those Improvements in Wisdom and Knowledge, which may render them easy to themselves, and useful to the World; hurrying, or being hurried away, over Part of the Continent, where they are unable to say any Thing material regarding the Beauties of their native Country !

To rouse such from an unpardonable Indolence, and to excite in them the laudable Curiosity of visiting their delightful native Country, as well as to afford Information to others, whose Avocations or Infirmities bid a

Denial

Denial to travel, the following Letters are publifhed: Not from Remarks *collected in the Clofet*, but from thofe taken in *actual Vifitations* of the Places which they defcribe. A Circumftance which muft neceffarily prove of great Inftruction and Ufe to thofe Foreigners, whom Curiofity or Bufinefs may induce to vifit this Ifland.

Confcious therefore of having endeavoured to ferve the Public, by laying before them an *Original Work*, actually written in the feveral genuine Tours, the Author has fome Reafon to flatter himfelf, that it will meet with a favourable Reception. The Manner and Execution of it, he freely fubmits to the Judgment of the Candid and the Judicious.

" Whofoever thou be (fays *Drayton* *)
" poffeffed with fuch Stupidity and Dulneffe,
" that rather than thou wilt take Paines to
" fearch into ancient and noble Things,
" choofeft to remaine in the thicke Fogges
" and Mifts of Ignorance, as near the
" common Layftall of a CITIE; refufing
" to walke forth into the *Tempe* † and Feelds
" of the Mufes, where, through moft de-
" lightful Groves, the angellique Harmony
" of Birds fhall fteale thee to the Top
" of an eafy Hill; where, in artificial
" Caves, cutt out of the moft naturall Rock,
" thou

---

* In his *Poly-Olbion*.

† A pleafant Valley, at the Foot of Mount *Hæmus* in *Theffaly*, celebrated by all the Poets as the *earthly Paradife*, and the moft delicious Place on the whole terreftrial Globe.

" thou fhalt fee the ancient People of this
" Ifle delivered thee in their lively Images;
" from whofe Height thou mai'ft behold,
" both the old and later Times, as in thy
" Profpect lying farre under thee : Then
" conveying thee downe, by a foule-pleafing
" Defcent, through delicate embroidered
" Meadowes, often veined with gentle glid-
" ing Brooks, in which thou mai'ft fully view
" the dainty Nymphs in their fimple naked
" Beauties, bathing them in chryftalline
" Streames; which fhall lead thee to moft
" pleafing Downes, where harmleffe Shep-
" herds are; fome exercifing their Pipes,
" fome finging Roundelaies to their gazing
" Flocks. If, as I fay, thou hadft rather re-
" maine where thou wert than ftraine thy-
" felfe to walk forth with the Mufes, the
" Fault proceeds from thy Idleneffe, not from
" any Want in my Induftrie."

England

England and Wales

DESCRIBED.

L E T T E R I.

From *Southampton*.

S I R,

THE two Promiſes which I had the Honour of making to you, when we left *Goſport*, I ſhall moſt punctually adhere to: Namely, in perſevering to ſerve you in your private Affairs, and in endeavouring to entertain you with the Accounts of my Travellings, ſo far as my future Obſervations, and the Remembrance of what I have read, will enable me. Theſe Taſks will be attempted with the more Alacrity, becauſe to oblige you is my Ambition; and in affording you Amuſement, I ſhall add to my own Pleaſures. According to your Requeſt, I ſhall tranſmit the Subjects upon different Papers, ſo that the one may employ your ſerious,

the

the other, your indulging Hour. You will not
fail, from Time to Time, to inform me of your
being at your beloved Retirement in the *Iſle of
Wight*, or that you are attending thoſe Employments in *London*, which you ſo worthily fill.

I think it was about Noon when I took my
leave of you, and your very agreeable Company:
And, together with Mr. *Charleton*, went on
board *Watſon*'s Hoy, bound to *Southampton*.
The Wind, I remember, was rather in your Favour, and, having hoiſted your little Sails, you
ſmoothly ſlid away; when, as Mr. *Whitehead*
prettily expreſſes it,

> —— We ſaw the riſing Gales
> Curl o'er the Deep, and ſwell the parting Sails:
> Swift glides the Bark, as ſwift our Eyes purſue,
> Catch the laſt Glance, and die upon the View.

Our Veſſel moved but ſlowly, which gave me
the better Opportunity of viewing (with my Glaſs)
the *Iſle of Wight*: This had an exquiſitely fine
Appearance, as had alſo *Calſhot-Caſtle*, and that
Part of the main Land of *Hampſhire* on our
Left; but what gave moſt Delight to my Eyes,
was the Ships of War, which gallantly rode at
Spithead, with the Admiral's Flag abroad.
Theſe I had with Pleaſure obſerved for many
Days, from the Ramparts at *Portſmouth*, but
now my Leave of them was nearly taken. Our
preſent Laureat, the ſame Mr. *Whitehead*, thus
addreſſes their Commanders.

> Chiefly you, who ride the Deep,
> And bid our Thunders wake or ſleep,
> As Pity pleads, or Glory calls——
> Monarchs of our wooden Walls!
> Midſt our mingling Seas and Skies,
> Riſe, ye *Blakes*, ye *Raleighs*, riſe!

Let

Let the fordid Luft of Gain
Be banifh'd from the liberal Main,
He who ftrikes the generous Blow,
Aims it at the public Foe.
Let *Glory* be the guiding Star,
Wealth and *Honours* follow her.

And afterwards,

If protected *Commerce* keep
Her Tenor o'er yon heaving Deep,
What have we from *War* to fear?
Commerce fteels the Nerves of *War*;
Heals the Havoc *Rapine* makes,
And new Strength from *Conquest* takes.

Soon after, our Veffel entered *Southampton* Water, the Banks of which are vaftly delightful.
Within a fhort Time we came in Sight of *Southampton*, and having left the Mouth of the River
Itchin on our Right, we drove up before a charming double Row of Trees planted on the Beach,
and, by Affiftance of a Boat, landed at the Key,
which is a very convenient one. The Officers
were not fo troublefome, but that I got the
fmall Prefent of Arrack you intended for the old
Gentleman, delivered fafe; and having fpent
the Evening very agreeably with him, the next
Morning he not only accompanied me about the
Town, and gave me many Informations regarding it; but alfo introduced me to Company,
who, for Politenefs and Good-Breeding, are
equal, I affure you, to any in *London*. I found
him to be much efteemed by the better Sort,
and one of thofe few, who, having known
the World, turn that Knowledge to its proper
Ufe. A late Author very judicioufly obferves,
" that, as there is nothing more ridiculous than
a trifling old Story-Teller, fo there is nothing
more venerable than one, who having gained
Expe-

Experience, turns it to the Entertainment and Advantage of Mankind." *Shakefpear*, in the Character of Juftice *Shallow*, has given us an high Picture of the Folly of old Fellows delivering Accounts of their youthful Vices : For he even makes *Falftaff* himfelf, in a Soliloquy, condemn and deny every Word that the Juftice had fpoken. But fo very fenfible and obliging is this Gentleman in the Day, and fo entertaining over the Bottle of the Evening, that I have continued at *Southampton* longer than really I intended. However, I purpofe proceeding farther in the Morning, after which you may expect fome Account of this agreeable Town. I have the Pleafure of fubfcribing myfelf, Sir,

Your moft humble and obedient Servant.

L E T T E R II.

From *Redbridge*, in *Hampfhire*.

S I R,

YESTERDAY in the Morning I left the pleafant Town of *Southampton* ; and arrived at this Place about Noon. *Southampton* is fituate between the Rivers *Teft* * and *Itchin*, the firft of which, after having paffed the Towns of *Stockbridge* and *Rumfey*, falls into *Southampton* Water, oppofite to the Window where I now write. The *Itchin* arifes above *Alresford*, and paffing that Place, moves on to *Winchefter*, and falls into the fame Water to the Eaft of *Southampton* Town.

---

* Mr. *Hanway* calls this River the *Tees*, and fays, it waters *Andover*. Thofe who have only read *Camden*, and confulted the Maps of this County, know him to be miftaken.

Town. Our Searchers into Antiquities tell us, that near it stood the *Roman Clausentum*, from whence they derive the name *Hanton*, or *Hampton*; and there are some Vestigia (perhaps) of a *Roman* Fort. But be that as it may, this however is certain, that *Southampton* has been frequently, and most grievously harrassed by those cruel Invaders the *Danes*; who at length became so pleased with its Situation, that, according to some of our Historians, their Kings made it a Place of their Residence, or, at least, they very often visited it. The Story of *Canute*'s sitting upon the Beach here at the rising of the Tide, is well known * : And his sycophantic Courtiers received a severe Check in that Action. Perhaps the Ministers of those Days had not read *Tully*'s

Account

---

* About the Year 1030, King *Canute*, commonly called the *Great*, being at *Southampton*, his Courtiers extolled him with the most fulsome Compliments, even at the Expence of Divinity itself. But *Canute* despising such Flattery, resolved, as an unanswerable Argument against all they had been saying, to give them ocular Proof that there was no more Divinity about the Person of a King, than about that of a Subject. For he ordered his Chair of State to be set within Flood-Mark, while the Tide was flowing; and then addressed the Sea in the following Terms: " Over thee, O Sea, I have Command, and the Strand on which I sit, is mine: Disobedience to me never goes unpunished; therefore upon thy Peril, advance no farther; nor presume to wet the Feet of thy Sovereign Lord." But the Waves, deaf to the Royal Voice, rolled on; at first besprinkled, then all over dashed the Royal Person; whereupon, *Canute*, as if surprized at the Disobedience of that Element, started up; and chiding his Courtiers for flattering him into a Belief of his Power, which might, upon Trial, have proved fatal to his Person, represented to them the narrow Limits of earthly Majesty, compared to that which can bind up the Ocean, and say to its Billows, *Thus far, and no farther, shall ye go.* He then, by Way of Penance, walked home wet-shod as he was, and never after wore his Crown, but commanded it should be put upon the Head of the Crucifix at *Winchester*.

Account of *Damocles,* and *Dionyſius* the Tyrant:
The latter of whom having been extolled as a
God by the former, cauſed him to be dreſſed in
the moſt ſplendid Manner, and commanded to
be laid before him the richeſt Viands that could
be obtained ; but, at the ſame Time, ordered a
drawn Sword to be hung over his Head, with the
Point downward, and ſuſpended only by a ſingle
Thread ; which ſo much affected him, that he
had no Enjoyment of his Dreſs, or Stomach to
eat. In the Reign of *Edward* the Third, this
Town was burnt down by the *French* ; but ſoon
after was rebuilt, and fortified with Walls, Battlements, and a deep Ditch ; which at high
Tides was ſupplied with Water ; and King *Richard* the Second built a ſmall, but ſtrong Caſtle,
which greatly added to the Defence of the
Town. In the Year 1410, it was in a very de-
fenſible State, as may be gathered from *William
de Langfelde,* then a Monk of *Reading.*

———— There is a gallant Town,
Well noted for her mighty Trade, I wis ;
Her Maidens Chaſtity hath moche Renoun,
Wel built, and very woondrous faire it is.
Her Walls with Battlements ful thicke I-ſtond,
And eke her Ditch ful wel ſecures the ſame.
So that no Foe mote hurt with hoſtil Hand ;
Her Sons for doughtie Dedes have laſting Fame ;
Cloſe by the Sea ſhe ſtonds, *Suthampton* is her Name.

When the heroic King *Henry* the Fifth had determined to invade *France,* he cauſed his Army to
rendezvous here : And having ordered the Earl
of *Cambridge,* the Lord *Scroop,* and Sir *Thomas
Gray,* to be executed for a Conſpiracy againſt his
Life , he wrote a Letter to *Charles* the Sixth of
France, and dated it from *Southampton by the
Sea-Side.* He ſoon after embarked his Men at
this

this Port, and our inimitable *Shakefpear* hath very finely defcribed that Royal Fleet, when juft got under Sail,

————— Suppofe that you have feen
The well-appointed King at *Hampton* Pier,
Embark his Royalty; and his brave Fleet
With Silken Streamers the young *Phœbus* fanning.
Play with your Fancies, and in them behold
Upon the hempen Tackle Ship-Boys climbing:
Hear the fhrill Whiftle, which doth Order give
To Sounds confus'd; behold the threaden Sails
Borne with th' invifible and creeping Wind,
Draw the huge Bottoms through the furrow'd Sea,
Breafting the lofty Surge. O, do but think
You ftand upon the Rivage! and behold
A City on th' inconftant Billows dancing;
For fo appears this Fleet majeftical,
Holding due Courfe to *Harfleur*.

The prefent Condition of *Southampton* is, that the Walls, as built in *Edward* the Third's Time, are in a great Meafure ftanding; as are alfo the Watch-Towers; and the Veftigia of the Ditch, which almoft encompaffes the whole Town, is very confpicuous. The Caftle, built by his Grandfon, King *Richard* the Second, is quite gone: But the Mount where it ftood is in the North-Weft Quarter, and feems to have been the Work of Art. It commands a fine Profpect over the Town, towards the Sea; as alfo over the Water to the *New Foreft*, and another towards the Eaftern Parts of the County. There is an old ftrong Building at the other End of the Town-Wall, which feems to have been intended for a Caftle; and erected at the fame Time with that Wall. This Fabric, were it more properly formed, and fortified with Cannon, might command the Entrance to the Key, by finking a Privateer or two, from whom only
they

they have any Thing to fear. But this Building is, I think, now ufed as a Jail. So that
Southampton hath no Fortification to defend it;
except we can fuppofe *Calfhot* fufficient for that
End, or lay any Strefs on fix or feven old Iron
Guns, and a Brafs one of *Harry* the Eighth,
which lie upon an old rotten Platform on the
Sea-Wall, near the Jail aforefaid. From this
Platform, almoft to where the River *Itchin* difembogues itfelf, runs the fame Sea-Wall, planted
with a double Row of Trees, fome Part of which
is a pleafant Walk ; but the whole might, with a
fmall Expence, be made vaftly delightful. So
alfo may another pretty Walk be made betwixt
the Bowling Green and the Town-Ditch, which
Ditch might be converted into agreeable Gardens. The old Gateway, which leads from the
Key to the principal Street, hath fomewhat venerable in its Appearance ; and feems to be of
like Antiquity with the Town-Wall. This Street,
which is as broad as *Cheapfide*, hath a gradual
Afcent of near half a Mile, thro' very handfome
Buildings, to a modern Gate, over which is the
Effigies of the late Queen *Anne*. On the other
Side of this Gate are the Arms of the Town,
and alfo the Supporters, which look almoft as
terrible as the Giants in *Guildhall, London*.

Here is a Bridge over the Town-Ditch, which
leads to the Suburb ; and this being on the
Summit of the Hill, and in general well built,
is the pleafanteft Part of *Southampton*. At the
Corner of the Road which turns towards *Redbridge*, and *Rumfey*, is a very grand Houfe now
building, that hath a moft charming Profpect.
In the Town are five Churches, but they have
nothing extraordinary in them. *Southampton* is
in general well built, and a deal of genteel Company

pany vifit it in the Summer Seafon, efpecially to bathe in the Sea. Its Trade, when all *Canary* Wines imported into *England*, (and then very much drank) were obliged to be landed here, was prodigious ! But after that Privilege was removed, the Town declined; though it now feems to be in a flourifhing Condition. Their Trade to *Oporto* is confiderable, and they are remarkable for importing the beft Wines from that Place; or, if you pleafe, for lighter Hands in the Bufinefs of Adulteration. To *Guernfey* and *Jerfey*, they deal very largely: Pretty much to *France* in Times of Peace, and fome to *Newfoundland*, and the *Streights*. Befides they have a good Coafting Trade, efpecially to the South of *Wales*. Provifions are cheap here in the Winter, but fomewhat otherwife during the Time of the *Country Gentry*, and the *Londoners* Vifitation. Fifh is in Plenty, but as many *French* Families are Inhabitants here, it is not extremely cheap, though I faw excellent Salmon fold for feven Pence a Pound. Here are feveral Conduits of good Water, but the Place is not fo well fupplied with that ufeful Article as fome others are.

The Town is a County in itfelf, and hath a Court of Judicature in all criminal Cafes. The Affize of Oyer and Terminer in general is held here once in three Years, by a Judge on the Weftern Circuit. Here is a Mayor, nine Juftices, one Sheriff, two Bailiffs, twenty-four Common-Council-Men; who, with twenty-four Burgeffes, have the Right to elect two Members to Parliament. The Mayor is Admiral of the Liberties of *Hurft*, near *Limmington*, to *South-Sea-Caftle*.

The Markets are on *Tuefdays* and *Fridays*, and their Fairs (which are chiefly for Horfes, Cattle and Leather) on the 25th of *April*, and *Trinity-Monday*.

Here is a Free-School, founded by King *Edward* the Sixth.

The Day being fine, the old Gentleman accompanied me in my Vifit to *Netley* or *Letley-Abbey*. We croffed the Mouth of the *Itchin*, and foon after came to this Piece of Antiquity, which was founded by King *Henry* the Third, and called *Letley*, or *Locum Sancti Edwardi*, but now by Corruption, has the Name of *Netley*. That King endowed it with Lands, in the thirty-fifth Year of his Reign. It was valued at the Diffolution of Religious Houfes, at One hundred and feventy-four Pounds Three Shillings *per Annum*. The Remains of it, which I had feen a Profpect of from *Southampton* Water, are very venerable, of which Mr. *Buck* has publifhed a beautiful View.

Southampton gave Birth to the able and honeft Sir *Thomas Lake*, Secretary of State to King *James* the Firft.

Among the Number of Perfons, to whom this Town has given the Title of Earl, I fhall only mention three. And firft of *Bogo*, *Beavois*, or *Bevis*. He was a *Saxon* Lord of much Power, and having a great Averfion to the *Normans*, in the Conqueror's Time, gathered an Army, and gave them Battle at *Cardiff* in *Wales:* From whence he fled to *Cumberland*, and what became of him afterwards we know not : For the Monks have fo dreffed him up, and loaded his Story with fuch Improbabilities, that the excellent *Drayton* thought proper to expofe thofe idle Tales, which he has finely done in the fuppofed Difpute at his Affembly of Rivers and Forefts.

There

There is at *Padworth*, not far from the Town, a Place called *Bevis-Mount*, now the Seat of Colonel *Mordaunt*, which I shall hereafter visit.

The Title of Earl of *Southampton* lay dormant 'till King *Henry* the Eighth conferred it on *William Fitz-Williams*, Grandson to *John Nevil*, Marquis of *Montacute*, after his having been his Ambassador in *France*, Admiral of the Fleet, Treasurer of the Houshold, Captain of *Guisnes*, Knight of the Garter, and Lord Privy Seal. I don't know, that (according to our best Historians) the Annals of *England* can shew us a more excellent Character than this Nobleman bore. In his Youth he had distinguished himself in successful naval Exploits, and when in the Cabinet of that unaccountable Monarch, maintained his Posts by Prudence and Magnanimity. He died in an Expedition against *Scotland*, universally beloved, esteemed, and regretted.

Henry Wriothesly, Grandson to the Chancellor of *England*, succeeded his Father as Earl of *Southampton*. He was a Person of Courage, and one of the gallant Soldiers at the taking of *Cadiz*, in the Reign of *Elizabeth* ; and so great a Patron to Learning and Men of Genius, that, according to Sir *William D'Avenant*, he made a Present of a thousand Pounds to *Shakespeare* at one Time. He was General of the Horse in *Ireland*, when *Essex* was Deputy of that Kingdom ; and afterwards joined him in his Insurrection in *London* ; for which they were both tried by their Peers, and condemned. *Essex* suffered, but *Southampton* was pardoned, and afterwards in much Favour with King *James* the First.

By this Time you may say, that I have employed my Pen as a Biographer, but as this is a Licence which you have occasionally allowed me, I have

no

no Cenfure to fear. The Title which this Place now gives is that of Duke, in the Perfon of *William Fitzroy*, Duke of *Cleveland* and *Southampton*, and Earl of *Chichefter*, who is Comptroller of the Seal or Green-Wax-Office; and Receiver and Comptroller of the Seals in the King's Bench and Common Pleas. He lives, when retired, at *Bayles* in *Buckinghamfhire*. I think to reach *Rumfey* this Evening, where I hope to receive your Difpatches; and am, Sir, *Yours.*

L E T T E R III.

From *Great-Bridge*, near *Rumfey*, in *Hampfhire*.

S I R,

I AM now again upon the Banks of the *Teft*: And the Houfe from whence this Letter is fent, hath one of the moft pleafing Situations that can be found in a Vale. Before its Front the River is divided into three Streams, and a fourth enclofes the Garden behind; indeed they may be called five fmall Rivers, for the fartheft of them, which is about the Size of the *New River* at *Iflington*, is feparated a little lower; and thofe two wafh the Streets of *Rumfey*. This Valley, where that Town alfo ftands, being very even, the *Teft* may, without Difficulty, be turned almoft to any Part of it; and the Quantity of Water is fo great, that a Navigation thereon might, with much Eafe, be completed. Millions of Beauties now decorate the fragrant Meadows, and the Induftry of the Hufbandman is exhibited on the verdant Slopes; while the allbounteous Hand of Nature is cloathing the Woods, which cover the gently-rifing Hills !

The

The Cuckow is pleafing the Farmer with Hopes of a ten-fold Encreafe, and the Milk-maid, with Mind undifturbed, fings chearfully *Nan of the Vale!* The Fifherman patiently waits for the Pike, or the rich-fpotted Trout, and thoufands of neighbouring Rooks attend on their unfledged Young.

But to return. Leaving the Town of *South-ampton*, on the Right-Hand Side of the Road is a Bank of what they call *Sea-Ore*, becaufe the Filaments of which it is compofed are thrown up by the Sea. They have the Appearance of pill'd Hemp, and are very tough and lafting; and where the Sea is not more agitated than at *South-ampton*, fuch a Fence may anfwer the End of breaking the Force of the Waves : But in Places more expofed, a Bank of this Sort would be of no Service*.

The Way from *Southampton* to *Redbridge* is vaftly rural and pleafing, the different Views over the Water are charming, and the ravifhing Mufic of the feathered Choir beyond Defcription ! *Redbridge* hath for many Years, as well as *South-ampton*, been famous for building of Ships, both for the Government and the Merchants; and there is at this Time a large Quantity of Timber on the Banks of the Water for thofe Purpofes. The Village itfelf is inconfiderable in Building. Indeed there is one large handfome Inn, and a Wharf for loading and difcharging Ships, for which together my Hoftefs told me fhe paid Two hundred Pounds a Year; but fhe obferves, that if the War continues, fhe muft decline the Occupation of the latter.

Venerable

---

* The Authors of the *Tour through Great-Britain* fay, " It performs its Work *better* than Walls of Stone or natural Cliff."

Venerable *Bede* calls this Place *Vadum Arundinis*, which he interprets *Reedford* : But by the Building the Bridge, the Name became changed to *Reedbridge* or *Redbridge*. This Building is of Stone, feems to be very ftrong, and leads the Traveller the direct Road from *Southampton* to *Salifbury*. *Camden* fays, that in the Infancy of the *Saxon* Church, here ftood a Monaftery of which one *Cymberth* was Abbot: When the Tide is in, the Woods, with intermixed Buildings on the oppofite Side, have, over this large Expanfe of Water, a moft delicious Effect ! Above the Bridge are many Wears for the catching of Salmon ; which Species of Fifh, I think, is here as high flavour'd as thofe of the *Severn* or the *Wye*.

Having left mine Hoftefs, I rode three or four Miles to an Hut-like Public-houfe, whofe Sign is the *Horns*, (in the great Road from *Southampton* to *Rumfey*) near which, on a large Common, was Part of the *Warwickfhire* Militia under Arms. Curiofity led me to the Place, and I was greatly furprized at their Dexterity in the manual Exercife. So much was I pleafed with them, that I continued there near an Hour, and on my Way to *Rumfey*, amufed myfelf with thinking on this laudable national Scheme : For as *Iflanders*, and *Lords of the Main*, what can we have to fear from foreign Enemies when the Militia becomes general ?

My Lord of *Denbigh* is Colonel of the Regiment of *Warwickfhire*, and I learn from the private Men, that he loves, and is beloved by his Soldiers ; they alfo are lavifh in their Praifes of the two Mr. *Greathceds*, Officers in the fame Corps ; this ought to be the Cafe with every Officer either at Land Sea. From the *Horns* to *Rumfey*, the Country is very beautifully diverfified with

Woods,

Woods, Lawns, Fields, enamelled Meadows, and gently-flowing Rills of cryftal Water. Near one of thefe, it being fomewhat hot, I alighted, and fat me down under the friendly Shade of a venerable Oak ; when the delightful Harmony of innumerable Birds foon carried my Memory to thofe fweet Lines of Mr. *Smart*, which are fo excellently fet to Mufic by Dr. *Boyce*.

> Near fome Cowflip-painted Mead,
>   There let me doze out the dull Hours,
> And under me let *Flora* fpread
>   A Sofa of the fofteft Flowers.

> Where, *Philomel*, your Notes you breathe
>   Forth from behind the neighb'ring Pine ;
> And Murmurs from the Stream beneath
>   Still flow in Unifon with thine.

I am inclined to think, that had *Rowe*, or *Addifon*, never vifited fuch Scenes as this, the World would be now without the two moft charming paftoral Songs in the *Englifh* Language. Having here folaced myfelf a full Hour, I arrived foon after at an handfome Building called *Broadlands* Houfe. It is fituate on a Bank of the River *Teft*, about half a Mile from *Rumfey*; and was erected by Sir *John Saint Barbe*, the Defcendant of that antient and illuftrious Family; and feems to be of about fixty Years ftanding. The Front, which looks through double Rows of venerable Chefnut Trees towards the high Road, is (as was the Cuftom before Light became fo much loaded) well ftored with Windows. The Gardens flope down to the River's Brink (which hath a large Share of various Fifh). Here is an Hot-Houfe and alfo a good Collection of Orange and other exotic Trees and Shrubs. The late Lord Vifcount *Palmerfton* purchafed this Seat for the Refidence of a younger Son, who

who dying without Issue, it reverted to his Nephew, the present Lord, a Minor; and his Trustees have let it out to the Earl of *Powis*, who visits it generally in the Season for shooting Partridge.

At the Post-Office in *Rumsey*, I had the Pleasure of receiving your Packet; and to the Contents thereof I shall be very attentive. This Town being situated in a Valley, and but few Miles from the Sea, is in the Winter much subjected to Fogs and hazy Weather; and the Soil being somewhat greasy, it is vulgarly termed *Rumsey in the Mud*. But since the Turnpike Roads are finished, it is rendered much more agreeable, and the People live to considerable Ages. The *Saxons* gave it the Appellation of *Rumseg*, or *Romseg*, and 'tis now indifferently spelt *Rumsey* or *Romsey*. King *Edward* the Elder built here a considerable Monastery of the Order of *St. Benedict*, in which his Grandson, King *Edgar*, in the Year 907, settled religious Nuns, under the Government of *Merwina*, their Abbess. *Edgar*, *Henry* III. and *Edward* I. were Benefactors to this House, and confirmed the Lands and Liberties to the same. At the Dissolution of Religious Houses, it was valued at Three hundred and ninety-three Pounds Ten Shillings and Ten Pence *per Annum*. The Remains of the Abbey are now very small, but the Church which belonged to it is almost entire. Mr. *Buck* has taken a View of the whole. This Building, which, according to Custom, is erected in Form of a Cross, with the Tower in the Midst, is strong and lofty, though not an elegant Fabric, even for those Times [*]. It has six heavy Bells

---

[*] The Authors of the *Tour through Great-Britain* say, that " The Roof of the South Cross is decayed, and, if not repaired

Bells, but not many Monuments of Note. There is indeed one, of curious Marble, to the Memory of one of the *Saint Barbe*'s, his Wife and Children, but 'tis the worst Piece of Sculpture I have ever seen, excepting that of Baron *Reynolds* at *St. Edmundsbury* in *Suffolk* Here is another for one Mr. *Kent*, who was a Silk-Throwster in *Spital-Fields, London;* and afterwards High Sheriff for this County ; and (the most remarkable Thing in the whole Church) in the same Isle, on a flat ordinary unpolished Stone, on the Floor, are these Words *literatim*, without any Date :

> *Here layes*
> *Sir William*
> *Pety* *.

I must own, that this poor Remembrance of so great a Man struck me with Surprize. He was Son of *Anthony Pety*, a Shalloon-Weaver in this Town ; was born in 1623, and, by the Power of an amazing Genius, acquired a Fortune of Fifteen thousand Pounds a Year! He was knighted by King *Charles* the Second, and died in 1689 ; and his Estate is descended to the present Earl of *Shelburn.* This Sir *William*, then Dr. *Pety*, was Surveyor-General of *Ireland*, under the Protector *Oliver* ; after whose Death, a Charge was brought against him in the Parliament of *Richard Cromwell*, by Sir *Hierome Sankey*, for embezzling Monies arising from the forfeited Estates. The Dr. came over from *Ireland* to vindicate himself, bringing with him a Letter from *Henry Cromwell*, then Lieute-

---

paired, will shortly fall in ". This might have been the Case when *Daniel De Foe* lived, but 'tis far from being so now.

* Mr *Hanway* calls this Gentleman Sir *William Pettit*. I am inclined to think it an Error of the Printer : For surely he could not mean *William Petyt*, Esq; who was of the *Inner Temple*, and Keeper of the Records in the Tower, in the Time of King *James* the Second! If he does, he is egregiously mistaken.

nant of that Kingdom, of which I have fubjoined a Copy; becaufe it fhews what an Opinion he had of the Dr. and, at the fame Time, affords us an Idea of his own Situation.

> Thefe for the Right Honourable *John Thurloe* Efq; Principal Secretarie of State, etc. at *Whitehall.*

SIR,

I have heretofore told you my Thoughts of Dr. *Petty*, and am ftill of the fame Opinion; and if Sir *Hierom Sankey* doe not run him down with Numbers, and Noife of Adventurers, and fuch other-like concerned Perfons, I believe the Parliament will find him as I have reprefented. Hee has curioufly deceived mee thefe foure Yeares if he be a Knave. I am fure the Juntoes of them who are moft bufie, are not Men of the quietteft Temper. I doe not expect you will have Leizure, or fee Caufe, to appeare much for him; wherefore this is onely to let you underftand my prefent Thoughts of him. The Activenefs of *Rob. Reynolds* and others in this Bufines fhews, that *Petty* is not the only Mark aimed at. But God's Will be done in all Things.

Pray let not the Bufines of my coming over wholy die, tho' it flumber for a While. It would be for the Conveniency of my own Affairs, to know whether it be probable, I may make a Step over this Summer. As for Things here, I refer you to the Bearer for the Accomt of them, and remane

April 11, 1659.   *Your very affectionat and humble Servant,*

H. CROMWELL.

Sir *William* gave the Rents and Profits of the Houfe in which he was born, with fome Addition, amounting in the whole to about twenty-feven Pounds a Year, to the Ufe of two Schools in this Town.   The

The Town of *Rumfey* is governed by a Mayor, fix Aldermen, twelve Burgeffes, &c. It is pretty well built. Here, in a fpacious Place, ftands the Market-Houfe, which is very neat. On *Saturdays* is a good Market, but the Farmers ufe a Cuftom, too much fuffered in *England*, of felling their Grain by Samples. The Fairs, which confift principally of Cattle, Horfes, Swine, and Cheefe, are held on *Eafter-Monday*, *Aug.* 26, and *Nov.* 8. The Tradefmen in general live very comfortably, and though the Number of Gentry is very fmall, the Town is not without a genteel and well-managed Boarding School for young Ladies. Here is carried on a large Manufactory of excellent Shalloons; but the pernicious and fcandalous Practice, fo much ufed in the Weft of *England*, of obliging the poor *Weaver* to take in Part of the Payment for his Labour what they call *Truck*, is not unminded here. For out of every ten Shillings earned by his Induftry, he is forced to lay out two in the Commodities which the Manufacturer or Mafter has to fell, who generally charges about thirty *per Cent.* more than the Market Price. It were to be wifhed, that the Parliament would look into this notorious Breach of *Britifh Liberty*.

On the different Streams of this Valley are many Mills for Corn, Paper, Leather, &c. which turn to good Account. The Church-yard being planted with fine fhady Chefnut Trees, is a very pleafant Place, having good Views over the Meads to delightful hanging Woods, which cover the gently-rifing Hills. And here I muft not forget an odd Production of Nature, which is an Apple-Tree that grows upon the Church, and bears Fruit every Year. The Church-Living is a pretty good one, but 'tis fuppofed that near one third Part of the Inhabitants are Diffenters, of the Prefbyterian Denomination. Lately that bufy Gof-

fip

fip Lady *Methodifm* has introduced herfelf here, and that too by the Means of fo inconfiderable a Perfon as a common *Drummer* in the Army! who, taking Advantage of the Credulity of a few Perfons, fo far prevailed, that they not only procured his Difcharge from the Parchment Rattle, and the murdering of Bodies, but fettled him in the more meritorious and peaceable Trade of Soul-faving; in which Occupation he holdeth forth with confiderable Applaufe, and hath many female Followers. Mr. *Cambridge* hath given us a droll Defcription of thefe modern Saints:

> The *Methodift*, in her peculiar Lot,
> The World forgetting, by the World forgot:
> Though fingle happy, though alone is proud,
> She thinks of Heav'n (fhe thinks not of a Crowd)
> And if fhe ever feels a vap'rifh Qualm,
> Some *Drop of Honey*, or fome *Holy Balm*,
> The pious Prophet of her Sect diftils,
> And her pure Soul feraphic Rapture fills;
> Grace fhines around her with fereneft Beams,
> And whifp'ring *W——* prompts her golden Dreams.

This Place being fo near the Coaft, is much burthened with Soldiers. Fifh and Port Wine are cheap, but Coals dear; the common People therefore burn Peat, with which the Valley abounds.

From *Rumfey* to *Great-Bridge* is an eafy, pleafant Mile, upon a good Road, between the Rivers, whofe pleafing Banks I fhall fpeedily leave, in order to purfue my Route to *Salifbury*. I am, Sir, Yours, &c.

LETTER IV.

From *Salifbury*.

SIR,

WRITING is now a greater Relief to me than I have ever found it before; for my

Obli-

Obligation to Punctuality in this Refpect, has been a fufficient Excufe for my leaving the Company of the moft unpleafing of Mortals ; I mean that of a *talkative old Batchelor.*

Leaving the Valley from whence my laft Letter was dated, I paffed through fome pleafing woody Lanes, to a wide and heathy Common : And having met with an agreeable Companion, we deviated from the direct Road to *Salifbury*, and paffed to *Poultons*, the Seat of Mr. *Stanley*, one of the Commiffioners of the Admiralty. The Road from a fmall Village to his Houfe is through a moft venerably delightful Grove of various Firs, other Trees, and Shrubs ; at the End of which, the Eye is fuddenly ftruck with a beautiful Lawn, almoft encompaffed by a large and fine Piece of Water; on the other Side whereof are other Lawns bordered with Woods, that afford a moft charming Contraft. The Houfe, though large, is but low, to which there is a Communication over a Bridge of a neat Conftruction. The modern Tafte of caufing *Art* to refemble *Nature* is here very excellent ; for the Water is formed fo as to reprefent a fmooth and noble River. From hence we proceeded to the *New Foreft*, as 'tis yet called, though completed near feven hundred Year ago.

In order to make this fpacious Foreft, *William* the Firft deftroyed no lefs than fix and thirty Parifh Churches ! a great Number of Villages, Hamlets, and Farms ; it therefore is, and will continue to be, a lafting Monument of *Norman* Tyranny.

Drayton was of Opinion, that he depopulated this Spot, that he might referve it as a Place for landing more of his Countrymen, if he fhould find their Affiftance wanting to continue his Seat upon the Throne.

Down

—— Down from *Sarum* Plains
Clear *Avon* coming in, her Sifter *Stour* doth call,
And at *New Foreſt's* Foot into the Sea do fall:
Which every Day bewail that Deed ſo full of Dread,
Whereby ſhe (now ſo proud) became firſt foreſted.
She now who, for her Site even boundleſs ſeem'd to lie,
Her Being that receiv'd from *William's* Tyranny.
Providing Laws to keep thoſe Beaſts here planted then,
Whoſe lawleſs Will from hence before had driven Men:
That where the Hearth was warm'd with Winter's feaſt-
    ing Fires,
The melancholly Hare is form'd in Brakes and Briars;
The aged rampick Trunk where Plowmen caſt their Seed,
And Churches overwhelm'd with Nettles, Ferne and Weed;
By conqu'ring *William* firſt cut off from every Trade,
That here the *Norman ſtill might enter to invade.*
That on this vacant Place and unfrequented Shore
New Forces ſtill might land, to aid thoſe here before.
                  POLY-OLBION,

But be this as it may, the late Mr. *Somervile*
thus extols *William,* as the firſt Improver of
Hunting in *England.*

      —— In this Iſle remote,
Our painted Anceſtors were ſlow to learn,
To Arms devote, of the politer Arts
Nor ſkill'd nor ſtudious; till from *Neuſtria's* Coaſts
Victorious *William,* to more decent Rules
Subdu'd our *Saxon* Fathers, taught to ſpeak
The proper Dialect, with Horn and Voice
To cheer the buſy Hound, whoſe well-known Cry
His liſt'ning *Peers* approve with joint Acclaim.
From him ſucceſſive Huntſmen learn'd to join
In bloody ſocial Leagues, the Multitude
Diſpers'd, to ſize, to ſort the various Tribes,
To rear, feed, hunt, and diſcipline the Pack.

The honeſt Monk, *Robert of Glouceſter,* was inclined to place the untimely Ends of Part of *William's* Family to the Account of his Tyranny; and it
muſt be confeſſed, that the Hand of Heaven, in
viſiting the Sins of the Father upon the Children,
ſeems to have been conſpicuous in theſe Inſtances,
                                  for

for here his Son, *William Rufus*, was fhot by an
Arrow from Sir *Walter Tyrrel*. Here, his Son
Richard was blafted with an Infection that killed
him; and here, his Nephew *Richard*, the Son of
Earl *Robert*, was, like *Abfolam*, catched in the
Bough of a Tree, which twifted him from his
Horfe, and broke his Neck.

The Warden of this Foreft has always been
fome Perfon of Rank and Diftinction. It did belong to the Earls of *Arundel* by Inheritance. One
of the prefent Rangers thereof is Mr. *Harry Bur-
rard*, of *Walhampton* near *Lymington*, Member of
Parliament for that Borough. In the *Foreft* are
nine Walks, to which belong one Keeper, two
Rangers, and a Bow-bearer. The Forefter of the
Bailiwic of *Tritham* is Lord *De la Warr*, who has
erected a Pillar with an Infcription, on the Spot
where *Rufus* was flain. This Infcription I fhall
hereafter fend to you.

At a Village called *White Parifh*, we came into
our Road again, which leads from *Rumfey* to *Sarum*; and about the fame Time left the County
of *Southampton* : The Lieutenant of which is
Charles Powlet, Duke of *Bolton*.

After our Departure from this Village, the
Country became more open, and here *Salifbury
Plains* begin. Having gained the Summit of a
Hill, we had a fine View of a charming champain
Country, in the Middle of which is a Valley,
where ftands the City of *Salifbury*; the lofty Spire
of whofe Cathedral, then about five Miles dif-
tant, had an excellent Effect. On our Right was
Clarendon-Park, near which is the Remains of a
Roman Camp, fuppofed to have been made by
Chlorus, the Father of *Conftantine*. From this
Fortification, doubtlefs, this Park had its Name
of *Clorendon* or *Clarendon*. King *Henry* the Second
held a Synod here, when Archbifhop *Becket*, and
the other Bifhops, fwore to the Articles of this
King's

King's Declaration; from whence they were call‑
ed the *Conſtitutions of Clarendon*. Here are the
Remains of two Palaces, called *King's Manor* and
Queen's Manor; the former was built by King
John.

King *Edward* the Second ſummoned another
great Council or Parliament to meet here, but the
Barons and *Commoners* diſobeyed, owing to a Diſguſt
taken at that King, on Account of his Favourites;
or, according to ſome Writers, for Fear of a
Plague and Famine, then raging in the Kingdom.
This Place gave the Title of Earl to the ever‑
famous Sir *Edward Hyde*, Lord Chancellor of
England, a Man of whom the World was then not
worthy. The Park is very large and beautiful;
which having left, in a ſhort Time we arrived at
this City.

Saliſbury, called in *Latin Saliſburia* or *Sariſburia*,
ſtands in the Midſt of a pretty and feitile Valley,
where the Rivers *Nadder* and *Willy* being joined,
fall into the *Avon*; whoſe detached Streams having
waſhed the Streets, it is augmented a little below
by the Waters of the *Bourne*; and, at *Hamham-
Bridge*, it begins to be navigable, and ſo continues
to *Chriſtchurch*, in the County of *Southampton*.
This Navigation was undertaken in the Year
1675, to which Dr. *Seth Ward*, then Biſhop of
this See, contributed largely.

The Situation of *Saliſbury*, though low, is ex‑
tremely pleaſant, and the Place is remarkably
clean; for there is ſcarce a Street in it which is not
waſhed by a clear and conſtant Stream of Water.
The Buildings are in general very good, eſpecially
thoſe in the Cloſe, near the Cathedral, and at the
Market-place. This laſt is a large and handſome
Square, where Five thouſand Men might be conve‑
niently drawn up, and, upon this fatal Spot, the
Tyrant *Richard* the Third, whoſe Court and Ar‑

rhy was then here, caufed the Head of his old Friend the Duke of *Buckingham* to be ftruck off.

In this Market-Place ftands the Town-Houfe, where, in the Council-Chamber, is an excellent original Picture of the late Queen *Anne*, drawn by the famous *Dahl*.

This City is the moft compact of any I have feen, excepting *Bath*; and owes its Rife to the Fall of *Old Sarum*, which was fituate about a Mile to the North of it, on a dry and barren Spot: To which Place (formerly a *Roman* Station) in the thirteenth Year of the Conqueror, the Bifhop's See was removed from *Sherborn* in *Dorfetſhire*: But afterwards King *Stephen*, having fome Difpute with the then Bifhop, feized his Caftle there, and the Citizens being much aggrieved with the Infolency of the Soldiery, diftreffed by the Scarcity of Water, and tired with the Keennefs of the Air, they removed their Habitations to the Vale where *Saliſbury* now ftands : Of which Matter Dr. *Walter Pope* thus merrily fings:

Old *Sarum* was built on a dry barren Hill,
    A great many Years ago :
'Twas a *Roman* Town, of Strength and Renown,
    As its ftately Ruins fhew.

Therein was a *Caſtle* for *Men* of *Arms*,
    And a *Cloyſter* for *Men* of the *Gown*;
There were *Friers* and *Monks*, and *Liars* and *Punks*,
    Though not any whofe Names are come down.

The Soldiers and Churchmen did not long agree :
    For the furly Men with the Hilt on
Made Sport at the Gate, with the Priefts that came late
    From fhriving the *Nuns* of *Wilton*.

Perhaps the Dr. is fevere : But, however, in the Year 1219, Bifhop *Poore*, having obtained Leave from the *King* and the *Pope*, began the Cathedral of *New Sarum* : When *Pandulph*, the Legate from *Rome*, laid the firft five Stones, *i. e.* for the *Pope*,

King *Henry* the Third, *William Longſpee,* Earl of *Saliſbury*; his *Counteſs,* and Biſhop *Poore.* The King and the Nobility contributed large Sums to this Work ; which, with Moneys raiſed by Indulgences, and the ſqueezing of dying Perſons by their Confeſſors, became completed in thirty-nine Years, at the Expence of Forty thouſand Marks. A prodigious Sum in thoſe Days !

It is now one of the moſt beautiful Gothic Buildings I have ſeen ; but, without believing Dr. *Pope*'s Tale of the Biſhop's Dream, one is at a Loſs to account for his beginning of it in ſo marſhy a Place.

> One Time as the Prelate lay on his Down Bed,
>   Recruiting his Spirits with Reſt,
> There appear'd, as 'tis ſaid, a beautiful *Maid,*
>   With her own dear Babe at her Breaſt.
>
> To him ſhe thus ſpoke (the Day was ſcarce broke,
>   And his Eyes yet to Slumber did yield) ;
> " Go build me a Church, without any Delay,
>   Go build it in *Merry-Field.*"

Merry-Field, according to *Camden,* was the Name of this Spot ; but it was then ſo very wet and unſtable, that they were forced to drive Piles for a Foundation ; and I am informed by ſome of the Inhabitants, that when a Grave is dug therein, it is frequently two Feet Depth in Water. It is built in the Form of a Croſs, or rather of a Lanthern, with a lofty Spire in the Center. The *Monument* at *London,* when I have ſtood upon *Fiſh-ſtreet-hill,* has ſtruck me with wonderful Surprize ; but this Spire (being Four hundred and ten Feet from the Ground to the Weather-Cock) is more than double the Height of that Column. The induſtrious Mr. *Browne Willis* meaſured this Church, and makes its Length Four hundred and ſeventy-eight Feet, of which, from the Weſt Door to the Entrance into the Choir, is about Two hundred and

forty-ſix

forty-fix Feet. The Length of the Choir is a-
bout One hundred and twenty Feet: and from
the High Altar to the upper End of the Virgin
Mary's Chapel, is about Eighty Feet more. The
Breadth of the Body and Side Ifles is Seventy-fix
Feet; and the Length of the lower Crofs-Ifle,
which is perhaps the lighteft, and one of the moft
beautiful of any Cathedral in *England*, Two hundred and ten Feet (each Tranfept being Sixty-
three Feet) and the Length of the upper Crofs-
Ifle is One hundred and fifty Feet. The Height
of the Vaulting is Eighty Feet. The Door and
Chapels of this Fabric are equal in Number to the
Months, the Windows to the Days, and the Pillars
added to the Pilafters, which are of fufile Marble,
to the Hours in a Year.

The Infide of this magnificent Building is not
equal to Expectation; the Paintings being but indifferent, and the Carvings few. Here are many
Infcriptions on old Monuments, which have already been publifhed; but that to the Memory
of *Thomas*, Lord *Wyndham*, Chancellor of *Ireland*, cut on a very beautiful one in the modern
Tafte, I have here enclofed:

Here lyeth
The Body of *Thomas* Lord *Wyndham*,
Baron Wyndham of *Finglafs*,
In the Kingdom of *Ireland*,
Youngeft Son of *John Wyndham*,
Of *Norrington*, in this County, Efq;
He was educated in the School of the
Canons of the *Clofe*,
From whence he went in 1698 to *Wadham-College*,
In the Univerfity of *Oxford*.
He removed from thence, to *Lincoln's Inn* in 1701;
And was there called to the Degree
Of *Barrifter at Law*, in 1705.
In the Year 1724, his Majefty
King *George* the *Firft*,
Was pleafed to appoint him
Chief-Juftice of the Court of *Commom-Pleas*

E 2

In

In *Ireland*;
Where he fate two Years.
In *December* 1726, he was advanced to the Office of
Lord High Chancellor of *Ireland*;
And conftituted one of the Lords *Juftices*
Of that Kingdom;
Into which laft Office he was fworn
Eight feveral Times.
On the Demife of King *George* the *Firft*,
His Majefty King *George* the *Second*
Renewed his Commiffion of
Lord High Chancellor:
And in *September* 1731,
In Confideration of his diligent and
Faithful Services,
Was pleafed to create him
A *Baron* of the Kingdom of *Ireland*.
He prefided in Six Seffions of *Parliament*,
As *Speaker* of the Houfe of *Lords* of
Ireland;
Where there is Seffion but once in two Years.
In *April* 1739, he fate as
Lord High Steward of Ireland,
On the Tryal of the Lord *Barry* of *Santry*;
Being the firft *Lord High Steward*
That ever was appointed in that Kingdom.
In *September* 1739, he refigned his Offices
At his Own Requeft,
On Account of an ill State of Health;
Contracted by a too intent, and too long Application
To the great Variety of Bufinefs he had been engaged in.
He was a Member of the *eftablifhed Church*,
A ftrenuous Affertor of Lawful Liberty,
A Zealous Promoter of Juftice,
A Dutiful Subject,
And a Kind Relation.
He was born on the 27th Day of *December* 1681,
He died on the 24th Day of *November* 1745.

I fhall juft mention the moft material Monu-
ments or Tombs here, namely, for the Bifhops
*Poore, Ofmund, Bingham, Audley, Salcot, Bridport,
Wyvil, Beauchamp, Hyde, Jewell, Uval, Gheft,* and
Ward. Dean *Gourdon,* Dr. *Sydenham,* and Dr. *Wil-*
fon.

fon. William Longfpee, William of York, a Duke
and Dutchefs of *Somerfet, Mary* Countefs of *Pembroke, Edward* Earl of *Hertford,* Lord *Cheyney,
Edward* Lord *Gorges,* Sir *Thomas Gorges,* and his
Lady, very neat; Sir *Richard Mompeffon* and his
Lady; and the Lords *Hungerford* and *Stourton,*
who were both hanged; Sir-*Giles Hungerford* and
his Lady; *Dawbigny Turberville* (a famous Ocu-
lift, the Epitaph wrote by Dr. *Walter Pope*); Mrs.
Elihoner Sadleir, a good Lady, defcended from
the illuftrious Family of *Saint Barbe*; *Thomas Saint
Barbe,* Sir *Henry Hyde,* Sir *Lawrence Hyde,* and
Sir *William Eyre.*

The Organ is very large, and has fifty Stops :
Some of the Windows of the Church are well
painted; and in *Hungerford* Chapel, at the Eaft
End of the Cathedral, is a very antient Painting
as large as the Life. In this grand Building are
depofited the Bones of feveral Earls of *Pembroke*;
particularly thofe of Earl *Thomas,* Grandfather to
the prefent Earl, of whom the learned Dr. *Stukeley* thus writes. " He was the Patron of my Studies, particularly thofe relating to *Stonehenge.*
Virtue, Piety, Magnanimity, Learning, Genero-
fity, all fublime Qualities, recommended and added to his illuftrious Defcent. Glorious will it be
for me, if thefe Pages live to teftify to another
Age, the Intimacy he was pleafed to honour me
with."

The *Cloyfter* belonging to this *Church* is a fine
Piece of Workmanfhip; and the *Chapter-Houfe* is
very curious, the Roof of it being fupported by
one fmall Pillar. In a large Tower, a little to
the North of the Cathedral, are eight Bells ; for
the Walls of the Spire, which is of Free-Stone,
are (near the Top) not five Inches thick, and
confequently unable to fuftain the Shock of
Ringing.

After

After the great Storm, which happened in the Year 1703, this Spire was suppofed to have received fome Damage, and therefore was furveyed by Sir *Chriftopher Wren*, who caufed it to be ftrengthened with Bands of Iron, which have quite fecured it.

There goes a Story, that when King *James* the Firft was here, a Perfon, in order to entertain him, flew, by means of a Rope, from the Top of this Spire to the Ground; and, expecting an handfome prefent, was introduced to his Majefty, who, turning to the Fellow, faid, " *Faith, Mon, I ha nae Money to gee thee, but that thou maift know I am pleafed with thy Performancé, Ife gee thee a Pottent."*

In this Church is the Figure of one *Bennet* (fome of whofe Defcendants are now living) who endeavoured to imitate our Saviour's Fafting, but expired on the feventeenth Day.

The Members of this Cathedral are a Dean, Chanter, Chancellor, Treafurer, three Archdeacons, a Sub-Dean, Sub-Chanter, forty-five Prebendaries at large (of which the Dean, with fix others, indifferently chofen out of the Dignitaries and Prebendaries, are Refidentiariés ; and commonly ftiled *Canonici Majores)* fix Petty, or Minor Canons, an Organift, fix Singing-Men, and fix Choirifters; befides Sextons, Vergers, and other inferior Officeis.

The Churches and Chapels in this Diocefe are Five hundred and fifty.

Befide Bifhop *Poore*, already fpoken of, I fhall juft trouble you with a Trifle relating to fome other Bifhops of this See : And firft of *Robert Wyvil*, who, in the Time of King *Edward* the Third, recovered the Caftle of *Old Sarum* from *Montacute*, Earl of *Salifbury*, together with *Sherborn*, and *Beere-Chafe*, which had been difmembered. He was was a Perfon of Spirit and Refolution.

lution. There is in the *Britiſh Muſæum*, among the *Harleian* MSS. this Book, *Succeſſio Epiſcoporum Sariſburienſium, a Ricardo Poore uſq; ad Robertum de Wyville, Number* 1761.

Richard Beauchamp, on whom the Chancellorſhip of the Order of the *Garter* was firſt conferred, his Succeſſors enjoyed it till Cardinal *Campegio*, made Biſhop of *Saliſbury* by *Henry* the Eighth, diſobliged that King in oppoſing the Divorce from Queen *Katherine*, loſt both his *Office* and *Biſhopric*, the former of which continued in Lay Hands for upwards of One hundred and thirty Years, when Dr. *Seth Ward* beforementioned, by Petition, had it reſtored to him and his Succeſſors. This Prelate, whoſe Life is written by Dr. *Pope*, built an Hoſpital here, for the Entertainment of Widows of poor Miniſters, in which lived and died the Mother of the wellknown Dr. *Sacheverel*.

The Murder of *William Aſkots*, Biſhop of *Saliſbury*, in *Jack Cade*'s Rebellion, is almoſt too ſhoeking to mention *.

Of this Dioceſe alſo was the famous Biſhop *Jewell*, ſo well known in Story.

The laſt that I ſhall mention is the celebrated Dr. *Burnet* ; a Perſon of great Abilities, whoſe Language, as a Writer, is perhaps equal, if not ſuperior, to any of his Time. His perſpicuous Judgment and pure Diction, together with an uncommon Knowledge of Men and Things, will cauſe his Hiſtories to be regarded by Poſterity, notwithſtanding the Falſities impoſed upon him by a Set of wicked Men then in Power.

The

* The *Wiltſhire* Men, upon the 29th of *June*, 1450, dragged *William Aſkots*, Biſhop of *Saliſbury*, from the high Altar, as he was celebrating Maſs in *Eaington* Church (having the Day before robbed his Carriage of the Sum of 10000 Marks) in his Albe, with his Stole about his Neck, to the Top of the Hill, and there inhumanly murdered him. *Truſſel*'s Hiſt. of *Engl.*

The two following Books in the *Cotton* Library, were burnt in the Fire which happened there the 23d of *October*, 1731.

De tranſlatione veteris Eccleſiæ SARISBURIENSIS; *per* GULIELMUM CROYLANDENSEM, *verſibus Elegiacis.*

And

La reule de Femmes religouſes et recluſes : ſive de vita ſolitaria et Anachoretica, per SIMEON DE GANDAVO, *Epiſcopum* SARISBURIENSEM, *in uſum Sororum ipſius.*

Beſides the Cathedral, and that at *Fiſherton*, there are three Churches at *Saliſbury*, which are dedicated to St. *Martin*, St. *Thomas*, and St. *Edmund*, the laſt of which is the Burial-Place of the honourable Family of *Windham*; and this is the Church where *Henry Sherfield*, Eſq; Bencher of *Lincoln's Inn*, and Recorder of *Saliſbury*, having for ſome Time been diſpleaſed with a ſuperſtitious Painting in a Window oppoſite to his Pew, he having agreed with the *Veſtry*, to new-glaze it with good white Glaſs, at his own Expence, and then broke it to Pieces; for which, in the eighth Year of King *Charles* the Firſt, he was tried in the *Star-Chamber*, fined Five hundred Pounds, committed to the *Fleet*, and obliged to make a public Acknowledgement of his Offence.

Saliſbury was incorporated by King *Henry* the Third, and is governed by a Mayor, High Steward (who is the Earl of *Pembroke*) a Recorder, a Deputy - Recorder, twenty-four Aldermen, and thirty Aſſiſtants or Common-Council-Men. Here is alſo a Town-Clerk, with three Serjeants at Mace.

This City, which contains about twelve thouſand Perſons, is quite open; nor do I note any Veſtiges of Fortifications. The *Lacedæmonians*, while they obſerved the Laws of *Lycurgus*, ſtood in as much need of Walls perhaps as the *Sariſburians*

rians do ; for our Hiftorians tell us, that the People of this Place have been always refpectful to
the Laws, and alfo remarkably brave in foreign
Wars.

The Manufactories of this City are chiefly
Flannels, Druggets, and what are called *Salifbury
Whites*, a confiderable Article in the Trade to
Turkey ; which, with the great Markets, Affizes,
Seffions, Cathedral, and Boarding-Schools, toge-
ther with its Situation on the great Weftern Road,
caufe it to be a very flourifhing Place.

In the Neighbourhood, as well as in the City,
are many Gentlemen of Family and Fortune ;
though I have feen in the *Harleian* MSS. now in
the *Britifh Mufæum*, a Lift of thofe who were
difclaimed here in *September* 1623, as Ufurpers of
the Titles of *Efquires* and *Gentlemen*, by *Henry St.
George*, *Richmond* Herald, and *Sampfon Lennard*,
Blue-Mantle, then upon a Vifitation of *Wiltfhire*,
as Marfhals and Deputies to the celebrated *Camden*, at that Time *Clarencieux King at Arms South
of Trent.*

The Markets here, which are extremely well
fupplied, are on *Tuefdays* and *Saturdays* ; and the
Fairs on *Tuefday* after *January* the 6th, for Cattle
and Woollen Cloth ; *Monday* before the 5th of
April, for Broad and Narrow Woollen Cloth ;
Whit-Monday and *Tuefday*, for Horfes and Pedlary ;
and *Tuefday* after *October* the 10th, for Hops, O-
nions and Cheefe. Here are three or four Charity-Schools, whofe Endowments are good.

I fhall end my Account of this City with a
few Notes relating to fome of thofe Perfons to
whom it hath given the Title of Earl. And firft
of *William*, furnamed *Longfpec* or *Longfpee*, from
the Sword he ufually wore ; who was the Son of
King *Henry* the Second, by his Miftrefs, the famous *Rofamund* · To him King *Richard* the Firft,

his half Brother, beſtowed in Marriage *Ela*, the Daughter and Heir of *William*, Earl of ·the ſame Place, and with her the ſaid Earldom ; this was about 1213. By King *John*, he was made Admiral of the Fleet, when he beat the *French* ; and afterwards commanded the *Engliſh* Troops in *Flanders*. At the Battle of *Bovines* he was taken Priſoner. He commanded an Army againſt the *Barons*, and at laſt was poiſoned, as ſuppoſed, by *Hubert de Burgh*, the Prime Miniſter of *Henry* the Third. This was afterwards written of him,

> *Flos comitum, Willielmus cognomine Longus*
> *Enſis vaginam cæpit habere brevem.*

William Mountacute, or *Mountague*, was created Earl of *Saliſbury* by King *Edward* the Third. He attended that King in *Flanders*, and was a ſtout and gallant Officer.—His Bravery at the memorable Battle of *Poictiers* added much to his Honour. He was afterwards made an Admiral, when he burnt the *Spaniſh* Fleet, relieved the Town of *Breſt*, and was honoured with the Government of *Calais*.

John Mountacute, or *Montague*, who, for his Loyalty to King *Richard* the Second, was degraded by Parliament. He was a Conſpirator againſt the Uſurper, *Henry* the Fourth, and in the Year 1400 was beheaded at *Cirenceſter*. 'Twas ſaid he died a *Wickliffite*.

Thomas Mountacute, or *Mountague*, was created in 1422. His Proweſs, Conduct, and Succeſſes in *Normandy*, *France*, *Maine*, and *Anjou*, are, to his immortal Fame, recorded in the Annals both of *England* and *France*. He was killed at the Siege of *Orleans*.

Richard Nevil, who married the Daughter and Heir of the laſt mentioned Earl. He joined the Duke of *York* againſt King *Henry* the Sixth ; and

was

was by that Duke made Chancellor. He defeated the Lord *Audley* at *Bloreheath*; · and kept *London* for the Duke of *York*, when that Prince was at the Battle of *Wakefield*; but he was afterwards beheaded at *Pomfret*. I shall speak of his Son hereafter.

Sir *Robert Cecil*, second Son of the famous Lord *Burleigh*, was, by King *James* the First, created Earl of *Salisbury*, (in the Morning of that Day, when the same impolitic King conferred the Title of Earl of *Exeter* on his elder Brother in the Afternoon) a Man whose great Abilities in the preceding Reign had been very conspicuous; and afterwards were manifest to all *Europe*. In this Family the Title still remains, in the Person of *James Cecil*, Viscount *Cranborn*. I am, Sir, *&c.*

L E T T E R V,

From *Yarnbury*, in *Wiltshire*.

S I R,

FEW Persons of Curiosity come to SALISBURY, without paying a Visit to *Wilton*, (which is situate in a pleasant Vale, near the Conflux of the Rivers *Nadder* and *Willey*). The Distance is trifling, and they are amply rewarded for their Trouble. The Town of *Wilton*, which, according to *Leland*, had twelve Parish Churches, is now inconsiderable, having one Church only; though it sends two Members to the *House* of *Commons*. The Manufactory of *English Carpets* was first established here, but many now bear their Appellation which are made in different Parts of the Kingdom.

About

About the Year 790, *Weolsthan* or *Wulstan*, Earl of *Wiltshire*, repaired an old Church here, and dedicated it to St. *Mary*; where he placed a College of Priests of the *Benedictine* Order. After the Death of *Wulstan*, his Widow, *Alburga*, in the Year 800, converted this Foundation into a *Nunnery of Virgins*. King *Alfred* built a new Monastery at *Wilton*; he dedicated the Church to St. *Mary* and St *Bartholomew*. In this religious House he placed an *Abbess*, and twelve *Nuns*; and also translated the *Nuns* from St. *Mary's* thither which caused the Number to be twenty-six. The Kings, *Edward* the Elder, *Athelstan*, *Edgar*, and *William* the Conqueror, were great Benefactors to this Monastery, which at the Diffolution was valued at Six hundred and one Pounds One Shilling and a Penny *per Annum*. *Camden* fays *Wilton* was anciently called *Elandunum*, and was the chief Town in the County. At this Place, in the Year 821, *Egbert*, King of the *West Saxons*, obtained a Victory over *Beorwulf*, a Monarch of the *Mercians*, when, according to the laft-mentioned Author, the River ran plentifully with the Blood of near Relations. And here alfo, fifty Years after, King *Alfred* fought a Battle with the *Danes*: At the Beginning of which, he had the Advantage, but in the End was driven out of the Field.

The House of the Earl of *Pembroke* here, was in a great Measure, built out of the Remains of the fuppressed Abbey, in the Reign of *Henry* the Eighth; but the great Quadrangle was not finished till the Time of the fucceeding Reign. The whole is a fquare Stone Building, with Turrets at each Corner. The Porch is after a Defign of *Hans Holbein*.

The famous *Inigo Jones* defigned those Parts which were rebuilt by the firft *Philip*, Earl of *Pembroke*, and alfo the Front towards the Garden. This

This Piece of Architecture is One hundred ninety-four Feet in Length, and vaftly fine. The Hall-fide being burnt down, was rebuilt in a very noble Manner by Earl *Thomas*, then Lord High Admiral of *England*.

Entering this Palace, on the Right-Hand is the Hall, where I was fhewn a fine Marble Shuffle-Board, and two large Marble Tables.

The great geometrical Stair-Cafe, which is extremely noble, is generally allowed to be the firft of its Kind in *England*. By the late Earl it was ordered to be painted in *Claro Obfcuro*, by *Van Rifquet*; and the Pictures which adorn it are fo various and excellent, that they are beyond Conception. The *Bacchus*, done in *Peloponnefian* Marble, at the Foot of the Stair-Cafe, is as large as the Life, and the young one on his Arm is finely executed.

In one of the firft Rooms, they fhew you the Piece of *Jefus* wafhing the Feet of his Difciples, which is finely done; and in another, *Little Shepherds*, and *Country Utenfils*, by *Bafon*.

The Grand Apartment, or Great Dining-Room, is vaftly noble and magnificent. Its Length is fixty Feet, the Breadth and Height are alike, that is, thirty Feet each. The Cieling is beautifully painted, and the Furniture almoft beyond Comparifon. This Room, together with the Salon, which is a Cube of thirty Feet, are looked upon as the two fineft Pieces of Architecture in *England*. The Buftos, which are placed oppofite to the Windows throughout the Length of the former, are extremely pleafing.

Over the Chimney-Piece is a Picture of *Charles*, Prince of *Wales*, and the Dukes of *York* and *Gloucefter*, Sons of King *Charles* the Firft. But that Piece which ftrikes the Eye in the moft amazing Manner is the famous Family Picture, placed at one End of this grand Apartment. It is twenty Feet long, and twelve high, containing thirteen Figures as large as the Life. It was executed by the celebrated *Vandyke*, who has so wonderfully approached to Nature, that our Imagination almoſt tells us it is real Life. The Figures of *Philip*, Earl of *Pembroke* (who was Lord Chamberlain of the Houſhold) and his Lady, Daughter and Coheir to *Edward Vere*, Earl of *Oxford)* ſeated in their Chairs, and that of the young Lady, Daughter of the Duke of *Buckingham* (who was ſoon to be married to *Charles*, their eldeſt Son, who ſtands by her) whom the Earl holds by the Hand, are ſo inimitably expreſſive, that no one can conceive. On the Right-Hand of the Earl and his Counteſs, ſtand their five Sons ; and the Earl of *Caernarvon*, with his Lady, their Daughter, on the Left. The placing the two ſtill-born Children in the Clouds, is a fine Thought, and as finely executed. They told me, that *Lewis* the Fourteenth offered as many Louis-d'ors for this Piece as would cover it ; and that even Sir *Godfrey Kneller* would have purchaſed it at the Price of Three thouſand Pounds. Two fine Portraits of King *Charles* the Firſt and his *Queen* are on each Side of this incomparable Piece. In this Room are alſo many Portraits of the *Pembroke* Family, by the ſame maſterly Hand.

In the Bottom Pannels of the Salon are ſome very indifferent Miniature-Paintings of ſeveral Incidents deſcribed in the *Arcadia* of Sir *Philip Sydney*, who wrote that incomparable Romance in this Houſe, and dedicated it to his Siſter *Mary*, Counteſs of *Pembroke*, Wife to the firſt Earl *Henry*. I ſhall not attempt a minute Deſcription of the aſtoniſhing Beauties in many more Rooms in this Houſe : The Labour would be endleſs. The Chimney-Pieces are chiefly of Marble, ſome

by

by *Inigo Jones*, others carved in *Italy*. The Workmanship of all these is exquisitely fine. In a black Marble, on the Chimney of one of the Garrets, one sees the Cathedral Church and Spire of *Salisbury* as plain as in a Looking-Glass. The numerous Statues, Basso-Relievos, and Paintings of celebrated Masters are incredible ; though it must be owned there are some Paintings but indifferently done. Among the Basso-Relievos, is a very ancient one of *Mantheus*, the Son of *Æthus*, giving Thanks to *Jupiter*. It was brought from *Smyrna*.

The lower Apartments are so crowded with curious Carvings in Marble, that they almost appear like grand Magazines of Sculpture. However, they are disposed in as elegant a Manner as the Room will admit of.

They shew the Head-Pieces, Coats of Mail, and Armour of the Kings *Henry* the Eighth, and *Edward* the Sixth ; together with the curious Suit of *Black Jack*, a Nick-Name given to the Earl of *Pembroke*, who took *Boulogne* in *France*; and also twelve more Suits of neat Work. The rest of the Armour was for about One hundred private Horsemen.

The River *Willey*, in the Front of the House, is formed into a beautiful Canal ; and in the Court-Yard, among other curious Pieces of Antiquity, is a grand Column of Porphyry, on the Top of which is a *Venus* : It is thirty Feet high, and the Sculpture is exceeding fine. They tell me it was bought in *Candia*, but came originally from *Alexandria* in *Egypt*. Near this Column is another Statue, with the Knee bent, and holding up a Sun-Dial.

The Stables and Offices are very handsome, and in the Bowling-Green is a *Loggio*, or *Banquetting-House*,

Houfe, with fine rufticated Pillars, and feveral cu⸗
rious Statues.

The Front of the *Grotto* is finely carved, and
'tis all Marble within : The Pillars are black, of
the *Ionic* Order, the Capitals of white Marble,
and Baffo-Relievos (which were brought from
Florence) are very curious.

On the South Side of the Houfe the Gardens
extend beyond the River *Nadder*, over which
Stream the late Earl erected a moft charming *Palladian* Bridge, on which is an open Co-
lonnade : The Order is *Ionic.* The Architecture
of this Building is greatly admired.

From this Bridge is a fine gradual Afcent to the
Summit of an Hill, where is a large equeftrian
Statue of the Emperor *Marcus Aurelius*; and a
Summer-Room, from whence is a fine View of
the fweet Valley below, Part of *Salifbury*, and
the North Side of the Cathedral ; which City being in fome Degree embowered with Trees, has
a charming Effect ; and the ferpentine Walks in
the hanging Wood on the South-Weft Side of the
Houfe, have a delightful Appearance.

South of the Gardens, the Great Park extends
over the Valley, till the Profpect opens to *Salif-*
bury Plain ; on the higheft Rife is *King-barrow*,
which is a large Tumulus. Dr. *Stukeley* fuppofes
it was that of *Carvilius*, a *Britifh* Prince, who
fought *Julius Cæfar.* This Barrow is planted with
four Trees, which is one of the Viftoes to the
Park ; and from hence is a very beautiful Profpect over *Wilton*, and the charming Valley in
which it ftands.

From *Wilton*, I rode to *Longford* or *Langford*,
the Seat of Lord Vifcount *Folkftone.* It is fweetly
fituated in a pleafant Valley, and through the
Gardens gently glides a fmall delightful River.

Inward View of STONEHENGE *from the High Altar*

ver. Here is a pleafing Lawn, and a delicious Plantation of flowering Shrubs; through which runs a neat Gravel Walk, terminated by a pretty Summer-Houfe. The Country around has gradual Afcents, and being much covered with Wood, appears extreamly charming.

The Houfe (which was built in the Reign of *James* the Firft) is in a triangular Form, with round Towers at the Corners. The Apartments are very elegant, and the Furniture and Decorations fhew an excellent Tafte; for, though they are extreamly neat, nothing tawdry is to be feen.

The Gallery, which, together with the Pictures and other Furniture, coft Ten thoufand Pounds, is very excellent; at each End of which are two of the beft Pieces of *Claude Lorrain*. They are a Rifing and a Setting Sun.

In one Corner is an octagonal Room, hung with modern Tapeftry from the droll Paintings of *Teniers*.

In another Corner is the Chapel, which is alfo an Octagon wainfcotted, and the Paintings in the Windows reprefent the Paffages of the Life of our *Saviour*, as expreffed in the Creed.

Among the various and handfome Furniture in the different Apartments, are many of green of different Manufactures and Shades.

Upon the whole, this Seat is one of the moft delightful in *England*, having the *Avon* flowing before its Front, and the Plain of *Salifbury* to the Weft of it; confequently it is finely fituated either for Fifhing or Hunting. According to a Meafurement ordered by Lord *Folkftone*, it is three Miles and a few Poles South-Eaft from *Salifbury*. From the Top of the Houfe is a fine View of Lord *Feverfham*'s Seat at *Barford*, which is fituate on a rifing Hill on the other Side of the

River ; as alfo of that which was Sir *George Van-deput*'s, who fold it to Mr. *Young*, but 'tis now in the Poffeffion of Mr. *Northey*.

From *Longford*, I rode to *Tanefbury*, or, as 'tis called by the Inhabitants, *Yarnbury Caftle*. Here is a large Camp, fortified with a deep double Ditch. *Camden* fays, we may eafily conclude it to be *Roman*, and obferves, that fome thought it to be formed by *Vefpafian*, who was Lieutenant of the twentieth Legion under *Claudius*. But Bifhop *Gibfon*, on Account of its oval Form, and the Outworks at the Eaft Entrance, with more Reafon, thinks it to be *Danifh*. It is 360 Paces long, and has two other Entrances, that is, on the North and South Sides.

I fhall fend this to the Poft-Office by a Gentleman, who is juft going to *Salifbury* ; and am, Sir, Yours, &c.

L E T T E R VI.

From *Stonehenge*, in *Wiltfhire*.

S I R,

THE Day was exceeding fine, and, after Dinner, I rode gently on over the charming Turf of *Salifbury* Plain ; which is not excelled by any in the World, for Drynefs of Soil, Sweetnefs of Grafs, and Wholfomenefs of Air. One cannot forbear thinking that fome of thefe fine fertile Lands might be turned to more Advantage than that of breeding Sheep ; but this I am certain, the Shepherds who attend them ftand in as much need of Cultivation as the Land does. I rode up to one of thefe (who was feated upon an Hillock, holding his Chin in the Palms of his

Hands,

Hands, and his Elbows refting upon his Knees)
and afked him, in a loud Tone of Voice, the
Way to *Stonehenge.* I waited fome Time for his
Anfwer, and, perceiving his Eyes ftaring me in
the Face, was convinced he was not afleep, and
therefore repeated the Queftion in a louder Tone;
which caufed his Dog to bark: Notwithftanding
which, the Fellow continued mute. I then,
thinking him unhappy in his hearing, halloo'd to
him as loud as I could; when he replied in thefe
Words, without any other Action than that of
nodding his Head, *Whot tha Divil does tha Mon
maak zich a Noife vor? Zure ya thinken I am deauf;!
Thicks the Way to Stonege.* I immediately left the
Fellow; but had it not been owing to my good
Fortune in meeting with a Traveller, I fhould
by the Time that I might have expected to be at
Stonehenge, have found myfelf at *Old Sarum.*
After turning fhort on my Left Hand, and keep-
ing the Point directed, I arrived at this amazing
Structure. But, as the Evening was now ap-
proaching, I chofe to proceed on to *Ambrefbury,* or,
as it is generally pronounced, *Amefbury,* being a-
bout three Miles and a half diftant, with a fixed
Refolution of paying my Vifit to *Stonehenge* in the
Morning.

The Sun had juft appeared in the Horizon;
and the melodious Lark was towring to the fleet-
ing Cloud. The general Bleating of Sheep proclaimed their Difcharge from the Imprifonment
of the Fold; and the ruftic Song of the Shepherd
drove Care from his fimple Heart, when I left
Ambrefbury, and my Horfe, behind, and entered
on Foot the foft verdant Turf of the Plain. A
more fweet and fatisfactory Morning I never paffed. The Air was extreamly refrefhing, and the
Grafs under my Feet had fuch a pleafing elaftic
Power, that I foon arrived at the ftupenduous

Building,

Building, which I am about to defcribe: And this perhaps I fhall be better enabled to perform, from the Information I gained by an Abftract (which I bought at *Ambresbury*) of the truely learned and ingenious Dr. *Stukeley*'s Account of this wonderful Temple.

His Grace the Duke of *Queensbury* is Lord of the Manor of *Little Ambresbury*, in which this Building ftands. It is fituate near the Summit of an Hill, on a moft charming and gentle Declivity towards the North-Eaft, which was on the Side I approached it by an Avenue; and when at about the Diftance of half a Mile, it had an auguft Appearance. As one advances nearer, the Greatnefs of its *Contour* (to ufe the Dr.'s Expreffion) fills the Eye in an aftonifhing Manner. The Awe and Veneration which affected me on my Entrance, I am not able to fet down, yet the more I traverfed and examined it, the more my Awe and Veneration encreafed.

Stonehenge is enclofed by a circular Ditch, which was originally thirty Cubits broad*. But the Length of Time, and numerous Coaches and Horfes, which come almoft every Day to fee the Temple, has in a great Meafure levelled it.

According to *Inigo Jones* and *Webb*, the whole Building was thirty-five Yards from the Ditch or Trench, over which there were three Entrances (but this is denied by Dr. *Stukeley*). The principal or grand one was from the North-Eaft. Thefe Architects, or rather Mr. *Webb* only, publifhed a

per-

---

* Take a Staff ten Feet four Inches and three Quarters long, divide it into fix equal Parts; thefe are Cubits Each Cubit is divided into fix Parts, and thefe are Palms; and this is the original Meafure of the Founders of *Stonehenge*. This Cubit is the old *Hebrew*, *Phœnician*, or *Egyptian* Cubit, and amounts to twenty Inches four fifths *Englifh* Meafure. *Dr.* Stukeley.

perſpective View of the Building from this Side,
as (ſuppoſed) it appeared in its perfect State; whereby the general Compoſure of the particular Parts of
the Uprights are ſeen altogether, and by which the
ſtately Aſpect and magnificent Greatneſs are very
conſpicuous. " At each Entrance on the Outſide of the Trench, ſays *Webb*, were two large
Stones gate-wiſe, ſeven Feet broad, three thick,
and twenty high ; parallel whereunto, on the Inſide, were two others, four Feet broad, and three
thick. But they lay ſo broken and ruined by
Time, that their Proportion in Height could not
be diſtinguiſhed, much leſs exactly meaſured by
them." This Account is alſo contradicted by the
Dr.

Through the Middle of the principal Entrance,
runs the principal Line of the whole Work, the
Diameter from North-Eaſt to South-Weſt. This
Line cuts the Middle of the *Altar*, Length of
the *Cell*, and the Entrance into the Court, and ſo
runs down the Middle of the Avenue to the Bottom of the Valley for almoſt Two thouſand Feet
together.

Nothing in Nature could be of a more ſimple
Idea than this vaſt *Circle* of *Stones*, with its *Corona*
or *Crown-Work* at Top, and yet its Effect is venerably majeſtic ; which is the principal Requi-
ſite in ſacred Structures. A ſingle Stone of the
Size of theſe is worthy of Admiration, but the
Boldneſs and great *Relievo* of the whole *Compages* can perhaps only be rightly apprehended
from a View of the Original. On the Outſide,
the Impoſts are rounded a little, to humour the
Circularity of the Deſign ; within they are ſtrait, ſo
that the *Crown-Work* on the Inſide makes a Polygon
of thirty Sides. But this Artifice, without leſſening
in the leaſt the Beauty of the Work, gives much
Strength

Strength to the whole, and to the Imposts in particular*.

That Part within the Trench, being an Eminence higher than the Plain without, gave it such an Advantage, that almost from whatever Part it was approached, it was by an easy Ascent; this must in its Perfection have had a fine Effect.

With respect to these outer Stones, they were intended to form a *Circle*, whose Diameter was to be sixty Cubits. Accordingly each Stone was to be four Cubits broad, and each Interval two Cubits : Now, as thirty Times four Cubits is twice sixty, and thirty Times two Cubits is sixty, consequently thrice sixty Cubits completes a *Circle*, whose Diameter is sixty Cubits. Thus, a Stone and an Interval in this outward *Circle*, makes three Squares; two allotted to the Stone, and one to the Interval, which for Stability and Beauty in such a Work as this, is an excellent Proportion. The seven Stones remaining at the grand Entrance sufficiently shew this general Design, and what was strictly the Intent of the Founders; and where they took the Liberty to relax of that Strictness, and that with Judgment too, so as to produce a very good Effect. The Inside of the Stones of this outer Circle are (according to the Practice of the polite Architects of the Eastern Part of the World) much smoother, better chisselled, and have a handsomer Appearance than the Outsides.

But to proceed. The Stones of the outer *Circle* are four Cubits broad, two Cubits thick, and

nine

---

* *Webb* says, that the inner Part of the Work, consisting of an *Hexagonal* Figure, was raised by due Symmetry upon the Bases of four equilateral Triangles (which formed the whole Structure) This inner Part was likewise double, having within it also another *Hexagon* raised. But this is proved by Dr. *Stukeley* to be false.

nine Cubits high ; and on the Top of every two
of them were placed two large Head-ftones by
Way of Architrave, or rather Impoft or Cornifh ;
for thefe Head-Stones are not made to fupport
any Thing above them, as is the Intent of an
Architrave, but for the Stability and Ornament
of what fupports them. Thefe Impofts are fix
Cubits long, two Cubits broad, and a Cubit
and half high. They are wrought or chiffelled in a perfectly plain manner, as are alfo
the Uprights that fupport them, excepting that
Part of them in the Earth, which is in the original natural Form. Thefe Uprights are very judicioufly diminifhed towards 'the Top, being there
but three Cubits and a half broad ; fo that the
Impofts project over them on both Sides. This
was an admirable Contrivance, both for the
Strength and Beauty of the whole. There is in
this outer *Circle* another curious Matter ; I mean,
an artful Variation from the ftrict Rules of Geometry. For the Aperture of the grand Entrance is fomewhat wider than the reft. This
Deviation arofe from true Reafon and good Senfe.
For the affording of this additional Beauty does
not in the leaft Degree affect the Stability of the
Work. In Strictnefs it ought to have been only
two Cubits, but they have advanced it to two Cubits and a half. This does indeed crowd the next
Intervals on each Side a very fmall Matter, but
the reft preferve their Diftance quite round the
whole. They farther manifefted their Judgment,
by making the Impoft over this Aperture confiderably thicker and fomewhat wider than the reft ;
this, without Doubt, was the more effectually to fe-
cure it from breaking ; but as they were fenfible,
that this Addition would have broke the noble
Cincture that furrounded the whole, if put at the
Top, therefore the additional Thicknefs is made
in

in the lower Part. The Length and Breadth of the hanging Stone here is aftonifhing. *Abraham Sturges*, an Architect, and Dr. *Stukeley* meafured it, in the Prefence of *(Heneage)* Lord *Winchelfea*. Its middle Length is eleven Feet ten Inches; which is fix Cubits four Palms; two Feet eleven Inches high, which is one Cubit and four Palms; and three Feet nine Inches, which is two Cubits and a Palm, in Breadth. The Stones that compofe this *Grand Front* are much deviated forwards from their true Perpendicular, and in much Danger of falling. Indeed nothing can prevent it, excepting the Mafonry of the Mortoife and Tenon of the Impoft. Thefe Tenons and Mortoifes fit each other very nicely; they are ten Inches and a half in Diameter, and their Form is fimilar to that of half an Egg, rather than to that of an Hemifphere; by this means they have fo preferved both the Uprights and Impofts from Laxation, that they muft have been thrown down with much Difficulty and Labour. The Height of an Upright and Impoft together is ten Cubits and an half.

The outer *Circle* in its Perfection (as I before obferved) confifted of fixty Stones, thirty Uprights and thirty Impofts. Seventeen of the former are now ftanding, eleven of which remain contiguous to the *Grand Entrance*, with five Impofts upon them. One Upright at the Back or South-Weft Side of the *Temple* leans upon a Stone of the inner *Circle*. On the Ground are fix more lying, whole or in Pieces. So that out of thirty Uprights, twenty-four are vifible. One Impoft more remains in its proper Place, and there are but two lying on the Ground. So that twenty-two have been carried away. Dr. *Stukeley* is of Opinion, that this *Temple* was not robbed and defaced upon the Introduction of *Chriftianity*, but

rather

rather by the Hands of thofe, who wanted the Stone for other Ufes.

It is five Cubits, or a little more than eight Feet, from the Infide of the exterior, to the Outfide of the interior *Circle* (between which is a noble and delightful Walk of Three hundred Feet in Circumference). This *Circle* was made by a Radius of twenty-four Cubits, drawn from the common Centers of the Work. The Stones, which were forty in Number, forming with the outward Stones a circular Portico, open to the Heavens (a fine Walk, with a charming Effect) excepting thofe two upon the principal Line of Diameter with the *Grand Entrance.* They do not precifely correfpond with thofe of the outward *Circle;* which caufes the Effect to be better than in fuch Cafe it would have been. The Stones are truly flat *Parallelograms;* their general and defigned Proportion is two Cubits broad, one Cubit thick, and four Cubits and an half high. It feems that the original Purpofe of the Founders was to have them the half of the outer Uprights; though 'twas not precifely executed. For in fome Places the Stones are broader than the Intervals, in fome narrower. There are fcarce any of thefe entire as to all thefe Dimenfions, and they alfo diminifh upward, as the Uprights of the exterior *Circle* do. It is further obvious, that the two Stones of the principal Entrance of this lefler *Circle* do indeed fomewhat correfpond to thofe of the outer *Circle* ; being fet at a greater Diftance from each other, and alfo more inward ; and are taller and broader than any other of this *Circle :* By which means they confpicuoufly point out the principal Entrance thereof. None of the Stones of this interior *Circle* have, or ever had, any Impofts upon them; for thofe would not have added to the Security or Ornament of them. Thefe Stones are of an harder Quality than thofe of the exterior *Circle* ; and the whole Number remaining of them is nineteen, eleven of which are ftanding *in fitu.*

It is probable, that the Founders of this *Temple* had no other meaning in thefe two *Circles*, than to make ufe of the thirty great Stones, and the forty leffer : And this produced a pleafing Variety, which certainly added much to the Solemnity of the Place, and the Duties performed there.

Having paffed the fecond *Circle*, I had a View of the *Adytum* or *Cell*, which is fo noble and beautiful an *Ellipfis*, that Dr. *Stukeley* thinks there is nothing like it in all Antiquity ; that it was certainly an Invention of the *Druids*, and a moft ingenious Contrivance to relax the inner and moft facred Part of the *Temple*, where they performed their religious Offices. The Infide of this Structure, when it was in its Perfection, muft have had a grand Effect produced by this *elliptical* Figure, included in a circular *Corona*, with a copious Hemifphere of azure Sky for its Canopy. This *Adytum* is formed of certain *Compages* of Stones, which the Dr. calls *Trilithons*. They are five in Number, each of which are made of two upright Stones, and one Impoft on the Top. The whole Number is yet remaining, but the vulgar Notion of their being factitious, has caufed many inquifitive though ignorant People to knock off Pieces with Hammers, in order to fatisfy a foolifh Curiofity.

This *elliptical Adytum* or *Cell* is formed by a Radius of twelve Cubits and a half from two *Centers*, as to the inward Curve ; as to its outward, that takes a Radius of fifteen Cubits ; for thefe Stones are two Cubits and a half thick. Thefe two Circuits are turned into an *Oval*, by a Radius

of

of thirty Cubits, fet in the two Centers, where the *Circles* interfect. It has been very pertinently obferved, that as fome of the Ancients thought the World to be of an Egg-like Shape, and a Circle was an Hieroglyphic of the Deity, it is not unlikely, that our ancient *philofophic Priefts* or *Druids* might have fome View to thefe prevailing Notions, in the Conftruction of this their *Temple*.

This *Oval Adytum* greatly ftrikes the Eye from the *Grand Entrance,* and would have been quite complete had there been a fixth *Trilithon*; but then the Defign of the whole *Temple* had been fpoiled. For that fixth *Trilithon* muft have ftood directly in the Way that leads from the *Grand Entrance*, and confequently would have prevented all View of the inner Part of the *Temple*. But their Judgment is manifefted in this Omiffion, for thereby the Opening to the *Adytum* is wonderfully noble; and by this contrivance, there is left a Space of five Cubits between the Jambs of the Opening of the *Adytum*, and the inner *Circle* in Front, being exactly the fame Diftance as between the inner and the outer *Circle*.

Dr. *Stukeley* was the firft Obferver of a curious Particular in the Conftruction of this *Adytum*, which is this: That being compofed of *Trilithons*, fet two and two on each Side, and one right before, they rife in Height and Beauty of the Stones from the lower End of the *Adytum* to the upper End; that is, the two *Trilithons* next the grand Entrance on the Right-Hand and on the Left, are exceeded in Height by the next in Order, and thofe are ftill exceeded by the *Trilithon* behind the *Altar*, at the upper End of the *Choir*. The Uprights of the *Trilithons* were caufed to diminifh confiderably towards the Top, with an apparent Defign to take off from their Weight, which was a Piece of true Judgment; becaufe it rendered

them

them more ftable, And this caufes the Interval of
the two upright Stones of the *Compages* to widen
fo finely upwards. In thefe different Degrees or
Orders of Altitude one exceeds the other by a
Cubit, the firft being thirteen, the fecond fourteen, and the laft fifteen Cubits high.

From all this, fays the Dr. the intelligent Reader muft needs fee, that our Founders had never
any Sight of *Greek* or *Roman* Pillars, and never
pretended to imitate them.

The Tenons and Mortoifes of thefe *Trilithons*
are finely contrived, and the Conformity they
bear to the outer *Circle* is furprizingly juft; for
every Thing is done according to true Geometry:
And though executed from plain and fimple Prin-
ciples, anfwers every Purpofe. In the bottom
Face of the Impoft, if divided into three Squares,
the two Mortoifes are made exactly in the Middle
of the two outermoft of thofe Squares. I have
before obferved, that if an Egg were cut a-crofs
its fhorteft Diameter, the one half reprefents the
Form of the Tenons of the outer *Circle*; fo, if
another Egg were cut a-crofs its tranfverfe Diameter, the one half of it would be the Shape of
the Tenons of the *Adytum*. The Meaning of this
is evident; the Tenons of the outer *Circle* are
higher in Proportion than the other, becaufe the
Impofts are lefs and lower, and on both Accounts
are more liable to be difturbed, either by Accidents or Violence than the others; and therefore
more Caution is ufed for their Prefervation.
This is an high Inftance of noble, yet fimple
Art.

Thefe greater Stones, as before noted, are all
on the Spot; that is, ten Uprights and five Impofts. The *Trilithon* firft on the Left-Hand is entire *in fitu*, but greatly decayed, efpecially the
Impoft, having fuch deep Holes corroded in fome
Places

Places that even the *Daws* make their Nefts in them. The next *Trilithon* on the Left-Hand is compofed of three moft beautiful Stones, and is almoft entire, for the Impoft being of a very durable Kind of *Englifh Marble*, is not much impaired by the Weather. The Earl of *Winchelfea* and Dr. *Stukeley* went on the Top of it, but found it a frightful Situation . Notwithftanding which, I fhould have been glad to have done the fame. The *Trilithon* of the upper End of the *Adytum* was an extraordinary Beauty ; but, owing in all Probability to fome Perfons digging on the Infide of the *Cell*, its noble Impoft is fallen upon the *Altar*, where its prodigious Bulk lies unfractured. The two Uprights which fupported it, are the moft delicate of the *whole Work*, being chiffelled, and finely tapered and proportioned. The Southward one lies upon the *Altar*, and is broke in two ; the other ftands pretty entire, but leans upon one of the Stones of the inward *Oval*. The unhewn, or originally covered Part of both, is raifed fomewhat above the Ground. The next *Trilithon* (that towards the Weft) is entire, except that fome Part of the Impoft is fallen off, and all the upper Edge much diminifhed by the Tooth of Time. The laft *Trilithon* (that on the Right-Hand of the Entrance into the *Adytum*) has fuffered much ; the outer Upright, being the Jamb of the Entrance, is yet ftanding ; but the other Upright and the Impoft are both fallen forward into the *Adytum*, and broke.

This famous *Temple* is compofed of two *Circles*, two *Ovals*, and an *Altar*. At the Diftance of two Cubits inward from the greater *Oval*, is the leffer, which is to be defcribed by two Cènters as before; the Stones are fixteen in Number (the *Altar* making twenty) at about the central Diftance of three Cubits. They are both in Breadth and Height one

one third of the great *Oval*; that is, a Cubit and a half broad, and four Cubits and four Palms in Height; but as they rife in Height, as nearer the upper End of the *Adytum*, their Height likewife is unequal, as the *Trilithons*. Thefe Stones are ftill harder than thofe that compofe the leffer *Circle* already mentioned. Of this *Oval* there are only fix Stones remaining upright. The Stumps of two are left on the South Side by the *Altar*. One (which was dug up, or thrown down by the Fall of the Upright there) lies behind the *Altar*. One or two were thrown down, probably by the Fall of the Upright of the firft *Trilithon* on the Right-Hand. A Stump of another ftill remains by the Upright there, yet ftanding.

The *Altar* is a fingle Stone of Blue coarfe Marble, fuch as is dug in *Derbyfhire*, and other Parts of the Kingdom, and frequently laid upon Tombs. This *Altar*, which is in Length ten Cubits (equal to the Breadth of the *Trilithon* before which it ftands) in Breadth two Cubits and a half, and in Thicknefs juft a Cubit, is placed in the *Adytum*, a little above the *Focus* of the upper End of the *Ellipfis :* At prefent 'tis flat on the Ground, or rather fqueezed into it by the great Weight of Ruins upon it. This Stone is harder than all the reft, as being intended to refift Fire.

Thus have I given you fome Account of the principal Part of this *ftupenduous Pile*, erected at fuch a Diftance of Time, and in fuch a Form, that all Searchers into its Antiquity have not been able to form a proper Idea of it, or fix any Period when or by whom it was built, 'till the ingenious and indefatigable Gentleman whom I have fo often mentioned, folved the mighty Problem, and broke the magical Spell, which has fo long deceived the Vulgar, who thought it an ominous Thing to count the true Number of the
Stones ;

Stones; infomuch, that whoever fhould do fo
would furely die foon afterwards; but here follows
the Dr.'s Inveftigation:

The great *Oval* confifts of ten Uprights; the inner *Oval*, with the *Altar*, of twenty. The great *Circle* of thirty; the inner *Circle*, of forty. Ten, twenty, thirty, forty, together make one hundred
upright Stones. Five Impofts of the great *Oval*,
thirty of the great *Circle*, two Stones ftanding upon the Bank of the *Area*, the Stone lying within
the Entrance of the *Area*, and that ftanding without, and one which feems to have lain upon the
Ground by the *Vallum* of the Court, oppofite to
the Entrance of the Avenue : All added together
make juft *One hundred and forty Stones*, the Number of which STONEHENGE, *a* TEMPLE *reftored to
the* BRITISH DRUIDS, *by Dr.* STUKELEY, *is compofed.* Upon one of thefe is the greater Part of
this Letter written, and from whence I beg leave
to declare myfelf, Sir, Yours, *&c.*

L E T T E R   VII.

From *Wallop*, in *Hampfhire.*

S I R,

MY laft was dated from the *Britifh Temple of
Stonehenge*, concerning which Piece of Antiquity I have yet fomewhat more to fay.

Having finifhed my Letter, I fat down upon
one of thofe enormous Stones in the *Adytum*,
when a pleafing Contemplation carried me fo far,
that I figured to myfelf the Scene of this primitive Congregation of *Druids*, performing their
Rites and Ceremonies. When the *Deity* was a-
dored without the Ornaments of Pride and Pa-
geantry, or the Ridiculoufnefs of modern Enthu-
fiafm,

fiafm, hère, in a fuperb Temple, dedicated to
the Honour of the Author and Preferver of the
Univerfe, they could, uninterrupted by a Roof,
lift up their Eyes to the Heavens, where the
Lord of All Worlds prefides. Carrying my Idea
farther, it was natural to figure on the Outfide of
the Temple, thoufands and ten thoufands of *Antient Britons*, our Progenitors, gathered together;
in oider to pay their annual or quarterly Adora-
tions to him, in whom they lived, and moved,
and had their Being.—But I have done,—

Upon the *Vallum* of the Ditch, which forms a
circular Terras on the Infide, are two Stones, and
two femicircular Hollows; thefe Matters puzzle
all Enquirers. Dr. *Stukeley* thinks them bowing
Stones, or Stones of filent Adoration; and that
the Hollows were Places in which Vafes were fet;
and fuppofes thefe religious Congregations might
ufe fome Wafhings, Luftrations, or Sprinklings;
but this is Conjecture only.

Stonehenge is in Diameter fixty Cubits; fixty
more reach to the inner Edge of the circular
Ditch of the Court. The Ditch was originally
thirty Cubits broad. The entire Diameter of the
Court reaching to the outward Verge of the
Ditch, four Times fixty Cubits, which is about
Four hundred and ten Feet.

The Views from this Temple are various, beautiful and extenfive. *Salifbury* Steeple appears at a-
bout fix Miles Diftance, and *Old Sarum* a Mile
nearer. The many Groups of *Barrows*, or
Places of Sepulture, fcattered upon the different
Rifings within its Sight, are a vaft Ornament to
thefe charming Downs. It is eafy to diftinguifh
fifty of thefe *Barrows* from hence, efpecially when
the Sun is juft arofe above, or finking below, the
Horizon.

The

The Avenue of *Stonehenge* is very apparent, and extreamly elegant. It anfwers to the *North-Eaft*, as I have obferved, being the principal Line of the Work, whereabouts the Sun rifes in our longeft Days. This Avenue extends itfelf, with a delicious Defcent, a thoufand Cubits, down to the Bottom of the Valley. The Ditches on each Side of it are forty Cubits afunder, and run perfectly parallel to the Bottom. The Earth of the Ditches is thrown inward. About the Mid-way is a pretty natural Depreffure, which has a fine Effect. At the Diftance of a thoufand Cubits from the Area of *Stonehenge*, it divides itfelf into two Branches, the one of which goes directly Eaft, pointing to an ancient Ford over the River *Avon*, called *Radfin*; but now difufed (on Account of the Bridge at *Amefbury* Town's End) and beyond that Ford, the Vifto of it bears directly to an Eminence, called *Harradon-Hill*. The Weftern Branch of this Avenue goes off at firft with a fimilar Sweep; but does not throw itfelf into a ftrait Line immediately as the other, but curves along the Bottom of the Hill, till it meets the *Curfus* or *Race-Courfe*. This *Curfus* or *Hippodrom* (as alfo the Avenue) was firft difcovered by Dr. *Stukeley*. 'Tis a noble Monument of Antiquity, and undoubtedly was the Place appointed for the Celebration of Feafts, Games, Exercifes and Sports, as has been the univerfal Cuftom at the more public and folemn Meetings to facrifice. This great Work is included between two Ditches, running Eaft and Weft, in a Parallel, which are Three hundred and fifty Feet afunder; and its Length is Ten thoufand Feet. A prodigious Work! formed to reach from the higheft Part of two Hills, and extended all the intermediate Diftance over a gently falling Valley: So that the whole *Curfus* lay conveniently under the Eye of the moft

numerous Spectators. And to render it still more
convenient for Sight, it is projected on the Side of
a rising Ground looking chiefly towards *Stonehenge.* It has two Entrances oppofite to each
other, and alfo to the ftrait Part of the Avenue
to *Stonehenge.* It feems as though the Turf of
the adjacent Ground on both Sides has been originally taken off, and laid upon the whole Length
of this *Curfus*, becaufe 'tis fomewhat higher.

The Eaft End is compofed of a great Bank of
Earth, thrown up nearly the full Breadth of the
whole *Curfus* ; and probably was the Place where
the Chairs or Seats of thofe were placed, who
were Judges of the Prizes, or principal Spectators. The Middle of the Valley is at prefent
fomewhat fteep ; but not fo but that a *Britifh
Charioteer* might have a good Opportunity of
fhewing that Dexterity which *Cæfar* fo much ap-
plauds ; and the exquifite Softnefs of the Turf
might prevent the bad Confequences of Falls.
The Weft End of the *Curfus* is curved into an
Arch, like the End of the *Circus's* of the *Romans* ; and here probably the Chariots ran round
in order to turn again, and there is an obfcure
Barrow round which they returned as it were a
Meta. The Imagination is here very great, when
we think of the delightful Profpect which was afforded from the *Temple*, when this vaft *Curfus* was
crouded with Chariots, Horfemen, and innumerable Multitudes of others, attending thefe ancient Solemnities.

The *Barrows* which I have mentioned, are in general upon elevated Ground. For the moft Part
they are of the Bell-Fafhion, but very elegant, and
even nicely finifhed. There is much Variety in
their Diameters, and Manner of Compofition. It
is therefore very ridiculous to fuppofe that thefe
were the tumultuary Burial-Places of thofe flain

in

in Battle, as some of our Writers have suggested; for they certainly were the Sepulchres of eminent Persons buried in the Days of Peace, and during a considerable Space of Time ; and as there are many Groups of them together, they were without Dispute the Burial-Places of Families. Most of these *Barrows*, even the small ones, have Ditches around them. Many circular Ditches are sixty Cubits, and others an hundred or more, in Diameter. They are frequently placed in equidistant Rows, and with some particular Regard to the *Temple*, the *Avenue*, or the *Cursus* ; so that from these Places they produce a regular and pleasing Appearance.

In the Year 1722, the Earl of *Pembroke* opened a *Barrow* situate to the South of the *Temple*, close by the Road to *Wilton*, in order to find the Position of the Body, as laid in those distant Days. On the West Side he made a Section from the Top to the Bottom, an entire Segment from Center to Circumference. The Matter of the Composition of the *Barrow* was good Earth quite through, except a Coat of Chalk about two Feet in Thickness, covering it quite over, under the Turf. Hence it appears, says the Dr. that the Method of making these *Barrows* was to dig up the Turf for a great Space round, till the *Barrow* was brought to its intended Bulk ; then with the Chalk dug out of the environing Ditch, they powdered it all over, so that for a considerable Time these *Barrows* must have looked white, perhaps for some Years ; and the Notion of Sanctity annexed to them forbade People trampling upon them, till perfectly settled and turfed over. From this the Neatness of their Form became, which continues to this Day. At the Center of this *Barrow*, Lord *Pembroke* found the Skeleton of

the

the Perfon interred, perfect, of a reafonable Size, with the Head lying towards *Stonehenge*.

In the following Year, by that Nobleman's Order, Dr. *Stukeley* opened one of the *Double Barrows*, which were conjectured to be the Sepulture of a Man and his Wife; and that the leaft of the two was the Female. A large Cut was made on the Top from Eaft to Weft. After the Turf was taken off, there alfo appeared a Layer of Chalk, and then fine Garden Mould. About three Feet below the Surface, a Layer of Flints, humouring the Convexity of the Barrow. This being a Foot thick, refted upon a Layer of foft Mould; in which was enclofed an Urn full of Bones. The Urn was of unbaked Clay, of a reddifh Colour, crumbled into Pieces. It had been rudely wrought, with fmall Mouldings round the Verge, and other circular Channels on the Outfide. The Bones had been burnt, and crouded altogether in a little Heap. The Collar-Bone, and one Side of the under Jaw, were entire. 'Twas imagined to have been a Girl of about fourteen Years old by their Size, and by the great Quantity of female Ornaments mix'd with the Bones, as Beads of many Sorts and Colours, particularly of Amber of various Shapes and Sizes; each having a Hole to run a String through. Several of the Button Sort were covered with white Metal, and one of them with a thin Film of pure Gold. But they had all undergone the Fire, fo that what would eafily confume fell to Pieces as foon as handled. This Perfon was probably a young *Heroine*, for there was found the Head of a Javelin in Brafs, at the Bottom of which are two Holes for the Pin that faftened it to the Staff, and a fharp Bodkin, round at one End, fquare at the other, where it went into the Handle. The Dr. preferved the Trinkets, and, as was his Practice,

recom-

recompofed the Afhes of the Defunct, covered
them with Earth, and left vifible Marks of its
having been opened, in order to prevent its being
opened again by any future Enquirers.

The next *Barrow* (which was fuppofed to be
that of the Hufband or Father of this Lady) being opened, at fourteen Inches deep, where the
Mould was mixed with Chalk, there appeared the
entire Skeleton of a Man. The Skull and all
the Bones rotted through Length of Time; the
Head lay to the North.

To the South-Weft of this, is (to ufe the Dr.'s
Expreffion) a circular Ditch-like Cavity, fixty
Cubits in Diameter, dug in the Chalk like a
Barrow reverfed. It is near a great *Barrow*,
one of the South-Weftern Group. This Cavity
is feven Feet deep in the Middle, very neatly
turned, and out of it, in all Probability, they dug
the Materials which formed the adjacent *Barrow*.
It feems to have been ufed as a Place for Sacri-
fice and Feafting in Memory of the Dead, as was
the ancient Cuftom. It is now over-grown with
the Shrub called *Erica vulgaris*, and (as when
Dr. *Stukeley* faw it) its Flower, which fmells like
Honey, is now in Bloom. The Dr. tells us,
that he made a crofs Section in the Center of this
Cavity, upon the cardinal Points; but found nothing but a Bit of a red Earthen Pot. He afterwards dug up one of thofe Tumulus's called the
Druids Barrows, and found the Bones of a Man,
but no Signs of an Urn. The Diameter of this
Ditch and Area is One hundred Cubits.

In fome other *Barrows* he found human Bones
burnt, as alfo thofe of various Animals; and
fince the Time of the Dr.'s digging there have
been found in fome of the *Barrows* near *Ambrefbury*, Pieces of Spears, and other warlike Inftruments,

ments, of which the Duke of *Queensbury* is in Possession.

The Earl of *Pembroke* told the Dr. that a Brass Sword was dug up in a *Barrow* here, and sent to *Oxford*. In one near *Little Ambresbury* was found a Weapon like a *Pole-Axe*; it weighed twenty Pounds, and was given to Col. *Wyndham*. In the most Northern *Barrow* from *Stonehenge*, was found one of these Brass Instruments, called *Celts*; it was thirteen Inches long. The Dr. supposes this *Barrow* to be that of an *Archdruid*, and. that this Instrument was used in cutting off the Misleto. It was given by Mr. *Stallard* of *Ambresbury* to the Earl of *Burlington*, and is now in the *British Musæum*. We must agree with Dr. *Stukeley*, that the Custom of burning dead Bodies was prior to the Name of *Rome*.

Having thus indulged myself with a Visitation of this *primitive Temple* and its Appendages, I returned in sweet Satisfaction to *Ambresbury*, from these extensive Plains; which are about fifty Miles in Length, and forty in Breadth. The Number of Sheep which annually graze on this delightful Turf are upon a Medium Two Million five hundred thousand; but Mr. *Hanway* was grosly imposed upon when at *Dorchester* (in the Neighbourhood of which I have spent more than two Years), he was told, that there were Six hundred thousand fed within the Circumference of six Miles round that Town*.

Before I enter upon the Description of *Ambresbury*, the Duke of *Queensbury's* Seat, or *Vespasian's* Camp, I shall just mention the Opinions of some Antiquaries regarding *Stonehenge*,

Gi-

---

* The Compiler of the *Tour through Great-Britain*, in his last Edition (copying Mr. *Hanway*) says, that *He* also was told this idle Tale. Those who write Works of this Sort, should be guarded against general Credibility.

Giraldus Cambrenfis, Geoffry of Monmouth, Matthew of Weftminfter, and other Fabulifts, have told ftrange Tales of the Stones that compofed this Building. As that *Merlin,* by his Magic, fetched them from *Ireland ;* by which Sort of Power they had been before brought from *Africa,* and that they had a medicinal Virtue in them. That they were erected at the Inftance of *Aurelius Ambrofius,* the laft *Britifh* King, in Memory of fome *Britons* murdered by the *Saxons.* And *Polydore Virgil* fays, 'twas erected as a fepulchral Monument for that King. *Sammes* conceits it to be a Work of the *Phœnicians. Camden* confeffes modeftly, that he is not able to give any accurate Account of it, but he could not perfuade himfelf that 'twas either *Roman, Saxon* or *Danifh.* The learned *Aubrey* thinks it to have been a Temple of the *Druids,* long before the *Roman* Invafion. But the Author of *Nero Cæfar* fays, 'twas raifed by the *Britons,* in Memory of Queen *Boadicea.* Others have been of Opinion, that it was a *Danifh* Monument, raifed either as a Trophy for fome Victory, or for the Election and Coronation of their Kings: And Dr. *Charlton* thinks the *Danes* erected it to keep their Men from Idlenefs. But of all the chimerical Notions regarding this Temple, that of *Inigo Jones,* or rather Mr. *Webb,* who makes it a Temple built by the *Romans,* to the God *Cælum* or *Terminus,* is the moft ridiculous ; for there is not the leaft Foundation for fuch a Conjecture.

Upon the whole, Dr. *Stukeley* has, with great Learning and clear Judgment, reftored this fuperb Temple to them, to whom it moft certainly belonged, namely, the *Britifh Druids.*

As to its prefent Name, that is plainly of *Saxon* Stock ; for even at the Time of their Encroachments upon this Iſland, it was in a decayed State, and had the Appearance of Hanging Stones.

I ſhall cloſe my Account of this wonderful Work, with obſerving that the Stones which compoſe it, were certainly brought from thoſe called the *Grey Weathers* upon *Marlborough* Downs, near *Abury* in this County, about ſixteen Miles diſtant. It has puzzled many who have attempted to point out the Manner of their Conveyance hither; but it would certainly puzzle them more, if they were to be aſked (as ſome have thought them factitious) how, and of what Materials they were formed? and ſtill farther, if in thoſe Days, they had not ſo much Knowledge of Mechaniſm as to draw theſe Stones from *Abury*, how could they raiſe the ponderous Impoſts that are upon the Uprights of the outer *Circle*; or thoſe whoſe horizontal Poſition contribute to form the *Trili-thons?*

I doubt I have ſtretched your Patience in dwelling ſo long upon this Subject, but I could not abridge it, without a Deviation from my Plan; and therefore I am ſure of your Indulgence,

The Place where the Town of *Ambreſbury* or *Ameſbury* now ſtands, probably took its Name from the famous Temple I have now deſcribed; for *Stonehenge* was originally called *Ambres*, or *Main Ambres*, which means the Anointed Stones, *i. e.* the conſecrated, the ſacred Stones: And it has been very judiciouſly obſerved, that the Buildings near *Veſpaſian*'s Camp (which I ſhall preſently deſcribe) were called *Ambreſburgh*, and therefore the Town now, according to common Corruption, *Ambreſbury*.

The Tale inſerted in a modern * Work, of *Aurelius Ambroſius* rebuilding a Monaſtery here, and filling it with Three hundred Monks, is ridiculous to the laſt Degree. That *Hengiſt* the *Saxon*
had

* *Tour through Great-Britain.*

had maffacred here Three hundred of the *Brtifh* Nobility in cold Blood, is mentioned by our Hiftorians, when King *Vortigern* was fo weak as to meet him with his Followers unarmed; but, according to Sir *William Dugdale*, the Nunnery at *Ambrefbury* was built by Queen *Elfrida*, by Way of Expiation for the Murder of King *Edward* the Younger, called St. *Edward*; of which fhe had been guilty. In the Reign of *Henry* II. A. D. 1177. the Nuns were expelled from hence, and fhut up in other religious Houfes, under ftrict Cuftody, for their fcandalous Incontinency; and other Nuns of *Font-Everard* introduced in their Stead, by the Authority of Pope *Alexander*, King *Henry* II. and *Richard*, Archbifhop of *Canterbury*; which King *Henry* gave to the faid Nunnery of *Font-Everard*, this Church as a Cell, with many other Lands and great Liberties. All which were confirmed by King *John*, in the firft Year of his Reign; and in the fifth Year of his Government he gave to it fifty Shillings *per Annum* out of the Exchequer for ever. *Eleanor*, Queen of *Henry* III. retired to, and died in this Nunnery : And the Princefs *Mary*, Daughter to King *Edward* II. and the Daughters of thirteen Noblemen, took the Veil together in this Houfe, which at the Diffolution was valued at Four hundred and ninety-five Pounds Fifteen Shillings and Two Pence *per Annum*.

This Town is pleafantly fituated upon the River *Avon*, has much Appearance of Antiquity, and fome good Inns; which are generally vifited by thofe who go to fee *Stonehenge*. The Market, which is but fmall, is held on *Friday*, and the Fairs on the 6th of *May*, the 11th of *June*, and the 13th of *November*.

Here is a Seat built by *Inigo Jones*, where live the Duke and Dutchefs of *Queenfbury* and *Dover*; who enjoy the Comforts of Retirement fo, as to caufe

the Hours of Age to slide smoothly on, dealing out
their Beneficence to the Indigent of the Neighbourhood. This is the illustrious Pair, who, in the
Life-Time of the modest, meritorious *Gay*, wiped
the Gloom of Sorrow from his Brow, and paid a
singular Regard to his Memory in *Westminster-*
Abbey. On this Occasion, says *Pope*,

> Blest be the Great! for those they take away,
> And those they leave me—for they left me *Gay*,
> Left me to see neglected Genius bloom,
> Neglected die! and tell it on his Tomb;
> Of all thy blameless Life the sole Return
> My Verse, and *Queensbury* weeping o'er thy Urn.

The Duke has made many fine Improvements
in his Gardens, through which the *Avon* sweetly
meanders; also at the Foot of a steep Hill,
which his Grace has enclosed, and beautifully
planted. Over this River is a Bridge, upon
which is built a delightful Room in the *Chinese*
Taste. He has also made Ridings over the
Downs from *Ambresbury* to *Stonehenge*, and planted
them with Clumps of ever-green Trees, which
would be a fine Ornament to these delightful open
Downs, provided the Country People could be restrained from damaging and destroying them.

Between *Stonehenge* and the Town, hanging over
the River upon elevated Ground, is a fine and ancient *Camp*, commonly called (with much more
Propriety than that at *Yarnbury*) *Vespasian's*. It
is an oblong Square, nicely formed upon a Flex-
ture of the River, which closes one Side and one
End of it. There is an old *Barrow* enclosed in it,
which doubtless was one of those belonging to
the Temple of *Stonehenge*, before this *Camp* was
made. It is observeable, that the Road from
Stonehenge to *Ambresbury* runs upon the true *Via
Prætoria* of the *Camp*; the General's Tent or *Præ-
torium* was in that Part South of the Road, be-

tween

tween it and the River, towards *Little Ambrefbury*. There is another Gate of the *Camp* at the lower End to the Northward.

From *Ambrefbury* I directed my Courfe over the Plain towards *Old Sarum*. This City filled up the Summit of an high Hill, at the Bottom of which the *Avon* glides in its Courfe from *Ambrefbury* to *Salifbury*. *Old Sarum* is by the Emperor *Antoninus* called *Sorbiodunum*, and the *Saxons* gave it the Appellation of *Searefbirig*. This City was erected in an orbicular Form, after a fine Defign. There is now a double Entrenchment, with a deep Ditch to each. That it was a *Roman Station* is generally allowed; but *Camden*, and his Continuator, are of different Opinions as to its having been *Britifh*. I have before obferved, that in the *Conqueror's* Time, the Bifhop's See was removed from *Sherborn* hither. In the North-Weft Angle of the City ftood the *Cathedral* and the *Bifhop's Palace*. I fhall not trouble you with the Particulars of a Council held here by King *Edgar*, or of its being plundered by the *Danes* in the Year after the *Danifh* Maffacre.

William the Firft fummoned the States of the Kingdom to fwear Fealty to him here; but, as I have already obferved, it was deferted in the Reign of *Henry* the Third, chiefly for Want of Water. Upon the whole, it appears to me an odd Situation to build a City upon, being a dry, barren and uncomfortable Hill, efpecially in the Winter-Seafon. Notwithftanding there is no Dwelling in, and but one Farm-Houfe near it, *Old Sarum* is called a Borough, and fends two Members to the Houfe of Commons.

I was fcarcely out of the Streets of *Salifbury* (which City is in 1 Deg. 55 Min. of Weftern Longitude from the Meridian of *London*; and its Latitude is 51 Deg. 6 Min.) when I found myfelf upon the Brow of an Hill, which com-

mands

mands a good View of the whole City. Here are many Tenter-Grounds for the Drying of Flannels, &c. This Situation is very fine, having a moſt charming open Country around, intermixed with ſweet cultivated Vallies.

Theſe Plains and Downs being very open, and their Surface not ſo liable to Alteration as that of a more encloſed Country, is probably the Reaſon of their having, at this Time, more antique Remains, than moſt other Parts of *England.* An ingenious Gentleman at *Saliſbury* informs me, that in this County are the Veſtigia of near ſixty *Britiſh, Roman, Saxon,* or *Daniſh* Encampments ; more of which I may hereafter viſit.

Having left this Spot, the Country became ſoon after a wide uncultivated Space, inhabited only by Shepherds and their Flocks : but in a ſhort Time, I found Fields of Wheat and Barley. *Gay,* in his Journey to *Exeter,* thus deſcribes this Part of *Wiltſhire,* and the Degeneracy of the preſent Shepherds from thoſe, who (perhaps) inſpired the all-accompliſhed *Sydney* to write his *Arcadia.*

—— The unbounded Plain
Where the cloak'd Shepherd guides his fleecy Train;
No leafy Bow'rs a Noon-Day Shelter lend,
Nor from the chilly Dews at Night defend ;
With wond'rous Art he counts the ſtraggling Flock,
And by the Sun informs you what's o'Clock.
How are our Shepherds fall'n from ancient Days !
No *Amaryllis* chaunts alternate Lays;
From her no liſt'ning *Echoes* learn to ſing,
Nor with his Reed the jocund Vallies ring.
Here Sheep the Paſtures hide, there Harveſts bend,
See *Sarum's* Steeple o'er yon Hill aſcend !

On theſe Plains I obſerved a confiderable Drove of fine Oxen, going from *Gillingham* Fair to *Wincheſter,* intended for the Nouriſhment of *French* Priſoners. Thus we ſee the *Britiſh* Government ſtill ftill fupporting our old unrivalled Character of Benevolence and Hofpitality, even to the Subjects of our moft dangerous Enemy.

My old Friend, the Landlord of the *Hutt*, entertained me, as ufual, with many Things in *his* Way. About a Mile Eaftward of this Inn, the Road parts; the Right-Hand leading through *Stockbridge*, the Left to *Andover* : And here are Infcriptions, which tell the Stranger, that *each* is the *neareft* and beft Way to *London*. From hence to *Wallop* the Country becomes more ufed to the Plough.

Wallop is a fmall Village (where I left *Wiltfhire*). This Place, which is pleafantly fituated in the County of *Hants*, gave Surname to the famous Sir *John* (Anceftor to the prefent Earl of *Portfmouth*) who, in the Year 1513, with Eight hundred Men, burnt twenty-one Towns in *Normandy*, and all the *French* Ships in the Ports of *Naples* and *Tripoly*.

A *Salisbury* Lady, who has two very young Gentlemen, her Sons, under the Care of a Pedagoguefs here, defired me to pay them a Vifit. I am juft returned from performing that Tafk, where, I faw the real Life of fuch a Picture, as is drawn by the Hand of the celebrated and accomplifhed Mr. *Shenftone*, after the Manner of *Spencer*; with which I fhall conclude this Letter.

> A Ruffet Stole was o'er her Shoulders thrown,
> A Ruffet Kirtle fenc'd the nipping Air;
> 'Twas fimple Ruffet, but it was her own!
> 'Twas her own Country bred the Flock fo fair:
> 'Twas her own Labour did the Fleece prepare,
> And footh to fay, her Pupils rang'd around,
> Thro' pious Awe, did term it paffing rare!
> For they in gaping Wonderment abound,
> And think, no Doubt, fhe been the *greateft Wight on*
>   Ground!

I am, Sir, Yours, &c.

L E T-

L E T T E R VIII.

From *Newbury*, in *Berkshire*.

S I R,

LEAVING *Wallop*, I turned a little to the Left, in order to fee the Remains of a Fortification at *Quarley-Hills*. *Camden* mentions this as a great Piece of Antiquity, having, in his Time, quadruple Works on one Side. The two outer Trenches are yet very plain, being a confiderable Diftance from each other : And at *Dunbury-Hill*, about a Mile from it, is another Fortification of fimilar Conftruction. From this Place 'tis about three Miles to *Weyhill*, where the famous annual Fair is held, of which I fhall prefently write. As Noon drew near, I continued my Courfe towards *Andover* ; which the *Saxons* called *Andeafaran*, that is, a Paffage over the River *Ande*. This inconfiderable Stream falls into the *Teft* fome Miles below the Town. It is a neat Market and Borough Town, governed by a Mayor, Aldermen, and Common-Council. It fends two Members to Parliament, and gives the Title of Vifcount to *Henry Howard*, Earl of *Suffolk* and *Berkshire*; whofe eldeft Son, lately called Vifcount *Andover*, a moft amiable Gentleman, met, in the Year 1756, with a fudden Death, by a Fall from his Chaife, greatly and juftly lamented.

By a Letter written by the Earl of *Leicefter* * to the Magiftrates of this Borough, it appears, that

Bailiffs

* " After my heartie Commendations. Whereas it hath pleafed her Majefty to appoint a Parliament to be prefentlie called : Being *Steward* of your Town, I make bould hartilie to pray you, that you would give me the Nomination of one

of

Bailiffs were the principal Officers here ; and alfo, that thinking them parfimonious, he endeavoured, with much Art, to play the ministerial Courtier upon them.

The Market-House here is fimilar to that of *Rumfey*; it has a very good Market on *Saturdays*, and a Fair on Mid-Lent *Saturday*, for Horfes, Cheefe, and Leather ; another on, the 12th of *May*, for millanery Goods and Leather ; and a third, on *November* the 16th, for Horfes, Sheep, Leather and Cheefe. But thefe are much eclipfed by that prodigious one held annually at *Weyhill*, in its Neighbourhood ; which is kept in an open Field, being perhaps the largeft Fair in *England*, that of *Stirbitch* near *Cambridge* not excepted, efpecially for Sheep, Hops, and Cheefe. As the Town of *Andover* is fituate on the Side of thefe delightful Downs, in an healthy Air, and upon the great Weftern Road, it is accommodated with fome very good Inns. And as here is a confiderable Manufactory of the beft Shalloons in *England*, it is a very populous and thriving Place.

William the Firft gave the Church of *Andover* (as a Cell) to St. *Florence* of *Saumurs* in *Normandy*, with many Lands and Revenues belonging to the fame

of your Burgeffes for the fame : And yf mynding to avoyd the Chardges of Allowance for the other Burgeffe, you mean to name aenie that is not of your Towne ; yf you will beftow the Nomination of the other Burgeffe alfo upon me, I will thank you for it : And will both appoint a fufficient Man, and fee you difchardged of all Chardges in that Behaulfe. And fo praying your fpeedie Anfwere herein, I thus bid you right hartilie farewell

From the Court, the 12th of *October*, 1584.

Your loving Friend,

R. LEYCESTER.

If you will fend me your Election with a Blank, I fhall put in the Names.

To my very loving Friends, the *Baliefes, Aldermen,* and the reft of the Town of *Andover*."

fame; which was confirmed by *Edward* the Second, in the eighth Year of his Reign.

The Church at prefent is very neat; and the People are genteel, though their Dialect is fomewhat broad. A *Saxon* Lady near this Place was rendered famous by the Impofition which fhe put upon King *Edgar*; who coming hither in or about the Year 964, and hearing of the Beauty of her Daughter; he, without any Ceremony, Courtfhip or Confent, ordered the Mother to bring her to his Arms. But the Lady artfully fent one of her Maids in her Stead, whom the King afterwards had great Affection for, till it was removed by the more powerful Charms of the Lady *Elfrida*.

Andover is famous for a Chriftening performed there in the Year 995, on the Perfon of *Anlaff*, King of *Norway*; who came from on board his Ships for that Purpofe; where he met King *Ethelred* the Second (the fecond Son of the faid *Edgar*) who ftood Godfather at the Font, when the Convert engaged to depart with his Forces from *England*, never to return, which he very faithfully performed.

In this Town is a Free-School, founded by *John Hanfdon*, in the Year 1569; and an Hofpital for fix Men, built and endowed by *John Pollen*, Efq; Member of Parliament for this Borough, in the Reign of King *William* the Third. Here was born *Robert Thomfon*, who went to *New Spain*; where being feized as an Heretic, he was fent to *Old Spain*, and put into the Inquifition; from whence he was releafed after three Years Imprifonment. He wrote a Defcription of *New Spain*, and the City of *Mexico*.

From hence in the Afternoon I bent my Courfe towards *Newbury*; and before the Evening came on entered a Common, on the Side of which was

a

a delightful Wood, through which an Herdſman, with much Chearfulneſs, directed me. The pleaſing Account the Fellow gave me of his happy State, put me in mind of a Poem, written above Two hundred Year ago, in which are theſe Lines ;

> I heard a Heardman once compare,
> That quiet Nights he had moe ſlept,
> And had moe mery Dayes to ſpare,
> Than he which ought the Beaſt he kept.

The Wood brought me, by a charming Path, to the Brow of an Hill, at the Foot of which lies a Village, called *Hurſbands* ; where is a Seat belonging to the Earl of *Portſmouth*. I quartered at the *Plough*, from whence departing in the Morning, I aſcended a white Hill, and paſſing through an irregular Road, came to an hilly Wood, and in the Bottom ſaw ſeveral ſuch pretty Dwellings as Mr. *Ambroſe Phillips*, the *Theocritus* of *England*, deſired. " To view (ſays he) a fair ſtately Palace, ſtrikes us indeed with Admiration ; and ſwells the Soul with Notions of Grandeur : But when I ſee a little Country Dwelling, advantageouſly ſituated, amidſt a beautiful Variety of Hills, Meadows, Fields, Woods, and Rivulets ; I feel an unſpeakable Sort of Satisfaction ; and cannot forbear wiſhing my kinder Fortune would place me in ſuch a ſweet Retirement." After a gentle Riſe, the Woods abounding with the Muſic of innumerable Birds, while the Milk-Maid's Song was chanting loud in the Meadows, and the Plowman's ſhrill Whiſtle in the ſloping Valley, I came to an Houſe of Entertainment, upon the Brow of an Hill, which fronteth the North, and overlooks a fine Valley, through which runs the River *Kennet*. Having deſcended, I paſſed through a delicious Country, till I arrived at the Town of *Newbury* ; which is built upon the Banks of that pretty River, the Navigation on whofe Bofom is of prodigious Service to this great Malting-Town, and the adjacent Country.

Newbury, notwithftanding its feemingly-modern Name, was, by the *Conqueror*, given to *Ernulph de Hefdin*, whofe Family, in or about the Year 1120, fold it to *William Marfhal*, Earl of *Pembroke*; but *Roger Bigod* forfeited it to King *Henry* the Third. This Town, which is very large, and well built, efpecially the principal Street, hath for many Ages been famous for its great Cloathing Manufactory; and (there is now a confiderable one of Shalloons) we are told, that one *John Winfchomb*, commonly called *Jack of Newbury*, in the Reign of King *Henry* the Eighth, had an hundred Looms in his Houfe, and was confidered as the greateft Clothier in *England*. He joined the Army of the faid King, then commanded by the Duke of *Norfolk*, and marching to the North, with an hundred of his own Men, armed and cloathed at his fole Expence; where, in that general Engagement with the *Scots* at *Flodden*, both his Men and himfelf behaved with diftinguifhed Bravery. The Church of this Town ftands near the Market-Place; the Tower and Pulpit were built by the faid Perfon, and on the North Ifle near the Chancel, under the Effigies of a Man and Woman, which I take to be thofe of the faid Clothier and his Wife, the following Words were infcribed upon a Plate of Brafs;

Of your Charite pray for the
Soule of *John Smalwood*, alias
Winchom, and *Alice* his Wife;
Which *John* died the 15th Day of
February, An. Dom. 1519.

Mr. *John Kendrick*, the Son of a Clothier, who became a Merchant in *London*, and of whom I fhall fay more hereafter, left by his Will Four
thoufand

thousand Pounds to encourage the Cloathing-Trade of this Town, and set the Poor of it to Work.

During the Contest between the Houses of *York* and *Lancaster*, the Earl of *Wiltshire* caused twenty of the former Party to be hanged and quartered in this Town of *Newbury*.

In 1643, this Place was rendered famous by a general Engagement, between the Army of King *Charles* the First, commanded by Prince *Rupert*, in which the King was present, and that of the Parliament, headed by the Earl of *Essex*. The Action was warm, obstinate, and bloody. Both Sides claimed the Advantage, but if there was any, it belonged to *Essex*. In this domestic Conflict was killed the Earls of *Sunderland*, and *Caernarvon*, and also the incomparable Lord *Falkland*, whom Mr, *Pope* thus laments;

Lo ! *Falkland* falls, the virtuous and the just !

In *October* the next Year, was another bloody Engagement, nearly upon the same Spot, in which the King narrowly escaped being taken, and Night only put a Period to the Battle, without any apparent Advantage on either Side.

The Town of *Newbury* is large, and very well built : And notwithstanding the Cloathing Business is removed to the West, is a genteel, flourishing, and populous Place. It is governed by a Mayor, High-Steward, Recorder, Aldermen and capital Burgesses. The Market is on *Thursdays*; the Fairs on *Holy Thursday*, for horned Cattle and Horses ; the 5th of *July*, for Cows, Horses, and Swine ; St. *Bartholomew*, *August* the 24th, for Cheese and Horses ; and St. *Simon* and *Jude*, the 28th of *October*, for the same Articles.

According to Dr. *William Twisse* (whose Father was a *German*, in the Cloathing Business at *Speen-*

hamland'

hamland) Polocutor of the *Assembly of Divines* ; the Reformation began in this Town, *Temp. Hen.* VIII.

Heie is a good Charity-School for forty Boys ; and there aie many good Inns in this Town, but as the *Bath* Road goes through *Speenhamland,* which is at the Noith End of it, that Place far eclipfes it in this Article. Indeed from the Remains of an ancient Town called *Spine,* this of *Newbury* arofe.

Near *Newbury* (which is as agreeable a Town as we generally meet with) is a good Houfe belonging to Lord *Craven.* I am now in Company with the worthy Mr. ——, of whom I fhall fpeedily take my Leave ; and am, Sir, Yours, &c.

L E T T E R IX.

From *Reading.*

S I R,

HAVING left *Newbury,* I paffed to the Remains of *Donnington-Caftle,* which *Camden* calls " very neat, feated on the Brow of a woody Hill, having a fine Profpect, and Windows on all Sides very lightfome." It is fuppofed to have been erected by Sir *Richard de Adderbury,* and under it was an Hofpital for poor Perfons. It became the Refidence of *Geoffry Chaucer,* the Father of *Englifh* Poetry ; afterwards of *William de la Pole,* Duke of *Suffolk,* who married his Granddaughter, *Alice,* from whom it defcended, and by a Grant from *Henry* the Eighth came to *Charles Brandon,* Duke of *Suffolk.* The aforefaid *Alice Chaucer* was the Daughter of *Thomas Chaucer,* Efq; who was High Sheriff of this County in

1400,

1400, and Speaker of the House of Commons in the ninth, tenth, and thirteen Years of the Reign of *Henry* the Fourth, and the second of *Henry* the Fifth. In the Beginning of the Civil War it was possessed by Mr. *John Packer*, and had a Garrison for the King, under the Command of Sir *John Boys*, and, being situate near the great Western Road, was of much Use. The Parliament's Forces under Colonel *Horton* laid Siege to it, who having raised a Battery at the Foot of an Hill near *Newbury*, demolished three of the Towers, and Part of the Wall. However, notwithstanding *Horton* was reinforced by General *Middleton* and the Earl of *Manchester*, the Garrison held out till they were relieved by the King. After the second Battle of *Newbury*, it was again besieged by the Forces of the Parliament, under the Command of the Earl of *Essex*; and that Siege was also raised: But it is now in Ruins. Below which runs the little River *Lambs-bourn*, or, as commonly pronouced, *Lambourn*, which falls into the *Kennet* at *Thatchem*. This Stream, which glides down from a small Town of that Name, is, contrary to all others, high in Summer, and low in Winter. It generally goes off about *Michaelmas*, and the Country People observe, that the sooner it leaves them the cheaper Corn will be that Season. This Phœnomenon has puzzled our Naturalists. *Joseph Sylvester*, who translated *Du Barta*'s Works, and lived at *Lambourn*, has these Lines;

And little *Lambes-Bourn*, tho' thou match not *Lers*,
Nor hadst the Honour of *Dubarta*'s Verse;
If mine have any, thou must needs partake,
Both for thine *Own*, and for thine *Owner*'s Sake *.
All Summer long (while all thy Sisters Shrink)
Then of thy Waters thousands daily drink;

Besides

* Sir *William Essex*.

Befides that Water, which in Haft doth run,
To wafh the Feet of *Chaucer's Donnington.*
But, while the reft are full unto the Top,
All Winter long thou doft not fhew a Drop,
Nor fend'ft a Doit of needlefs Subfidy,
To cram the *Kennet's* wantlefs Treafury ;
Before her Store be fpent, and Springs be ftaid,
Then thou alone, thou lendft a liberal Aid.
Teaching thy wealthy Neighbours (mine of late)
How, when, and where to right participate
Their Streams of Comfort to the poor that pine,
And not to greafe ftill the two greafy Swine ;
Neither for Fame, nor Form (when others do)
To give a Morfel, or a Mite or two ;
But feverally, and of a felfly Motion,
When others mifs, to give the moft Devotion.

The People here fhewed me where ftood a great
Oak, which they told me ufed to fhade its celebrated Owner, while he compofed his Poems. But
this is mere Tradition ; and I am inclined to think
that the Tree which went by *Chaucer's* Name was
one of his own planting : For that great Natu-
ralift and Philofopher, *John Evelyn,* Efq; fays,
there were three Oaks in this Park planted by
Chaucer himfelf *.

From

---

* One of thefe was called the *King's,* the other, the *Queen's,*
and a third, *Chaucer's* Oak. The firft was fifty Feet in Height
before any Bough or Knot appeared , and cut five Feet fquare at
the *But-End,* all clear Timber. The *Queen's* was felled fince
the (civil) Wars, and held forty Feet excellent Timber, ftrait
as an Arrow in Growth and Grain, and cutting four Feet
at the *Stub,* and near a Yard at the Top; befides a Fork almoft ten Feet clear Timber above the Shaff, which was crowned with a fhady Tuft of Boughs ; amongft which, fome were
on each Side curved like Rams Horns, as if they had been fo
induftrioufly bent by Hand. This Oak was of a Kind fo excellent, cutting a Grain clear as any Clap-board (as appeared
in the Wainfcot which was made thereof) that a thoufand Pi-
ties it is fome *Seminary* of the Acorns had not been propagated
to preferve the Species *Chaucer's* Oak, though it was not of
thefe Dimenfions, yet was it a very goodly Tree. This Soil
is a Sort of gravelly Clay, moiftened with fmall and frequent
Springs. Evelyn *on Foreft Trees.*

From *Donnington* I returned to *Spinhamland*, and entered the dusty Road which leads from *Bristol* and *Bath* to *London*. The Country on each Side was extreamly pleafant, efpecially the rifing Lands on the North. I paffed through *Thatchem* and *Woolhampton*, or rather *Woodhampton*, according to *Camden*, which alfo depends on the Road, and came to the Banks of the *Kennet*, where the Bargemens Oaths were both abundant and uncommon; it were to be wifhed, that the Punifhment of this Practice was more fevere. The Veffels upon this River are drawn by Horfes. The Fields were extreamly fine, and the Day as hot as any Traveller would wifh.

A little on the Left-Hand of the great Road is *Beenham*, of which Church Living the worthy Dr. *Zinzan* is Patron, and the late Mr. *Thomas Stackhoufe*, Author of the *Hiftory of the Bible*, was Incumbent, in Praife of whofe moral Character the Inhabitants are not very lavifh.

The nearer I drew towards *Reading*, the more improved the Country feemed. On my Left were Hills, upon which ftand many delightful Seats, ornamented with delicious Woods; and in the Vale on my Left appeared many others equally charming. Here I ftopped fome Time to attend the Nightingale's Lay, and here, through a fine Avenue of Trees, the gently-cooling Breeze afforded a pleafing Enjoyment. At *Theale*, where are more Inns, I had about four Miles to *Reading*; which I found to be a very large Town. We have the *Latin* Word *Readingum* for this Place, but it is only given to the *Britifh* Appellation *Redin* or *Reading*, that is Fern, with which this Neighbourhood yet abounds. A little below the Town the *Kennet* falls into the *Thames*, which *Drayton* thus mentions;

At *Reading* once arriv'd, clear *Kennet* overtakes
Her Lord the ſtately *Thames*, which that great Flood again
With many Signs of Joy doth kindly entertain.

The *Danes* moſt grievouſly oppreſſed this Place
about the Year 871 : And thoſe barbarous *Scandinavians* were now ſo terrible, that the *Engliſh* in
their Litany uſed theſe Words,

From the Fury of the *Danes*, good Lord deliver us ! *

In the Year 1126, King *Henry* the Firſt
founded a magnificent Abbey in this Town, between the Rivers *Kennet* and *Thames*. He endowed it with the Privileges of enjoying all the
Churches and Chapels, and alſo all the Pleas of
Suits, within and without the Borough, beſides
other great Immunities. He dedicated it to the
Holy Trinity, the Virgin *Mary*, St. *James*, and St.
John Baptiſt (which Endowments were confirmed
by King *Henry* the Second). In a Word, for
Grandeur and Riches, it was ſcarcely equalled in
England. In the Year 1135 this Monarch died,
and his Bowels were buried in the Church of St.
Mary de Pres, at *Roan* in *Normandy* : When his
Body, being wrapped up in Ox-Hides, was ſent
to *Caen* ; where, according to his own Orders, it
lay till there was an Opportunity of conveying it
to *England*. It was afterwards buried in this Monaſtery, and the Monks erected over him a moſt
noble Monument†. His Queen was alſo buried
here :

* The *Danes*, ſays *Henry of Huntingdon*, by frequent Fits
and Starts, ſought, not to poſſeſs, but to plunder, and thirſted
not after Dominion, but after Deſtruction : Even when they
were conquered, the Victors had no Joy in their Succeſs ; ſince
another and a larger Fleet and Army ſtill ſtarted up to ſupport
the Invaders.

† *Hugh*, Abbot of *Reading*, and his Convent, reciting by
their Deed, that King *Henry* the Firſt had erected that Abbey
for the Maintenance of Monks there devoutly and religiouſly
ſerving

here : And the Abbots fat in Parliament till the Diffolution : When this Abbey was valued at One thoufand nine hundred and thirty-eight Pounds Fourteen Shillings and Three Pence *per Annum*. After which Time the Monument was defaced, and his Bones, or rather Duft, thrown out to make room for a common Stable for Horfes.

In the feventh Year of King *Edward* the Firft, a Council of the Clergy was held at *Reading*; and in the Chamber of the Refectory in this Abbey, in the thirty-firft Year of King *Henry* the Sixth (befides others) was held a Parliament from the 6th of *March* till the 18th, when feveral Laws were enacted.

In the Year 1643, the Earl of *Effex* took this Town in ten Days Time (which greatly alarmed the King, who lay at *Oxford*) and his Army was quartered here all that Winter.

In *Reading* are the Parifh Churches of St. *Mary*, St. *Lawrence*, and St. *Giles*; and it is by much the largeft and beft built Town in the County. The Trade of it is very large and extenfive. Here are fome Linen-Dapers that return great

serving God, for the Reception of Strangers and Travellers, but chiefly *Chrift*'s poor People, they therefore erected an Hofpital without the Gate of the Abbey, there to maintain twenty-fix poor People ; and to the Maintenance of Strangers paffing that Way, they gave the Profits of their Mill at *Leominfter* (in *Herefordfhire*). Alfo *Aucherius*, Abbot of *Reading*, built near this Abbey an Houfe for Lepers, which was called St. *Mary Magdalen*'s, allotting for their Suftenance fufficient of all Things, as well for Diet, as other Matters. If any Brother of this Houfe were guilty of Adultery, or of ftriking his Brother in Pride, Anger, or Hatred, he was to be expelled the Houfe. None were to go abroad without a Companion ; and what Charity happened to be given to any one was to be common to all. Thefe, and feveral others, were the Rules obferved in the Lepers Houfe of St. *Mary Magdalen*.

Sums to *London* for the Article of blue Linen, which is an *Ofnabrig* dyed, for the Shirts of Bargemen, and Farmers Servants. The Bufinefs of Malting is very confiderable. The Cloathing Trade is indeed removed from hence ; but, on the whole, 'tis an agreeable, populous, and flourifhing Place ; for Veffels of near an hundred Tons may come up to the Bridge. The Market at *Reading* is held on *Saturdays* ; and a Fair for Cheefe and Horfes on the 1ft of *February* ; another for Horfes on the 1ft of *May* ; a third for Horfes and other Cattle on the 25th of *July* ; and a fourth for Cheefe on the 21ft of *September*.

It is governed by a Mayor, twelve Aldermen, twelve Burgeffes, and other Officers, and fends two Members to Parliament.

This Town gave the Title of Baron to the famous Soldier, Sir *Jacob Aftley*, as it does now to *Charles* Lord *Cadogan*.

Here was born *William of Reading*, Archbifhop of *Bourdeaux* Alfo the good Sir *Thomas Whyte*, Alderman and Lord-Mayor of *London* ; and the famous *John Kendrick*, befoie mentioned.

The former of thefe two, Sir *Thomas Whyte*, chief Magiftrate of *London* in the Year 1554, was of the *Merchant Taylors* Company, and, being a Lover of Learning, founded *Gloucefter-Hall*, and St. *John Baptift's College* in *Oxford*. He erected a School at *Briftol*, another at *Reading*, and a College at *Higham Ferrers*. He alfo gave to the City of *Briftol* Two thoufand Pounds in Truft ; Eight hundred of which was, by the Mayor and Citizens, to be lent to fixteen poor Clothiers for feven Years certain, without Intereft, upon their giving fufficient Security : And then was to pafs to fixteen other Clothiers, according to the Difcretion of thofe in Truft. And two hundred Pounds were referved to buy Corn for the Ufe of
the

the Poor of that City, in cafe of Scarcity. He
alfo by his Will left an hundred Pounds to be
lent, (for two Years) to four young Clothiers of
the City of *York*, after that in the fame Manner,
to thofe of *Canterbury, Reading*, the *Merchant-
Taylors, Gloucefter, Worcefter, Exeter, Salifbury,
Chefter, Norwich, Southampton, Lincoln, Winchefter, Oxford, Hereford, Cambridge, Shrewfbury,
Lynn, Bath, Derby, Ipfwich, Colchefter*, and *New-
caftle* ; and fo alternately for ever. He gave to
the City of *Coventry* Fourteen hundred Pounds in
Truft, to pay to twelve old poor Inhabitants forty
Shillings yearly, and to lend to four young Men
of that City, without Intereft, for nine Years,
and then to be fo employed in ferving four more
fuch Perfons, and many other fuch good Charities. In the Council Chamber of the Corporation at *Reading* is a Picture of this worthy Gentleman, drawn in his Alderman's Gown and Gold
Chain, under which is this Infcription ;

Thomas Whyte Miles, Aldermannus
Civitatis *London.* natus apud *Read-
ding*, in Comitatu *Berks*, Fundator Collegii Sancti *Johannis Baptifte*, et Aule
Gloucef Oxon. cum 24 Civitates at
Villas hujus Regni *Anglie* ditaffet ope-
ribus. Obiit An. Dni. 1566. Ætatis
fuæ, 72.

Auxilium meum à Domino.

In the fame Chamber is the Picture of Mr.
Kendrick, and at the Head of the Frame are thefe
Words ;

Congeries amplum, complebat copia cornu
At cum quinque fuos decies numeraverat annos,
Et fine conjugio cælebs fine prole deinque
Munificum reputans, ftudii moribundus adhæfit.

On the Right Side,

Languida nativa reparare repagula villæ
Sic meditans, dedit huic nummorum millia septem,
Et plus eo ut soles operantes pascat egenos :
Structuras fieri varias mandabat ad artes.

On the Left Side,

Natus in hac villa fuit*, hunc posuere parentes
Musæis deditum, post hæc intentus ad urbem.
Londini sortem res mercatoria fixit
Magna erat in quæstu longo conamine rerum.

At the Foot,

Atque hæc Majori et Burgensibus omnia recte
Constituenda dedit nullumque abolenda per ævum.

On the Right Hand in the Picture,

Johannes Kendrick, Civis, et Dra-
per de *London*.   Anno Ætatis suæ 50.
Obiit 30 Die *Decembris*, Anno Dni.
1624.

On the Left Hand of the Picture,

Pauperibus in Vita
Munificus,
In Morte
Munificentissimus.

This Mr. *John Kendrick* was the eldest Son of a
considerable Clothier here, and, according to an
Inscription in St. *Mary*'s Church, on the Monument of his Brother, they were descended from a
Royal *Saxon* Family.

John Kendrick* was an eminent Merchant in
London; by whose Will, bearing Date the Day
preceding his Death, he left Seven thousand five
hundred Pounds in Trust, to the Mayor and Corporation of *Reading*, as a common Stock, for the
Use

* The Writers of the *Tour through Great-Britain* erroneously
say, his Name was *Kenrick*, and that he was the Son of a Clothier of *Newbury*.

Ufe of the Poor, and fetting them to work, either in making coloured Clothes or Whites, working of Wool, Hemp, Flax, or Iron, grinding of *Brazil* Woods, and other Stuffs for Dying, &c. as to the faid Mayor and Burgeffes, and their Succeffors for ever, fhould feem meet and convenient. And to the Mayor, Aldermen, and Burgeffes of the Town of *Newbury*, Four thoufand Pounds, for the fame Purpofes. And if the latter Corporation fhould be guilty of Non-Performance of the Intent and Meaning of his Will, the Money was to go to the Mayor and Burgeffes of *Reading*, as an Addition to their common Stock as aforefaid. And if the Corporation of *Reading* fhould become guilty of neglecting to put in Execution the Intent and Meaning of his Will, in fuch Cafe the whole Sums were to be paid to the Mayor, Commonalty and Citizens of *London*, to the Ufe of *Chrift's Hofpital*. He gave a great many other charitable Legacies, and was buried in St. *Chriftopher's* Church, *London*.

In the Council-Chamber at *Reading* are alfo painted the Arms of the Corporation, with this Infcription. " Thefe are the auntient Armes, and
" Seale, apperteyning and belonging to the Mayor
" and Burgeffes of the Towne and Borough of
" *Reading*, in the County of *Berks*, and at this my
" prefent Vifitacion was *Edward Butler* Mayor;
" the Right Honourable *Robert* Earl of *Leicefter*,
" Knight of the Moft Noble Order of the Gar-
" ter, Mafter of the Horfe to the Queen's Majefty,
" and one of her Highnefs Privy Councell, High
" Steward of the Towne and Borough. *Robert*
" *Bowyer*, *Thomas Aldworth*, *Thomas Turnor*, *John*
" *Ockham*, *Robert Fylbie*, and *Richard Watlington*,
" Head Burgeffes; and late Mayors of the faid
" Town and Burrough; *John Ockham* aforefaid,
" Steward of the Courts of the faid Burrough.
" Which

" Which Armes I *Clarenceux* King of Armes, have
" ratified and continued unto the said Mayor, and
" Burgeffes of the Towne and Burrough of *Reading*
" in the County of *Berks.* In Witnefs whereof I
" have herereunto fubfcrybed my Name, the 6th
" of *October* 1566, *Will. Henry, Clarencieux* King
" of Armes."

On another Tablet with the fame Arms are
thefe Words, " Infignia Natalitia Villæ et Corpo-
" rationis de *Radinge*, in Monumentis Collegii
" Regii Heraldorum tempore Vifitationis ejufdem
" Comitatus, Anno Salutis a Chrifto 1623, re-
" lata, fecundum fidem eorum Antiquitatis, Tef-
" tamur hoc *Hen. Chittinge, Chefter*; *Joh. Phil-*
" *pott*, de Rubeo Dracone, Marifcalli ac Deputati
" *Willelmi Cambdeni, Clarenceux* Regis Armorum in
" partibus auftralibus citra ripam fluvii de *Trent*."

The famous *William Laud*, Archbifhop of *Canterbury*, was the Son of a Clothier in this Town,
to which he was a Benefactor. He procured a
new Charter for the Corporation, and erected an
Hofpital here, which he endowed with Two hundred Pounds a Year. And here drew his firft
Breath the upright Lord Chief Juftice *Holt*.

Reading is fituated in 51 Deg. 25 Min. of North
Latitude, and in 1 Deg. of Weft Longitude from
the Meridian of *London*. I am, Sir, Yours, *&c.*

L E T T E R X.

From *Maidenhead*, in *Berkfhire*.

S I R,

AFTER leaving *Reading* and its delightful
Neighbourhood, I rode to *Catfgrove Hill*,
to fee that wonderful continued Body of Oyfter-
Shells. The Account of it given by Dr. *Brewer*,

in

in the *Philosophical Transactions*, is, I believe, very juft*; but whether thefe Shells are mere *Lufus Naturæ*, or were thrown into this Order by the great Deluge, remains ftill a Doubt.

Having paffed a good Bridge over the *Thames*, I came to the Village of *Caverfham*, where is the Seat of *Charles*, Lord *Cadogan*, which Place gave the Title of Vifcount to his elder Brother.

Caverfham was antiently the Demefne of *Gilbert de Clare*, Earl of *Gloucefter* and *Hertford*; who married *Joanna*, commonly called *Joan* of *Acres*, the fecond Daughter of King *Edward* the Firft. She was after-

---

* Near *Reading* in *Berkfhire*, for many fucceeding Generations, a continued Body of Oyfter-Shells has been found through the whole Circumference of five or fix Acres of Ground   The Foundation of thefe Shells is a hard rocky Chalk ; and above this Chalk, the Oyfter-Shells lie in Beds of green Sand, upon a Level, as nigh as can pofiibly be judged. This Stratum of green Sand Oyfter-Shells is (as I meafured) nigh two Feet deep.   Now immediately above this Layer or Stratum of green Sand and Shells, is a Bed of a blueifh Sort of Clay, very hard, brittle, and rugged ; they call it a pinny Clay, and is of no Ufe   This Bed or Layer of Clay, I found to be nigh a Yard deep ; and immediately above it is a Stratum of Fuller's Earth, which is nigh two Feet and a half deep . This Earth is often made ufe of by our Clothiers. And above this Earth is a Bed or Layer of a clear white Sand, without the leaft Mixture of any Earth, Clay, &c which is nigh feven Feet deep   Then immediately above this, is a ftiff red Clay (which is the uppermoft Stratum) of which we make our Tiles.   The Depth of this cannot be conveniently taken, it being fo high a Hill ; on the Top of which hath been, and is, dug up a little common Earth, about two Foot deep.
I have, with a Mattock, dug out feveral whole Oyfters, with both their Valves or Shells lying together, as Oyfters before opened   In their Cavity there is got in fome of the forementioned Sand.   Thefe Shells are fo very brittle, that in digging for them one of the Valves will frequently drop from its Fellow ; but 'tis plainly to be feen, that they were united together, by placing the Shell that drops off to its *Fellow Valve*, which exactly correfponds : But I dug out feveral that were entire, nay fome double Oyfters, with all the Valves united. Lowthorp's *Abridgement of Philofoph Tranfact*.

afterwards the Wife of *Ralph de Monthermer*. In the Reign of *Henry* the Sixth, *Henry de Beauchamp* had a Seat here; where, *Anne*, his Daughter, by *Ifabel*, his fecond Wife, the Daughter of *Thomas le Difpenfer*, Earl of *Gloucefter*, was born. During the late civil Wars, *Caverfham Lodge* was the Seat of the Lord *Craven*, Earl of *Kildare* in *Ireland*. At which Time in the Year (1647) the Head Quarters of the Parliament's Army was at *Reading*, and the King a Prifoner at *Windfor*. But by the Mediation of General *Fairfax*, the Parliament permitted him to pay a Vifit to all his Children then in *England*, who were at *Caverfham*, in the Cuftody of the Earl of *Northumberland*. They went with their Father to *Windfor*, and ftayed with him two Days, after which they returned to *Caverfham*, in the Cuftody of the fame Nobleman.

The Houfe is large and handfome, the Situation is a rifing Ground, where is a commodious Park, planted with lofty Woods, and well ftocked with Deer. From whence I paffed through fome fine Fields of Grain, to a fmall Common. In a fhort Time I entered fome Woods, where the various Mufic of Birds, rejoicing at the Return of a fine Morning, and, after a moft melancholly, wet Evening, reminded me of the beautiful Defcription of a modern Poet;

A Grove I reach'd, where tuneful Throftles fung,
The Linnet here did ope his little Throat;
His twitting Jefts around the Cuckow flung,
And the proud Goldfinch fhewd his painted Coat,
And hail'd me with no inharmonious Note.
The Robin eke here tun'd his Sonnet fhrill,
And told the foothing Ditty all by Rote,
How he with Leaves his pious Beak did fill,
To fhroud thofe pretty Babes, whom *Sib* alone would kill.

In the thickeft Part of the Wood ftands a little defireable Dwelling, where the Inhabitants courteoufly

ETON

COLLEGE.

teoufly put me in the Way for *Henly*; and in about half an Hour, following a fteep but extream pleafant Road, down the Wood, was brought into a fine Valley, covered with the promifing Payment for the Ufe of the painful Plow. The hanging Woods above had a pleafing Appearance : And now purfuing a winding Road, between a Wood and a Gentleman's Seat, I foon arrived.

The Town of *Henley upon Thames* is the moft ancient in the County. The Derivation of its Name is from the *Britifh* Word *Hen*, or *Old*, and the Word *ley*, in that Language ufed for our Word *Place*. The Inhabitants were called *Ancalites*, and this Town was the Head of thofe People when they revolted to *Cæfar*. The *Saxons* called the Place *Henlega*, in whofe Times it was of confiderable Note. It now contains about Six hunred Houfes, many of which are well built. The Church is a very handfome Edifice, near the River Side; within it, in the North Ifle, is a Monument to the Memory of Lady *Elizabeth Periam*, who liberally endowed a School for the Teaching, Cloathing, and putting out poor Children Apprentice. On her Monument is this Infcription;

Memoriæ facrum Digniffimæ
Dominæ Dominæ *Elizbe Periam*,
Viduæ quondam Uxoris Primo
Roberti Doyley,
Denuo *Henrici Nevile*,
Ultimo *Gulielmo Periam*, Militum :
Quæ in hoc Oppido Scholam fundavit
Educandis Pauperum filii viginti,
Et *Bailioleum* Collegium in inclyta
Academia *Oxon*,
Unius Socij;
Et duorum Scholarium acceffione detavit ;
Obijt autem anno Domini Mileffimo
Sexcenteffimo viceffimo Primo *Maij* tertio.

In the oppofite Ifle is a Monument thus infcribed;

Hic jacet Reliquiæ
Viri vere Reverendi *Johan. Cawleij*, T. D.
Archidiaconi de *Lindo*, Rectoris de *Dicdcott*,
In Agro *Bercherienfi*, & de *Henley ad Thamifin*.
Qui extremū vitæ diem morte confecit
13º Augufti, MDCCIX.
Natos Annos 77.

John Cawley, D D.
Dyed *Aug^t*. the 13, 1709;
And was buried near this Place.
To whofe Memory
This Monument is offered
With Gratitude, Affection, and Honour,
By his Daughter;
Dame *Sufanna Kneller*.

J. Cawley, Official of *Lincoln's Inn*,
And Son of *J Cawley*, D. D.
Dyed *Jan*. 24, 1722, aged 58,
And was buried near this Place.

In copying this laft I have obeyed your Commands, which to do is my beft Pleafure. Befide
the School founded by the Lady abovementioned,
here is a free Grammar School, erected in 1604,
by King *James* the Firft, who endowed it with
Lands, out of the Rents of which the Mafter is
paid a Salary of fifty Pounds, and the Under-
Mafter twenty Pounds *per Annum* , and, as many
Benefactions have been added, 'tis now fomewhat
confiderable. On the Eaft Side of the Town, in
the Road to *London*, is a very good Bridge over
the *Thames*, which Bridge, as alfo the Church,
are kept in Repair by the Profits of an Eftate ap·
propriated to that Purpofe. Here are twenty
two Alms-Houfes for as many poor People, and
the late unfortunate Mr. *Blandy*, who was Town-
Clerk, recovered feveral Charities that had either
been loft or neglected.

It

It were needlefs to remind you of the Fate of that unhappy Man, for his fad Cataftrophe has been known to all.

The Town of *Henley* is a Corporation, governed by a Warden, High Steward (at prefent the Earl of *Macclesfield*) Burgeffes, Town-Clerk, and other Officers. The Situation is very pleafant, on the Banks of the *Thames*, efpecially the Weftern Part, which runs gradually up a Hill, from whence the Profpect is very fine. A little below the Town, on the Side of the *Thames*, is the Seat and Gardens of Mr. *Giffelham Cooper*, a Banker in the Strand, who has here a fine Eftate, in Right of his Wife, a moft excellent Lady. Her Maiden Name was *Whitelock*, I believe, of the Family of the famous *Bulftrode Whitelock*, well known in the Libraries.

From Mr. *Cooper*'s the River glides gently down to an Ifland belonging to that Gentleman, on which is a beautiful Summer-Houfe, in Sight of the fine Seat of Mr. *Sambrooke Freeman*, which commands a fine View of the *Thames*, the Town of *Henley*, the charming tufted Hills, and the fweet luxuriant Meadows, to which beautiful Objects nothing can add more than the proud and noble Swans*, that ride upon the Bofom of the Stream. Mr. *Philips* thus finely compared *William*, Duke of *Gloucefter*, the Son of Queen *Anne*.

As milk-white Swans on Streams of Silver fhow,
And filv'ry Streams to grace the Meadows flow;
As Corn the Fields, and Trees the Hills adorn,
So thou to thine an Ornament was born.

A

* In fome of our old Law Books we find, that he who fteals Swan's Eggs out of the Neft, fhall be imprifoned for a Year and a Day, and fined at the King's Will, one Moiety to the King, the other to the Owner of the Land where they lay. That all white Swans, not marked, which have gained their natural Liberty, and are fwimming in an open or common River,

ver,

A more modern Poet hath thefe Words, in Imitation of *Spencer*'s Manner.

See the fair Swans on *Thamis* lovely Tide !
The which do trim their Pennons Silver bright,
In fhining Ranks they down the Waters ride,
Oft have mine Eyes devour'd the gallant Sight.

When I had travelled about a Mile to the Southward of the Town, I came to a Lock, through which the Veffels are drawn, when the Fall is great : Indeed the Locks, Flafhes, and Flood-gates on the *Thames* are numerous, confequently very expenfive ; but in this I fhall be more particular hereafter. Oppofite to this Lock is a new Plantation, on the Hill, which from the Bridge at *Henley* has a pretty Appearance : As indeed is every View heieabouts, on account of the many tufted Hills.

The Trade of this Town is very confiderable in the Articles of Malt, Wheat, and Wood; the Market, which is on *Thurfdays*, is frequently large, efpecially in the fecond mentioned Commodity : And its Fairs are on *February* the 24th, for Horfes ; on *Thurfday* after *Whitfuntide*, for Horfes and Sheep; and on the *Thurfday* fe'nnight before *October* the 10th, for Horfes and Cheefe.

Here are large Wharfs for lading and unlading Goods, and the Bargemen who inhabit here, and conduct the Navigation from hence to *London*, and up the *Thames*, are very numerous. Yefterday there was one of thefe Gentlemen married to a Girl, whofe Paths had not always been thofe of Virtue, upon which Account, they had this

Morn-

Morning an extraordinary Serenade of rough Mufic; fuch as Frying-Pans, Salt-Boxes, Marrow-Bones and Cleavers, for the Amufement of the Town.

Here are many Diffenters of the *Prefbyterian* Denomination, and no inconfiderable Number of the People called *Quakers*; the beft Inns are the *Red-Lion*, the *Catherine Wheel*, and the *Bell*.

Having paffed the Bridge, I came to fome promifing Hop-Gardens; and afcended a fteep Hill, by the Road which leads to *London*, and, after riding a few Miles through much Duft, turned on the Left-Hand to *Hurley*; which Village is pleafantly fituated on the Southern Bank of the *Thames*, being Part of the large Peninfula here formed by that charming River. Here was a Cell of *Benedictine* Monks, dedicated to St. *Mary*, which *Godefridus de Magnavilla* or *Mandeville*, in the Reign of *William* the Firft, gave to the Abbey of *Weftminfter*; and *William*, Bifhop of *London*, confirmed the fame. In the Year, 1258, *Godefridus*, Prior of *Hurley*, and his Convent, made an Exchange of fome of their Revenues, with *Abfolon*, Abbot of *Walden*; but this Religious Houfe was, at the Diffolution, valued at One hundred and twenty-one Pounds Eighteen Shillings and Five Pence.

In the Chancel of the Church here is a Monument, with this jingling Infcription;

Lovelace, thy Name layes downe a lafting *Love*,
Thy Title, Worfhip, Juftice, and Efquire,
Thy wedded *Grace* gives *Graces* from above,
Her Father *Sampfon*, Vertues to afpire.
Joyne thine and hers, the Difference is not odd,
Grace only *Grace*, and *John* the Grace of *God*.
Bleffing the Poore more bleffed thou didft thrive,
Six Sons, two Daughters, bleffed was thy Bed;
Thy Lyfe in *Chrift*, then bleffed thou alive,
Thy Death in *Chrift*, then bleffed art thou dead;
Bleffed thy Name, by Title, and by Wife,
By Father, Children, Poore, by Death, and Lyfe.

On

On a Ledge near the Bottom of the Monument,

Johannes Lovelace, Armiger,
Mortem, obiit 25 *Augusti*, 1558,
et Uxor ejus, obiit 12º *Novembris*,
Anº 1579.

On the Right Side of the Monument is the Statue of a Man kneeling, and over him is thus inscribed;

Richard Lovelace, Son of *John
Lovelace*, Esq, lived verteously, and
departed this Lyfe the 12th Day of
March, An. Dni 1601

And on the Left Side is another with these Words ;

Sir *Richard Lovelace*, Knighted in the Wars, Son of *Richard
Lovelace*, Esquire, lived worthily, and departed this Lyfe....
Anno Dni.........

This Sir *Richard Lovelace*, in the Reign of *Eli-zabeth*, eminently distinguished himself in the War against *Spain* · And, in 1627, was by King *Charles* the First, created Lord *Lovelace* of *Hurley*. His Grandson, *John*, Lord *Lovelace*, was very active in bringing about the *Revolution*, but greatly wasted his Estate ; Part of which was after his Death, sold by a Decree of the Court of *Chancery*. With him expired the last Male Heir; but his Daughter married Sir *Henry Johnson* of *Black-wall*.

Bisham or *Bystleham* is distant about a Mile from *Hurley*, upon the same Bank of the *Thames*. The Situation is delightful, and the Country around it very fertile. *Bisham* was an Estate of the Knights Templars ; but, in the Year 1138, *William de Mountacute*, Earl of *Salisbury*, Lord of *Denbigh* and *Man*, founded a Priory here (of
which

which there 'are yet fome Remains) for Canons
Regular of St. *Augustine*'s Order, and endowed it
with Lands, Churches, and Rents; and granted,
that, upon the Death of the Prior, neither he,
nor his Heirs, fhould intermeddle with the Cuftody of the Houfe, or any of their Poffeffions.
Henry the Fifth, in the eighth Year of his Reign,
gave a Licence to *Matilda*, Widow of *John de
Mountacute*, Earl of *Salifbury*, to remove the
Bones of her Hufband, buried in the Abbey of
Cirencefter, to this Priory; which, at the Diffolution, was valued at Two hundred and eighty-five
Pounds Eleven Shillings.

In this Monaftery was interred both its Founder
and his Countefs, who was a Daughter of the
Lord *Grandifon*. Alfo *Richard Nevil*, Earl of *Salifbury*, *Alice*, his Wife, and *Thomas*, his Son;
likewife the unhappy *Edward*, Earl of *Warwick*;
the remaining Heir Male of the illuftrious Family of *Plantagenet*, who, on the 28th of *November*,
1499, was notrioufly facrificed on *Tower-Hill* to
the ambitious Timidity of *Henry* the Seventh.
The Lordfhip and Eftate at *Bifham* came afterwards to a Branch of the *Hobyes*, of *Leominfter*,
in the County of *Hereford*.

In a Chapel built on the South Side of the
Chancel, are many Monuments of this honourable and illuftrious Family, among which is a
fquare pyramidal one, fupported by four Swans,
and at the Top is a bleeding Heart. There is an
Infcription to the Memory of *Margaret*, Wife of
Sir *Edward Hoby*. She was Daughter to *Henry*,
Lord *Hunfdon*, Kinfman to Queen *Elizabeth*.
Concerning this Sir *Edward Hoby*, *Camden* expreffes
himfelf to this Purpofe. " That *famous and worthy Knight, Sir Edward Hobey*, a Perfon to whom
I owe a very particular Refpect, and whofe more
than ordinary Obligations are, and always will be

fo

fo much the Subject of my Thoughts, that I can never poffibly forget them."

Againft the South Wall is erected a noble Monument, whereon, in white Marble, lies the Statues at full Length of two Knights (his Sons) in complete Armour: Their Heads refting upon their Helmets, and beneath the upper Ledge is this Infcription, which I could not forbear to copy.

Sir *Philip Hobye* married Dame *Elizabeth*,
Daughter to Sir *William Stoner*, Knight.
And after worthy Service done to his Prince and Country,
Dyed without Yffue, the 31 of *May*, 1558,
being of the Age of 53 Yeares, at his Houfe in *London*;
And from thence was conveyed hither.

Sir *Thomas Hobye* married with Dame *Elizabeth*,
Daughter to Sir *Anthony Cooke*, Knt.
By whome he had Yffue foure Children;
Edward, *Elizabeth*, *Anne*, and *Thomas Pofthumus*.
And being Embaffador for Queen *Elizabeth*, in *France*;
Died at *Paris* the 13th of *July* 1566, of the Age of 36.
Leaving his Wife greate with Childe in a ftrange Country,
Who brought him honourably home,
And built this Chapell,
And layd him and his Brother in one Tomb together.
Vivit poft funera virtus.

On the Fore-Part of the Monument is an Infcription, written in Honour of the two worthy Knights above named, confifting of thirty Lines of indifferent Poetry.

Within a beautiful Arch, which rifes from the upper End of this Monument, againft the Wall is written;

Elizabetha Hobœa conjux, ad *Thomam Hobeum*, Equitem Maritam.

O dulcis conjux, animæ pars maxima noftræ,
Cujus erat vitæ, vita medulla mea, &c. &c. &c.

Here

Here is alſo a Monument for this learned Lady, who was (after the Death of Sir *Thomas Hoby,*) married to *John,* Lord *Ruſſell)* and a Tomb for two of her Daughters. This is yet the Burial-Place of the *Hoby* Family; though their Seat is in the County of *Dorſet.*

From *Byſham* I came to a Village called *Cookham,* in which Pariſh is Part of the Town of *Maidenhead;* and here, for many Years, the Family of *Babham* have had a good Eſtate. In the Chapel, on the South Side of the Chancel, is an Alabaſter Monument, with the following Inſcription ; in which the good Widow does not forget her own Praiſe.

1561, 6 Aprilis:

To chriſtall Skies let Fame reſound, the vertous Praiſe aright,
Of *Arthur Babham,* here depicted in Albaſter bright.
Of antient Race he did deſcend, and thereto as you heare,
He took to Wife a worthy Dame, *Alice* the Daughter deare
Of Sir *John Brome,* in *Oxfordſhire* ; a Knight of worthy Fame,
Of whome ſix Children did proceede, as herein this doth name,
John, the firſt, deceaſed is ; *Chriſtopher* next the Heire,
Elizabeth and *Colubree,* *Urſula* and *Elunerre,*
Loe, this Dame *Alice* hath erect this Work in coſtly Stone,
For her ſweete *Arthur Babham's* Sake, though he be dead and gone ;
Farewell, renouned, true Eſquire, my Huſband, and my Friend,
I hope in Heaven to meete with thee when all Things here have End.

From *Cookham,* keeping the *Thames* on my Left, I ſoon came to this Town of *Maidenhead,* which, *Camden* ſays, was formerly called *South Ealington.* It is ſituate on the Weſtern Side of the *Thames,* and had its preſent Name from the Head of one of thoſe Maidens who ſuffered Martyrdom with St. *Urſula* at *Cologne.* It was firſt incorporated in the twenty-ſix Year of King *Edward* the Third, by the Name of the Fraternity or Guild of the Brothers and Siſters of *Maidenhithe.* The Reformation being finiſhed, it was incorporated by the Appellation of the Warden and Burgeſſes; but King *James* the Second granted it a new Charter, by the Name of the Mayor, and Aldermen; with Power to chuſe an High-Steward, and Steward, ſo that it now conſiſts of an High-Steward, a Mayoi, a Steward, and ten Aldermen; out of which laſt, two Bridge-Maſters are annually choſen. The Mayor is not only Clerk of the Market, but Coroner, and Judge of the Court, which he is obliged to hold once in three Years. He alſo holds a Seſſion twice in the Year, and, with the Aldermen, has the Power of making Bye-Laws for the Well-Being of the Corporation. The Town is not very conſiderable, but chiefly depends on the great Road to *London.*

I have before obſerved that 'tis partly in the Pariſh of *Cookham,* the other Part belongs to that of *Bray,* a Village about a Mile off, where the celebrated time-ſerving *Vicar* lived, in the Reigns of *Charles* the Second, *James* the Second, *William* the Third, and Queen *Anne,* of whom the Verſes were written, which have this Beginning;

> Of *Bray* the Vicar long I have been,
> And many a Teſt and Tryal
> Have ſtood, and various Changes ſeen,
> But never prov'd diſloyal;
> For with the *Crown* I always clos'd,
> Whatever Perſon wore it,
> And when an Oath the *State* impos'd,
> I moſt devoutly ſwore it.
> And this is Law, which I'll maintain until my dying Day, Sir,
> That whatſoever King ſhall reign, I'll be Vicar of *Bray,* Sir.

The

The Bridge over the *Thames* at *Maidenhead* is very neat, and the Barge Pier divides the Counties of *Berks* and *Buckingham*. This Bridge is maintained by the Corporation, who have a Toll allowed them, befides three Trees annually out of *Windfor Foreft*, for that Purpofe. One Mr. *John Smith*, a Salter in *London* (who died in 1589)' and his Wife, left here a comfortable Subfiftance for eight Poor Men and their Wives.

The Market here is held on *Wednefdays*; and on *Whitfun-Wednefday* and the 30th of *November* are Fairs for horned Cattle and Horfes: And another on the 29th of *September*, for the fame Purpofes, as alfo for hiring of Servants. The Lieutenant and Cuftos Rotulorum of the County of *Berks* is the Duke of St. *Alban's*.

I purpofe feeing *Chefden* and *Eton* this Afternoon, and intend to take *Cooper's Hill* in my Way to *London*. I am, Sir, Yours, &c.

L E T T E R XI.

From *Brentford*, in *Middlefex*.

S I R,

HAVING been to fee the elegant Buildings which the late Duke of *Marlborough* erected upon a little Ifland near the Town of *Maidenhead*, as a Fifhing-Houfe, or Place of Sequeftration from the noify World; I paffed into the County of *Buckingham*. At the End of the Bridge I had a fine View of *Chefden*, the Seat of the illuftrioufly-amiable *Frederic*, late Prince of *Wales*. Bifhop *Gibfon*, in his Edition of *Camden*, calls this Place *Clifton*. It was built by the witty *George Villers*, Duke of *Buckingham*, on the Top of a fine Hill; and afterwards came to the Earl of *Orkney*. The

O 2

Build-

Building is regular and grand, and the Apartments noble, especially that which is called the *Grand Chamber* : Where, in Tapestry, the Battles of the great Duke of *Marlborough* are finely depicted. The Terrace before the Front of the House has, I think, Prospects almost equal to those from that at *Windsor Castle*. Perhaps our prudent Travellers, who have seen the Beauties exhibited here, before they made the *Italian* Tour, are not so lavish in their Encomiums of the Appearance of the *Valdarno* from the *Appenines*, as our *English* Travellers, who are ('tis too true) almost Strangers to the charming Scenes which abound in their native Country. Under this Terrace, the Duke erected twenty-six Niches, in which he intended to place as many Statues large as the Life. The Additions, Enlargements, and Improvements, both of the House and Gardens, made by the late Royal Owner, are extremely fine; particularly in Avenues, Parterres, and Lawns ; which, with the delicious Exhibition made by the Bosom of the *Thames*, must cause an Emotion even in the Soul of a *Stoic*. From hence I rode to *Dorney*, a Village sweetly placed upon the Side of the silvery *Thames*. Here was born the famous Dr. *Mountague*, late Bishop of *Chichester* ; whose Father was Incumbent of this Living.

After passing through some sweet sequestered Lanes, I came to *Eton*, which is rendered famous by the noble College founded there, by that pious Monarch, who was a great Encourager of Learning, *Henry* the Sixth, by his Charter, bearing Date at *Windsor*, *September* the 12th, in the nineteenth Year of his Reign.

In order to carry on this Work, he appointed three Procurators and Agents. At its first Institution it consisted of one Provost or Præposit, ten Priests, four Clerks, and six Boys Choiristers ; twenty-

twenty-five poor and indigent Grammar-Scholars, and twenty-five poor and decrepid Men; also a Master to teach Grammar Learning to the aforesaid poor Scholars, and others coming from any Part of *England*, freely and without any Manner of Exaction. The King made *Henry Sevor*, Clerk, the first Provost of this Foundation, and incorporated it by the Name of the *Provost*, and *Royal College* of the blessed *Mary* of *Eton*, near *Windsor*. He gave to it the Advowson of the Parish Church of *Eton*, to be made Collegiate, and entirely united to their own proper Use, without endowing a Vicar, or appointing a competent Sum to be yearly distributed to the Poor of the Parish out of the same, the Statute *non obstante*, with Licence to purchase Lands to the Value of One thousand Marks a Year, the Satute of *Mortmain non obstante*; and discharged them from the Payment of *Corrodities*, or any Pensions or Annuities whatsoever. The said King also granted to this College several Rents arising out of alien Priories, with the Reversions of the said Estates, and all Liberties and Franchises belonging to those alien Priories, in as full and ample a Manner as they were used by the former Possessors; with Warranty, &c.

The same Prince founded *King's College* in *Cambridge*, whither Scholars from *Eton* are annually removed; of this I shall say more when I come to that *University*. The College of *Eton* suffered much from King *Edward* the Fourth, who seized on several of its Manors, and would have taken more, had not his religious Concubine, Mistress *Shore*, prevented it.

The Situation of *Eton* is low, and the Lands very moist in the Winter Season; though the Air is wholesome, and the Inhabitants of the Village long-lived. The *Thames* gently glides between

tween this Place and the Town of *Windſor* ; to which there is a Communication by a Bridge, whoſe Barge Pier (as that of *Maidenhead)* ſepa-rates the two Counties of *Buckingham* and *Berks.* The great School-Room at *Eton* is modern, but all the other Buildings are in the ſame Form as when the College was founded, though lately re-paired out of the common Stock. The Chapel is a noble Gothic Structure, which has a very ve-nerable Appearance from the Terrace at *Windſor.* In this ſacred Pile are depoſited, under a Monu-ment, the Aſhes of that truly noble, illuſtrious, and learned Gentleman, Sir *Henry Savile,* ſo well known in the Republic of Letters : He died in the Year 1621. And in this Chapel alſo is a Mo-nument for the famous Dr. *Richard Allſtree,* who was Provoſt here, and died in 1680. A later Provoſt, Dr. *Goldolphin,* Dean of St. *Paul's,* cauſed to be erected, in the great Court, a large Copper Statue of the Founder, which is well executed.

Here is an handſome Library, which has re-ceived large Benefactions from Dr. *Waddington,* Biſhop of *Chicheſter* ; *Richard Topham,* Eſq; who had been Keeper of the Records in the Tower ; Mr. *Reynolds,* and *Nicholas Man,* Eſq;

The Gardens are both large and handſome, ex-tending down to the *Thames* ; of theſe the Provoſt has not only the Uſe, but alſo a fine Garden and noble Houſe for himſelf.

This College at preſent has a Provoſt, a Vice-Provoſt (who is alſo a Fellow) ſix other Fellows, and ſeventy Scholars upon the Foundation, toge-ther with a full Choir for the Chapel, Officers, and Servants.

Here is an upper and lower School, each of which is divided into three Claſſes ; and in each School is one Maſter, who has four Aſſiſtants or Uſhers. In the lower School, Children are re-

ceived

ceived very young; but none are taken into the upper School before they can make *Latin* Verses, and have some Knowledge of *Greek*. Besides those on the Foundation, here are upwards of Three hundred Scholars, many of whom are Children of Persons of Quality, and other opulent People; who are boarded in the College, or in Houses in the Town, where many Housekeepers find great Advantages from them. They are kept under as strict Discipline as possible; but are as excursive from it, when out of School, as their Competitors of *Westminster*.

The annual Election of Scholars for *King's College* in *Cambridge* is on the first *Tuesday* in *August*: when the *Provost*, one senior, and one junior *Poser*, Fellows of that College, are deputed from thence, who, being joined by the *Provost*, *Vice-Provost*, and *Head-Master* of that of *Eton*; they call before them the Scholars of the upper Class; and having examined them in their several Parts of Erudition, they chuse out twelve of the best qualified, and enter them on a Roll, and according as they stand upon that Roll, they are taken to *King's College*, as the Vacancies happen there. Upon the whole, this is one of the largest and best Schools in *Europe* for Grammar-Learning.

From *Eton* I crossed the Bridge into the lower Part of *Windsor* (of which, and the Royal Castle, I shall treat in a future Letter) and rode between the *Thames* and the Park-Wall, till I came to *Datchet-Bridge*, which was built over the *Thames* in the Reign of Queen *Anne*. The Village is on the North, or *Buckinghamshire* Side of the River, and has a fine View of *Windsor-Castle* and *Park*. It has been much frequented at its Horse-Races, and is now as famous for finding Dogs (especially of the Pointer Breed, before they are really lost) as it formerly has been for furnishing the
Pastry

Paſtry Cooks of London with good and cheap Veniſon ; the Vicinity of the Park accounted for this laſt mentioned Trade.

In this Pariſh is a Seat called *Ditton-Park* : The Houſe, which is ancient and venerably noble, was built by Sir *Ralph Winwood*, Secretary of State to King *James* the Firſt, in the Middle of a pleaſant and well-timbered Park. Its Form is that of a Caſtle, and 'tis ſurrounded by a large Moat. The Apartments are commodious, and beautifully painted ; and in the Gallery is a good Collection of Pictures by the beſt Maſters. This Seat and Manor became the Property of the noble Family of *Mountague*, but, upon the Death of the late Duke of that Name and Title, it came to the preſent Earl of *Cardigan.*

I now directed my Courſe to that celebrated Spot in the County of *Surry*, called *Cooper's Hill :* Sir *John Denham's* Poem on this enchanting Place has rendered it famous to the poetic World ; as the Choice of the Place itſelf hath given a manifeſt Proof of that Gentleman's excellent Taſte of a proper Subject for his Muſe.

Leaving *Englefield-Green*, where Nightingales greatly abound, eſpecially about the Seat of Mr. *Kingdom*, I turned down a private Lane, which brought me to the Brow of this moſt delightful Hill , which is ſo ſuperlatively charming, that no Pen but that of *Denham* was ever equal to ſuch a Taſk. However, I ſhall juſt ſketch down the Proſpect, as I enjoyed it. Standing upon its Brow, which faces the North, on my Left-Hand appeared the Royal Palace of *Windſor*, and this Way I had a delightful View of *Datchet-Bridge* ; and to my Right, that of *Staines* was conſpicuous : Beyond this was ſuch a Variety of Matter, even to St. *Paul's*, and many Spires in *London,*

don, that the Beauties are beyond Credibility. Directly before me, in the fweet Meads through which the *Thames* flows in fuch ravifhing Meanders that cannot be either conceived or expreffed, ftands *Anchorwick*, an Hamlet belonging to the Village of *Reftry*, or, as *Morden* fpells it, *Wyrardfbury*, the Spire of whofe Church has a charming Effect. Beyond this laft mentioned Place the View continued as it were unbounded, to which *Salthill*, *Slough*, and *Cliefdon* gave fine Additions.

Looking over *Anchorwick*, *Harrow on the Hill* appears extreamly plain to the Eye, and between that and *London*, *Primrofe*, *Hampftead* and *High-gate* Hills are very confpicuous. In the Bottom the River *Coln* comes gliding through the Meadows ; and on the Back of the Village of *Egham*, full in my View, lay the ever-famoufly-memorable Spot, called *Runny*, or *Charter Mead* ; and ftill more to the Right, an Hill prefented itfelf at fome Diftance, on which ftands two or three lofty Trees ; this is called St. *Anne*'s Hill. Without faying more of my own Obfervings, I'll give you a Specimen from the Poem already mentioned. You will, I am perfuaded, excufe the Length of the Quotation, for the Sake of the inimitable Picture it prefents you with.

My Eye, defcending from the Hill, furveys
Where *Thames* amongft the wanton Vallies ftrays,
Thames, the moft lov'd of all the Ocean's Sons
By his old Sire, to his Embraces runs,
Hafting to pay his Tribute to the Sea,
Like mortal Life to meet Eternity.
Though with thofe Streams he no Refemblance hold,
Whofe Foam is Amber, and their Gravel Gold ;
His genuine, and lefs guilty Wealth t' explore,
Search not his Bottom, but furvey his Shore ;
O'er which he kindly fpreads his fpacious Wing,
And hatches Plenty for th' enfuing Spring.

Nor then deſtroys it with too fond a Stay,
Like Mothers which their Infants overlay.
Nor with a ſudden and impetuous Wave,
Like profuſe Kings, reſumes the Wealth he gave.
No unexpected Inundations ſpoil
The Mower's Hopes, nor mock the Plowman's Toil.
But God-like his unwearied Bounty flows;
Firſt loves to do, then loves the Good he does.
Nor are his Bleſſings to his Banks confin'd,
But free and common as the Sea or Wind,
When he to boaſt, or to diſperſe his Stores,
Full of the Tributes of his grateful Shores,
Viſits the World, and in his flying Tow'rs
Brings home to us, and makes both *Indies* ours.
Finds Wealth where 'tis, beſtows it were it wants,
Cities in Deſerts, Woods in Cities, plants.
So that to us no Thing, no Place is ſtrange,
While his fair Boſom is the World's Exchange.
O could I flow like thee, and make thy Stream
My great Example, as it is my Theme !
Though deep, yet clear, though gentle, yet not dull,
Strong without Rage, without o'erflowing full.
Heaven her *Eridanus* no more ſhall boaſt,
Whoſe Fame in thine, like leſſer Currents loſt,
Thy nobler Streams ſhall viſit *Jove*'s Abodes,
To ſhine amongſt the Stars, and bathe the *Gods*.
   While the ſteep, horrid Roughneſs of the Wood
Strives with the gentle Calmneſs of the Flood ;
Such huge Extreams when Nature doth unite,
Wonder from thence reſults, from thence Delight.
The Stream is ſo tranſparent, pure, and clear,
That had the ſelf-enamour'd Youth gaz'd here,
So fatally deceiv'd he had not been,
While he the Bottom, not his Face, had ſeen.
But his proud Head the airy Mountain hides
Among the Clouds, his Shoulders, and his Sides
A ſhady Mantle cloaths ; his curled Brows
Frown on the gentle Stream, which calmly flows,
While Winds and Storms his lofty Forehead beat :
The common Fate of all that's high or great.
Low at his Foot, a ſpacious Plain lies plac'd,
Between the Mountain and the Stream embrac'd :
Which Shade and Shelter from the Hill derives,
Where the kind River Wealth and Beauty gives ;

An

And in the Mixture of all thefe appears
Variety, which all the reft endears.
This Scene had fome bold *Greek* or *Britifh* Bard
Beheld of old, what Stories had we heard,
Of Fairies, Satyrs, and the Nymphs, their Dames,
Their Feafts, their Revels, and their am'rous Flames!
'Tis ftill the fame, although their airy Shape
All but a quick poetic Sight efcape.
There *Faunus* and *Sylvanus* keep their Courts,
And thither all the horned Hoft reforts,
To graze the ranker Mead, that noble Herd,
On whofe fublime and fhady Front is rear'd
Nature's great Mafter-Peice, to fhew how foon
Great Things are made, but fooner are undone.
Here have I feen the King, when great Affairs
Gave leave to flaken, and unbend his Cares,
Attended to the Chace by all the Flower
Of Youth, whofe Hopes a nobler Prey devour:
Pleafure, with Praife and Danger, they would buy,
And wifh a Foe that would not only fly.

This Hill belongs to one Mr. *Edgware* of *Eg-ham*, and is let to one Farmer *Plim*. The late General *Honywood* was fome Time fince the Te-nant of it, when he built a Seat upon its Brow; but that is now gone.

From the Summit of this delicious Place, I de-fcended by a green, unfrequented Lane, through a fmall Wood, in which I was entertained by de-lightful Songs of many Nightingales: And here it was that I made my firft Obfervations of the Ro-bin's Imitation of their ravifhing Notes, which that little Songfter performed to a confiderable Degree of Perfection. In a few Minutes after, I found myfelf on that ever-to-be-remembered Spot, *Runny-Mead*, where the Tyrant, King *John*, was compelled to fign the famous *Charter of Liberties*, and alfo the *Charter of the Forefts*. As the Names of the principal of thofe illuftrious Barons, who, fo compelled him, ought to be remembered by every Lover of Liberty, I have here fet them

P 2   down,

down, as I copied them from the *Cotton* Library, not for your Information, but to let you know, that, as an *Englifhman*, I hold their Memories dear in my own Bofom.

Ricus Comes de *Clara.* Com. *Aubemarl. Gaufrid.* Comes, *Effex* et *Glouc. Saber, Comes Winton. Henr.* Comes *Hereford. Roger Bigod, Norff.* et *Suff. Robtes.* Come *Oxon.* Comes *Marciallus,* junior *Robt.* Fit *Walter. Gill.* de *Clara. Euftach* de *Vefcy. Hugh le Bigot. Willielmus de Mobray.* Major de *Londonio. Willus de Lawvalay. Robtus* de *Ros. J. Conftabular. Geftn. Robtus de Percy. Johes,* Fit *Robti. Willus Malet. Gaufridus de Say Rogerus de Mobray Willus de Huntingfield. Ricus de Manfichet. Willus de Albiniac.*

The Mead contains about One hundred Acres of Grafs-land, and belongs (together with *Long-Mead,* and *Yard-Mead)* to the Parifh of *Egham* ; the Gardens from which Village adjoin to *Runny-Mead,* which terminates Eaftwardly at *Egham* Turnpike. *Egham* is a confiderable Village, and here many of the *Denham* Family are interred ; from whence to *Stains* I had pleafant Travelling, over the Caufeway that was fome Years fince repaired by Authority of Parliament ; and refrefhed myfelf at the *Swan,* an Inn at the *Surry* End of *Stains-Bridge.*

The *Swan* at *Stains* (or rather *Egham,* for 'tis in this Parifh) is fweetly fituated on the Southern Bank of the *Thames* ; which here gently glides between the Counties of *Middlefex* and *Surry.* A Perfon who had never feen this River above *Chelfea,* would be aftonifhed to find it fo confiderably fmaller at *Stains,* which is, only nineteen Miles by Land from *London. Camden* fays, that *Stains* or *Stanes* had its Name from a Boundary-Stone, fet up here, to diftinguifh the Extent of the Jurifdiction, which the City of *London* had in the River. The Bridge is of Wood, which, together

with

with *Egham* Caufeway, as obferved above, became very ruinous, and therefore an Act paffed in the Year 1739-40, for the Reparation and Prefervation of both; and they are now in excellent Condition. Having paffed the Bridge, I entered the Town of *Stains*, which is a very good one, and, though the Situation is low, yet the Soil being a Gravel, it is tolerably clean. It has a very good Weekly Market for Corn: and the Farmers who attend it, appear and behave vaftly different to thofe in Markets at great Diftances from the Metropolis. The River is a fine Convenience here. The Fairs are on the 11th of *May* and the 19th of *September*.

The Church ftands at fome Diftance from the Town. The civil Officers here; are two Conftables, and four Headboroughs; who, as it is a Lordfhip belonging to the Crown, are appointed by the King's Steward.

From this Place to *Belfound* is the pleafanteft public Road that I have feen near *London*; the Village is alfo pleafant, but I cannot fay the fame of *Hounflow-Heath*, becaufe one has more Apprehenfions than upon fuch Commons at a greater Diftance from *London*. This Heath hath been famous for Encampments, efpecially that of the Parliament's Army, when King *Charles* was in Cuftody; and alfo that of King *James* the Second, who was fo weak as to have public Mafs faid in his Tent here, which gave the Soldiery fuch a Difguft, that they never had any Affection for him afterwards. I cannot forbear thinking, that if this Heath was inclofed, it would turn to good Account: for the Soil is not bad, and *London* is fo near, that Manure muft come cheap to it, either by Barges or returning Hay-Carts: And indeed, if feveral other Commons near *London* were put to the Plough, they would certainly an-

fwer

fwer better than at prefent; befides, the Conveniences for Highway Robberies would not be fo great, as thefe wafte Lands afford. *Houn-flow* is a large Village, that depends upon the Weftern Roads.

From *Hounflow* I am arrived at this Place, one of the moft difagreeable in *England*; but as my Letter is dated here, I muft fay fomewhat of it. *Gay*, in his Journey to *Exeter*, has thefe Words;

Three dufty Miles reach *Brentford's* tedious Town,
For dirty Streets, and white-legg'd Chickens known.

The Situation of *Brentford* is, where the fmall River *Brent* falls into the *Thames*. The Town is long, dirty, and indifferently built; and fince the great Ufe of Poft-Chaifes, is much upon the Decline: For the Stage upon this Road, being from *London* to *Hounflow*, without ftopping here, it has fo much affected the Inns, that even the *famous Red Lion at Brentford* is fhut up. The Chapel here, which is an old indifferent Building, belongs to the Parifh of *Great Ealing*. On the oppofite Side of the *Thames* are the Royal Gardens of *Kew*, and indeed fome Part of *Brentford* being upon a bold Bank of that River, might be made vaftly pleafant and clean. Perhaps you now expect fome Account of *Sion* or *Ofterley* Houfes, the Seats of the Earl of *Northumberland* and Mr *Child*; but of thefe I fhall not fail to be mindful in my future Difpatches, when I come to defcribe *London*, and the Environs of that unrivalled City.

The following Lines of Mr. *Pope*, in Imitation of *Spencer*, are a true Painting of the Scenes exhibited in the Alleys of this Town of *Brentford*.

In

In ev'ry Town where *Thamis* rolls his Tyde,
A narrow Pafs there is, with Houfes low ;
Where ever and anon the Stream is ey'd,
And many a Boat foft-fliding too and fro.
There oft' are heard the Notes of Infant Woe,
The fhort, thick Sob, loud Scream, and fhriller Squall,
How can ye, Mothers, vex your Children fo ?
Some play, fome eat, fome cack againft the Wall.
And as they crouchen low, for Bread and Butter call.

I think to reach *London* this Evening, and bend
my Courfe towards *Hertfordfhire* very foon. I am,
Sir, Yours, *&c.*

L E T T E R XII.

From *Stevenage*, in *Hertfordfhire.*

S I R,

HAVING paffed *Turnham-Green*, I came to
the Spot where the Confpirators againft the
Life of King *William* the Third intended to have
put their Plot into Execution. The Place was
favourable, the Road being narrow and far from
any Houfes ; but, as their Intention was that of
fpilling innocent Blood, the Hand of Heaven
prevented it : the happy Confequences of which,
the Annals of our Times can teftify. Leaving
Hammerfmith, Kenfington, and *Knightfbridge* behind ;
I ordered my Horfe to *Grays-Inn-Lane*, where he
now is, and the following Morning rode one of
Sir *John*'s, attended by *Charles*, to *Pancras*, a
Place remarkable for its Wells, which are of a
purgative Quality, and much reforted' to in the
Spring and Summer Seafons, and alfo for its
Church-yard ; where more Perfons of the *Romifh*
Religion are interred, than in any other perhaps
in *England.* Here was depofited the mortal Part
of

of that illuftrious *Pruffian*, *John Erneft Grabe*
(whofe Learning was famous all over the *Chriftian*
World). The Honourable Mr. *Thomas Arundel*,
the Honourable Mrs. *Amey Conftable*, Daughter of
Hugh, Lord *Clifford* of *Chudleigh*, a Lady, whofe
Qualities were truly amiable, as appear to have
been thofe of one Mifs *Mary Bafnet*, to whofe
Memory is erected an handfome Monument, fimilar to that dedicated to the Virtues of Lady
Henrietta Beard, late Wife of Mr. *John Beard*,
whofe great Merits, as a Servant of the Public, are
far excelled by thofe of his private Life.

On the laft mentioned Monument are thefe
Words;

Sacred to the Remains of the Lady
Henrietta Beard,
Only Daughter of *James*, late Earl of *Waldegrave*.
In the Year 1734, fhe was married to Lord
Edward Herbert,
Second Son to *William*, Marquis of *Powis*;
By whom fhe had Iffue one Daughter,
Barbara, now Countefs of *Powis*.
On the 8th of *Jan.* 1738-9, fhe became the Wife of
Mr. *John Beard*:
Who, during a happy Union of 14 Years,
Tenderly loved her Perfon, and admired her Virtues:
Who fincerely feels, and laments his Lofs,
And muft for ever revere her Memory;
To which he confecrated this Monument.
Ob. 31 *May*, 1753, Ætat. 36.

Having left *Pancras*, I came to *Kentifh-Town*, a
Village remarkably rural, confidering its near Vicinity to *London*. This Place is an Hamlet to *Pancras*, but here is a Chapel of Eafe to the Inhabitants.
At the farther End, a fteep Road leads to the
Brow of *Highgate-Hill*, which affords exceeding fine
Views of *London* and *Weftminfter*, down the *Thames*
below *Greenwich*, *Shooter's Hill* in *Kent*, and of
the lofty Elevations in the County of *Surry*. Numerous

merous are the neat Houfes erected on this Hill,
efpecially thofe of Mrs. *Crafteign*, Mr. *Freemantle*,
and Mr. *Edwards*; which command Profpects,
that cannot in Idea touch the Mind of any Man
who never vifited *London*. On the upper Part of
the Hill is a Gate, from whence the Village of
Highgate took its Appellation. Some Hiftorians
tell us that the Gate here was erected about Four
hundred Years fince, in order to receive Toll, for
the Ufe of the Bifhop of *London*, on account of
the Road from *Grays-Inn-Lane* being turned
through his Park. But *Drayton*, who was an excellent Antiquary, as well as *Poet Laureat* to King
James the Firft, hath thefe Lines ;

Then *Highgate* boafts his Way, which Men do moft fre-
    quent,
His long continued Fame, his high and great Defcent,
Appointed for a Gate to *London* to have been.

From which one is led to fuppofe the Gate here
was erected prior to the faid Alteration of the
Road. Where the Chapel ftands (which belongs
to the Parifh of *Hornfey*) formerly ftood an Hermitage ; near which, in the Year 1562, the Lord
Chief Baron *Cholmondeley* erected and endowed a
Free-School, and eight Years afterwards Dr. *Edwin Sandys*, Bifhop of *London*, enlarged it, and
alfo added a Chapel to it.

In this Village the glorious and immortal
Queen *Elizabeth*, in her Way from *Hatfield* to
London, was met by the Bifhops, and a numerous
and illuftrious Train of Noblemen and Ladies,
attended by an immenfe Crowd of People, teftify-
ing their unfeigned Joy, by the loudeft Acclama-
tions.

Over the Signs of many Public-Houfes here,
are large Pairs of gilt Horns, and 'tis a Cuftom,
that when the Country People coming to *London*,

especially Waggons, stop for Refreshment, they
have a large Pair of Horns fixed at the End of a
long Staff brought out to them; when they are
so earnestly pressed to be sworn, that they are told
there is no dispensing with the Custom : And
when they are prevailed with, a Sort of burlesque
Oath is administered, Part of which is, that they
will never eat brown Bread when they can get
white ; nor (if a Man) will kiss they Maid, when
they can kiss the Mistress ; and a deal more such
Stuff. This is repeated *verbatim* after the Person
who adminsters it, the Country Person holding
one of the Horns in his or her Hand. This silly
Ceremony is altered according to the Sex so sworn,
but they are allowed to add to each Particular the
Words, " Except I like the other better." The
whole Ceremony of Words being repeated, they
kiss the Horns, and pay a Shilling each, to be
spent among their Company.

I soon reach'd *Finchley* Common, which is remarkable for a large Hog-Market : and here
many a Road Collector's Carcase has been hung
up to public View. From thence I rode to *Whet-
stone* Turnpike, and leaving Sir *John Wolf*'s
House and Rookery on the Right-Hand, came
to *Chipping-Barnet.* This is a long Town, eleven
Miles from *London*, and consists chiefly of one
Street, in which are some good Inns, particularly
the *Mitre*, and *Red-Lion*, The Church, which
is a Chapel of Ease to *East-Barnet*, is old, and
stands too near the Street. It contains three Isles.
Here is a large monumental Inscription on *Thomas
Ravenscroft*, Esq; his Wife and Children. In
this Town, in the Year 1672, *James Ravenscroft*,
Esq; founded six Almhouses for six poor Widows,
with some Furniture to each ; and here Queen
Elizabeth erected a Free-School, where nine Children are instructed *gratis*.

This

This Town fubfifts partly by Travellers that ftop upon this Road, which leads both to *Scotland, Ireland,* and *North Wales*; and partly from the Quantities of Cattle and Sheep, which are here refrefhed in their Way to *Smithfield.* It were to be wifhed, that foreftalling and regrating were not fo much in Practice here as it moft manifeftly is.

At *Barnet* is a Market on *Mondays*; a Fair on the 8th, 9th, and 10th of *April*, for Toys; and another on the 4th, 5th and 6th of *September*, for *Englifh, Scotch,* and *Welch* Cattle.

In the Times of our *Saxon* Kings, the Place where this Town ftands, and alfo its Neighbourhood, was one continued Wood: Which was granted to the Church of St. *Alban,* by the Name of the Woods of *Southaw, Borham* and *Huzchege*; and is fince (owing to its Situation) been confirmed by fucceeding Kings, by the Name of *Bergnet,* which, in the Language of the *Saxons,* fignifies a little Hill.

They have here an annual Horfe-Racing, which doubtlefs affords high Diverfion to the Gentlemen of the Turf, and other good Horfemen; for fuch an Exhibition of bad Horfes, and worfe Riders, are (perhaps) not to be feen at any other Courfe in *England!* And 'tis notorious, that more Misfortunes generally happen at *Barnet Races,* than at any other Horfe-Race whatever.

Having left this Town fcarce a Quarter of a Mile, I came to the Place where the Road feparates, that on the Right-Hand leading to *Edinburgh,* and the Left to *Chefter, Wales,* and *Glafgow*; and here, on an Obelifk, erected by the late Sir *Jeremy Sambrooke,* Bart. in the Year 1740, are engraven thefe Words;

Q 2

Here

Here was
Fought the
Famous Battle
Between *Edward*
the 4th, and the
Earl of *Warwick*,
April the 14th,
Anno 1471,
In which the Earl
Was defeated
And flain*.

The fame Obelifk alfo tells us, that 'tis eight Miles and three Quarters from St. *Alban*'s, and feven Miles and three Quarters to *Hatfield*. This is a Part of a Common, then called *Gladmore Heath* ; and our Hiftorians inform us, that on that memorable *Eafter-Day*, the Army for King *Henry* the Sixth, was commanded by the great Earl of *Warwick*, together with the Earl of *Oxford*, and the Marquis *Montacute*. That of the Enemy was headed by *Edward* himfelf. The Engagement was exceffively furious, in which were killed Ten thoufand three hundred. Men : Among whom was the Earl of *Warwick* (nick-named the *King-maker*) the Marquis *Montacute*, the Lords *Cromwell*, *Say*, and *Montjoy* ; Sir *Henry Bourchier*, and Sir *William Terrill*. I muft confefs it almoft makes me fhudder, to think what a prodigious Number of Lives were loft in the Difpute between thofe two Houfes of *York* and *Lancafter* : for, according to good Accounts, they amounted to Eighty-five thoufand fix hundred and twenty-eight ! in which were two Kings, one Prince, ten Dukes, two Marquifes, twenty-one Earls, twenty-feven Lords,

* The Compilers of the *Tour* erroneoufly fay, that this Battle was fought in 1468, " And here, Anno 1740, a Stone Co-
" lumn was erected, on which is a *long Infcription*, giving a
" *particular* Account of that Battle."

two Vifcounts, one Lord Prior, and one Judge, befides Gentlemen.

From hence the Road continues fine, with large Commons and *Enfield-Chace* on the Right-Hand, till you come to *Potters Barr*, a ftraggling Hamlet, about two Miles and an half from whence, I found myfelf at another Hamlet in the Parifh of *Mims*, called *Bell-Bar*. Here, at a civil Houfe, whofe Sign is the *White Hart*, I took fome Refiefhment; and then proceeded to vifit the Gardens at *Gobions*, or as vulgarly called *Gubbins*, late the Seat of Sir *Jeremy Sambrooke* before mentioned. In my Way thither, which is about a Quarter of a Mile, I paffed before the Front of a good Houfe (facing the Heath called *Mims* Common) lately the Property of an amiable young Gentleman, who, being in his twentieth Year, went a Volunteer on that unfortunate Expedition to St. *Cas* in *Britany*, where he was killed. He was Heir to an Eftate of Five thoufand Pounds a Year.

Turning to the Right, I came to a Stile, which put me into a very beautiful Walk through a double Row of Trees, and having paffed feveral fmall Gates, the Trees and beautiful Walk ftill continuing, I croffed the Road which leads to *Gobions-Houfe*, and foon after turning to the Left, entered a delightful Path, which conducted me into a charming Wood. This Walk is irregularly cut through the Underwood, but the lofty Oaks which overfhadow it are not difturbed. After being pleafed with this pretty Sort of Labyrinth for fome Time, I came fuddenly into the moft ravifhing Spot that can be imagined. It is a perfect *Rotunda*, about the fame Diameter with the *Ring* in *Hyde-Park*. Here the Underwood is entirely taken away, but the Oak Trees, which are very ftrait, and vaftly high, remain entire. They are a great many, and the Ground between them

them is entirely covered with a thick, fhort Mofs of the Colour of Gold. The whole is furrounded by a Gravel Walk, about eight Feet wide. On one Side is a large Alcove ; where, fitting down, I could not forbear thinking, that if their fairy Majefties, *Mab* and *Oberon*, have not found out and enjoyed this Place in their nocturnal Gambols, they are but Sovereigns of fmall Divination, or true Tafte. Oppofite to the Place of my Entrance into this fweet Recefs, is another Avenue, which brought me to a large Alcove, fituate at the End of an oblong Piece of Water ; on each Side of whofe Banks are fine Gravel Walks, lined with Rows of Trees. This Pond is fo formed, that a Part of it is deep, and therefore the Bottom not eafily feen ; but the other Part is fhallow, and it may be filled and emptied (as may the other Refervoirs here) at Pleafure. The Grafs at the Bottom, when covered with Water, hath a fweet Effect. Having feated myfelf under the Alcove, I had a View over the Water to a fine large Figure of *Time*, rifing from the Bafe, with his Wings prepared for Flight, and holding a large Sun-Dial in his Hands ; beyond whom, through a Vifta, the Eye is infallibly led to an Obelifk, at a confiderable Diftance, beyond the Gardens. Having left this Spot, I turned to the Right, through a beautiful Walk of Trees, that led me to the Manfion-Houfe, which did not excite my Curiofity, though I am told there are fome good Family Pieces in it ; the Front is towards the Wood, from whence I was conducted by one of the Gardeners through a moft fuperb and elegant Walk, which terminated at a Summer-Houfe, built of Wood in the Lattice Manner, and painted green. We then turned to the Left, through meandering Walks, cut through the Underwood (the umbrageous Oaks alfo here being entire) to

a very affecting Grotto ; which having paffed, a
large Arch prefented itfelf acrofs the Walk, and
through that I beheld a moft ravifhing Cafcade.
The Retirednefs of the Situation, the Effect
which the Arch, and winding Grotto gave to the
Waterfall, the Mufic of the feathered Choir, and
the Coolnefs afforded by the overfhadowing Oaks,
failed not to remind me of *Thomfon's* Lines ;

> Hence, let me hafte into the mid-wood Shade,
> Where fcarce a Sun-Beam wanders through the Gloom,
> And on the dark-green Grafs, befide the Brink
> Of haunted Stream, that by the Roots of Oak
> Rolls o'er the rocky Channel, lie at large,
> And fing the Glories of the circling Year.

Continuing with my Guide, I turned to the
Right, when a winding Walk brought us to a
Seat, where the Cafcade has a more diftant Sound.
This is a very contemplative Situation, abounding with thofe Trees of which our antient Druids
and Bards were fond, and applicable to the Words
of Mr. *Francis Coventry.*

> Hark ! I hear the Echoes call,
> Hark ! the rufhing Waters fall ;
> Lead me to the green Retreats,
> Guide me to the Mufes Seats ;
> Where antient *Bards* Retirement chofe,
> Or antient *Lovers* wept their Woes.

I don't remember to have found fo many Wood-
Pigeons and Squirrels, as this Place affords.
From the laft mentioned Seat a pretty Walk
brought me to a good Statue of *Hercules*, in his
leaning Pofition ; from whence, through a verdant Arch, appears a beautiful Canal ; at the End
of which is an handfome Temple, whofe Front
is fupported by four Pillars. In this Temple are
two Buftoes of the two Ladies who now are the
Poffeffors of this defireable Place ; that is to fay,
according to the Words of my Guide, *Madam*

Sam-

Sambrooke and *Madam Betty :* They seem to have employed a masterly Statuary; but I could not forbear wishing, that the Back, rather than the Face, of that athletic *Greek* had been turned towards them, which would have been more consistent with Decency.

On one Side of the Canal is a *Roman Gladiator*, very well done. I never look on one of those Representations of *Roman Brutality* without some Horror. To think that Men, who were able to attend the Leaders of the *Roman* Arms, should, for a Livelihood, be hack'd and hew'd upon a Stage! Yet that such Exhibitions were the Delight of many *Roman* Spectators is well known; and *Suetonius* says, that those of the *Equestrian Order*, and even *Senators*, have been engaged in these bloody Conflicts. *Horace* tells us of one *Mænius*, a *Roman* Consul, who having been a great Spendthrift, sold all his Estate, excepting a Pillar, or rather Balcony, of his House, which Reserve was made only, that he might indulge himself in seeing the *Gladiators*. Alas what a Taste! But what can we say? How can we account for the Dispositions of Mens Minds? Pray is not our *English* Taste for Boxing, or, as 'tis more modernly termed, Bruising, equally shocking? That two Fellows should expose themselves on a Stage, and fight, even to the Danger of Life and Limb, for the Sake of a few Pounds? Nay, I have known them do it for a few Pence!

Leaving this Canal, I ascended a strait Walk, which brought me, on the Left-Hand, to a *Cleopatra*, as stung with an *Asp*. This Figure stands upon a Pedestal, in a Meadow, at some Distance; and, on our Right, appeared a very large and beautiful *Urn*. The Top of our Walk terminated at a large Oak, from whence there is a View over the Canal just mentioned, to the *Gladiator*;

diator; and from thence, through a Grove, to a lofty Pigeon-Houfe. Turning to our Right, we came to the neateft and moft retired Bowling-Green I ever faw; at one End of which, is the *Urn* before mentioned, and at the other a Sum-mer-Houfe, full of Orange and Lemon-Trees, with fine Fruit upon them. On one Side of the Green is a Statue of *Venus*, and on the other, one of *Adonis*. Leaving this Place, I gently de-fcended, through fome pleafant, though (I think) too regular Walks, to the Figure of *Time*, already fpoken of: And here my Guide unlocked a Gate, which brought me to the Piece of Water firft abovementioned. However, he accompanied me to the *Rotunda* before defcribed, which, he was of Opinion, would be much prettier, if the Trees in it were cut down; " Though that, continued " he, cannot be done; for my Ladies fall no " Trees, but thofe that are rotten." Poor filly Fellow! He little thought, that, if the Mofs was robbed of its Shade, the Sun would foon burn it away. The Ladies here live in a very genteel Manner, keep a Set of Horfes, and are vifited by much Company in the Summer-Seafon.

This Eftate, in the Reign of *Stephen*, belonged to that famous Baron, Sir *Richard Gobion*, or *de Gobion*, as did two other Places of the fame Name; the one of which is *Higham Gobion*, in *Bedfordfhire*; and that which Sir *Henry Chauncy*, in his Map of this County, calls *Gubbins*, to the North of *Hertford*. A Daughter of this Sir *Richard* married with one of the ancient Family of *Boteler*, to whom thefe Eftates defcended. In the Reign of *Henry* the Seventh, this (near *North Mims*) the Gardens of which I have juft defcribed, came into the Family of the *Mores*, and then was called *More-Hall*; but, by the At-tainder of that celebrated Scholar, great Lawyer, and accomplifhed Gentleman, Sir *Thomas More*, (whofe Refidence it was) Lord Chancellor to the Tyrant *Henry* the Eighth, it was forfeited to the Crown, and fettled upon the Princefs *Elizabeth* who held it till her Death. After which Period, it was poffeffed by feveral Families : At laft, it was purchafed by the late Sir *Jeremy Sambrooke*, who dying a Batchelor, his Sifters now enjoy it*.

From *Gobions* to *Hatfield* I had the great North Road, which is the beft in *England*. The Corn in this Country looks very well : Notwithftanding the Backwardnefs of the Spring. As Sir *John*'s Horfes were good Travellers, I came foon to *Hatfield*, called by the *Romans*, *Hatfeldia*, or *Campus Altus*; at which Place, in the Year 681, *Theodore*, Bifhop of *Canterbury*, held a Synod againft the *Eutychean Herefy*. The Manor of *Hatfield* belonged to the *Saxon* Kings, till King *Edgar* prefented it to the Monks of *Ely* ; who continued to be Lords of it till *Henry* the Firft converted that Monaftery into a Bifhopric, and then the Bifhop enjoyed it with all its Privileges and Liberties, together with thofe of Free-Warren, Soc, Sac, Toll, and Forfeitures, added by the Kings *Henry* the Firft, *Richard* the Firft, and *John*.

After thefe Donations, the Kings of *England* had a Palace at *Hatfield*, where *Edward* the 6th having been educated, was waited on by the Earl of *Hertford*, and a numerous Concourfe of Nobility and Gentry ; who attended him to *London* in order to be his being crowned. In this Palace
th

* The Compiler of the *Tour* (one cannot avoid Rifibility) fays, this Place is a *little North of* Hertford And to ufe his own Words, " It was, *when I was laft there*, the Property of " Sir *Jeremy Sambroke*, Bart. fince deceafed : Who, with regard " to the Beauty of its Gardens, &c has made the Place on " of the moft remarkable Curiofities in *England*." There is no thing like travelling at home.

the Princefs *Elizabeth* alfo refided at the Death of her Sifter *Mary*, when fhe removed to *London* as before mentioned. She afterwards bought this Manor of the Bifhop of *Ely*, and her Succeffor, King *James*, in the fifth Year of his Reign, exchanged it for *Theobalds*, with his Favourite Sir *Robert Cecil* (who built the prefent Houfe) Anceftor of *James Cecil*, at this Time Earl of *Salifbury*, whofe Refidence it now is. I can't fay, that this Building is in excellent Repair, but the Gardens and Park, through which laft runs the River *Lea*, are very fine, as to Situation : In the Year 1647, the unhappy King *Charles* the Firft was removed from this Houfe to *Holmbye*.

The Town of *Hatfield* is pretty large, and not ill built : The Church is one of the beft Rectories in *England*, being worth about Eight hundred Pounds a Year. The Earl of *Salifbury* is the Patron. This Building, which is in the Form of a Crofs, hath a Chapel adjoining to the Chancel. The Tower is handfome, and the Bells in it heavy, but tuneable. On *Thurfdays* here is a good Market, if we confider its Vicinity to *London* ; but the Market-Houfe is rather in the Way of Travellers. The Fairs are on the 23d of *April*, and the 18th of *October*, both chiefly for Toys.

From *Hatfield* to the River *Lea* is about five Miles, where I croffed it at *Leamsford*; and rode through a fine Country to *Welwyn*. The Evening began to approach, but your Commands obliged me to reach *Stevenage* before I enjoyed the Refrefhment of Sleep. I met indeed with an Innkeeper at *Welwyn*, who preffed me much to take up my Lodgings at that Village, without giving me to underftand that he dealt in the public Trade. However, on my Arrival at his Door, the Difcovery was made, and then we

R 2 parted:

parted : Nothing could be finer than the Clofe of this Day, which was like that defcribed by *Milton*.

> Now came ftill Evening on, and Twilight gray
> Had in her fober Livery all Things clad .
> Silence accompany'd ; for Beaft and Bird,
> They to their graffy Couch, thofe to their Nefts,
> Were flunk, all but the wakeful *Nightingale* ;
> She all Night long her amorous Defcant fung ;
> Silence was pleas'd : now glow'd the Firmament
> With living Saphires. *Hefperus,* that led
> The ftarry Hoft, rode brighteft ; till the Moon,
> Rifing in clouded Majefty, at length,
> Apparent Queen, unveil'd her peerlefs Light,
> And o'er the dark her filver Mantle threw.

Nothing can be more pleafant than travelling in a fine Summer Night.

It was about twelve o'Clock when we arrived at the *Swan,* the beft Inn in *Stevenage,* where, after fome Refrefhment, I took my Reft, and fent *Charles* back with the Horfes, at Ten in the Morning.

Stevenage, formerly called *Stevenhaught,* is a ftraggling fmall Market-Town, in the Mid-Way between *Welwyn* and *Baldock.* As its Situation is on the great North Road, 'tis much frequented, and has fome good Inns. The Manor of it belonged to the *Saxon* Kings, till *Edward* the Confeffor granted it to the Abbot of *Weftminfter.* In Doomfday Book is this Record, " In *Broadwater* " Hundred Abbas de *Weftmonaft.* tenet *Stigenace* " pro octo Hidis defendebat, *&c.*" After the Diffolution, when *Henry* the Eighth changed the Monaftery of *Weftminfter* into a *Bifhopric,* Dr. *Thirleby* being the firft *Bifhop,* enjoyed this Manor ; but King *Edward* the Sixth diffolving the *Bifhopric,* granted the Manor to Dr. *Ridley,* then Bifhop of *London,* and his Succeffor, Queen *Mary,* vacated this Grant, difplaced *Ridley,* and put *Bonner* in

his

his ftead. But afterwards fhe got the Grant confirmed by the *Pope*, and firmly fettled it on this
See, on paying One hundred Pounds annually into the Exchequer, in which State it now is.

The Church, which ftands upon an Hill, contains two handfome Ifles, a large Chancel, and
two Chapels. Here is a Ring of Six Bells, and a
large Spire.

King *James* the Firft granted to the Bifhop of
London, and the Inhabitants of *Stevenage*, a week-
ly Market, to be held on *Mondays*; and annual
Fairs on *Afcenfion-Day*, St. *Swithin*'s, and the *Fri-
day* before *Palm-Sunday*; but in the fifth Year of
William and *Mary*, the Market was changed to
Fridays.

The Fairs are now held nine Days before *Eafter*,
nine Days before *Whitfuntide*, the 15th of *July*,
and the firft *Friday* in *September*, at which are
many Hawkers and Pedlars, and fome Sellers of
Cheefe. I am, Sir, Yours, *&c.*

L E T T E R XIII.

From *Eaton*, in *Bedfordfhire*, near St. *Neot*'s, in
the County of *Huntingdon*.

S I R,

FROM *Stevenage* I purfued my Rout to *Baldock*. This is a tolerable Market-Town, fituate
in a whitifh Soil, in a very fine Corn Country. In
the Reign of King *Stephen*, *Gilbert*, Earl of *Pembroke*, who was Lord of this Manor, gave about
One hundred and twenty-eight Acres of Land to
the *Knights Templars*, on which they built this
Town, and gave the Name of *Baudac*. King
John gave them fome Privileges; and his Son,
Henry the Third, granted them an annual Fair
and

and a Market on *Wednefdays*. After the Diffolution, King *Henry* the Eighth gave the Manor to
Thomas Rivet, of *London*, Mercer ; who furrendered up his Patent to Queen *Elizabeth*; for
which Confideration, fhe granted to him and his
Heirs, a Market on *Saturdays*, and Fairs on the
Days of St. *James*, St. *Andrew*, and St. *Mathew*;
but both the Market and Fairs are now altered,
the former to *Thurfdays*, and the latter are held
upon *Wednefday* after the 24th of *February*, the
laft *Thurfday* in *May*, the 6th of *Auguft*, the 6th
of *October*, and the 11th of *December* ; and they
are all confiderable for Cheefe, Houfhold Goods,
and Cattle. The Market is large, efpecially in
the Article of Malt.

The Church is a Rectory, in the Gift of the
Crown. This Building is in the Middle of the
Town, 'Tis a confiderable Fabric, to which belong three Chancels, and a good Tower, with a
mufical Ring of fix Bells. In one of the Chancels, among many other Monuments, is one for
Margaret Bennet, Mother of *Robert Bennet*, Bifhop of *Hereford*; and, in the Church, a Tomb
for Mr. *Jofias Bird*, who died aged Eighty-eight,
having been Rector here Fifty-three Years.

There have been many Donations to the Poor
of this Town, particularly Eleven thoufand
Pounds given by one Mr. *John Winne*, to build
fix Alms-Houfes, and purchafe Annuities of forty Shillings *per Annum*, for each Perfon who
fhould inhabit the fame.

From *Baldock* I went in a Poft-Chaife to *Bigglefwade*. On my Road, I paffed the old *Roman*
Way, called the *Icknield-ftreet*, and overtook a
Troop of light Horfe, who were well mounted,
and in general very clever-looking Fellows ; they
were quartered at *Baldock*. I am of Opinion,
that this Improvement in the Army will be very
ufeful,

useful, as well as ornamental. The Lord Lieutenant and *Custos Rotulorum* of this County is *William*, Earl *Cowper*. Nothing very material happened to me on the Road to this Place, from
whence I again send you a Tender of my best Services.

I am 'much pleased with the Behaviour of Mr.
Smith; nothing seems wanting to make him a polite Gentleman. The Observations which he has
made abroad have, by an excellent Judgment,
been turned to great Advantages at home. I
like his Manner vastly, and he seems to have in
Nature what the *French* call *Je ne scai quoi*; in a
Word, his Understanding is great, his Address
engaging, and, if I am not a very pitiful Judge,
his Heart is honest. I therefore congratulate you
on your Happiness in his Friendship. Sir *John
Denham* says,

> Well chosen Friendship, the most noble
> Of Virtues, all our Joys makes double,
> And into Halves divides our Trouble.

Bigglefwade is a small Market-Town on the
York Road ; the Market is held on *Thursdays*,
when a deal of *Barley* is sold ; and they have
Fairs on *February* the 13th, *Saturday* in *Easter-
Week*, *Whitfun-Monday*, *July* the 22d, St. *Simon*
and *Jude*, and *October* the 28th, for all Sorts of
Cattle.

The Situation of this Place is extreamly agreeable.

In the Chancel of the Church is a large Marble Monument, in Memory of *John Ruding*, Batchelor of Laws, who had been Prebend of *Bigglefwade*, and afterwards Dean of *Lincoln*. His
Effigies are done in Brafs, and on some Plates are
Latin rhyming Infcriptions, but Part of them are
ftolen away. His Arms are a Crefcent, within a
Bordure

Bordure of five Mullets : This is the Motto, *All may God amende.* He died in the Year 1481.

- The River *Ivel* is here navigable, which is of prodigious Service to all the Neighbourhood. Here are several good Inns, especially the *Star*, and the *Royal Oak*.

From this Town I paffed by the Side of the *Ivel*, to a Bridge over the fame, where is a Sluice for the Service of Navigation ; for which an Act paffed in the Year 1758, intitled, an Act for making the River *Ivel*, and the Branches thereof, navigable, from the River *Ouse* at *Tempsford*, in the County of *Bedford*, to *Shotling-Mill*, otherwife called *Burnt-Mill*, in the Parifh of *Hitchin*, in the County of *Hertford* ; and to *Black-Horfe-Mill*, in the Parifh of *Byegrave*, in the faid County of *Hertford* ; and to the *South* and *North* Bridges, in the Town of *Shefford*, in the faid County of *Bedford*. The Veffels here are very long, and frequently four or five are tied together : Thofe that went down at this Time were laden with Wheat and Barley. The Country now became very flat, the Fields large, and the Grain promifing. I here met Abundance of poor People of various Ages ; they had come fiom the North, and were going to the Hay-Harveft about *London*. Having croffed the River *Ouse* (which comes down from *Bedford)* a little above its Conflux with the *Ivel*, in a fhort Time I came to the Village of *Eaton* ; which confifts of indifferent Houfes, excepting fome few Inns, but thofe being on the great North Road, are well accuftomed. The Church is large, but has nothing extraordinary in it. The People here, and for many Miles round, are moft grievoufly afflicted with a very peftilential Diforder, which is fatal to many. Perhaps you conclude, as the Lands near it are low, and in fome Places marfhy, that this Difor-

der

der is the Ague. No, Sir, that unwelcome Companion only affects the *Body*; but this deftructive Poifon attacks the more valuable Part, the *Mind*: And is commonly called or known by the Name of *Methodifm*. I am told, that fome of the Haberdafhers of this Sort of Mifchief deal it about fo effectually, that the Inhabitants ftand in need of a Building as large as *Bedlam*. It were to be wifhed, that the legiflative Doctors would find out fome Remedy for this ravaging Malady. At *Eaton* was formerly a Caftle, the Seat of Part of the *Beauchamp* Family; and at *Biffemead* or *Bufhmead*, about a Mile to the Weft of it, in the Reign of *William* the Conqueror, two Brothers, *Hugo* and *Roger de Beauchamp*, founded a Priory for *Black Canons*. From *Eaton* to St. *Neot*'s is about a Mile. I entered this Town by a Bridge over the *Oufe*, which here is a pretty River, having been augmented by the *Ivel*, and a large Brook from the Eaft of *Huntingdonfhire*.

The Name of this Town arofe from its being the fecond Burial-Place of the learned, pious and benevolent *Neotus*, or St. *Neot*, who furpaffed all the lettered Men in the Court of the glorious King *Alfred*. Yet the Fame of his Piety, and the Authority of his Example, eclipfed his Learning. He was an Abbot, defcended from the Blood-Royal of the *Eaft Angles*, and confequently in Confanguinity with the King; this gave him a proper Afcendancy over him, and he frequently reproved him for the Sallies of his Youth: In a Word, to him it was in a great Meafure owing, that that mildeft, jufteft, moft beneficent of Kings, who drove out the *Danes*, fecured the Seas, promoted Learning, eftablifhed Juries, crufhed Corruption, guarded Liberty, and was the Founder of the *Englifh Conftitution*, continued fo unftained by perfonal Vices. This goodly Abbot was the firft Reader of Divinity in *Great Univerſity Hall*, now *Univer-ſity College*, in *Oxford*. His Death happened about the Year 883, at a Place called *Gaineſbury* in *Cornwall* (where he had ſettled, after being forced to fly out of the Country of the *Eaſt Angles*) where, in the Church of St. *Guerirſ*, being interred, he not only ſupplanted that Saint in the Name of the Church, but a religious Houſe was there dedicated to him, and called *Neotſtow*, or *Neotſtock*. After this, the Report of his Zeal for Religion was ſuch, that his Body was, by Order of the King, who greatly honoured his Memory, removed to the Palace of Earl *Alric*, or *Elfrid*, here, then converted into a Monaſtery for that Purpoſe; which cauſed the preſent Name of this Town. This religious Houſe having been ſpoiled and burnt down by the *Danes*, was, in 1113, rebuilt, and greatly endowed by *Roiſa*, or *Roheiſa*, the Lady of *Richard*, Earl of *Clare*; about which Time it was given as a Cell to the Abbey of *Bec* in *Normandy*. By the Bull of Pope *Celeſtine*, directed to the Biſhop of *Lincoln*, it appears that the Prior and Convent of St. *Neot*'s, having their Houſe ſituate on a great Road, uſed to beſtow Meat and Drink on all Travellers that deſired it. To which Purpoſe ſolely they appropriated the Rents and Penſions which they yearly received from the Churches of *Eyneſbury* and *Torney*. According to ſome of our Hiſtorians, *Henry*, Abbot of *Croyland*, in the fifteenth Year of King *John*, took up the Bones of this good Man from this his ſecond Place of Interment, and beſtowed them in *Croyland* Minſter.

In the Reigns of *Henry* the Fourth and Fifth, this Monaſtery was diſcharged from its foreign Subjection to the Abbey of *Bec*, and converted into an *Engliſh* Priory; which, at the Diſſolution, was

was valued at Two hundred and forty-one Pounds Eleven Shillings and Four Pence *per Annum.*

In the Year 1648, the Earl of *Holland,* with a Party of Horse, being pursued by the Troops of the *Parliament,* came to this Town, where a sharp Skirmish ensued, in which Colonel *Dalbier* was slain, and the Earl of *Holland* taken; from whence he was sent a Prisoner to *Warwick* Castle. The Duke of *Buckingham,* the Earl of *Peterborough,* and other Persons of Quality, escaped.

The Town of St. *Neot's* is well-built, and considerably large; the Stone Bridge over the *Ouse* is strong and handsome. The Church is large, and pretty elegant; the Workmanship of the Steeple is very curious.

As this Town is situate on a navigable River, among other Things, great Quantities of Coals are brought hither, and afterwards carried to the neighbouring Towns and Villages. The Grain and other Commodities, which are sent down this River, are also considerable.

On the whole, St. *Neot's* is the second, if not the best Town, in the County of *Huntingdon.*

This Town gave the Title of Baron to *Edward Montague* (the Son of Sir *Sydney Montague,* the youngest Son of *Edward Montague,* of *Hynfington,* Esq; and Brother to *Edward,* the first Lord *Montague* of *Boughton*) who having had the Command of the Navy, so effectually served King *Charles* the Second, that he created him a Knight of the Garter, Baron *Montague* of St. *Neot's,* Viscount *Hinchinbrooke,* and Earl of *Sandwich.* This brave and gallant Gentleman was killed in the Engagement in 1672 with the *Dutch* Fleet in *Solebay,* in the forty-seventh Year of his Age; the same Titles are now descended to his Great-Grandson, *John Montague,* Earl of *Sandwich.*

The Market at St. *Neot's,* which is very plentiful of Corn and other Provisions, is held on *Thursdays;*

days;

days; and the Fairs are on *Afcenfion Thurfday, June* the 13th, *Auguft* the 1ft, and *December* the 13th, for all Sorts of Cattle.

As this Town is in the Hundred of *Tofeland*, I muft not omit the merry Conceit of the Gentleman that ferved the Office of Sheriff for this County in Year 1618, who being, by Judge *Dodderidge*, reprimanded for impannelling Perfons not qualified for the Grand Jury, did, at the next Affizes, emphatically read thefe Names, according as I have pointed them, being the Jurors by him then impannelled.

Maximilian, King of *Tofeland*,
Henry, Prince of *Godmanchefter*,
George, Duke of *Somerfham*,
William, Duke of *Wefton*,
William, Marquis of *Stukeley*,
Edward, Earl of *Hartford*,
Robert, Lord of *Warfley*,
Richard, Baron of *Bythorpe*,
Robert, Baron of *Winwich*,
Edmund, Knight of St. *Neot*'s,
Peter, Efquire of *Eufton*,
George, Gentleman of *Spaldock*,
Robert, Yeoman of *Barham*,
Stephen, Pope of *Wefton*,
Humphry, Cardinal of *Kimbolton*,
William, Bifhop of *Bugden*,
John, Archdeacon of *Paxton*,
John, Abbot of *Stukeley*,
Richard, Friar of *Ellington*,
Henry, Monk of *Stukeley*,
Edward, Prieft of *Graffham*,
Richard, Deacon of *Catfworth*.

The Lord Lieutenant and Cuftos Rotulorum of this County is the Duke of *Manchefter*.

I purpofe fetting out for *Bedford* in the Morning, and am, Sir, Yours, &c.

L E T.

LETTER XIV.

From *Shefford* in *Bedfordshire.*

S I R,

FROM my Lodging at *Eaton,* I returned, by the *Bigglefwade* Road, for two or three Miles; and then turning to the Right, paffed through a fine Country, where the Wheat is the ftrongeft I have feen : Indeed 'tis fo rank that the Blade is of an extream dark-green Colour. Some few Miles farther I ftopped, according to your Defire, at a fweet Cottage, where Happinefs feems to have taken up her Seat. Your Queftions which I had to afk of the venerable Matron were anfwered with the kindeft natural Simplicity. She intreated my taking a Refrefhment of her homely Fare, which I accepted ; and, on my offering a trifling Return, fhe feemed greatly difpleafed. She told me her Manner of Life, and the Happinefs which fhe enjoyed in the Health and Tendernefs of her Hufband, who, added fhe, notwithftaning his being fixty-one, can earn ten Pence a Day, and goes twice to Church on the *Sunday.* The old Woman's Face is as florid as if but thirty Years old ; and fhe exhibited Marks of Induftry and Cleanlinefs by every Thing within her ftraw-covered Manfion. She then took me into the Garden, where Rofes abounded in remarkable Profufion.

> Obferve the fragrant blufhing Rofe,
>   Though in the humble *Vale* it fpring ;
> It fmells as fweet, as fair it blows,
>   As in the Garden of a *King !*
> So calm Content as oft is found compleat
> In the *low Cot,* as in the *lofty Seat.* DODSLEY.

From

From an Eminence near *Goldington*, I had a fine Prospect of the Valley, through which the River *Ouse* glides gently by the Village of *Willington*; which stands upon a wholesome gravelly Soil. This Manor was formerly the Property of the *Beauchamps*, Barons of *Bedford*: From them the *Mowbrays* inherited it, but in the Reign of *Henry* the Eighth it was purchased by the Family of *Gostwyrke.*

The Day was very hot; my Road strait and good to the ancient Town of *Bedford*; through which the *Ouse* runs towards the East. This was the *Lactodurum* of the *Romans*, by the *Saxons* it was called *Bedanford*, and *Beduanford*; but the *British* Name was *Lletudwr*, from *Lletu*, Inns or Lodging Houses, and *Dwr*, a Water. This Town, which is in 52 Deg. 10 Min. from the Equator, and in 20 Min. West Longitude from *London*, was rendered famous by its being the Place of Interment of the great *Mercian* King, *Offa.* In the Year of Christ 571, here was a general Engagement between the *Saxons*, commanded by their King, *Cuthwulf*, the Brother of *Ceaulin*, and the *Britons*; in which the former were victorious. In the Reign of *William* the Second, *Paganus de Beauchamp*, Baron of *Bedford*, built a strong Castle here; but that, together with the whole Town, was razed to the Ground on the following Account. In the Year 1224, one *Fowkes de Brent* was Governor of the Castle; a Person who had been so far guilty of Mal-Practices, that he had thirty Verdicts found against him, at the Assizes held before the general Judges at *Dunstable* in this County. Upon which he sent his Brother, with a Party of Men, to seize the Judges; two of whom escaped, but the third, *Henry de Bebroc*, fell into their Hands; and, after being treated with great Ignominy, was carried

Prisoner

Prifoner to the Caftle. Upon which, the King
(*Henry* the Third) laid Siege to it, and, after a
Defence of nine Months, obliged the Garrifon to
furrender at Difcretion, when the Governor, with
all his Knights and Soldiers, fuffered the igno-
minious Death of Hanging.

This Caftle had indeed undergone another
Siege, for in the Year 1137, *Milo de Beauchamp*,
the then Governor, declared himfelf in Favour of
the King of *Scots* ; and, having repaired it, refolved to defend it to the laft Extremity. But
King *Stephen* foon afterwards fat down before it,
and took it on *Chriftmas Day* that Year.

Here was an Hofpital for Lazars, dedicated to
St. *Leonard*, and another Hofpital to the Honour
of St. *John*, a curious Particular of which laft,
containing Two hundred and forty-fix Pages, was
burnt in the Fire at the *Cotton* Library.

In this Town is a Free-School, founded by Sir
William Harper (who was born here) Lord-Mayor
of *London*. Mr. *Thomas Chrifty*, formerly a Re-
prefentative in Parliament for this Borough, alfo
founded an Hofpital here for eight poor People,
and a School for forty Children.

Here are five Churches, dedicated to the following Saints, *Paul, Peter, Cuthbert, John*, and
Mary ; the firft of which is the largeft and moft
beautiful, where was interred the Body of the celebrated Dr. *Thorne*, and to whofe Memory is this
Infcription ;

> Underneath lies buried the Body of *Giles Thorne*,
> Doctor in Divinity, Chaplain in Ordinary to King
> *Charles* the II^d, Archdeacon of *Buckingham*,
> Rector of St. *Mary*'s and St. *Peter*'s here in *Bed-
> ford*, who deceafed *June* 25, 1671.

In that of St. *Peter*, near the Communion Table, are thefe Words ;

Here

Here lie the Remains of
Sufanna, Wife of *Thomas Knight* of this Town;
And Daughter of *Jofeph*, and *Sufanna Winwood*
of *London*.
She died in Child-Bed the 24th Day of *April*, 1754,
Aged 19 Years, 11 Months, and 7 Days.

Mortals, behold ! and tremble at this Shrine!
    Where *perfect Beauty* moulders into Duft ;
The late Companion of a *Soul* divine,
    Whofe Thoughts were pure, and ev'ry Action juft.

Sweet *Modefty* fat fmiling on her Cheek,
    And *Virtue*'s Dwelling was her peaceful Breaft ;
Where fpotlefs *Innocence*, ferenely meek,
    Attendant liv'd, and brighten'd up the reft.

But ah! fhe's gone; 'twas Heaven's confirm'd Decree!
    Remember, Matrons, what you owe to Heaven ;
Be thankful, O ! be more, be good as fhe ;
    And hope the Payment which to her is given.

This Epitaph was written by your humble Servant, as a Memorial of a young Perfon every
Way deferving of it. It is publifhed at the End
of the fecond Volume of my Collections.

The Town of *Bedford*, though large, is not
very elegant ; the Buildings in general are old,
and the Streets but indifferent. The Bridge over
the *Oufe* is not very broad, therefore the Gateway upon it is an Inconyenience.

On account of the Navigation of the River
Oufe, this Town hath a Communication with the
Counties of *Hertford*, *Huntingdon*, *Cambridge*, and
Norfolk : where, at *Lynn*, the River difembogues
itfelf into the *German* Ocean. The Quantities of
Wheat fent down this River from *Bedford* is prodigious. The Concourfe of People, and Bufinefs
tranfacted here on Market-Days, which are *Satur-*
days, is very confiderable ; though here too much
Corn is fold by Sample. The Fairs are on the
firft *Tuefday* in Lent, the 21ft of *April*, the 5th
of

The South West View of the ABBY CHURCH of St. ALBANS.

of *July*, the 22d of *Auguſt*, the 11th of *October*, and the 19th of *September*, for Cattle of every Sort.

The Corporation of *Bedford* is governed by a Mayor, Aldermen, a Recorder, two Bailiffs, two Chamberlains, a Town-Clerk, and three Serjeants. The Town ſends two Members to Parliament: The Number of Voters is about One thouſand. Near the Town of *Bedford*, and in many other Parts of this County, the Plant called *Glaſtum Sativum*, or *Woad*, is much cultivated. With the Tincture of this Plant the ancient *Britons* uſed to paint their Bodies, that they might appear more terrible to their Enemies. It is much uſed in dying Blue, and is raiſed after this Manner.

They ſow it about the Beginning of *March*, and cut it, for the firſt Time, about the Midſt of *May*. They generally cut or crop it four or five Times a Seaſon, as it grows up; but the firſt Crop is the beſt, the ſecond a little inferior, and ſo on, the laſt being the worſt. *Woad* is beſt in a dry Summer; but they gather more of it in a wet one. After cropping they carry it directly to the *Woad-Mill*, where 'tis ground ſo as to be fit to ball. When 'tis made into Balls, they lay them upon Hurdles to dry, and when 'tis quite dry, they grind them to a Powder as ſmall as poſſible. Then they throw it upon a Floor, and water it, which they call Couching, and let it ſmoke and heat, turning it every Day, till it is perfectly dry and mouldy, which they call Silvering. They then weigh it, putting Two hundred Weight in a Bag, as fit for Sale. The beſt is generally worth eighteen Shillings an hundred Weight. It is to be obſerved, that they ſow the Seed every Year, and pluck up the old Woad, unleſs 'tis ſaved for the

Seed; But never fow it more than two Years together upon the fame Land.

The People of *Bedford* are very well behaved,
and live in a happy Manner, neither abounding in
Luxury, nor griped by the cold Hand of Indi-
gence. The Bowling-Green here is extreamly
pleafant, and fo indeed is the Country all around.

This Town hath given the Titles of Earl and
Duke to many illuftrious Perfons, efpecially to *In-
gelram de Guifnes*, Baron of *Coucy*, and Earl of *Al-
bemarle* (who had married the Lady *Ifabella*, of
England). He was, by King *Edward* the Third,
in the Year 1366, created Earl of *Bedford*, with
a Salary of One thoufand and thirty Marks a
Year.

In the Year 1412, King Henry the Fourth
created his third Son, *John Plantagenet*, Duke of
Bedford. All the World hath known the Fame of
this gallant and great Man, whofe Bravery was
fcarce excelled by his eldeft Brother, *Henry* the
Fifth ; and whofe Goodnefs was almoft as much
celebrated as that of his other Brother, the *good
Duke Humphry*. The *French* called him the *Fire-
brand of France* ; of which Kingdom he was both
Conftable and *Regent* for many Years. Hiftory is
fo full of his Exploits, great Conduct, and matchlefs Integrity, that I fhall clofe my Account of
him with the Words, if I can remember them,
of a modern Writer.

" The Treaty of *Arras* portended the fudden
" Ruin of the *Englifh* Affairs in *France* ; and this
" was compleated by the unhappy Death of the
" illuftrious Duke of *Bedford* ; who died at
" *Rouen*, on the 14th of *September*, in the Year
" 1435, and was buried in the Church of *Notre
" Dame* in that City. He had all the Qualities
" of a great Prince, and a brave General ; his
" own Enemies confeffed his Worth : For when
" *Lewis*

" *Lewis* the Eleventh, Son of *Charles* the Se-
" venth, was looking at his Tomb, he was ad-
" vifed to demolifh that ftanding Monument of
" the Difhonour of *France*. But the King re-
" plied, *No, let the Afhes of a Prince reft in*
" *Peace, who, if he was alive, would make the*
" *boldeft of you tremble ; and I rather wifh a more*
" *ftately Monument was erected to his Memory.*"

After the Battle of *Bofworth*, in the Year
1485, King *Henry* the Seventh created his Uncle,
Jafper Tudor, who was already Earl of *Pembroke*,
Duke of *Bedford*. He was the fecond Son of Sir
Owen Tudor, who fprang from an original Branch
of *Cadwallader*, the laft King of the *Britons*, who
died in 689, by *Catherine* of *France*, Widow of
King *Henry* the Fifth of *England* ; which Sir *Owen*
Tudor, in the Year 1460, had been taken Prifoner
in the Engagement (near *Mortimer-Crofs*, in the
County of *Hereford*) between the Forces of the
Houfes of *York* and *Lancafter* (the latter of which
were commanded by the faid *Jafper*) and, with
feveral others, was executed, in Revenge for the
Death of the Earl of *Salifbury*.

In the Year 1549, King *Edward* the Sixth, conferred the Honour of Earl of *Bedford* on *John*,
Lord *Ruffel*, Lord Prefident, Lord Privy-Seal,
and Lord Admiral. This was a Nobleman above
the low Intrigues of a Court. He had been
much entrufted by *Henry* the Eighth, to whom
he was of fingular Service. He owed to Sagacity
what others acquired by Cunning ; the Diftinction paid him by his Sovereigns arofe entirely fiom
his Merit. No Nobleman of that Time fteered
fo happily as he ; for he wore his Honours uncon-
taminated. Though he was not fo bufy, yet he
was more ferviceable than any of his Rank in the
Caufe of Reformation. His Sentiments feem to
have been for bounding the Prerogative ; but

when

when he undertook the Service of the Crown, he discharged it with Zeal, and generally with Success. In a Word, he preferred his Duty to his Country to all his private Obligations.

In this Nobleman's Line the Title continued till the Year 1694; when King *William* the Third created *William Ruffel*, Duke of *Bedford*; whose great Grandson, the present Duke, is Lord Lieutenant and Custos Rotulorum of this County.

I shall end my Account of the Town of *Bedford* with observing, that *John Bunyan*, the Author of that well-known Book, the *Pilgrim's Progress*, was a Brasier there; and lies interred in the *Diffenters* Burying-Ground in *Bunhill-Fields*, *London*.

From *Bedford* it is about a Mile to *Elstow*, which is the corrupted Name of *Helenstow*, where, in the Reign of *William* the First, *Judith*, the Lady of *Waltheof*, Earl of *Huntingdon*, built a Priory for Nuns of the Order of St. *Benedict*, and dedicated it to the Honour of the *Holy Trinity*, the Virgin *Mary*, and St *Helen*, Mother of *Constantine* the Great. At this Village are annual Fairs on the 14th of *May*, and the 25th of *November*, for Cattle of all Sorts.

About three Miles farther I left *Hawnes*, the handsome Seat of the Earl of *Granville*, on my Left-Hand; near which is *Southill*, the Seat of the Lord Viscount *Torrington*, Nephew of the unfortunate Admiral *John Byng*; and continued my Course by *Chickfand*, a Seat belonging to the *Ofborn* Family; of these Seats I shall say more. I soon came to *Shefford*, a small Town, whose Market is on *Fridays*, and Fairs are held on the 23d of *January*, *Easter-Monday*, the 19th of *May*, and the 10th of *October*, for Cattle.

The Situation of Part of this Town is between the River *Ivel*, and another large Stream, which falls into that River a little below. The Country about

about this Town, though low, is not much subjected to Fogs or unwholesome Air ; for here are
no Fens or stagnated Waters. The Land in
these Parts of *Bedfordshire* is extreamly fertile,
and on the steril Hills, especially about *Luton* and
Dunstable, among various Sorts of Manures, they
find the greatest Advantage from the Shavings
and Chips of *Horn*, which they buy in *London*,
and have afforded to give fourteen Pounds a
Load for it. I am told that there is a Farmer,
at or near the last mentioned Town, who buys
many hundred Pounds worth of this Commodity
annually : But the present Price is only about ten
Pounds a Load, which contains twenty Sacks.
One would be almost inclined to conclude, that
the Farmers could not make the Return of such
an Expence, but Experience shews the contrary.
I am, Sir, Yours, *&c.*

L E T T E R   XV.

From *Welwyn*, in *Hertfordshire*.

S I R,

ABOUT two Miles from *Shefford* is an old, but
magnificent Seat, called *Wrest-House*. This
was the Residence of the illustrious Family of
Grey, Dukes of *Kent*; but the late Duke dying
without Male Issue, it descended, together with a
fine Estate, to his Grand-Daughter, the Lady *Je-
mima Campbell*, only Child of his eldest Daughter,
by her Husband, Lord *Glenorchy*; which young
Lady, after the Death of her Grandfather, the
Duke of *Kent*, was, in the Year 1742, created
Marchioness of *Grey*, by King *George* the Second.
She is now married to *Philip*, Lord *Royston*, a
Gentleman, whose Love of Learning, and Regard
for

for Men of Letters, is remarkable ; and his Taste is manifested in his beautiful Park, Gardens, and Buildings. Here is an Hermitage, formed after the Manner of true Simplicity, on which are the following Lines ;

Stranger or Gueſt, whom e'er this hallow'd Grove,
   Shall chance receive, where ſweet Contentment dwells,
   Bring here no Heart, that with Ambition ſwells,
With Av'rice pines, or burns with lawleſs Love.

Vice-tainted Souls will all in vain remove
   To ſylvan Shades, and Hermits peaceful Cells ;
   In vain will ſeek Retirement's lenient Spells,
Or hope that Bliſs, which only good Men prove.

If Heaven-born Truth, and ſacred Virtue's Lore,
   Which chear, adorn, and dignify the Mind,
Are conſtant Inmates of thy honeſt Breaſt ;
   If, unrepining at thy Neighbour's Store,
Thou count'ſt, as thine, the Good of all Mankind,
   Then, welcome, ſhare the friendly Groves of *Wreſt.*

Near the Mid-Way from *Shefford* to *Hitchin,* I again croſſed the *Pretorian Roman* Way, or *Ick-nield-Street,* near a Place called therefrom *Ickleford.* This Road was very good to *Hitchin,* a Town and Manor formerly poſſeſſed by the Kings of *Mercia.* This is pretty manifeſt by the Extenſion of the latter into the Pariſh of *Offley,* ſituate a little to the Eaſt of this Town ; where was the Court of the famous King *Offa.* There too he died, and was buried at a Place before ſpoken of. The Appellation of this Town aroſe from *Hiz,* the Stream which runs through it. King *Edward* the Confeſſor gave it, together with the Manor, to Earl *Harold,* afterwards the ſecond King of that Name (who ſo gallantly and bravely loſt his Life in the memorable Battle of *Haſtings*). *William* the Firſt poſſeſſed it in Right of the Crown, for in *Doomſday-Book* are theſe Words, " In dimidio Hundred de *Hiz* Rex Wil-
                     " lielmus

" *lielmus* tenet *Hiz* pro quinq; Hidis fe defende-
" bat," *&c.·* His Son, *William,* gave the-Manor
to *Bernard de Baliol,* Baron of *Biwel,* in the County of *Northumberland*; in whofe Family it continued, till *John de Baliol* became King of *Scotland,*
when it devolved to *Edward* the Firft, as King of
England, and remained in the Crown till the
fourteenth Year of his great Great-Grandfon,
King *Richard* the Second, who beftowed it on his
Uncle, *Edmund de Langley,* the fifth Son of his
Grandfather. In the Reign of *Henry* the Seventh,
it again reverted to the Crown ; where it now
continues.

In the Parifh of *Hitchin* are fome fmall Manors
dependant on this ; there are alfo three Hamlets
belonging to the Parifh ; they are, *Minfden, Wede-
lee,* and *Temple-Dinefley,* the two latter of which
belonged to the *Knights-Templars.*

The Town of *Hitchin* is large, well-built, and
very populous.

Formerly it was confiderable for the ftaple Commodities of the Kingdom, and many Merchants
of the Staple of *Calais* were Inhabitants there ;
but there is now no Manufactory worth Notice.
The Market, which is held on *Tuefdays* by Prefcription, is free from the Payment for any Sort
of Grain, and is remarkable for Malt. The
Fairs are on the 2d of *April,* the 30th of *May,*
and the 12th of *October,* all chiefly for Cattle.

The Church of *Hitchin* is a Vicarage, of which
the Mafter and Fellows of *Trinity-College* in *Cambridge* are Patrons, and they have augmented it
ten Pounds out of the impropriate Tythes. The
Building is handfome. It was originally dedicated
to St. *Andrew,* but, on its being rebuilt, to the
Mother of Chrift. It is in Length about One
hundred and fifty-two Feet, and in Breadth about
fixty-eight. To this Church belong three Chancels ;

2

cels ; the Tower is twenty-one Feet fquare, in which hang a good Ring of fix Bells. In two of the Windows are fome tolerable Paintings, and in the Church many Monuments ; particularly one with long Infcriptions relating to the *Radcliffe* Family: That to the Memory of Mr. *Kempe* I have copied, according to your Requeft ; he was buried in the Middle of the Chancel.

3 *Auguft* 1654.
Senam fuam hic depofitum
Exuit
Magni Nominis
Jofephus Kempe.
Qui

Omnes Terras fuas Ædes ac Redditus in *Hitchin* ad valorem Librarum plus mille in Egenorum iftius Oppidi Liberorum in bonis Literis et Artibus ingenuis provectionem nec non Viduarum fuftentationem pie confecravit et in perpetuum munificè donavit.

Nec pereat Populas populires condidit olim
Egypti Jofeph nofter at ille fuas.
Cujus Opes ditant inopes tenet Offa Sepulchrum
Atque Animam Omnipotens Anglie nomen habet:

Hoc Mnemofynum
Anna
Relicta ejus Obfervantiffima
Lachrymis pofuit
1655.

In a Window in the North Ifle are painted *Faith*, *Hope*, and *Charity*, and the four Cardinal Virtues ; and the Beatitudes are well done in the next North Window. Here are fome other Paintings that were damaged in the civil War.

This Town hath a good Free-School, and other charitable Donations, for the Relief of the Poor.

From *Hitchin* the Road is fine to the little Village of *Minfden*. I afterwards came to the Side of of *Knebworth* Park, which belongs, as I am told, to Mr. *Litton*; whofe Anceftor, *Robert Litton*, of *Derby*, Efq; Under Treafurer in the Court of Exchequer, Keeper of the King's Ward, and a Privy Counfellor to *Henry* the Seventh, purchafed this Manor of that King. His Family has flourifhed here ever fince.

Between this Place and *Welwyn* is *Codicot*, *Codicet*, or *Caldecote*, a large Village, where is now a Tinker, who has nine Sons living, and all are Soldiers in the *Englifh* Army.

The Manor was anciently Part of the Poffeffions of the Monaftery of St. *Alban*. The Church is fituate upon a dry Hill, near the Manor Houfe; it is covered with Lead, and at the Weft End is a fquare Tower, with a Ring of five Bells.

This Parifh is famous for the great Walnut-Tree, regarding which Sir *Henry Chauncy* has two extraordinary Certificates *.

* *Edward Wingate*, Efq; one of the Juftices of the Peace for this County, did certify, under his Hand, Anno 1627, That there was a great Walnut-Tree grew on *Sciffivernes Green*, in this Parifh, which was of that great Extent, that the Branches thereof covered feventy fix Poles of Ground. Mr. *Penn* (who was Lord of the Manor) fold fo much of it to a Gun-Stock-Maker in *London*, as he would carry thither for ten Pounds, which he paid, and fawed out into Planks of two Inches thick and half, as much as filled nineteen Carts and Waggons. Mr. *Penn* had thirty Loads more, which the Man left, with the Roots and Branches; with the End of one Root, he wainfcotted a fair Room, made a Portal, many Chairs, and Stools of the Remainder; and Mr *Penn* averred to myfelf and others, that he had, divers Times, been offered fifty Pounds for this Tree. Edward Wingate.

The other Certificate is,
Jafper Docwra, born in *Hallwood* in *Codicote*, doth aver, that in the Year 1622, he meafured the Circumference of Mr. *Penn*'s Walnut-Tree, he being then fifteen Years old; and it was eight of his Fathoms, of both Arms, in Compafs round the Body. Jasper Docwra.

From *Codicot* the Road is fine to *Wellwyn*, at which Place the Maſſacre of the *Danes* firſt began, in the Reign of King *Ethelred*, on St. *Brice*'s Day.

The Church here is dedicated to the Virgin *Mary*; it conſiſts of two Iſles, and a Chancel: The Covering is Lead. Here is a long Inſcription to the Memory of that great and good Divine, Dr. *Gabriel Towerſon*, who was Rector of this Pariſh; and the following Words are cut on another Tomb-ſtone; the Author of them may eaſily be known, from the ingenious, yet ſimple Stile, but the two laſt Letters afford us a plain Demonſtration that they were written by the preſent Incumbent.

Reader !
If fond of what is rare, attend,
Here lies an *Honeſt Man !*
Of perfect Piety,
Of lamb-like Patience,
My Friend, *James Barker*.
To whom I pay this mean Memorial ;
For what deſerves the greateſt.
An Example
Which ſhone through all
The Clouds of Fortune.
Illuſtrious in low Eſtate.
The Leſſon and Reproach of thoſe above him.
To lay this little Stone
Is my Ambition ;
While others rear
The pompous Marbles of the Great ;
Vain Pomp !
A Turf over Virtue charms us more.
E. Y. 1749.

This large Village, which is ſituate upon the ſmall River *Mavan*, or *Minevum*, that falls into the *Lea* near *Hertford*, is bleſſed with the Reſidence of that moſt excellent Divine, celebrated Poet, accompliſhed Preacher, and truly good Man, the Reverend Dr. *Edward Young*. Such a Tide of Praiſes,

and

Applauſes, and ſincere Wiſhes, that are poured out here, by all Ranks and Degrees, as Gratitude for his Benevolence of Heart, and the Liberality of his Hand, exceeds all Example! How amiable! I am unwilling to ſay, how uncommon is this Clergyman's Goodneſs?

In this Village is a Spring of Water, whoſe Virtues are ſimilar to that of *Tunbridge* in *Kent*. It was firſt diſcovered about ſixty two Years ſince; and about the Year 1751 was revived by an all-accompliſhed Gentleman, whoſe Name I have mentioned. The Accommodations were then but indifferent, but now they are very good, and much frequented by the neighbouring Gentry; if we conſider that Water-Drinking ſeems to have had its Day.

A Servant of Mr. *Smith* is this Moment come into the Inn, who I find is to be in *London* this Evening; I ſhall, therefore, take the Opportunity of ſending this Letter by him, and am, Sir, Yours, &c.

L E T T E R XVI.

From St. *Alban's*.

S I R,

FROM *Wellwyn* to *Wheathamſted* is about three Miles.

This latter Place had its Name from the great Quantity of Wheat which it produced; and with this Commodity it ſtill abounds. The Manor was poſſeſſed by King *Edward* the Confeſſor, who, during Part of his Reign, kept it, as furniſhing Part of the Proviſion of his own Table; but he afterwards preſented it to the Abbot and Convent of *Weſtminſter*. On the Diſſolution of

Religious

Religious Houſes, it became veſted in the *Dean* and *Chapter* of that collegiate Church, who enjoy it at this Time. This Village is rendered of ſome Note by being the Birth-Place of *John Boſtock*, commonly called *John of Wheathamſtead*, a Perſon of *Learning* and *Piety*, who was firſt Monk of *Tinmouth Priory*, in the County of *Northumberland* ; he was afterwards made Prior of the Abbey of St. *Alban's*, in which he continued about twenty Years, and then reſigned to *John Stock*, Prior of *Wallingford*; who poſſeſſed it ſix Years, when *John Wheathamſtead* was re-elected, but ſoon after died. At *Redburn* he rebuilt the Church, and furniſhed it with Books. At St. *Alban's* he erected St. *Andrew's* Chapel, and another in the Monks College at *Oxford*. This Village ſtands upon the River *Lea*, from whence I paſſed on to *Sandridge*, the Manor of which belonged to the Family of *Jennings*, or rather *Jenyns*, who lived at this Place, and deſcended to *Sarah Jenyns*, Dutcheſs of *Marlborough* ; it alſo gave the Title of Baron to her illuſtrious Conſort the Duke.

From *Sandridge* I ſoon came to St. *Alban's*, a Town built out of the Ruins of *Old Verulam*, which was ſituate on the other Side of the little River *Ver*. Our Hiſtorians think that *Verulam* was the Seat of the famous *British* King, *Caſſibelan*, and tell us, that the Inhabitants thereof became the firſt civilized *Britons*, or rather the fondeſt of *Roman* Luxury; inſomuch that the enraged *Boadicea*, Queen of the *Iceni*, treated them as Enemies, razed their City, and even *Dio* himſelf ſays, that ſhe cauſed to be hanged, crucified, and cut to Pieces, upwards of *Fourſcore thouſand of them*. After the Defeat and Ruin of that Queen by *Suetonius*, they lived in Eaſe and Proſperity, built more Houſes and Temples, and eſtabliſhed Courts

of

of Juſtice, learnt the *Roman* Eloquence, wore their Habits, ſtudied the liberal Arts and Sciences, and greatly improved their Trade, until the Year 293, when aroſe the Perſecution of *Diocle-ſian*, and *Alban*, the *Britiſh Proto-Martyr*, ſuffered for the *Chriſtian* Religion, in a moſt exemplary Manner.

The *Saxons* gave it the Name of *Werlamceſter*, and *Watlingaceſter*, from the *Roman Pretorian Way* which paſſed through it. About the Year 498, the old Name, *Verulam*, was reſtored ; but after ſome Years it became quite loſt, and the Place entirely neglected.

Our excellent *Spencer* thus cauſes her to lament her Condition.

> I was that City which the Garland wore
> Of *Britain*'s Pride ; delivered unto me
> By *Roman* Victors, which it won of yore,
> Though nought at all but Ruins now I be ;
> And lie in mine own Aſhes, as you ſee.
> *Ver'lam* I was, what boots it that I was,
> Sith now I am but Weeds and waſteful Graſs ?

It was in 793, more than Two hundred Years after this, that *Offa*, the renowned King of the *Mercians*, built on a Hill, at a Place called *Holmehurſt*, on the oppoſite Side of the River (where the Remains of St. *Alban* had been ſuppoſed to be found) a Monaſtery to his Memory, and there depoſited the Bones of that Saint.

Offa, for the Support of this Religious Houſe, (in which he placed One hundred Monks of the Order of St. *Benedict*) did, by Charter, dated in the Year abovementioned, grant to the ſaid Monaſtery ſeveral Lands, and great Privileges. In the Year 1154, *Nicholas*, Biſhop of *Alba* (who was born near this Monaſtery, being choſen *Pope* by the Name of *Adrian* IV. granted to the *Abbot* of this *Abbey*, that, as St. *Alban* was the firſt Martyr

tyr

tyr of *England*, fo the *Abbots* fhould be the firft in Order and Dignity of any in *England*. By *Domef-day-Book* it appears, that the Manor of this Town was held by the *Abbot* for ten Hides of Land.

King *John* gave to this Church, and its Monks, many Lands, and great Liberties. In the Year 1218, Pope *Honorius*, by a Bull, confirmed to this Church, all the Lands and Liberties granted to it by former *Popes*, Kings, and others: And granted to the *Abbot*, and his Succeffors, Epifcopal Rights, and the Epifcopal Habit; and that he and his Monks fhould be exempt from the Jurifdiction of the *Bifhop*, with other Exemptions, *&c.* referving only the annual Payment of an Ounce of Gold to the Apoftolic See, for thefe Liberties.

The *Abbots* of this Houfe fat in Parliament till the Diffolution, when it was valued at Two thoufand one hundred and two Pounds feven Shillings and one Penny *per Annum*.

The *Abbots* of St. *Alban*'s were in Number forty-one, the thirty-ninth was *Thomas Woolfey*, and the laft *Richard Boreman*; who was, after he had furrendered, allowed a Penfion of Two hundred and fixty-fix Pounds thirteen Shillings and four Pence for Life.

In the Fire which happened in the *Cotton* Library were burnt;

Regiftrum Chartarum Abbatiæ S. Albani, de pof-feffionibus, libertatibus, privilegiis redditibus, aliif-que rebus ad idem Monafterium fpectantibus.

La vie S. Alban, le primier Martyr d' Angleterre, & de S. Amphibal.

Alfo another Book bearing this Title;

Metra varia; puta de mifera forte Regni Angliæ, de bello commiffo infra villam S. Albani. Item Epitaphia varia.

Our

Our Hiftories of *England* are circumftantial as to the two Engagements between the Houfes of *York* and *Lancafter*, near this Town. In the firft, which happened in the Year 1455, on the Part of the *Yorkifts* the Earl of *Warwick* commanded, and prevailed. Among five thoufand *Lancaftrians* killed, were the Duke of *Somerfet*, the Earls of *Northumberland* and *Stafford*, and the Lord *Clifford*. The fecond Action was in 1461 (ten Years before that of *Barnet*) when the *other Houfe* was victorious, and the *Yorkifts* loft near Three thoufand Men.

The Church of the Monaftery of St. *Alban* is ftill a large Pile of Building; it is not much more valuable for its Antiquity than Beauty. The Corporation purchafed it of King *Edward* the Sixth, for Four hundred Pounds; when it became a Parifh Church by the Name of St. *Alban*'s. The Tooth of Time, and Power of Weather, have indeed caufed it to appear like Stone, but, on an Experiment of breaking a Bit of it, the Rednefs of Brick is confpicuous.

The High Altar is in the *Gothic* Tafte, but very fine; and fome Years fince, one Mr. *Polehampton* made this Parifh a prefent of a petty Altar-Piece, whofe Subject is the Lord's Supper.

In the Eaftern Part of this Church are fix Holes in the Pavement, in which the Pillars were fixed, that fupported the Shrine of St. *Alban*; which Building is now entirely gone, but this Infcription remains;

S. Albani Verolamenfis Anglorum
Protomartyr, xvii Junii CCXCIII.

On the North Side of the Entrance into the Church, is a Picture of King *Offa* on his Throne, under which are thefe Words;

Fun-

Fnndator Ecclefiæ circa annum Chrifti 793.
Quem mala depiƈta et refidentem cernis alte
Sublimen folio Mercius *Offa*, fuit.

In a Wall on the South Ifle is the Monument of
Humphry, Duke of *Gloucefter*, Uncle and Protector to King *Henry* the Sixth, with the Arms of
England and *France* quartered, and a ducal Coro-
net. In Niches on the South Side are the Effigies of feventeen Kings, but thofe of the other
Side have none.

Here is an indifferent *Latin* Infcription to his
Memory, which does, not deferve copying. In
the biographic Work at your Houfe in the *Ifle
of Wight*, the Charaƈter of this Prince is well-
drawn *.

The

---

* *Humphry Plantaganet*, furnamed the *Good*,
Was the fourth Son of King *Henry* the Fourth,
Son, Brother, and Uncle of Kings!
Duke of *Glocefter*, Earl of *Henault, Holland, Zealand* and *Pembroke*,
Lord of *Frifeland*, great Chamberlain of *England*,
Proteƈtor and Defender of its Church and Kingdom.
Thus great, thus glorious, by Birth and Creation,
Was he in his honourable Titles and Princely Attributes:
But far more great and illuftrious
In his vertuous Endowments, and inward Qualities.
He was a ftriƈt Obferver of Juftice,
And furnifhed his noble Wit with the better and deeper
Kind of Studies.
And under *Henry* the Sixth governed the Kingdom
Five and twenty Years; with Prudence, Honour,
Integrity, and a Charaƈter fair and fpotlefs:
So that no good Men had caufe to be difpleafed,
No bad Men had Room to find Fault.
In a Word, he was the Father of his Country,
And the Idol of the People.
He built the Divinity School in the Univerfity of *Oxford*,
And was a great Benefaƈtor to the Abbey at St. *Alban*'s.
But O! (how uncertain are human Enjoyments!)
By the Envy, Malice, and Cruelty of the Queen, and
Her Accomplices,
This Moft Excellent and beloved Prince
Was cut off in St. *Saviour*'s Hofpital at St. *Alban*'s.
A. D. 1446.

Sir

The People here tell me, that in the Reign of Queen *Anne*, as they were digging a Grave, some Stairs were found, which led down to a Vault, where, in a leaden Coffin, they found his Body. It was preserved by a Pickle, excepting the Legs, from which the Flesh had wasted, owing to the Pickle at that End being dried away. In the Vault, which has no offensive Smell, is a Crucifix painted on the Wall : on each Side of the Head is a Cup, a third at the Hip, and a fourth at the Feet.

In the Windows of the Cloyster of this Abbey were formerly painted many historical Passages out of the Bible, with *Latin* Verses under each Story, explaining the same. In like manner were the Windows of the Library and Presbytery painted with the Pictures of famous Men, with explanatory Verses ; but these are all gone.

A little to the South of St. *Stephen*'s Church, are the Remains of the Church and House of St. *Julian*, which was founded for *Lazars* by *Gaufridus*, *Abbot* of St, *Alban*'s, with the Advice and Consent of his Convent; and endowed it with several Tythes and Parcels of Tythes in St. *Alban*'s, *Bradeway*, &c. which were confirmed by King *Henry* the Second. For the Government of the Monks, several Orders were made, among which were these. That their Habit should be a *Tunic* and *Super-Tunic* of plain Russet. That they should be single ; or, if married, to separate from their Wives, both Parties being willing. That no Woman should enter into the House, except the common Laundress, or a Mother, or Sister, to visit their Relation when sick, with Licence of the *Custos*. That every Brother, at his Admittance, should make an Oath to obey the Abbot of St. *Alban*'s, and his Archdeacon, &c.

In this Town, befides this of St. *Alban*, are the Parifh Churches of St. *Peter*, St. *Stephen*, and St. *Michael*. St. *Peter*'s, which is a good Building, ftands on the Eaft Side of the Town ; in this Church is a Monument for *Robert Pemberton*, Efq; who built fix Almfhoufes, and endowed them with an Eftate of thirty Pounds a Year, for the Maintenance of fix poor Widows. In this Parifh alfo are nine Almfhoufes, built by *Sarah*, Dutchefs of *Marlborough*, for thirty-fix Perfons, with an Allowance of fifty Shillings a Quarter, and a Piece of Garden-Ground, to each. This Lady had an Houfe, called *Holywell*, in St. *Stephen*'s Parifh, on the River *Ver*, or *Verulam*, built by her Confort the Duke*.

In the Church of St. *Michael* are many Monuments, particularly that of the celebrated Lord *Bacon*, and *George Grimfton*, Efq; the former of whofe Effigies is in Alabafter, feated in an Elbow Chair, with this Infcription ;

H. P.
Francifc. Bacon, Baro de Verulam, Sanct. Albani Viceco'
Seu notioribus Titulis
Scientiarum Lumen, Facundiæ Lex,
Sic fedebat :
Qui poftquam omnia naturalis fapientiæ
Et civilis Arcana evolviffet,
Natura decretum explevit,
Compofita folvantur.
Anno Dom. MDCXXVI.
Ætat. LXVI.

Tanti

* In a Work called the *Tour through Great-Britain*, the Compiler has not only told us of a Statue being erected at St. *Alban*'s, by the late Dutchefs of *Marlborough*, to the Memory of Queen *Anne*, but has even given us a Copy of the Infcription. Now this is to inform the *Public*, that the fame is entirely void of Truth, for the Statue and Infcription, which he means, happen to have been erected at *Blenheim*, in the County of *Oxford* (which I fhall hereafter defcribe) near feventy Miles from the Town of St. *Alban*'s.

Tanti viri
Mem.
Thomas Meautys
Superſtitis Cultor.
Defuncti Admirator.

In the Middle of the Town ſtands one of thoſe
magnificent Croſſes, erected by King *Edward* the
Firſt, between *Lincolnſhire* and *Weſtminſter*, to
the Memory of his beloved and meritorious
Queen, *Eleanor*. This Building was re-erected in
the Year 1703, and repaired in the Years 1731
and 1744.

The Borough of St. *Alban's* is a Liberty, and
in Matters both eccleſiaſtical and civil, hath a
peculiar Power in itſelf, which Juriſdiction extends to the Pariſhes of *Watford, Rickmanſworth,
Norton, Ridge, Hoxton, Abbots Walden, Abbots
Langley, Sarret, Elſtree, Buſhy, Cudicot,* or *Codicot,
Shepehale, Sandridge, Redburn,* and *Barnet,* for
which there is a Gaol-Delivery at this Town, on
the ſucceeding *Thurſday* after every Quarter Seſſions held at *Hertford.*

The Town is divided into four Wards. The
Corporation is governed by a Mayor, Aldermen,
and other Officers.

The Market is held on *Saturdays*; and the
Fairs on the 25th of *March*, the 17th of *June*,
and the 29th of *September*, chiefly for Cows,
Horſes and Sheep.

In the Reign of *Edward* the Firſt, it once ſent
Burgeſſes to Parliament, four Times in the Reign
of his Son, and five in that of his Grandſon, but
the Abbot having obtained Leave, in the fifth
Year of this laſt King's Government, to have it
exempted from that Service, it did not ſend any
Repreſentatives to that auguſt Aſſembly, till a
Charter granted to it by King *Edward* the Sixth be-

X 2 came

came in full Force. But since the Reign of
Queen *Mary*, there appears upon the Records a
continual Election of Burgesses for St. *Alban*'s.

In this Town are two Charity-Schools, one of
which is for twenty-eight Boys, and the other for
twenty-one Girls.

There are nine contiguous Manors, that also
belonged to the Abbots of the Monastery; the
Names of these Manors are, *Newland, Squillers,
Butterwick, Becch, Kingsberry, Gorhamberry, Child-
wick, Windridge, Weldrandolfes*, and *Newberrys*.

This Town has had the Honour of giving the
Title of Viscount to that eminent Man, Sir *Francis Bacon*, Lord *Verulam* (Son of Sir *Nicholas Bacon*, Lord Keeper) once Lord High Chancellor of
England, the first Reviver of Experimental Philoso-
phy. His Abilities as a Statesman are well
known to the World, and he had so many amiable
Qualities that 'tis wonderful we have Authority to
say,

> What a falling off was there !

That he was guilty of conniving at the Extortions of his Servants is out of Question: In his
Essays are these Words, " If *Judges* are easy and
" corrupt, you shall have a Servant five Times
" worse in catching at such Gains than a Wife."
Bacon was certainly guilty of conniving at Bribery;
and Sir *Henry Chauncy* tells us, that one Day as he
passed through the Hall, where his Servants were
at Dinner, they arose up from their Seats; when
the Chancellor spoke aloud, " *Sit you down, my
Masters, sit you down: Your Rise is my Fall*. He
certainly was a striking Example of the Depravity
of human Nature. The best Thing that the Pen
of Mr *Mallet* ever produced, is the History of the
Life of this great, unfortunate Man.

St.

' St. *Alban*'s gave the Title of Earl to *Richard de Burgh* (Earl of *Clanrickard* in *Ireland*) and to *Henry*, the second Son of Sir *Thomas Jermyn*, of *Rufbroke* in *Suffolk*, Knt and afterwards that of Duke to *Charles Beauclerk*, the Grandfather of the Nobleman who at present enjoys the same.

In this Town was born, and, about the Year 1372, was also buried here, the well-known Sir *John Mandevill*, a Traveller, who dealt much in the Marvellous; and St. *Alban*'s gave Birth to *John of Hertford*, and *William Alban*, both Priors of the Monastery here, and both Persons of Learning and Abilities ; Sir *Francis Pemberton*, Lord Chief Justice of both Benches, and the celebrated Sir *John King*, who is buried in the *Temple* Church in *London*. I am, Sir, Yours, &c.

LETTER XVII.

From *Gravefend*, in *Kent*.

S I R,

AFTER leaving St. *Alban*'s, I came to *Colney*, where are some good Inns. The *Blounts* (who are of the same Family with those of *Sedington*, in *Worcefterfhire* ; *Kinlet*, in *Shropfhire* ; and *Elwafton*, in *Derbyfhire*) have a neat House and Gardens here, called *Titenhanger*. At *Colney* I dined, and came that Evening to *London*.

We set out early by Water, and, having got clear of the Hawfers of the numerous Ships which ride from the *Tower* to *Limehoufe*, we had on the Left-Hand Wall, or Bank of the River, a great many Windmills, which have a pleasing Appearance. A little lower, on the Right, is *Deptford*, of which Mr *Buck* has published a very

pretty

pretty View, including the Docks and Yards, where are feveral large Ships of War upon the Stocks. The new Church, and the Houfes upon *Blackheath*, intermixed with Trees, have a charming Effect. The Village of *Deptford*, of which I fhall hereafter be more particular, contains upwards of Two thoufand Houfes; it was in the Yard here, that the *Ruffian* Emperor, *Peter* the Firft, informed himfelf of the practical Part of Ship-building.

We landed at *Greenwich* (I wonder you have not vifited this delightful Place!) The College or Hofpital here, for the comfortable Subfiftence of old and difabled Seamen, is one of the moft fuperb Buildings in the Univerfe. I wifh the Palace at St. *James*'s were equal to it.

The firft Wing of this magnificent Building, which King *Charles* the Second intended for a Palace, coft Thirty-fix thoufand Pounds. In the Year 1694, King *William* the Third granted it, together with nine Acres of Ground, to be turned into an Hofpital for the Purpofe it is now put to, and gave Two thoufand Pounds a Year towards finifhing it; which, however, has not been done till within a few Years. Upwards of Sixty thoufand Pounds have been received in private Benefactions towards this Charity, and on three Tables in the Hall are the Donors Names. In the Year 1732, the Parliament gave Six thoufand Pounds a Year, being Part of the unfortunate Earl of *Derwentwater*'s Eftate, for the fame Ufes. It is built of Free-ftone, in a Tafte remarkably grand, and the two Cupolas on each Wing afford it an inconceivable Ornament.

In the *Great Hall*, which is a very noble Building, is an Alcove, and under it, a beautiful Painting, being a Group, confifting of the Princefs *Sophia*, King *George* the Firft, and King

George

George the Second, Queen *Caroline*, the Queen of *Pruffia*, the late Prince of *Wales*, the Duke of *Cumberland*, and his five Sifters. In the Cieling over the Alcove, are thofe of Queen *Anne*, and Prince *George* of *Denmark*; and on the Cieling over the Hall, thofe of King *William* and Queen *Mary*, with many emblematic Figures ; the whole was done by the celebrated Sir *James Thornhill*. Oppofite to the Great Hall is the Chapel, which, for curious Carving and Gilding, is perhaps the moft elegant in the World. The Statue of his late Majefty, which ftands upon a Pedeftal between the two Wings facing towards the *Thames* and the *Ifle of Dogs*, is well executed.

The two Globes at the Weftern Entrance are vaftly large. On the whole, *Greenwich* Hofpital, for Magnificence of Building, is fcarcely to be equalled.

One hundred difabled Seamen, in the Year 1705, were the firft that were taken into this Hofpital, but now the Number is upwards of a Thoufand. Six Nurfes, the Widows of Seamen, are allowed to every hundred Men, with a Salary of ten Pounds each ; and an Addition of two Shillings per Week, if they attend the Infirmary. The Uniform of the Penfioners is blue Cloth, with Brafs Buttons.

At this Town is alfo an Hofpital, which is called the Duke of *Norfolk*'s College, but it was founded by his Brother, the illuftrious *Henry*, Earl of *Northampton*, who, in the Year 1613, endowed it by the Name of *Trinity Hofpital*. In the Chapel which belongs to it is this Infcription ;

Inclytus hic Comes tria Hofpitalia
Fundavit et latifundiis dotavit unum
Greenwici in Cantio in quo xx egeni et
Praefectus alterum Cluni in comitatu
Salopiae in quo xiɪ egeni cum praefecto
                              Tertium

Tertium ad Caftrům Rifing in comitatu
Norfolciae in quo XII pauperculae
Cum Gubernatrice in per
Petúum alantur.

This Monument, containing the Body of
The Right Honourable *Henry Howard,*
Earl of *Northampton,* Baron of *Marnhill,*
Keeper of the *Privy Seal,*
Guardian of the *Cinque Ports,*
Conftable of the Caftle of *Dover,*
Chancellor of *Cambridge,*
And *Knight of the Garter;*
Was firft erected in the Chappel of the
Caftle of *Dover*
Anno Domini MDCXIV.
But the faid Chappel falling to Decay,
The worfhipful Company of *Mercers, London,*
Governors of this *Hofpital,*
Founded Anno MDCXIII.
By the aforefaid Earl of *Northampton,*
Caufed this Monument, together with
The Body of the faid Earl of *Northampton.*
To be removed into this Chappel ;
By the Permiffion of
The Archbifhop of *Canterbury,*
Henry, Duke of *Norfolk,*
And *Henry,* Earl of *Romney.*

William Ivat, Efquire, Mafter, M. *Jafper Clotter-
booke,* jun. M. *William Bridges,* M. *John Archer,*
Wardens of the Company of Mercers, An
MDCXCVI.
By the Care of M. *Francis Barry, Mercer.*
John Stow, then Warden of this Hofpital.

℟ This Town contains about Fifteen hundred
Houfes, many of which are inhabited by Peo-
ple of Fafhion, who have ferved their Country at
Sea, and now enjoy the Comforts of Eafe and
Tranquillity. One of the fifty new Churches is
lately built here. 'Tis a good Fabric of Free
Stone, and dedicated to St. *Alphage.*

Sir

Sir *William Boreman* founded a Free-School at *Greenwich*; and one Mr. *John Roan* left an Eftate, for the Cloathing and Teaching twenty Boys Reading, Writing, and Arithmetic: And here alfo is a well-conducted School for Girls, maintained by the voluntary Subfcription of Lady *Creed*, and other Ladies; a laudable and meritorious Charity!

We dined at the *Greyhound*, oppofite the *Park-Gate*. The Park is excellently laid out, after Defigns of the celebrated *Le Notre*. The Wall round it was built by King *Charles* the Second. The old Palace here, of which are no Remains, was erected by the good Duke *Humphry*. King *Henry* the Seventh enlarged it, and his Son, *Henry* the Eighth, who was born here, compleated it. The Princeffes, *Mary* and *Elizabeth*, his Daughters, were alfo born here; and here his Son, *Edward* the Sixth, died. King *James* the Firft gave the Palace to the before mentioned Earl of *Northampton*, who much enlarged and beautified it, but King *Charles* the Second pulled it down to the Ground; and alfo a Tower began on the Top of the Hill, by the fame Duke of *Gloucefter*, and finifhed by King *Henry* the Seventh, on which Spot the faid King *Charles* built an Obfervatory, and furnifhed it with many excellent mathematical Inftruments. He alfo caufed a deep dry Well to be dug for the Obfervation of the Stars in the Day-Time. It is now called *Flamftead* Houfe, on Account of the famous Aftronomer of that Name, who poffeffed it; as did alfo the well-known Dr. *Edmund Halley*. 'Tis now ufed by the celebrated Dr. *Bradley*. The Views are fine from this *Park*, efpecially that of *London* from *One-Tree-Hill* is far out of the Power of Words to exprefs, and that down the River is exquifitely charming.

In the Year 1737, a Market was eſtabliſhed here, the Profits of which are appropriated to the Uſe of the *Grand Hoſpital.* The Gun-Powder Magazine, which was ſo dangerous to this Town, is lately removed to *Purfleet* in *Eſſex.*

The *Captain,* contrary to his Intention or Deſire, being obliged to call at *Woolwich,* we walked thither, leaving the *Thames* and *Blackwall* on our Left-Hand. The Town of *Woolwich* is but indifferently built ; but the fine Yards and Docks for building large Ships of War make it at preſent a very flouriſhing Place. It is almoſt inconceivable what a Number of People are here employed! Among others, here is one Ship almoſt built, which is nearly equal to that unfortunate one, called the *Victory* : Some think that it will be impoſſible to compleat her before next Year, though ſhe has been ſeven Years in building.

In the Reign of *Edward* the Firſt, *Woolwich* belonged to *Gilbert de Mariſco,* who alſo held (by the Rent of a Knight's Fee) a conſiderable Part of the adjoining Marſh, of *Warren de Montchenſy,* Baron of *Swanſcampe.*

In the Days of our matchleſs Queen *Elizabeth,* the ſmall Docks and Launches at this Place were greatly enlarged ; and as here is a greater Depth of Water than at *Deptford,* the largeſt ſized Ships are more the Buſineſs of the Place. All the *Yard,* in which are the Docks, Store-Houſes, and many other appurtenant Buildings, is encloſed on the Land Side by a lofty Wall, and is one of the moſt compleat and well-appointed belonging to the King.

Between the Yard and the Rope-Walk, in which are made the largeſt Cables, is the Church, which is one of the fifty intended by the late Queen
Anne.

Anne. It ftands upon a Hill, and is built with Brick, fomething in the Manner of that at *Iſling-ton:* But that Place, which is called the *Gun-Park* or *Warren,* is the moſt pleaſing of any Thing at *Woolwich* to a Traveller's Eye. Here is an amazing Quantity of Cannon, both for Ships of War and Batteries ; Mortars of all Sizes ; the Balls and Shells are almoſt out of Number. Here is the *Royal Foundery* for caſting Cannon, and the Laboratory, where the Engineers prepare the Ma-terials, and charge Bombs, Carcaſſes, and Grena-does for the Navy, as well as Army. Here is al-fo an Academy, where the Art of Gunnery is taught as a Science, the Head-Maſter of which is Mr. *Muller,* and the next is the celebrated Mr. *Simpſon,* a Perſon well known in the mathematic World. To the Eaſtward of the Buildings is a Mount, where the Officers and Soldiers of the Train of Artillery try or fcale their Cannon ; and farther off, and nearer the River Side, is fixed a Target, where they practiſe in the Art of Gun-nery. Having ſpent the Evening very temperate-ly, conſidering the Cuſtom of fuch Partings, we went on board the Captain's fix-oared Boat, at the Weſt End of the Yard; where almoſt all the Sand uſed by the *Houſewives of London* is put on board Barges from Carts, which bring it down from the neighbouring Hill.

As we were rowed down the *Thames,* the Docks, Yards, Ships upon the Stocks, Store-Houſes, the Church, and the Warren, formed a pleaſing Ex-hibition.

The River at High-Water was about a Mile broad, and, as the Reach is three or four Miles long, the Day being fine, the Scene was extream-ly delightful.

The next Place of Note that we paſſed was *Erith* ; which looked very pleaſing through a

Glaſs.

Glafs. At *Erith* the *Eaft-India* Ships generally unload, and when they arrive, 'tis filled with the Wives, Friends, and Acquaintance of thofe who are returned from that diftant Quarter, together with Jews, Slop-Sellers, and Cuftom-Houfe Officers. In about an Hour, having *Purfleet* Hills on our Left, we faw *Grais* on the *Effex* Side, and in lefs than half another came on board our intended Ship, then at Anchor between *Gravefend* and that powerful Fortification *Tilbury* Fort.

Contrary to our Expectation, the Captain refolved to go out that Tide, and, having fettled Matters, Mr. *Johnfon* and myfelf took our Leaves, and were put on Shore at *Gravefend*; from whence we faw the Ship get under Sail, and foon after fhe was out of our Sight.

From the Landing-Place at this Town, the Fort of *Tilbury* has a formidable Appearance. In it are upwards of One hundred great Guns mounted, and, if it is properly repaired, muft always be a fufficient Fortification to prevent any Ships of an Enemy paffing up the River. The Town of *Gravefend* is in general well built, and, as all outward-bound Ships are obliged to ftop, and clear out from hence, 'tis a very thriving Place. Here is a Blockhoufe, where a Centinel puts obftinate Captains in Mind of bringing-to, which if they refufe, they may expect the Thunder of *Tilbury* Guns.

The Manor was formerly the Eftate of the Lords *Cobham*, but now belongs to the Duke of *Lenox*. In the Reign of *Richard* the Second, this Town was plundered and burnt by the *French*; but the Abbot of St. *Mary le Grace* upon *Tower-Hill*, to whofe Abbey the fame King having given the Manor of *Parrocks* belonging to this Town, he obtained of that Monarch the Privilege that none but the Inhabitants of this Place,

3   and

and thofe of *Milton*, fhould carry Paffengers by Water to *London*, at two Pence a Head, or four Shillings the whole Fare; but the Prices are now nine Pence each in the Tilt-Boat, and twelve Pence in the Wherry : The former are reftrained from taking in more than forty Paffengers at a Time, and the latter moré than ten. According to an Act of Parliament, the Company of Water-men are obliged to provide Officers at *Billingfgate* and *Gravefend*, who, at every Time of High-Water, whether by Day or Night, are, at their refpective Places, to ring a Bell (fet up for that Purpofe) for a Quarter of an Hour, which gives Notice to the Tilt-Boats and Wherries to put off; and Coaches ply at *Gravefend*, to carry Paffengers from thence to *Rochefter*.

Gravefend is a Corporation, governed by a Mayor, Jurats, and other inferior Officers. The Markets held here, on *Wednefdays* and *Saturdays*, are very plentiful, efpecially in Afparagus Time; of which Article there is more fent to *London* from hence, than from any other Place. The Fairs are on the 23d of *April*, and the 25th of *November*, for Horfes, Cloaths, Toys, and other Com-modities.

The Church, which is dedicated to the Virgin *Mary*, being burnt down, with the greateft Part of the Town, is rebuilt as one of the fifty new ones. Here is a Charity-School for twenty-four Boys; and, in the Year 1624, one Mr. *Pinnock* gave twenty-one Dwellings, and an Eftate to keep them in Repair, alfo an Houfe for a Mafter-Weaver, to employ the Poor.

Mr. *Johnfon* is fetting off immediately for *London* in a Poft-Chaife, and carries this Letter to the Poft-Office there, directed to you, by Sir, Yours, *&c.*

L E T-

L E T T E R   XVIII.

From *Rochester*, in *Kent*.

S I R,

AFTER difpatching my laft to you, I went in the Coach to *Rochefter*. As *Virgil* fays, " *Si parvis componere magna folebam,*" *Stroud*, or *Strode*, is to this City, what *Old Brentford* is to that called the *New*. In other Words, it is a long difagreeable Place, confifting chiefly of one dirty Street, that terminates eaftwardly at the fine River *Medway*; over which is a very handfome Bridge, ornamented with neat Iron Rails. The Church of *Stroud* is dedicated to St. *Nicholas*, and ftands in the principal Street. It was formerly a Chapel, belonging to the Parifh of *Frendfbury*; but now it hath a Cemetery, and, according to the Records of *Rochefter*, the Incumbent is intitled to all Tythes, excepting Corn. This Manor was, by King *Henry* the Third, granted to the *Knights Templars*, but that Order being fuppreffed, it reverted to the Crown: And King *Edward* the Third gave it to *Mary*, Countefs of *Pembroke*, who prefented it to the Abbey of St. *Denny*, in the County of *Cambridge*. At the Diffolution of this Abbey, King *Henry* the Eighth gave it to one Mr. *Edward Elrington*, who difpofed of it to *George Brooke*, Lord *Cobham*; whofe Grandfon being concerned with Sir *Walter Raleigh* in a Sort of Plot, forfeited it to King *James* the Firft, who gave it to his Favourite, Sir *Robert Cecil*, Earl of *Salifbury*, whofe Son fold it to Mr. *Bernard Hyde*, and from him it came to the *Blagues*.

Dr. *Gilbert Glanville*, formerly Bifhop of *Rochefter*, founded an Hofpital in this Village, dedicated

cated to the Virgin *Mary* and St. *Andrew*, which fell at the Diffolution; and then was valued at fifty-two Pounds nine Shillings and ten Pence. But there is now one for fick and lame Soldiers, near the Bridge over the River *Medway*.

In this Village is annually a Fair for Toys on the 26th of *Auguft*.

According to *Camden*, *Simon de Montefort* cut down the wooden Bridge here, inftead of which a curious arched one of Stone was built, with Money raifed out of the *French* Spoils, by *John Cobham* and *Robert Knowles*; the latter whereof raifed himfelf by his warlike Courage from nothing, to the higheft Pitch of Honour. The Railing was done at the Expence of *William Warham*, Archbifhop of *Canterbury*. Through this Bridge, which is fupported by eleven lofty Arches, the *Medway*, on the Return of the Tide, rufhes with great Impetuofity; but foon after becomes calm, forms the fine Dock and Ridings for Ships of War at *Chatham*, and falls into the *Thames* at *Shirenefs*.

The *Medway* rifes in the North-Eaft Part of *Suffex*, and enters the County of *Kent* near *Penfhurft* (the Place which gave Birth to that Patron of Poetry, that Example of Virtue, that Lover of Learning and learned Men, that brave Soldier, and moft gallant Gentleman, the Darling of Mankind, Sir *Philip Sydney*) and having wafhed *Tunbridge*, runs through a fine Country to *Maidftone*, above which Place it is navigable. Upon its charming Shores are many Gentlemens Seats, and almoft innumerable Plantations of Hops, whofe beautiful Appearance may be ideally formed after reading thefe elegant Lines in *Smart*'s Poems;

Now are our Lab'rers crown'd with their Reward,
Now bloom the florid *Hops*, and in the Stream
Shine in their floating Silver, while above

Th'

Th' embow'ring Branches culminate, and form
A Walk impervious to the Sun ; the Poles
In comely Order ftand, and while you cleave,
With the fmall Skiff, the *Medway*'s lucid Wave
In comely Order ftill their Ranks preferve,
And feem to march along the extenfive Plain
In neat Arrangement.

Drayton, in finging this River, thus delivers
himfelf ;

> *Medway*, with her attending Streams,
> Goes forth to meet her Lord, great *Thames* ;
> And where in Breadth fhe her difperfes,
> Our famous *Captains* fhe rehearfes ;
> With many of their valiant Deeds.

And afterwards,

> —— For her more Renown,
> Her only Name fhe leaves to her only chriften'd Town* :
> And *Rochefter* doth reach, in entring to the Bower
> Of that moft matchlefs *Thames*, her princely Paramour.

And then expreffes the Honour fhe hath had
of fending out our gallant Fleets ;

> This *Medway* ftill hath nurs'd thofe *Navies* in her Road,
> Our *Armies* that had oft to Conqueft borne abroad ;
> And not a Man of ours for Arms hath famous been,
> Whom fhe not going out or coming in hath feen.

Rochefter is indifputably the moft difagreeable
City in the whole *Kingdom*. In good Truth it is
but little better, either for Situation, Building,
Cleanlinefs, or Company, than *Wapping* or *Rat-cliff-Highway*. Yet the Hofts and Hofteffes of
Inns in this uninviting Place are full as high in
their Bills as at *Richmond*, *Hampton-Court*, or *Bath*.
This in fome Degree is a national Concern. Be-caufe, in the Bofoms of thofe Gentlemen-Strangers
who come to *London* from *Italy*, *Swifferland*,
France, *Flanders*, &c. it raifes falfe Ideas of the
Britifh People in general.

This

* *Maidftone.*

This City is one of the moft ancient in *England*. By *Antoninus*, in his *Itinerary*, it is called *Durobus*, or *Duro-brovæ*; and in the Foundation Charter of the Cathedral Church, 'tis called *Durobrovis*. The *Saxons* gave it the Appellation of *Rhouceafter*. It took Rife from a Caftle built there, as appears by the *Saxon* Name; and *Bede* himfelf calls it *Caftellum Cantuariorum*. Numerous have been the Misfortunes that this Place hath undergone. In the Year 676, *Ethelred*, King of *Mercia*, almoft deftroyed it; and in the Year 839, it was facked by the *Danes*; and in, or about, the forty-fourth Year afterwards, thofe Ravagers caft Works round the Caftle, and befieged it in the beft Form of thofe Times; particularly they raifed a large Wooden Machine in Height equal to the Walls, fomething after the Conftruction of the *Romans*; from which they greatly diftreffed the Place. However the Refiftance of the Befieged was fo gallant, that they held it out till the brave, the great, and the good King *Alfred*, whofe Name was a Terror to the *Danes*, raifed the Siege fo precipitately, that they ran in the utmoft Confufion to their Ships, which lay in the River *Medway*; leaving their Horfes, Baggage, and other Booty to the *Englifh*; of which Difcomfiture, *Richard of Rochefter*, a Monk of *Feverfham*, thus wrote;

Then weren the *Danes* fo furis and bold,
  That everich *Englifhman* weren in moche Fere;
They feken for Plunder of Silver and Gold,
  And al els yat gode is, yat they can come nere,
They eaten ure Metes, and dronken ure Wines,
  And all y-dronke ufid ure Maydins perforce,
Ure Wives alfo, O woe the fad Tymes,
  When Man colde not fave ne his Houfe ne his Horfe!
Ure Houfes they brened, the Cattle weren flain
  In the Contre, then cam they to *Rochefte*,
And fighten againft her Caftil Wals, but in vain,
  For the gode Kyng *Alfrede* he fone dyd apere;

Then the barbrous *Danes* were in Fright ful fore,
  " Fly, *Alfrede*, yat Devil is coming," they fayd;
And renn to ther Shippes ful quickly therefor,
  And leven ther Booty and eke al ther Dede.
Then weren moche Meriment in *Rocheſtre* made,
  That we bin fo fone deliveryd from Evil
Of thefe furis *Danes*; our Herts weren glad,
  That they feren ure gode *Kyng* more then *God* or the
    Devil.

The Caftle, of which there are now confiderable Remains, was built by King *William* the Firſt; and *Odo, Biſhop of Bayeux*, defended it for fome Time againſt his Son, King *William* the Second; but it being furrendered, this King rebuilt it. In the Year 1215, *William de Albiney* was, by thofe Defenders of Liberty, the *Barons*, fent with a Detachment to defend this Caftle, which he found ill provided for his Purpofe. However, as they had fworn to relieve him, if he ftood in need of it, he entered upon his Command with the Refolution of a Soldier: And it was foon invefted by King *John*, and his numerous Army of Foreigners. The Army of the *Barons*, intended for its Relief, went no farther than *Deptford*, while the King preffed the Siege with much Vigour, and the Place was bravely defended by the Governor; to whom an Engineer and excellent Markfman, who faw the Perfon of *John* from the Walls, faid, " I have an Arrow here ready in my Hand; is it " your Pleafure that with it I pierce the Heart of " the King?" " By no means, thou Wretch, re- " plied *Albiney*; far be it be from me to feek the " Death of the Lord's Anointed." At length, all the Provifions of the Befiegers being fpent, the very Horfes eaten up, the Wall either battered down or undermined, they, on the 30th of *Novem-* *ber*, were obliged to furrender: When *John*, ir-
                                                        ritated

ritated by their Bravery, was mean enough to order both *Albiney*, and his Garrison to be put to Death : Such was the scandalous Difposition of *John*, notwithstanding he had been informed of *Albiney*'s generous Behaviour, in sparing his Life from the Walls. Upon which, *Savary de Mallion*, who was a general Officer under the King, strongly remonstrated against so cruel, so ungrateful, so impolitic a Proceeding; and did indeed so far prevail, that *Albiney*, and those who had been of the greatest Note under him, were sent Prisoners to *Corf-Castle* in *Dorsetshire*; but all the rest of the Garrison, excepting the *Cross-Bow-Men*, were hanged over the Walls of the Place.

The Cathedral of *Rochester* was first built in the Year 600, by *Ethelbert*, the first Christian King of *Kent*, who dedicated it to St. *Andrew* the Apostle; and making it an Episcopal See, appointed *Justus* the first Bishop thereof. He endowed it with many Lands, to which *Eadbert*, King of *Kent*, and *Offa*, King of the *Mercians*, added many more; and denounced heavy Curses and Imprecations upon those who should violate their pious Donations.

About the Year 1080, a *Norman* Bishop of this See, named *Gundulphus*, greatly repaired it, put out the secular Canons, and introduced Monks in their Stead. To this Church, this Prelate and his Monks, King *Henry* the First confirmed all the said Lands and Liberties. And, besides these Monarchs, *William* the First, and *William* the Second; *Rodbert*, Son of King *Henry*, *Robert Fitz Hamon*, and *William de Albiney*, were great Benefactors. At the Dissolution it was valued at Four hundred eighty-six Pounds eleven Shillings and Five Pence.

According to the Establishment made by *Henry* the Eighth, in the Year 1541 (who, as he had done at *Canterbury*, converted the Prior and

Z 2

Monks

Monks here into a College of Seculars) this
Church hath a Dean, six Prebendaries, or Major
Canons, six Minor Canons, a Deacon, Subdea-
con, Master of the Choiristers, eight Choiristers,
two Masters of the Grammar-School, twenty
Scholars, six Alms-Men, two Sextons, two Vergers, two Cooks, a Porter, and a Barber. The
Churches and Chapels in this Diocese are One
hundred and seven.

The late worthy and patriotic Dr. *Herring*,
Archbishop of *Canterbury*, when Dean of this Cathedral, in the Year 1742, considerably repaired
the Inside of the Building, but the Outside is not
in the best Condition. The Choir is neat, the
Organ small, the Chapter-House handsome, and
the Library large.

Here is a Monument, erected to the Memory
of Dr. *Walter de Merton*, Bishop of *Rochester*, and
Lord High-Chancellor of *England* in the Reign
of *Henry* the Third, and *Edward* the First; who,
having founded *Merton College* in *Oxford*, died the
27th of *October*, 1278. 'Twas done at the Expence of Sir *Henry Savil*, in the room of an ancient one, which was much defaced and broken.

Here is also one for Dr. *Lowe*, Bishop of this
See in the Reign of *Henry* the Sixth; and three
for Dr. *Warner* (who was also Bishop of *Rochester*)
his Son, and Grandson. In the Body of the
Church, they shew us a flat Stone, on which is
carved an Axe, where they tell us, that Dr. *Fisher*,
Bishop of this Church, was buried, after (in the
Year 1535) he had suffered Martyrdom, for de-
nying the Supremacy of King *Henry* the Eighth.
To this good Man, Confessor to the Countess of
Richmond, are owing the Foundations of *Christ's*
and St. *John's* Colleges in *Cambridge*. On the
South Side of the Choir is an Inscription, under
the Effigies of an old Man.

Sacred

Sacred to the Memory of *Richard Watts*, Efq;
who, by his Will, dated *Auguft* 22, 1579,
founded an Alms-Houfe for the Relief of poor
People, and for the Reception of fix poor Travellers
every Night, and for the Employing the Poor of
this City.

The Family of *Weldon* have enjoyed a great Advantage by the Grant made by King *James* the
Firft, of the titular Guardianſhip of the ruined
Caſtle here. This, perhaps, you'll think I ſhould
have mentioned before.

In the Center of the City ſtands an old Building, though in very good Repair, being that
erected purſuant to the Will mentioned in the
above-named monumental Inſcription. 'Tis now
called by the Name of *Bridewell*, and over the
Door is a Stone thus inſcribed;

Six poor Travelling Men,
Not *contagiouſly diſeaſed*,
Rogues or *Proctors*,
May have Lodging here one Night free;
And four Pence each when they depart in the Morning.

The Tickets for Admittance are delivered by
the Mayor; ſometimes he allows eight Perſons to
lodge, but there are only fix Groats divided
amongft them.

This City is governed by a Mayor, Recorder,
and twelve Common-Council-Men. The Town-
Houſe, which was built in the Year 1687, during
the Mayoralty of *Richard Bryant*, Efq; is a large
Brick Structure over the City Gaol. In the Front
of the Market-Houſe is this Inſcription;

This Building and Clock were given by
The Honourable Sir *Cloudeſley Shovel*,
In the Year 1706.

The Markets at *Rocheſter* are on *Fridays*, and
the Fairs on the 30th of *May*, and the 11th of
December,

December, for Horfes, Horned Cattle, and various Commodities.

The Mayor, and Citizens of *Rochefter*, hold occafionally what they . call an *Admiralty-Court* ; which is to prevent Abufes in the Oyfter Fifhery in the Branches and Creeks of the *Medway*, that are within their Jurifdiction. This Court has the Power to appoint the Times when Oyfters fhall, or fhall not, be taken, and alfo the Quantity each Dredger fhall take in a Day.

Any Perfon, who, being free of this City, and has ferved feven Years Apprenticefhip to a Fifherman or Dredger, who was alfo free of the faid City, has a Right to take Oyfters, for which he has a Licence, paying for it fix Shillings and eight Pence annually.

The Court has Cognizance of all Mal-Practices, fuch as catching too many Oyfters, or deftroying the *Brood* or *Spat* ; and by two Acts, paffed in the Reign of *George* the Second, their Power is augmented, fo that this Fifhery flourifhes well, and is under good Regulation.

This City gave Title of Vifcount to that profitting Scholar of King *James* the Firft, *Robert Carr*, of infamous Memory ; and that of Earl to the profligate and witty *John Wilmot* : Since which it hath been in the Family of *Hyde*, but now is extinct. *Rochefter*, which is in the Latitude of 51 Deg. 22 Min. and 34 Min. of Eaft Longitude from the Meridian of *London*, fends two Members to the Houfe of Commons. I am, Sir, Yours, &c.

LETTER XIX.

From *Greenstead* or *Green-Street*, in *Kent*.

SIR,

AS *Stroud* is a *Western* Suburb to *Rochester*, so is *Chatham* towards the *East*; and indeed the whole may be called one of the longest and most disagreeable Streets in *Europe*. This Town of *Chatham* has nothing in it worth Notice, save a Victualling-Office; which is an handsome and convenient Building. From the Church, which stands on a Precipice, is a beautiful and extensive Prospect up and down the River *Medway*, where ride the Ships of War, and many other Vessels.

Below the Church-Yard, and on the Side of the River, lies the *Gun-Yard*; where a great Number of Cannon are deposited, and fit for immediate Use. The Manor of *Chatham*, which is partly in the Parish of *Gillingham*, was held in the Time of the Conqueror by *Hamon de Crevequer*, who was stiled *Domini Chetham*. But his Descendants forfeited it to the Crown, and King *Edward* the Second gave it to *Bartholomew*, Lord *Bedelsmere*, for *Adresley*, in the County of *Salop*; whose Descendants also forfeited it, when King *Edward* the Fourth gave it to *Roger*, Lord *Wentworth*. Here was formerly an Hospital for Lepers, which had many large and noble Benefactions, but it fell at the Dissolution of Religious Houses. Here is still an Alms-House for old or maimed Sailors or Shipwrights: 'Twas built by the famous Sir *John Hawkins*; and on the 27th of *August*, in the 13th Year of Queen *Elizabeth*, was incorporated by her Letters Patent, by the Name of the Hospital of Sir *John Hawkins*, Knt. in *Chetham*.

The

The Market in this Place is held on *Saturdays*, and the Fairs on the 15th of *May* and 19th of *September*, for Cattle and various Commodities.

The Dock at *Chatham* was built by Queen *Elizabeth*, being then the beſt in the World. Her Succeſſors, the Kings *Charles* the Firſt, *Charles* the Second, and *James* the Second, made great Improvements therein ; and, at this Time, if we conſider the Docks and Yards at *Chatham*, in their ample Light; that is, the Launches, Maſt-Houſes, Boat-Houſes, Boat-Yards, Anchor-Yards, Founderies, Forges, Canals, Streets of prodigious large Warehouſes and Storehouſes, where are laid up the Sails, Rigging, Ammunition, great Guns, great and ſmall Shot, ſmall Arms, Swords, Cutlaſſes, *&c.* which belong to the Ships of War that ride at their Moorings ; all which Furniture or Stores are placed in ſuch a Manner, that they may be taken out without Confuſion, in the utmoſt Emergency. I ſay, if this be conſidered, together with the general Warehouſes and Magazines of Tar, Pitch, Hemp, Flax, Tow, Oil, Tallow, Roſin, Standing and Running Rigging, Sail-Cloth, unfitted Cordage, Blocks, Tackles, Runners, Boatſwain's, Gunner's, and Cook's Stores ; Anchors of all Dimenſions, Grapnells, Chains, Balls, wrought and unwrought Iron, Spikes, Pots, Caldrons, Furnaces, Boats, ſpare Maſts and Yards, and many other Neceſſaries ; it will be found to be one of the largeſt and beſt appointed Arſenals in the Univerſe.

The Fortifications at *Gillingham, Cookham* Wood, the *Swamp*, and *Brumpton*, where are many new Works, together with the large, ſtrong, and regular one of *Shireneſs*, are in ſuch Condition, that our old Friends the *Dutch*, who once viſited and burnt ſeveral Ships in the *Medway*, and endangered the Yards and Docks, would now find ſuch

an

an Attempt attended with more Difficulties than in the Reign of such an indolent King as *Charles* the Second. The Commissioner of this Yard has a Salary of Five hundred Pounds a Year; the Clerk of the Checque, Store-Keeper, Master-Shipwright, and Clerk of the Survey have Salaries of Two hundred Pounds a Year each; the Master-Ropemaker has One hundred Pounds a Year, and the Master-Caulker has the same Salary.

There are many other Officers belonging to this famous Yard, and both those within and without Doors are, and act in, Subordination to one another respectively, according to their several Degrees and Employments. It is almost unnecessary to say, that the Watch, with Bells over their Heads, is set every Night, with which they toll the Hour, as in other Royal Yards.

A Guard-Boat also rows its Rounds, to take Care that no Duty in the Ships be neglected.

Notwithstanding the Building-Yards, Docks, Timber, Deal and Gun-Yards, seem to be much in a Hurry, yet every Thing is so ordered, and each Person is so well acquainted with his particular Province or Employ, that there is not the least Confusion : But since the Government have gone upon the Experiment of having Ships of War built at private Docks, and caused so many lately to be built at *Woolwich*, *Deptford*, and *Portsmouth*, *Chatham* has greatly fallen off in that Particular.

About six Years since, the Inhabitants of *Chatham-Dock*, from a Place called the *Hill-House*, to the Entrance of *Smithfield Bank*, were obliged to leave their Dwellings, in order to make room for those large Intrenchments which have been compleated by the Soldiery, who had the additional daily Pay of six Pence each Man ; by which and other means, the Fortifications of the

Dock-Yard are both extended, and more defenfible. On the Side of *Brumpton* they are in Circumference near three Miles, which Works are defended by a ftrong Barricado of Timber, a deep dry Ditch, and well-finifhed Baftions of Stone and Sods, fo contrived, that provided an Enemy was to get Poffeffion of the firft towards *Gillingham*, it is much expofed to the Fire of the fecond, and fuch Annoyance would continue progreffively to the large Fort, which joins to the Town of *Chatham*. A great Part of *Brumpton-Hill* is enclofed in thefe new Fortifications, where is built three parallel Streets of Houfes, which are three Stories high, with fafhed Garrets ; thefe are Barracks for the Soldiers.

Before I leave this Place, I fhall only mention that what is called the *Cheft* at *Chatham* is of great Utility to the Navy. It had its Inftitution in the Year made memorable by the Defeat of the *Armada* of *Spain*, when the Seamen in the Service of Queen *Elizabeth*, by the Advice of Sir *Francis Drake*, Sir *John Hawkins*, and other illuftrious Commanders, voluntarily affigned a Part of each Man's Pay, for the Relief of their then wounded Brother Seamen, which falutary Inftitution is continued to this Day.

The Hill near *Brumpton* commands a fine Profpect of the River, the City of *Rochefter*, *Chatham*, and *Stroud*, together with *Upnor-Caftle*, the *Dock*, and the Woods on the oppofite Shore.

I now turned my Courfe towards *Sittingbourn*, and foon came, through a fine Country, to the Village of *Rainham*, where, in the Church, are fome Monuments of the Earl of *Thanet*'s Family.

Nothing can be more pleafing than travelling on this Coaft, where, on one Side, is a charming cultivated

cultivated Country, and, on the other, continued Views of the Sea, with Ships failing to or from *London*.

The Church at this Place is a ftrong old Building, and the Steeple is a Sea-Mark to Veffels that enter or go out of the *Thames*. From this Village the Country continues fine, with the Sea very near, and the approaching Harveft feems to enliven the Hearts of the Yeomen and Farmers of *Kent*. Near *Key-ftreet* is a very beautiful Seat and Park, in a pleafing Situation; but, owing to its Vicinity to the Sea, that Diftemper called the *Kentifh* Ague, at the Seafons of Spring and Autumn, is a conftant Vifitor. From hence I came to *Chalkwell* and *Sittingbourn*. This is near to the famous Oyfter-Town called *Milton*, or *Melton*, which I purpofe feeing on my Return to *London*.

Sittingbourn is a large well-built Village; it was once both a Corporate and Market-Town, but, notwithftanding thefe Privileges are loft, it ftill has Fairs on *Whit-Monday* and *October* the 9th, for Linen and Woollen-Drapery, Hardware, and Toys.

In the Year 893, *Hafting*, the *Danifh* Pirate, having fortified a Caftle near *Milton* (the Remains of which are called *Caftle Ruff*) King *Alfred* coming againft him, fortified himfelf on the other Side of the Water near *Sittingbourn*; the Ditches, and a fmall Part of the Stone-Work, ftill remain; it is now called *Bavord-Caftle*.

The Church is a good one, in which is an old Monument that was erected to the Memory of Sir *Richard Lovelace*, a great Soldier; who was Marfhal of *Calais* to King *Henry* the Eighth. Here are fome good Inns, one of which is the *Red-Lion*, where Mr. *John Norwood*, a Gentleman of this

Neigh-

Neighbourhood, entertained the heroic King *Henry* the Fifth, as he returned from *France*. Our Hiftorians tell us, that the Feaft, though very elegant, coft no more than nine Shillings and nine Pence.

In a Coppice in the Manor of *Tunftal*, near *Sittingbourn*, in the Month of *January*, 1757-8, a poor Boy found a great Number of Gold Broad-Pieces, and, being ignorant of their Value, played with them at the Houfe of a neighbouring Farmer, who got them from him; but, being unable to keep the Secret; Sir *John Hales*, who lived near, and whofe Anceftor was fuppofed to have concealed them in the civil Wars, laid Claim to them, as Lord of the Manor; as did alfo the Lord of the Manor of *Milton*, which is Paromaunt to that of *Tunftall*. But the Crown interfering, the Farmer refunded Six hundred and twenty-four of them to it : A fufficient Mortification for his Folly.

From *Sittingbourn* I came to *Greenftead* or *Green-Street*, in whofe Neighbourhood is *Tenham*, a Place famous for Cherries, even in the Days of *Drayton*, who fays,

Where *Thames*-ward to the Shore which fhoots upon the Rife,
Rich *Tenham* undertakes thy Clofets to fuffice
With Cherries ; which we fay the Summer in doth bring,
Wherewith *Pomona* crowns the plump and luftful Spring.

Tenham was formerly given by *Kenulf*, King of the *Mercians*, to the Church of *Chrift* in *Canterbury*, at the Eftimate of twelve Plow-Lands. Dr. *Crammmer* exchanged it with the Crown, and King *James* the Firft granted it to Sir *John Roper*, whom he created Baron of *Tenham*, in the Year 1616. This Gentleman, who had diftinguifhed himfelf as a loyal Subject to Queen *Elizabeth*,

zabeth, was the firſt that openly proclaimed the
ſaid King in the County of *Kent*. His Deſcendant
is *Henry Roper*, Baron of *Tenham*, whoſe Seat is
at *Linſtead-Lodge*, but on Account of his Religion, he cannot ſit in the Houſe of *Peers*.

At this Hamlet of *Greenſtead*, where is held a
Fair for Cattle on the 1ſt of *May*, and where the
People were moſt grievouſly afflicted with the
Ague, was once the Seat of the famous *Apul-
dorfield*, who, in the Time of King *Richard* the
Firſt, ſo eminently diſtinguiſhed himſelf in the
Holy War, and whoſe Armour was hung up in
the Church of *Lenham* in this County. I am,
Sir, Yours, *&c.*

L E T T E R   XX.

From Canterbury.

S I R,

LEAVING *Greenſtead*, and paſſing through a
rich Country, I came to *Boughton*, and afterwards to *Harbeldown* or *Harbledown*, a Village
delightfully ſituated in a pretty Valley. In this
Place Archbiſhop *Lanfrank* erected an Hoſpital
for lame and diſeaſed Perſons : He dedicated it to
St. *John*, and annexed to it a Priory of *Black Canons*, which together, at the Diſſolution, was valued at Two hundred and twenty-ſix Pounds four
Shillings and five Pence. In this Religious
Houſe was kept as a Relic, the Upperleather of
one of *Thomas a Becket's* Shoes, it was ſet in
Copper and Cryſtal, and offered to all Paſſengers
to kiſs, which was always complied with in much
Devotion.

Here are many Hop-Gardens, but as I nearer approached *Canterbury*, theſe Plantations became more
abundant

abundant; and are in a moſt promiſing Condition.
As this Part, and within the Diſtance of about
twenty Miles, is the moſt famous in *England* for
Hops, I ſhall feaſt you here with a few Lines
from Mr. *Smart's* poetic Hop-Garden. The Intent of his Poem is thus beautifully told;

> The Land that anſwers beſt the Farmer's Care,
> And ſilvers to Maturity the *Hop*;
> When to inhume the Plants, to turn the Glebe,
> And wed the Tendrils to th' aſpiring Poles;
> Under what Sign to pluck the Crop, and how
> To cure, and in capacious Sacks infold,
> I teach in Verſe *Miltonian*. Smile the Muſe,
> And meditate an Honour to that Land
> Where firſt I breath'd and ſtruggled into Life *;
> Impatient, *Cantium*, to be call'd thy Son.

In pointing out the different Species of Hops,
he uſes theſe Words;

> The nobleſt Species is by *Kentiſh* Wights
> The *Maſter-Hop* y-clep'd. Nature to him
> Has giv'n a ſtouter Stalk, patient of Cold,
> Or *Phœbus*; ev'n in Youth, his verdant Blood
> Indefinently vigorous: The next
> Is arid, fœtid, infecund, and groſs,
> Significantly ſtyl'd the *Fryar*. The laſt
> Is call'd the *Savage*; who, in ev'ry Wood,
> And ev'ry Hedge, unintroduc'd, intrudes.

The Diverſion (in the Time of *Hop-picking*) of
what in *Kent* is called *Binning*, and in *Herefordſhire*, *Cribbing*, he thus deſcribes;

> —————— The emulating Mob
> Strive for the Maſtry—Who firſt may fill
> They bellying *Bin*, and cleaneſt cull the *Hops*.
> Nor aught retards, unleſs invited out
> By *Sol's* declining, and the Evening's Calm,
> *Leander* leads *Lætitia* to the Scene
> Of Shade and Fragrance—Then th' exulting Band
> Of *Pickers*, male and female, ſeize the *Fair*
> *Reluctant*,

* Mr. *Smart* was born at *Margate* in *Kent*.

Reluctant, and with boift'rous Force and Brute,
By Cries unmov'd, they bury her in the *Bin*.
Nor does the *Youth* efcape—Him too they feize,
And in fuch Pofture place, as beft may ferve
To hide his Charmer's Blufhes. Then with Shouts
They rend the echoing Air, and from them both
(So Cuftom has ordain'd) a *Largefs* claim.

The City of *Canterbury*, which the *Britons* called
Caer-Kent, the *Romans*, *Dorovernum*, and the
Saxons, *Cantwarabyric* (1. e. the *Kentifh Men's City*,
or *Court*, or *Burgh*) is fituate in a good Air, upon
the River *Stour*; which falls into the Sea below
Sandwich. That *Canterbury* was originally built
by the *Britons*, may be learnt, not only from the
Monk of *Huntingdon*, but from the *Itinerary* of
Antoninus. In the Time of the *Saxon Heptarchy*,
it was the Capital and Refidence of the Kings of
Kent, till King *Ethelbert*, by the preaching of *Au-*
guftine the Monk, became a Convert to the *Chrif-*
tian Religion; and not only gave his Palace to
him, but alfo the Royalties of the City and its
Territories : And that Miffionary being made an
Archbifhop by Pope *Gregory* the Firft, who alfo
removed the Archiepifcopal Dignity from *London*
to *Canterbury* (which Settlement was confirmed
by fucceeding Popes) it became the Seat of him
and his Succeffors. On the Spot where ftands the
prefent magnificent Cathedral, St. *Auguftine* built
a Chriftian Church, and confecrated it to the Honour of *Chrift*. He alfo, at the Expence of the
King, erected a Monaftery * adjoining to it, for
Secular Canons, which was handfomely endowed.
                                                From

---

* Among many curious Tracts, relating to that of St. *Au-*
guftine (and of which I fhall prefently write) which were burnt
in the *Cottonian* Library, were thefe two. *Regiftrum Chartarum*
Monafterii S. Auguftini Cantuarienfis. And *Epitome Privilegio-*
rum Monafterii S. Auguftini Cantuariæ a prima fundatione per Re-
gem Athelbertum, ex variis Regum Chartis. Vixit Auctor tem-
pore R Henrici 5, Regis Angliæ.

From the Time of the Confecration of *Chrift-Church*, till the Irruptions of the *Danes*, it continued in Peace and Profperity; when, in the Year 1011, it was rifled and burnt by that favage People, together with almoft the whole City. However, their King, *Canute*, afterwards rebuilt both it and the Monaftery ; but not many Years after, it was again deftroyed by Fire, with moft of the Charters of Privileges, and Records relating thereto. In this ruined State it continued, till Archbifhop *Lanfrank*, a *Norman*, pulled down the Remains of the Church, and in feven Years Time rebuilt it after a new Model; together with the Palace and Monaftery. It was now called the Church of the *Holy Trinity*. His Succeffor, *Anfelm*, contributed much to the Completion of his Defign, but *Conrad* the Prior, and the Monks, by the Encouragement of King *Henry* the Firft, finifhed it in a magnificent Manner : When, in a pompous Sort, before the Kings of *England* and *Scotland*, it was again dedicated by the Appellation of *Chrift-Church*. Between forty and fifty Years after this, happened another Fire, which brought it to Ruin. But the Monks being zealous for its Glory, were indefatigable : And the Pope allowed all the Offerings made at the Shrine of the new-canonized Saint, *Thomas a Becket*, fhould go towards the Repair; which, together with the Contributions of the Archbifhops, *Simon of Sudbury, Courtney, Arundel,* and *Chicheley,* and others, it became what it now is, one of the fineft and largeft Gothic Buildings in *England.* The Tower and Spire at the Weft End and Weft Front have but fmall Beauty or Symmetry, but the Tower in the Middle is extremely handfome. This Church is in Length Five hundred and fourteen Feet, in Breadth feventy-four, and fourfcore in Hight, from the Area of the Nave to the Canopy. The Tomb

WORCESTER CATHEDRAL.

Tomb of *Thomas a Becket*, of which Mr. *Dart* has publifhed a Print, is ftill remaining ; and one cannot look upon it without condemning the idle Superftitions of thofe Days.. That *Becket* was an obftinate, proud Prieft, is without Difpute, but the gallant Knights of King *Henry* the Second * had no Right from hence to murder him, any more than the Pope had to make him a Saint.

Mr. *Nelson* thus relates the Punifhment inflicted upon the conniving King. " On *July* the 12th,
" 1174, King *Henry* the Second alighted from his
" Horfe three Miles from *Canterbury*; and pulled
" off his Boots, and went barefoot to the Tomb
" of *Thomas a Becket*, and fell before it : And
" was whipped by all the Bifhops and Abbots
" then prefent ; and every Monk of *Chrift-Church*
" had a Lafh at him. He afterwards continued
" fafting and praying all that Day and Night,
" and would not fuffer a Carpet to be put under
" his Feet, to keep them from the Stones. But
" it is to be noted, that this was done in warm
" Weather." The Riches afterwards offered by Pilgrims and other Votaries were fo great, that *Erafmus*, who was an Eye-Witnefs, tells us,
" at this Shrine, all fhined, fparlked, and glit-
" tered with rare and very large Jewels ; and even
" in the whole Church appeared a Profufenefs
" above that of Kings." At the Diffolution, the Plate and Jewels belonging to this Shrine

---

* *Hugh Morvil*, *William Tracey*, *Hugh Brito*, and *Richard Fitz-Urfe*, hearing King *Henry* the Second (who was juftly offended at the Infolence of *Becket*) fay, " I am very unhappy,
" that among the great Numbers I maintain, there is not a
" Man that dares undertake to revenge the Affronts I perpe-
" tually receive from the Hands of a wretched Prieft," fet out immediately for *Canterbury*, and murdered the Archbifhop at the Altar of the Cathedral.

filled two large Chefts, each of which required eight Men to carry them out of the Church.

In this Cathedral is a very affecting Matter to the Eye of the Difcerning, namely, in the Ifle on the North Side of the Choir ; where (among the numerous ones in the Gothic Tafte, with which this fuperb Edifice abounds) are erected fome Pillars in the *Roman* Manner.

The Monument of *Edward* the *Black Prince*, Son of King *Edward* the Third, is very magnificent ; and here is a plain one for Henry the Fourth, the Dethroner of his Son, King *Richard* the Second. Here are alfo Monuments for the Cardinals *Courticello* and *Pole*; the Archbifhops *Chicheley*, *Peckham*, *Langton*, and many others : Drawings of which have been publifhed by Mr. *Dart*, and fince the Publication of his Work, are many handfome Monuments erected ; but, like thofe in *Weftminfter-Abbey*, they are fhamefully covered with Duft. I cannot forbear wifhing, that, after Families have erected Monuments at a great Expence to the Memories of their Relations, they would alfo leave a fmall Pittance to keep them clean : Or indeed, that the Bifhop, Minifter, or Minifters, and Churchwardens of each Church, fhould caufe the fame to be brufhed from their Duft, in order to their properly anfwering the End for which they were intended. The Nave of this Church is much lighter, and kept in better Order, than that of *Weftminfter-Abbey*: The Front here is a fine one ; 'twas built by Dr. *Warner*, Dean of *Rochefter*.

The Metropolitan Chair is of grey Marble, and ftands behind the High Altar. The Cloifters are not excellent ; but near them is a large Chapel, or Sermon-Houfe, as 'tis commonly called, wainfcotted with Oak from *Ireland*.

Under

Under the Cathedral is a large Church, given by Queen *Elizabeth* to the *Walloons*, who fled hither from *Artois*, and many Parts of the *Netherlands*, owing to the perfecuting Spirit of that unchriftian *Spaniard*, the Duke of *Alva*. This Congregation was much increafed by other Refugees, who left *France* in the oppreffive Reign of *Lewis* the Fourteenth, on the fame Account.

In the Cathedral Church, according to the Foundation, Anno 1541, is a Deacon, twelve Prebendaries, or Major Canons, fix Preachers, fix Minor Canons, fix Subftitutes, twelve Lay Clerks, or Singing Men, one of which is Organift, a Mafter of the Choiriflers, which are ten in Number; two Mafters of the Grammar-School, fifty Scholars, twelve Almfmen, two Vergers, two Veftry-Keepers, with other junior Officers, as Bell-Ringers, &c.

The Churches and Chapels in this Diocefe are Three hundred and eighty-two.

In the Clofe are many handfome Houfes and Gardens for the Prebendaries, &c.

Befides the Cathedral and St. *Martin*'s (which was alfo the Cathedral of fuffragan Bifhops Three hundred and forty nine Years) are fifteen other Churches in this City. Two Gates, which belonged to St. *Auguftine*'s Monaftery, like thofe of St. *Edmundfbury*, are almoft entire.

This Religious Houfe, which was built and endowed by King *Ethelbert* (or, more properly fpeaking, by St. *Auguftine*) who granted it many Privileges, and denounced Cenfures and Curfes againft thofe who fhould violate the fame, was ufed alfo for the Burial-Place of the Archbifhops, Monks, and others, till *Cuthbert*, the eleventh Archbifhop from St. *Auguftine*, obtained Leave of the Pope for having Burial-Places within the Cities of *England*.

The

The Monaſtery of St. *Auguſtine* at *Canterbury*, whoſe Abbots ſat in Parliament, and whoſe Monks were of the Order of St. *Benedict*, was, at the Diſſolution, valued at One thouſand four hundred and thirteen Pounds four Shillings and eleven Pence. Venerable *Bede* ſays, that the Founder was buried in the Poich of the Church of this Monaſtery, and over him was thus inſcribed;

HIC REQUIESCIT DOMINUS AUGUSTINUS DOROVERNENSIS ARCHIEPISCOPUS PRIMUS, QUI OLIM HUC A BEATO GREGORIO ROMANAE URBIS PONTI-FICE DIRECTUS, ET A DEO OPERA-TIONE MIRACULORUM SUFFULTUS, ET ETHELBERTHUM REGEM AC GEN-TEM ILLIUS AB IDOLORUM CULTU AD FIDEM CHRISTI PERDUXIT, ET COM-PLETIS IN PACE DIEBUS OFFICII SUI DE-FUNCTUS EST SEPTIMO KALENDAS JUNIAS, EODEM REGEM REGNENTE.

There are ſome Remains of the Caſtle Walls and Towers, which were built for the Defence of this City, but in general they are now in a ruinous Condition; though ſome of the Gates are in good Repaii *.

This ancient City is very large, and pretty well built. Here are ſome People of Faſhion, and Trade is as well as may be expected in ſo large an inland Place; for though the *Stour* runs through it, there is no Navigation. *Drayton* thus mentions the Courſe of this River;

—— *Stour*, which coming down by *Wye*,
And towards the goodly Iſle his Feet doth nimbly ply,
To *Canterbury* then as kindly he reſorts,
His famous Country thus he gloriouſly reports.
O noble *Kent* ! quoth he, this Praiſe doth belong,
The hardſt to be controul'd, impatientſt of wrong.

Here

---

* The Author of the *Tour* ſays, untruly, that " this City is " ſtrongly walled about."

Here is a good Silk Manufactory, which was firſt begun by the *Walloons* beforementioned, but 'tis now not ſo great as formerly *, and the moſt Brawn made up, and ſold, of any Place in the Kingdom ; it is worth more in the *London* Market than that made at *Shrewſbury*, though 'tis far from being ſo excellent either as to Taſte or Sight.

The City is governed by a Mayor and Aldermen, whoſe Charter was granted in the 26th Year of King *Henry* the Sixth, and it ſends two Members to Parliament.

The Markets here, held on *Wedneſdays* and *Saturdays*, are plentifully ſupplied ; and the Fair is on the 29th of *September*, for Toys. The Races of *Barham-Downs* bring a fine Appearance of Perſons of Diſtinction and Figure to *Canterbury*, where the Aſſemblies are generally very brilliant.

Here are ſeveral Charity-Schools, beſides that which is called the *Free* or *King's School*.

Canterbury is ſituated in the Latitude of 51 Deg. 16 Min. and its Longitude is 1 Deg. 15 Min. from London.

Beſides another Hill, which overlooks the City, is that, which is very corruptly called the *Dungeon-Hill*, for it is very conſpicuous by the Trenches, that it was thrown up in order to facilitate a Siege after the *Daniſh* Manner ; and as the *Danes* beſieged this City in the Reign of King *Ethelred*, without all Doubt, it was from thence called the *Danes* or *Danian-Hill*. The Lord Lieutenant and Cuſtos Rotulorum of this City, and alſo of the County of *Kent*, is the Duke of *Dorſet*. *Kent* has given the Titles of Earl and Duke to many illuſtrious Perſons, but now they are extinct. I purpoſe taking *Feverſham* and *Milton* in my Way to *Upnor-Caſtle* ; and am, Sir, Yours, &c. LET-

---

* A Gentleman, who has been a Manufacturer here for many Years, tells me, that there are about Four hundred Looms, all in the rich Way.

LETTER XXI.

From *Dartford*, in *Kent*.

S I R,

FROM *Canterbury* I rode to the Town of *Fe-versham*, situated upon a Creek, which *Camden* calls a Bay, in a very plentiful Part of this fine County. It consists chiefly of one large Street: The Market-House is a good one.

This Town is known in our Histories for the Meeting of a Parliament * here, in the Reign of King *Athelstan*, Anno 903. In the Year 1148, King *Stephen* founded an Abbey here for *Cluniac* Monks, and dedicated it to the Honour of *Christ*. He endowed it with many Manors, Lands, Liberties, and free Customs, to hold in perpetual Alms, discharged and free from all Secular Exactions. In this Monastery the said King, his Wife *Maud*, and his Son *Eustace*, were buried. *Henry* the Second not only confirmed to the Monks here all their Lands and Franchises, but also granted them an annual Fair for eight Days, beginning at the Feast of St. *Peter ad Vincula*. These Privileges and Advantages were likewise confirmed by the Kings, *John* and *Henry* the Third.

As this Abbey from the Beginning had held its Lands *per Baroniam*, the Abbots had a Right to sit in Parliament, provided they were summoned by the Royal Letters; and, according to the learned *Selden*, they sat in thirteen Parliaments in the Reigns of *Edward* the First and Second; but afterwards, owing either to Age, Laziness, or Poverty, they were discharged from

that

---

* *Camden* writes *Prudentum Conventus.*

that Attendance. At the Suppreffion of Religious Houfes by *Henry* the Eighth, when this was found to be one of the moft diffolute in *England*, it was valued at Two hundred and eighty-fix Pounds twelve Shillings and fix Pence *per Annum.* The Manor, together with all its Privileges, continued to be a *Royal Demefne*, till King *Charles* the Firft gave it to Sir *Dudley Digges* of *Chilham-Caftle*, whofe Son demifed it to Sir *George Sonds*, Knight of the *Bath*, of *Leez-Court*, both in this County, which laft was created Earl of *Feverfham* by King *Charles* the Second, with Remainder to *Lewis*, Lord *Duras*, who had married his eldeft Daughter. This laft-mentioned Gentleman was Commander of the Army of *James* the Second, at the Time of the Landing of the Prince of *Orange* in 1688. In the Year 1747, the late King created *Anthony Duncombe*, Efq; Lord *Feverfham*, Baron of *Downton*, in the County of *Wilts*, whofe Seat at *Barford* I have already fpoken of.

This Town was firft incorporated by the Name of the *Barons* of *Feverfham*, and afterwards by the Title of the *Mayor* and *Commonalty* ; and laftly, by that of the *Mayor*, *Jurats*, and *Commonalty* of the Town of *Feverfham*.

The Creek here is a Member to the Port of *Dover.* The Town is now in a good Condition, and is one of thofe who fupply the Markets of *London* with Apples, Cherries, and large Oyfters; for which laft Commodity the *Dutch* alfo are their great Cuftomers.

The Church here was formerly given to the Abbey of St. *Auguftine*, in the City of *Canterbury.* 'Tis dedicated to St. *Mary*, and in it are many Monuments.

Here are two Markets, but the moft confiderable is on *Saturdays* ; the other is held on *Wednefdays :* And two Fairs for ten Days each, the one

begins

begins upon the 25th of *February*, and the other on the 12th of *August*. The Goods fold are chiefly Linen, Woollen Drapery, and Toys. Here is also a Charity-School for ten Boys and ten Girls, who are cloathed and taught at the Expence of the Inhabitants.

It was by some Fishermen of this Town, that the pusilanimous King James the Second was stopt, and boarded near *Shellness*, at the East End of the Island of *Sheepy*; when he first attempted escaping to *France*.

The Custom here is, that no Fisherman can take up his Freedom, unless he is married, and they are restrained from bringing Oysters into the Town, but at some particular Times.

As I intend making a Voyage down the Side of this Coast, I have now omitted visiting the Island of *Sheepy*, which lies off this Town, and rode to *Milton*, which by old Writers is called *Middeton* ; in ancient Records it is stiled a *Royal Village*, on Account of a Palace which the Kings of *Kent* had in it, till it was burnt down by Earl *Godwin*, at the Time of his Rebellion against *Edward* the *Confessor*.

The Manor was granted by King *James* the First to *Philip*, Earl of *Pembroke*, and his Heirs for ever ; but the Royalty was exempted on Account of its having been given by King *John* to the Abbey of *Feversham*. The Church of *Milton* stands near a Mile from the Town : And Bishop *Gibson*, in his Additions to *Camden*'s *Britannia*, thinks the latter was removed after its being burnt as abovesaid, to the Head of the Creek, where it now stands. In the Church, which is dedicated to the Holy Trinity, are many Monuments of Antiquity, especially for the *Norwoods* : Some of whom being represented cross-legged, had probably undertaken the *Crusade*. *Milton* is a large Town, governed by a *Portreve*, who is annually

chosen

chosen on St. *James*'s Day, and has a Right to su-
pervise and examine the Weights and Measures
not only in the Town, but throughout the whole
Hundred of *Milton*. The Market here was
granted by King *Edward* the First : 'Tis held on
Saturdays, and confists chiefly of Corn and Fruit;
and on the 24th of *July* is a Fair for Toys. But
what this Place is most famous for, are the Oyster-
Grounds, which produce the finest and best Oysters
that are found in the *London* Markets.

Near this Town are the Remains of *Tong-Caftle*,
formerly the Seat of the illustrious Family of *Ba-
dilfmere*.

From *Milton* I continued my Course Westward-
ly; but having no Inclination to ride over the
difagreeable Stones of *Chatham*, *Rochefter*, and
Stroud, already treated of, I alighted at the Bottom of the Hill, at the Entrance of the first of
these Places; sent my Horse to the last; and, after
walking over *Brumpton-Hill*, paffed over the *Medway* in the Ferry to *Upnor-Caftle*. This Fortification was erected by Queen *Elizabeth*; it commands two Reaches of the River, but is of no
confiderable Strength. Here are some convenient
Barracks, and a small Garrifon, of which Mr.
Robert Heath, a celebrated Mathematician, is an
Officer. This Gentleman treated me in a friendly
Sort, and accompanied me to *Stroud* : From
whence, having met with two Gentlemen of my
Acquaintance, we rode to *Chalkftreet*, near *Gravefend*, and soon after to *Northfleet*. At *Swanfcomb*,
in this Neighbourhood it was, that the brave *Men
of Kent* met *William* the First, after the Battle of
Haftings, having *Stigand*, Archbifhop of *Canterbury*, and *Eglefine*, Abbot of St. *Auguftine*'s Monaftery in that City, at their Head. All the
whole Army carried Boughs of Trees, as well as
Arms, in their Hands, and so suddenly surprized

VOL. I. C c the

the Conqueror, that they obtained feveral Privileges, particularly that of *Gavel Kind*; which their Defcendants, and other *Men of Kent*, now enjoy *.

The Day had been extreamly fine, and my Companions very facetious, fo that though we paffed *Gadfhill*, a Place famous in Story for robbing, it gave us little Concern. The Sun was funk below the Horizon before we reached *Dartford*; and *Hefperus* became our Attendant on this charming Evening, which afforded a Scene fimilar to that painted by *Gay*;

——— See, at the Call of Night,
The Star of Evening fheds his filver Light
High o'er yon Weftern Hill : The cooling Gales
Frefh Odours breathe along the winding Dales.

This Town of *Dartford*, or more properly *Darentford*, is fituate upon the fmall River of that Name ; upon which Stream was erected the firft Mill in *England* for flitting of Bar-Iron : And in the Reign of *Charles* the Firft, Sir *John Spillman* built here the firft Paper-Mill in this Kingdom, and, for his Encouragement, the faid King gave him a Patent, with a Salary of Two hundred Pounds a Year.

In the Reign of *William* the Firft, this Town was in the Poffeffion of *Hamo*, a *Norman*, who gave the Church, then dedicated to the *Holy Trinity*, to the See of *Rochefter* ; which was confirmed by King *Henry* the Firft. Upon the Return of the glorious King *Edward* the Third out of *France*, a

grand

* By *Gavel-Kind* is meant, that all Lands of that Nature are divided among the Males by equal Portions, or, in Default of Male Iffue, among the Females. By this, they enter upon the Eftate at fifteen Years of Age, and have Power to make over to any one, either by Gift or Sale, without Confent of the Lord. By the fame, the Sons fucceed to this Sort of Lands, though their Parents be fentenced for Theft, *&c.* Bifhop. *Gibfon*'s *Camden.*

grand and general Tournament was held here, when the King and his Nobility performed with great Gallantry.

The fame King founded a Nunnery here of the Order of St. *Auguſtine* (the Nuns of which were to live under the Care of the Friars of the Order of *Preachers*) which he endowed with Lands and Revenues in this County and elſewhere, together with ſeveral Houſes and Rents in *London*; all which was confirmed to them to hold in *Frankalmoine*, by the ſaid King's Grant, dated in the forty-ſixth Year of his Reign. *Richard* the Second, in the eighth Year of his Reign, granted to the Prioreſs and Convent of this Houſe, the Manor of *Maſſingham* in *Norfolk*, together with conſiderable Privileges, for the finding a Chaplain to celebrate in the Chapel of the Infirmary of this Houſe, and for the Relief and Suſtentation of the Siſters and Brethren in the ſaid Infirmary. This Houſe at the Diſſolution was valued at Three hundred and eighty Pounds nine Shillings *per Annum*.

Some Hiſtorians tell us, that the Rebellion of *Wat. Tyler*, *tem. Ric.* II. began at *Deptford*; but that is a Miſtake, for it was certainly in this Town of *Dartford*; and, if ſome of our beſt Writers are to be credited, the original Oppoſition was to be juſtified: For the Collector of the King's Tax was ſo far from being ſatisfied with diſtraining the Goods of *Tyler*, that he even attempted the deflowering of his Daughter. 'Tis true, the Cruelties committed by this tumultuous Mob are not to be vindicated; but the Servants of the Crown ſhould always take *Juſtice* with them as a Guide, and then they will never be led to Precipices, that may be fatal to their Necks.

In this Town, where is a Fair on the 22d of *July*, for Horſes and Bullocks, are two Church-

Yards,

Yards, one of which is higher than the Tower of the Church. · At *Dartford* the *Canterbury* Stage-Coach takes a Guard, armed with a Blunderbufs and Piftols, which goes with them to Town, and returns in the Morning. Otherwife it would be very dangerous paffing over *Shooter's Hill*, and *Blackheath*. I am, Sir, Yours, &c.

LETTER XXII.

From *Beconsfield*, in *Buckinghamfhire*.

SIR,

IN the Morning I rode to *Crayford*. *Camden* fays it was called *Creccanford*, being a Ford over the little River *Crecce*, which alfo gives Names to the neighbouring Villages of *Paul's Cray*, *Foote* or *Votes Cray*, *North Cray*, and to the Town of St. *Mary Cray*, and falls into the *Darent* between *Dartford* and the *Thames*. At *Crayford*, eight Years from the firft Landing of the *Saxons*, a Body of that People, commanded by *Hengift*, engaged the *Britons*, wherein moft of the Leaders of the latter were flain, and the Victory on the Side of the *Saxons* was fo complete, that he afterwards eftablifhed his Kingdom in *Kent*, without any Difturbance from them. From hence we had a pleafant Ride to *Shooter's Hill*, where the Profpects are various, extenfive, and delightful: That towards *London* is beautiful beyond Conception or Defcription. This Place hath its prefent Name from its being a Spot where Butts were caft up, for the Exercife of Archery. Upon the Top of the Hill is a Spring of excellent Water, which, I am told, never freezes. Leaving this Hill, we came foon after to *Blackheath*, where we paffed *Morden* College, and riding by

the

the Side of *Greenwich-Park* Wall, faw the fine
Houfe of Sir *Gregory Page* (both which Buildings
I fhall hereafter defcribe) and foon after defcended
the Hill into Part of the Town of *Greenwich*, and
thence came to *Deptford*, where I was left by my
Company.

This Place was formerly called *Weſt-Greenwich*,
and is built where the Stream called *Ravenſbourn*
falls into the *Thames*. The Deepnefs of the Ford
here gave Name to the Place. Over that Brook
now is a good Bridge, near one of the largeſt
Malt-diſtilling Houfes in *England*: I think, it belongs to Mr. *Bryant*, and on the oppofite Side of
the Street is a very beautiful Garden, which has
the fame Owner.

In *Deptford*, which is far from being an agreeable Place, is a Church dedicated to St. *Nicholas*;
but the Number of Inhabitants becoming too numerous to attend divine Service there, another is
lately erected, and dedicated to St. *Paul*; this is
built of Free-Stone, is very handfome, and one
of the fifty new ones intended by Queen *Anne*.

King *Henry* the Eighth, in the fourth Year of
his Reign, fettled a Corporation at *Deptford*, the
Officers of which were called the Maſter and Wardens of the *Holy Trinity*. They were to infpect
the Building, Preferving, and Management of
the King's Navy: He alfo enabled them to begin,
to the Honour of the *Holy Trinty*, and St. *Clement*,
a perpetual Guild or Brotherhood, concerning the
Craft or Cunning of the Mariners, and for the
Increafe of the Ships of this Realm. Their
Houfe was adjoining to the Church, and the Treafurer of the Navy had an Houfe in the Dock-
Yard for himfelf.

This Body Corporate ſtill continues, under the
Name of the *Trinity-Houſe* of *Deptford-Stroud*;
but without having any Truſt or Authority in the
Royal

Royal Navy. The Building of the said Corporation, was erected by them, though 'tis not contiguous, nor was it built at the same Time. The old Part consists of twenty-one Houses, and that of the new is thirty-eight, both for the Use of decayed Pilots or Masters of Ships, or their Widows.

The Manor here antiently belonged to the Barons of *Mamigniot*, but having been possessed by many others, it now belongs to the *Evelyn* Family.

The King's Dock at *Deptford* has been made upwards of Two hundred and thirty Years, and though the larger Ships are built at *Woolwich*, yet very much Business is done in the Yard here: The Area of which has been enlarged some Years since. Here are also many additional Store-Houses and other Buildings, and also naval Officers established, as at *Chatham*, &c.

The *Red-House*, so called from the Redness of the Bricks it was built with, and in which were laid up vast Quantities of Hemp, Flax, Pitch, Tar, &c. &c. was entirely consumed by Fire in *July*, 1739.

We returned from the Yard to the Sign of the *Centurion*, where we left our Horses: The Host of which House (lately dead) was one of those few Sailors who sailed the long Voyage with the present Lord *Anson*, that did not spend their Money.

The Road from *Deptford* to *London* is, to the Honour of the Commissioners, in the best Condition of any which leads into that Metropolis.

I intend to set out soon for a longer *Tour*, namely, into the Counties of *Middlesex*, *Buckingham*, *Oxford*, *Gloucester*, *Worcester*, *Salop*, and *Warwick*, and I must freely confess to you, that since I have made these Excursions, *London* is not so pleasing

to

to me as before ; but I cannot hold it in that
Light which Mr. *Johnson* does : I think these are
his Words ;

> —— Who would leave, unbrib'd, *Hibernia's* Land,
> Or change the Rocks of *Scotland* for the *Strand?*
> There none are swept by sudden Fate away,
> But all, whom Hunger spares, with Age decay.
> Here Malice, Rapine, Accident conspire,
> And now a Rabble rages, now a Fire.
> Their Ambush here relentless Ruffians lay,
> And here the fell Attorney prowls for Prey,
> Here falling Houses thunder on your Head,
> And here a female Atheist talks you dead.

It is but a melancholly Road, when by one's
self, to *Acton* ; but the Village is very prettily situated upon a rising Ground, and the Country
around is very pleasant, and finely cultivated.
The Church is neat, and, in it are many Monuments, particularly one for the famous Sir *Thomas
Cornwall*, who died in 1537. In this Neighbourhood is a Spring, which, some Years since, was
much frequented by the Water-Drinkers of *London*. Dr. *Rutty* has wrote some Account of its
Virtues, but 'tis now neglected.

From *Acton* to *Hillingdon* the Road is excellent.
The Air of this last Place must be extreamly good,
though the Church-Yard is almost as full of
Grave-Stones as the Dissenters Burying-Ground at
Bunhill-Fields. Upon a flat Tomb-Stone near the
Church, is an Inscription to the Memory of the
Widow of the heroic Lord *Aubrey Beauclerc*, and
another for Lieutenant-General *Francis Columbine*.

The Weather, which most of the Day had
been very wet, now became fine, when I came to
the pleasant Town of *Uxbridge*. Here are many
good Inns, which are much frequented, being at
a proper Distance for the Breakfasting of a Traveller

veller from *London*. The Gardens near the Mill, upon the River *Coln*, are very neat. This Water rises near *Mims* in *Hertfordshire*, and having passed by *Rickmansworth*, runs to this Place: About four Miles below it reaches *Colnbrook*, and disembogues itself into the *Thames*, as I have observed in a former Letter. Leaving *Uxbridge*, which is famous for the Treaty held here in 1645, and gives Title of Earl to *Henry*, Lord *Paget*, I came to *Gerrard's Cross*, a Village in the County of *Bucks**. Here is a Charity-School, erected and endowed by the late Duke of *Portland*, for twenty Boys and fifteen Girls, who are taught and cloathed; and two of them are annually put out Apprentice.

The Road soon led me to the Park-Wall of the Duke of *Portland*, which, after continuing on my Left for a considerable Way, brought me to a View of his Grace's House, called *Bulstrode*. This was once the Property of the well-known Chancellor *Jefferies* †. Its Situation is very pleasant, upon an Eminence in the Park; which is a very fine one, and well stocked with Deer. From hence I came to the Town of *Beconsfield*, which is situate upon a dry Hill, hath a Market on *Tuesdays*, and Fairs on the 13th of *February*, and *Holy Thursday*, for Horses, Cows, and Sheep.

It consists of one long and broad Street, in which are several good Inns. At the West End of the Town stands the Church, near which Building, in the Yard, is erected a very beautiful pyramidic Marble Monument, enclosed with Iron Rails; on the Sides of which is inscribed, a *Latin* Epitaph, written by the learned and ingenious Mr.

---

* The Author of a Work, called *London and its Environs*, says untruly, this Place is twenty-eight Miles from *London*.

† Bishop *Gibson*, in his *Addenda* to *Camden*, erroneously places this Seat near *Eton*.

Mr. *Rymer*, to the Memory of the celebrated Poet, *Edmund Waller*, Eſq;

He was born at *Hall-Barn*, the Family Seat near this Town, where his Anceſtors had long continued. Perhaps he was the moſt accompliſhed Gentleman of that Age, and ſo excellent a Poet, that he had the Appellation of the *Engliſh Tibullus*. In his Poem, called the *Battle of the Summer-Iſlands*, he hath left us theſe extreamly beautiful Lines;

O! how I long my careleſs Limbs to lay
Under the *Plantain*'s Shade! and all the Day,
With am'rous Airs my Fancy entertain,
Invoke the *Muſes*, and improve my Vein!
No Paſſion there in my free Breaſt ſhould move,
None but the ſweet, and beſt of Paſſions, Love.
There, while I ſing, if gentle Love be by,
That tunes my Lute, and winds the Strings ſo high,
With the ſweet Sound of *Sacchariſſa*'s Name,
I'd make the liſt'ning Savages grow tame.

Mr. *Waller*'s Conduct as a Politician is ſomewhat inconſiſtent. For, after the Trial of his Uncle, the famous Mr. *Hampden*, for his Refuſal to pay *Ship-Money*, he, on the 22d of *April*, 1640, made an excellent Speech in the Houſe of Commons (of which he was a Member) concerning the Heart-Burnings of the People on that Occaſion. After this he impeached Sir *Francis Crawley*, one of the Judges, for his Conduct in that Matter againſt Mr. *Hampden*.

In the Year 1642, the Parliament ſent Mr. *Waller*, as one of the Commiſſioners, to treat with the King at *Oxford*, concerning a Peace.

The King, who privately knew, that this Gentleman was at that Time not only attached to him, but actually contriving a Plot, in Conjunction with the City of *London*, in his Favour, received him very kindly : However, the Treaty came to nothing, and the Plot alſo failed. But this latter Attempt had been fatal to Mr. *Waller*, had he not found many real Friends; notwithſtanding which, ſome of his Party loſt their Lives, and himſelf was forced to pay *Ten thouſand Pounds*; he was alſo loaded with many public Reflections. One of his beſt Poems is a Panegyric on *Oliver Cromwell*, which being obſerved to him by King *Charles* the Second, after he had produced one on that *Monarch*'s Reſtoration, *Waller* ſmartly returned, " O " Sir, we Poets never ſucceed ſo well in writing " Truth as in Fiction."

In the latter Part of his Life, he was thus addreſſed by Mr. *Wycherley*;

> As you *Apollo*'s eldeſt Offspring are,
> You of his Spirit claim a double Share ;
> Still warm, though old, like your immortal Sire,
> Your Flame of Wit is an eternal Fire ;
> Your Bays ſhall never fade, your flowing Vein
> *Phœbus*, with all his Heat, can never drain !

Over his Monument grows a Walnut-Tree, which, in a rainy Autumn, ſtains it conſiderably: But I am told, that the Tree being produced from a Nut planted by his Hands, the Family will not by any means have it cut down or removed.

There is nothing very pleaſing in the Appearance of the Houſe at *Hall-Barn*, but a ſweet View of the Banquetting or Aſſembly-Room from the Fields.

This Eſtate is now in the Poſſeſſion of *Edmund Waller*, Eſq; Member of Parliament for *High* or *Chipping-Wycomb*, which Town I intend ſoon to viſit ; and am, Sir, Yours, *&c.*

L E T T E R XXIII.

From *Bleachington*, in *Oxfordshire*.

S I R,

FROM *Beaconsfield*, after descending an Hill, I came to the charming Valley, in which the two *Wickhams* stand, and through it runs a delightful Stream, which, after having turned a great Number of Paper and other Mills, falls into the *Thames* at *Hedsor*, near *Great Marlow*. This Vale is extreamly pleasing, being diversified with Meadows, and Fields of various Sorts of Grain, in a very fine Condition. On the Summits of the Hills are such beautiful Woods as those near *Henley*, in the County of *Oxford*. My Course was directed through the Bottom of the Valley to the Town of *Chipping-Wycomb*, or, as it is more commonly called, *High-Wycomb*, or *High-Wickham*. The Name is taken from *Wick*, a *River*, and *Comb*, a *Vale*. This is one of the best built Towns in the County of *Buckingham*. At the West End of the principal Street is lately erected a very neat Market-House, where, on *Fridays*, is held the Market, which is one of the largest to be found so near *London*, especially for Corn and other Grain, and there is a Fair on the 25th of *September*, for hiring Servants. The Church, which stands near the Market-House, is a very good Building.

The Lord of this Town and Manor, in the Time of the Conquest, was *Wigod de Wallingford*; but falling to the Crown, it was by King *John* divided between *Alan Basset*, and *Robert de Vipont*. Here has been a small Monastery of *Black Monks*, dedicated to St. *Margaret*; and also two Hospitals,

D d 2   one

one for Lepers, dedicated to St. *Margaret* and St, *Giles*, the other to St. *John*; to which belonged feveral Lands about the Town: Thefe, after the Diffolution, Queen *Elizabeth*, in the fourth Year of her Reign, gave to the Corporation, in order to maintain a free Grammar-School, and fome Alms-People, which laft, by Improvements and Advance of Rents, are become more numerous.

This Borough, which is perhaps the firft in the County that ever fent Burgeffes to Parliament, is governed by a Mayor, Recorder, Aldermen, Bailiffs, and Burgeffes, or Common-Council.

Near the Church is a Piece of Water in a triangular Form, and the Borders being planted with Trees, it has a pretty Appearance.

From this Place to *Weft Wickham* is about a Mile, the River continuing on the Left-Hand. Before one enters this Village, appears a fine View of the Seat, Park, and Gardens of Sir *Francis Dafhwood*, Bart. and, above all, is a thick Wood, which crowns the Profpect on that Side. Purfuing the Road, on the Left-Hand is a charming Shrubbery, at the End of which the Garden Wall begins, and this is the Support of a delightful Terrace, though not fo fine as that of the Duke of *Devonfhire* at *Chifwick*. At the Eaft End is a pretty Temple, fupported by neat Pillars, very near to which, in the high Road, Sir *Francis* has erected an handfome Obelifk, on three Sides of which we are directed to the City (i. e. *London*) to the County Town, and to the Univerfity; the fourth gives Information by whom it was erected.

Richard, Earl *Temple*, is Lord Lieutenant of this County of *Buckingham*, and Colonel of its Militia; of which Corps the faid Sir *Francis Dafhwood* is Lieutenant-Colonel.

The

The Church of *Weft Wickham* is built on the Brow of the Hill, on the North Side of the Valley, which Situation is fo extreamly high, and the gilt Ball on the Top of the Steeple fo large, that it affords a very pleafing Sight. Having reached the Village, I afcended the Hill to the Church-Yard, from whence the View is furprizingly fine, both up and down the Valley, efpecially towards Sir *Francis Dafhwood*'s : For here I had the Houfe in Front, which is an handfome modern Building, and below a fine Piece of Water, on which was a beautiful Yatch, mounted with ten or a Dozen Cannon. The Profpect of the Park was very ample, and the whole Landfcape vaftly charming. There are two modern Views of this Seat in the Print-Shops ; they were done by *Hannam*. In the Church are fome Monuments, one in particular to the Memory of the Right Hon. Lady *Mary Dafhwood*, eldeft Daughter to the Right Hon. *Vere Fane*, Earl of *Weftmorland*, and Wife to Sir *Francis Dafhwood*, Knt. and Bart.

I now bent my Courfe to the Right of the *Oxford* Road, and paffed over a long, dreary Common, called *Bedlowe-Ridge*. In about two Hoyrs I entered a fmall Wood, which I foon paffed, and found myfelf on the Brow of a fteep Hill, from whence is a moft extenfive Profpect of the Vale of *Aylefbury*. So fine a Bottom, with various Sorts of excellent Grain waving in the gentle Breeze, and promifing even an overflowing Fulnefs to the Farmer's Barn, could not fail of reminding me of *Whitehead*'s Addrefs to Liberty.

——— O deign to fmile,
Goddefs of *Britannia*'s Ifle !
Thou, that from her Rocks furvey'ft
Her boundlefs Realms, the wat'ry Wafte;
Thou, that rov'ft the Hill and Mead,
Where her Flocks and Heifers feed;

Thou

Thou, that chear'ft th' induftrious Swain,
While he ftrews the pregnant Grain ;
Thou, that hear'ft his caroll'd Vows,
While th' expanded Barn o'erflows ;
Thou, the Bulwark of our Caufe ;
Thou, the Guardian of our Laws,
Sweet *Liberty* !—O deign to fmile,
Goddefs of *Britannia*'s Ifle !

To this let me fubjoin *Philips*'s Defcription of Property ;

But who advances next, with chearful Grace,
Joy in her Eye, and Plenty in her Face ?
A wheaten Garland does her Head adorn ;
O *Property* ! O Goddefs *Englifh*-born !

This Vale extends from *Leighton* upon the River *Lowfel* in *Bedfordfhire*, to *Dorchefter*, in the County of *Oxford*, where the *Thames* and *Ifis* join : 'Tis thus poetically defcribed by *Drayton* ;

Aylfbury's a Vale that walloweth in her Wealth ;
And (by her wholfome Air continually in Health)
Is lufty, frim, and fat ; and holds her youthful Strength,
Befides her fruitful Earth, her mighty Breadth and Length
Doth *Chiltern* fitly, which mountainoufly high
And being very long ; fo likewife fhe doth lye
From the *Bedfordian* Fields, where firft fhe doth begin
To fafhion like a Vale to th' Place where *Tame* doth win
His *Ifis* wifhed Bed, her Soil throughout fo fure
For Goodnefs of her Glebe, and for her Pafture pure ;
That as her Grain and Grafs fo fhe her Sheep doth breed,
For Burden, and for Bone, all others that exceed.

The *Chiltern-Hills*, of which *Bledlow Ridge* is a Part, are very high : And alfo the Eaftern Boundary of the whole Vale.

Having alighted, and defcended from this Summit, I foon came to *Chinner*, one of the many Villages that are fituated in this rich Valley : It ftands juft within the County of *Oxford*, and in this Parifh the *Roman* Way, called *Ikenild-Street*,

enters

enters this County from that of *Buckingham.*
Here is a ſtrong old Church.

From this Village to *Tame* or *Thame* is about
four Miles, which Town ſtands near the ſmall River of that Name, that here bears its Courſe Weſtward, and ſo continues almoſt to *Wheatley-Bridge,*
and then runs Southward till it falls into the *Tha-*
mes or *Iſis.* This Town is of ſome Antiquity:
It was of Note in the Time of the *Saxons,* and the
Danes fortified it againſt King *Edward* the Elder;
who, having took it, put both the *Daniſh* King,
and the Garriſon, to the Sword; but the Town
ſoon after (i. e. in 1010) felt their revenging
Hands.

In the Year 1138, Sir *Robert Gait,* a Knight,
founded and endowed a Religious. Houſe here,
and furniſhed it with *Ciſtercian* Monks from *Wa-*
verley. *Henry* the Second, in the firſt Year of his
Reign, confirmed their Eſtate to them, as did
Edward the Second, in the tenth Year of his
Reign. This Houſe at the Diſſolution was valued
at Two hundred fifty-ſix Pounds thirteen Shil-
livgs and ſeven Pence *per Annum.* There are yet
ſome Ruins of this Building.

In *Henry* the Third's Reign, the Biſhop of *Lin-*
coln, whoſe Name was *Lexington,* brought the
great Road through this Town, which was of
much Service to the Inhabitants. Sir *John Wil-*
liams, of *Burfield* in *Berkſhire* (Steward of the
Biſhop of *Lincoln*'s Lands in this Country) who
had been created Lord *Williams,* of *Tame,* by
Queen *Mary,* founded here a fine Free-School, and
an Almſhouſe. The Church is a very good one,
at the End of which is a very ridiculous Inſcription to the Memory of one *John Kent,* who
changed his Religion. The Town is large, and
the Street where they hold their Market very
broad, and indifferently well built. This Market

ket is held on *Tuefdays*, and the Fairs on *Eafter-Tuefday*, for all Sorts of Cattle ; *Michaelmas* (October the 10th) for hiring Servants, and felling Horfes and fat Hogs.

My Inn here was the *Crown*, where, it being Market-Day, I was well enough entertained with fome of the honeft Farmers.

At *Tame* Park is the Seat of Lord *Wenman*.

Having left *Tame* with an agreeable Companion, we paffed by *Rycot*, where is a Manfion-Houfe, Chapel, and a fine Park, belonging to the Earl of *Abingdon*. I now was conducted to *Wheatly-Bridge*, which is built over the *Tame*, upon the great Road to *Oxford*. Not far from the Bridge is the Village of that Name, where the neareft Road to *Worcefter* feparates from that which leads to *Oxford*; the former of which we followed, and, in about an Hour, found ourfelves upon a Common near *Iflip*, at the Entrance of which Place is a large Bridge over the River *Bur*.

In the Month of *April*, in the Year 1645, *Oliver Cromwell*, having met General *Fairfax* at *Windfor*, was difpatched with a Party of Horfe into this Country, to prevent the Junction of another large Body of Horfe (that was detached from the Army of Prince *Rupert* in *Worcefterfhire*) with the Army of the King, which lay about *Oxford*. *Cromwell* was fo fortunate, that, at this Bridge, he met with five of the Royalifts beft Regiments, commanded by the Earl of *Northampton*, whom he routed, and took Four hundred Horfes, and Two hundred Men Prifoners.

In the Church of this large Village of *Iflip* was born and baptifed King *Edward* the Confeffor : The Font ufed in that Chriftian Duty was fome Years ago fet upon a Pedeftal in the Garden of Sir *Henry Brown*, of *Nether-Kidlington*. The Donations of the famous Dr. *South* to this Town, of

which

which he had been Rector, were, according to his monumental Inscription in *Westminster* Abbey, for the Re-building the Chancel, and the Rector's House, and the Erection and Endowment of a School for poor Children.

This Place is more populous than handsome.

The next Village we arrived at was *Blechington*, where is a Seat belonging to the Earl of *Anglesea*, a well-known Nobleman. In the civil Wars, this House was garrisoned by the King, and the Governor was Colonel *Windebank*. But *Cromwell*, immediately after his Success at *Islip-Bridge*, summoned him to surrender, with which he immediately thought proper to comply, and for that Act was soon after shot to Death at *Oxford*.

Dr. *Daniel Fairclough*, commonly called *Featley*, was born in this Village. His Father was Cook of *Corpus Christi College*, *Oxon*. He was Chaplain to Sir *Thomas Edmunds*, Ambassador to *France* ; where he so defended the *Protestant Divines* against the *Sorbonnists*, that they gave him the Character of *Accutissimus & Accerrimus*. By Archbishop *Abbot* he was preferred to the Rectories of *Acton* and *Lambeth* ; he was also made Chancellor of the Diocese of *Salisbury*. In the civil Wars he was a great Sufferer, and died in 1664.

The Companion which I met with at *Tame*, is a Gentleman whose Seat is in the Neighbourhood of *Blechington*. His Treatment was very genteel. He obliged me to stay a Night with him, and the next Morning took a Ride with me to *Woodstock*, after I had promised to spend also the ensuing Evening at his House. The Ride was extreamly agreeable, and the Country fine.

Woodstock is a tolerable good Town, pretty well paved, but not elegantly built. It has convenient Inns, and some Persons here are remarkable for polishing Steel, especially steel Chains for Watches.

It

It is governed by a Mayor, High Steward, Recorder, four Aldermen, two Chamberlains, and sixteen Common-Council-Men. The Market is held on *Tuesdays*, and the Fairs on *March* 25, *Whit-Monday*, *June* 21, *September* 21, and *December* 6.

Bishop *Fell* built here a large House for the Incumbents. Here is a Free-School, with a Salary for the Master of twenty Pounds *per Annum*, some Almshouses for eight poor Persons, and a Library, under the Care of the Corporation. The People of this Place will have it, that *Chaucer* was born here, and that he lived in an House, of which there are some ruinous Remains, between the Park Wall and the Town ; but this is a doubtful Matter. That there was a Royal Palace at *Woodstock*, in which King *Ethelred* held a Witagemot or Parliament, and that the Palace also continued in the Time of King *Alfred*, is allowed : For Dr. *Plot*, who wrote a Natural History of this County, says, that that King translated *Boetius de Confolatione Philosophiæ* (which Manuscript is now in the *British Museum*) in his Palace here. King *Henry* the First made Additions to the Palace, and walled in the Park, which is between ten and eleven Miles in Circumference, in which, according to some Writers, he kept Lions, Tigers, Panthers, and other savage Beasts.

That *Henry* the Second resided principally here, appears from many public Transactions with the Princes of *Wales*, and here he gave his Cousin, the Lady *Ermengard*, Daughter of *Richard*, Viscount *Beaumont*, in Marriage to *William*, King of *Scotland*. But what our Historians relate of a Labyrinth made here for his Concubine, *Rosamond*, the Daughter of the Lord *Clifford*, has rendered it most famous. This romantic Hiding-Place was formed in the Valley, somewhat to the North-West of the Bridge ; it was called *Fair Rosamond*'s
Bower,

Bower, and near the Spot is now a Spring or Bath, called *Rofamond*'s *Well*.

However, they tells us, that the Queen found her out, which brought on the Death of *Rofamond*, who was buried at *Godftow* in this County.

At the Royal Palace here was born *Edmund*, the fecond Son of King *Edward* the Firft, and the famous *Black Prince*, Son of King *Edward* the Third. In this Houfe the Princefs, afterwards the glorious Queen *Elizabeth*, was kept a Prifoner fome Time, under the Care of the Lord *Tame* and Sir *Henry Bennifield*, when fhe narrowly efcaped being burnt to Death.

The Splendor of this Palace continued till the unhappy Days of *Charles* the Firft, and the grand Ruins of it remained within the Memory of fome People now living. Its Situation was to the North of the Bridge, upon a Spot where two Elm Trees are planted, as a Mark where it ftood.

The Manor being Royal, Queen *Anne*, in the fourth Year of her Reign, and with the Concurrence of Parliament, granted all the Intereft of the Crown in the Honour and Manor of *Woodftock*, and Hundred of *Wotton*, to *John*, Duke of *Marlborough*, and his Heirs, as a Reward for his eminent and unparalelled Services, in gaining, by his Courage and Conduct, divers Victories over the *French* and *Bavarian* Armies at *Schellenberg* and other Places, but more efpecially at *Blenheim*: By which the Frontiers of *Holland* were fecured and enlarged, and the Empire faved from immediate Ruin. And as a lafting Monument of the Glory and Importance of that unparalelled Victory, a Palace was erected here, at the public Expence, and the Queen gave it the Name of *Blenheim*.

From the Town we entered the Park, through a large and elegant Portal, or triumphal Arch, of

the

the *Corinthian* Order. This Building was erected
at the Expence of *Sarah*, Dutchefs-Dowager, to
the Memory of her illuftrious Confort. From
hence is an oblique View of the Palace, which
appears to vaft Advantage. Here is alfo a grand
Profpect of the Valley, Lake, and Bridge (which
I fhall hereafter mention) and other charming
Scenes in the Park.

The Palace of *Blenheim* is of Free-Stone, the
Front adorned with a grand Balluftrade, and many
excellent Statues ; it is extended to the Length of
Three hundred and forty-eight Feet from Wing to
Wing. The Architecture of it is various, noble,
and beautiful. Some Connoiffeurs have with
Juftice thought, that Sir *John Vanbrugh*, the Architect, was to blame in his having confulted
Multiplicity of Ornament, rather than Unifor-
mity of Defign. The South Front is towards the
Garden, and, in refpect to noble Simplicity, has
been thought to have the Preference. On the
Pediment of this Front is a fine Bufto, larger
than the Life, of *Lewis* the Fourteenth, taken
from the Gate of the Citadel of *Tournay*.

We entered this magnificent Building on the
Eaft Side, through a Portal built in the Manner
of martial Architecture, which led us into a Quadrangle, confifting chiefly of Arcades and Offices,
and from whence we paffed into the grand Area.
In the Center of the Front is a moft noble Portico, fupported by lofty and maffy Columns ; and
from hence we entered the grand Hall, which
reaches to the Height of the Palace, with a
Breadth proportionable. The Roof, which is
fupported by *Corinthian* Pillars, was painted by
Sir *James Thornhill*. The Piece is allegorical,
and reprefents the Duke of *Marlborough*, crowned
with Victory, who points to a Plan of the Battle
of *Blenheim*. In the Receffes between the Pillars
are

are placed fome excellent Cafts from the antique
Statues of the *Roman Slave*, the *Venus of Medici*,
the *Athletæ*, and *Saltator*.   Above thefe are the
Loves of the Gods.   Thefe Paintings were a Prefent made to *John*, Duke of *Marlborough*, by the
King of *Sardinia*, and are afcribed to the Pencil
of *Titian* ; but this is not allowed by nice Critics.
Notwithftanding which, the mafterly Strokes both
of Defign and Expreffion caufe them to be confidered as done from Sketches of that Mafter ; and
'tis certain they came from the *Venetian School*.
In the Arcades on the Right and Left, the Arrangement of Marble *Termini* is very fine.

From the Hall, we were conducted into the
Apartments on the Left.   In the Hangings of the
firft of which begins a Suit of Tapeftry, exhi-
biting the Victories and Atchievements of *Alexander* the Great, from *Le Brun*.   Thefe are, his entering the Tent of *Darius*, and his Converfation
with the *Magi* and *Diogenes*.   In this Room are
the Pictures of St. *Auftin*, when young, and Pope
Gregory; both done by *Titian*.   The *Woman taken
in Adultery*, by *Rembrandt* ; and *Mary of Medici*,
by Sir *Peter Paul Rubens*.   Here were two mafterly
Crayon-Pieces, which were removed by the Lady
Bolingbroke, Sifter to the prefent Duke.   In the
fecond Apartment are in the Tapeftry fome fine
Pieces ; the Subjects are *Claffical Allegory* ; and
here is a Picture of the *Holy Family*, by *Rubens*;
St. *Jerome*, by *Tintoret* ; and the late Duke at full
Length, by *Vanloo*.   In the Tapeftry of the third
Apartment, the Hiftory of *Alexander* is refumed,
being the Battle of *Arbela*, and the Defeat of *Po-
rus*.   In this Room is that celebrated and capital
Picture of *Rubens's Family*, done by himfelf ;
the Dutchefs of *Portfmouth*, Mrs. *Ellen Gwynn*,
and Lord *Strafford*, dictating to his Secretary, all
three

three by *Vandyke*. The Earneftnefs of the Speaker, and the Attention of the Writer, are fo wonderfully heightened by each other, that 'tis confidered as one of the principal Portrait-Pieces of that great Mafter. In the Fourth Apartment *Alexander*'s Battles are continued, with his Paffage of the *Granicus*, and clofed with his Entry into *Babylon*. In this Room is the Picture of *Rubens*'s *Wife*, and *Catherine de Medicis*, both by *Rubens*; and *Mary*, Queen of *Scots*, by *Vandyke*. Some have fuppofed this laft to be a Copy, or, at leaft, unfkilfully cleaned. The next Apartment is a curious Cabinet of eminent Mafters; among which is a *Holy Family*, the Offering of the *Magi*, the Angel directing *Lot* out of *Sodom*, the Flight into *Egypt*, an *Head*, and a Piece, which has little more than the firft Colouring, all by *Rubens*. A *Madona*, by *Carlo Maratti*, *Mary Magdalen*, by *Carlo Dolci*. Two *Madona's*, in different Attitudes, by *Titian*. *Herod*'s Cruelties, and Queen *Efther*, by *Paul Veronefe*. A *Head*, by *Hans Holben*. The *Paffage of the Red Sea*, by *Old Franks*. The *Deftruction of Troy*, by *Bruhl*. A *Holy Family*, by *Carracci*. Here are four fmall Pieces, and a Dutch Piece, by *Teniers*: And two fmall Pieces, by *Philippi Lowther*; with many other fmall Pieces. In the fixth Apartment, the Tapeftry begins with the Battles of the *Duke of Marlborough*. They are introduced by a ftriking Reprefentation of a Suttling-Booth, Foragers, a Battle, and a Siege. Here are the Pictures of *Chrift* receiving the Children, by a Scholar of *Rubens*. The Earl of *Sunderland*, by Sir *Godfrey Kneller*. And (which is a fine Piece, in the old correct Manner) *Dobfon*, an *Englifh* Painter, in the Reign of King *James* the Firft, with his Family, done by himfelf. The Tapeftry in the feventh Apartment reprefents the Battles of *Wynendale,*

dale, *Bouchain*, and *Oudenarde*, with the Siege of *Donawert :* And in this Apartment is a Picture of *Jupiter* and *Europa*, by *Paul Veronese*. The Countess of *Sunderland*, by Sir *Godfrey Kneller*; and a Piece of *Beasts*, &c. by *Bassan*. In the next Apartment are the *Three Graces*, cloathed; *Venus* and *Adonis*; *Silenus*, *Agle*, and *Satyrs*, &c. and the *Roman* Charity, all by Sir *Peter Paul Rubens*; and are astonishing Specimens of the Luxuriancy of his Pencil. Here is a Piece of *Ægyptian Foretune-Tellers*, by M. *Angelo Caravaggio*. Two Battle-Pieces, by *Bourguignon*; and six Landscapes, by *Wootton*. The Clock in the Corner of this Apartment is of excellent Workmanship; the Dial-Plate is enamelled : It stands upon a Pedestal of Mahogony, carved in exquisite Taste. It was brought from *France* by the Earl of *Sunderland*, Uncle to the present Duke.

Over the Door that leads into the *Saloon* is a Bust of the *Great Duke of Marlborough*, with a *Latin* Inscription. This Room in Breadth, Heighth, Furniture, and Ornaments, is agreeable to the Magnificence of the Rest. The lower Part is lined with Marble, on account of affording a cool Retreat in hot Weather.

The Walls and Cieling are painted by *La Guerre :* On the former are the different Habits and Modes of Dress in all Nations; and in one of the Copartments the Painter has introduced himself. The Cieling is an allegorical Piece, finely executed; it is a Representation of *Peace*, stopping the Duke in his Career; and *Time*, admonishing him of the Rapidity of his *own Flight*. In the Tapestry of the ninth Apartment, are the Battles of *Blenheim* and *Malplaquet*, and the Siege of *Lisle*. Here is painted two Hunting Pieces, by *Schneider*, and a *Dutch* Piece, by an unknown Hand. The Tapestry in the tenth Apartment completes the
Suite

Suite of the Duke's *Battles*, with the March to, and Siege of, *Bouchain*. Here are the Pictures of *Isaac blessing Jacob*, by *Rembrandt*. The Great Duke, by Sir *Godfrey Kneller*. And a Fruit-Piece, by *Michael Angelo*. In the eleventh Apartment (which, with those already described, completes the East and South Fronts of the Palace) are two Pieces of *Still Life*, by *Maltese*, and the late *Dutchess*, by Sir *Godfrey Kneller*.

Turning now to the Right-Hand, from these smaller, though magnificent Apartments, we were surprizingly struck, on our entering that most noble Room, which originally was intended as a Gallery for Paintings. Its Length is One hundred and eighty Feet; to which the Heighth and Breadth are proportionate. The Pilasters, with the complete Columns, are of Marble, and support a most curious, rich, and expensive Entablature. The Window Frames are very fine, and there is a Basement of black Marble quite round : Which, with the stuccoed Compartments of the vaulted Cieling, are all designed and finished in the highest Taste. I have observed, that this Room was intended as a Gallery, but 'tis now called the *Library*; for the late Duke, whose Taste for, and Encouragement of, Learning was conspicuous, furnished it with the grand Collection of Books, gathered by his illustrious Father, the Earl of *Sunderland*. They are about Twenty-four thousand Volumes ; and are perhaps the best private Collection in *England*. On the Tops of the Cases are placed *Bronzes*, and the Books are kept under gilt-wire Lattices. Here are a fine *Orrery* and *Planetarium*, placed by the late Duke. And at the upper End of the Room, is a Statue of Queen *Anne*, finely done, by *Rysbrack*, with this Inscription ;

To the Memory of Queen ANNE,
Under whose Auspices,
JOHN, Duke of MARLBOROUGH,
Conquered;
And to whose Munificence,
He, and his Posterity,
With Gratitude,
Owe the Possession of *Blenheim.*
A.D. MDCCXXVI.

Above the Book-Cases are these Paintings following · *Cartoons*, copied by *Le Bland. Lot and his Daughters*, by *Rubens*. A *Crucifixion*, by *Vandyke.* A *Dutch* Piece, by *Bassan*. A *Landscape*, by *Claude Lorrain:* And a View of *Antwerp*, by *Vanderhoot.*

We had now gone through the Body of the Palace, and from the Bow-Windows of this Room, the Prospect of the Water, and the Ascents and Woods beyond it, are extreamly fine.

The *Chinese Closet* is below Stairs. This Room is furnished (besides some beautiful and expensive Jars, collected by the old Dutchess) with an elegant Collection of *Dresden China*, sent to the *Great Duke* by the King of *Poland*, in Return for a Pack of *Stag-Hounds*. They consist of *Turenes*, Sets of *Plates*, and many *fantastic Figures*. The Colours are fine, and the Representations somewhat natural.

In the Chapel, which is one of the Wings to this Palace, is a noble Monument by *Rysbrack*, to the Memory of the *Great Duke* and his *Dutchess*. They are represented with their two Sons, who died young, as supported by *History* and *Fame*. And in the Basso-Relievo is represented the Taking of Marshal *Tallard*.

On the whole, the Gardens of this House, and its Furniture, of which the fine Marble Chimney-

Pieces are confiderable, exceeds the Expectation of any curious Traveller.

Some of the Offices are fo large, that they are capable of entertaining Three hundred Perfons, and the Out Houfes can conveniently lodge a Regiment of Horfe. The Gardens originally confift of upwards of One hundred Acres of Land: They are finely laid out, or rather augmented and improved by the late Duke. There is a noble Defcent to the Water on the South and Weft Sides, where the Flowering-Shrubs and other natural Beauties are charming; and the diftant Views are vaftly fine. Formerly there was an Echo acrofs the Valley, which, before the old Buildings were removed, would repeat fix Times.

The Afcent to this Palace is through a long and wide Avenue, over a Bridge of one Arch, after the Manner of the *Rialto* at *Venice*. It is One hundred and ninety Feet in Diameter, and coft Twenty thoufand Pounds. A fine Stream of Water falls into the Canal that runs under it. This was done alfo at the Expence of the old Dutchefs Dowager. And, in 1738, fhe caufed a Statue of Queen *Anne*, cut by the ingenious Mr. *Ryfbrack*, to be erected, in a Bow-Window of the Houfe, and, upon the Pedeftal, this Character of that Princefs to be written*;

    " Queen *Anne* was very graceful and majeftic in her
     " Perfon. Religious without *Affectation*. She al-
     " ways meant well. She had no *falfe Ambi-*
     " *tion*; which appeared, by her never complain-
     " ing at King *William*'s being preferred to the
     " Crown before her, when it was taken from the
     " King her Father, for following fuch Counfels,
     " and purfuing fuch Meafures, as rendered the
     " Revolution neceffary. It was her greateft Af-
         " fliction

* This is the Infcription placed by the Author of the *Tour* at St. *Alban's* in *Hertfordfhire*.

" fliction to be forced to act against him, even for
" Security. Her Journey to *Nottingham* was ne-
" ver concerted, but occasioned by the great Con-
" sternation she was under at the King's sudden
" Return from *Salisbury*.

" She always paid the greatest Respect to King *Wil-
" liam* and Queen *Mary*; never insisted upon any
" one Circumstance of Grandeur, more than
" what was established in her Family by King
" *Charles* II. though, after the *Revolution*, she
" was Presumptive Heir to the Crown, and, after
" the Death of her Sister, was in the Place of
" Prince of *Wales*.

" Upon her Accession to the Throne, the *Civil List*
" was not *encreased*. The late Earl of *Godolphin*,
" Lord High Treasurer of *England*, often said,
" that, from Accidents in the Customs, and Le-
" nity in the Collection, it did not raise, one Year
" with another, more than 500,000 l. a Year.

" She had no Vanity in her Expences, nor bought
" any *one Jewel* in the whole Time of her Reign.

" She paid out of her Civil List many Pensions
" granted in former Reigns, which have since been
" *thrown upon the Public*.

" When a War was necessary to secure *Europe* a-
" gainst the Power of *France*, she contributed in
" one Year, towards the War, out of the Civil
" List, 100,000 l, in Ease of her Subjects.

" She granted the Revenue arising from the First-
" Fruits to augment the Provision of the poorer
" Clergy.

" She never refused her private Charity to proper
" Objects.

" Till a few Years before her Death, she never
" had but 20,000 l. a Year for her Privy-Purse;
" at the latter End of her Reign, it did not
" exceed 26,000 l. a Year, which was much
" to her Honour, because it is subject to no Ac-
" count. And as to her Robes, it will appear
" by the Records in the Exchequer, that, in nine
" Years, she spent only 32,050 l. including the
" Coronation Expence,

She

" She was extreamly well-bred, treated her chief
" Ladies and Servants as if they had been her
" Equals.
" Her Behaviour to all that approached her was de-
" cent, and full of Dignity, and shewed *Conde-*
" *scension* without *Art* or *Meanness.*
" *All this I know to be true,*
" SARAH MARLBOROUGH.
MDCCXXXVIII."

In the principal Avenue before mentioned, at a
considerable Distance beyond the Bridge, is a prodigious large Obelisk, being One hundred and thirty
Feet high, on the Top of which is the Statue of
the Duke. On this Pillar, the following Account
is inscribed. It was written by Dr. *Hare,* formerly Chaplain to the Duke, and afterwards Bishop of *Chichester* *, who died in the Year 1740.

The Castle of *Blenheim* was founded by Queen ANNE,
In the fourth Year of her Reign,
In the Year of the *Christian Æra* 1705,
A Monument designed to perpetuate the Memory
Of the signal Victory
Obtained over the *French* and *Bavarians,*
Near the Village of *Blenheim,*
On the Banks of the *Danube,*
By JOHN, Duke of MARLBOROUH,
The Hero, not only only of this Nation, but of his Age,
Whose Glory was equal in the Council, and in the Field.
Who, by Wisdom, Justice, Candour, and Address,
Reconciled various, and even opposite Interests .
Acquired an Influence which no Rank, no Authority can give,
Nor any Force, but that of superior Virtue;
Became the fixed, important Center,
Which united in one common Cause
The principal States of *Europe.*
Who, by miltary Knowledge, and irresistable Valour,
In a long Series of uninterrupted Triumphs,
Broke the Power of *France,*
When

---

* The Author of the *Tour* says, " it is supposed to be written
" by the late Lord Viscount *B.*" Who this Lord *B* was, after
knowing the *real Author,* will not be thought worth an Enquiry.

When raifed to the higheft, when exerted the moft:
Refcued the *Empire* from Defolation,
Afferted, and confirmed, the Liberties of *Europe*.

Philip, a Grandfon of the Houfe of *France*, united
to the Interefts, directed by the Policy, fupported
by the Arms of that Crown, was placed on the
Throne of *Spain*. King WILLIAM the Third
beheld this formidable Union of two great, and
once rival Monarchies.—At the End of a Life,
fpent in defending the Liberties of *Europe*, he faw
them in their greateft Danger. He provided for
their Security in the moft effectual Manner. He
took the Duke of MARLBOROUGH into his
Service.

Embaffador-Extraordinary and Plenipotentiary
To the *States-General* of the *United Provinces*.

The Duke contracted feveral Alliances before the
Death of King *William*. He confirmed and improved thefe. He contracted others, after the Ac-
ceffion of Queen ANNE; and re-united the
Confederacy, which had been diffolved at the End
of a former War, in a ftricter and firmer League.

Captain-General and Commander in Chief
Of the Forces of *Great-Britain*.

The Duke led to the Field the Army of the Allies.
He took with furprizing Rapidity *Venlo*, *Ruremonde*,
Stevenfwaerc, and *Liege*. He extended and fecured the Frontiers of the *Dutch*. The Enemies,
whom he found infulting at the Gates of *Nimeg-
hen*, were driven to feek for Shelter behind their
Lines. He forced *Bonne*, *Huy*, *Limburgh*, in another Campaign. He opened the Communication
of the *Rhine*, as well as the *Maes*. He added all
the Country between thefe Rivers to his former
Conquefts. The Army of *France*, favoured by
the Defection of the Elector of *Bavaria*, had pene-
trated into the Heart of the Empire. This mighty Body lay expofed to immediate Ruin. In that
memorable Crifis, the Duke of MARLBO-
ROUGH led his Troops, with unexampled Cele-
rity, Secrecy, and Order, from the Ocean to the
Danube.

Danube. He faw; he attacked; nor ftopped, but to conquer the Enemy. He forced the *Bavarians*, fuftained by the *French*, in their ftrong Entrenchments at *Schellenberg*. He paffed the *Danube*. A fecond Royal Army, compofed of the beft Troops of *France*, was fent to reinforce the firft. That of the Confederates was divided. With one Part of it, the Siege of *Ingoldftadt* was carried on; with the other, the Duke gave Battle to the united Strength of *France* and *Bavaria*. On the 2d Day of *Auguft*, 1704, he gained a more glorious Victory than the Hiftories of any Age can boaft. The Heaps of Slain were dreadful Proofs of his Valour. A Marfhal of *France*, whole Legions of *French*, his Prifoners, proclaimed his Mercy. *Bavaria* was fubdued ; *Ratisbon, Augsbourg, Ulm, Meminghen,* all the Ufurpations of the Enemy, were recovered. The Liberty of the *Diet*, the Peace of the *Empire*, were reftored. From the *Danube* the Duke turned his victorious Arms towards the *Rhine* and the *Mofelle, Landau, Treves, Traenbach*, were taken. In the Courfe of one Campaign, the very Nature of the War was changed. The Invaders of other States were reduced to defend their own. The Frontier of *France* was expofed in its weakeft Part to the Efforts of the Allies.

That he might improve this Advantage, that he might pufh the Sum of Things to a fpeedy Decifion, the Duke of MARLBOROUGH led his Troops, early in the following Year, once more to the *Mofelle*. They, whom he had faved a few Months Months before, neglected to fecond him now, They, who might have been his Companions in Conqueft, refufed to join him. When he faw the generous Defigns he had formed fruftrated by private Intereft, by Picque, by Jealoufy, he returned with Speed to the *Maes*. He returned ; and Fortune and Victory returned with him. *Liege* was relieved, *Huy* taken. The *French*, who had preffed the Army of the *States-General* with fuperior Numbers, retired behind Intrenchments, which they deemed impregnable. The

Duke

Duke forced thefe Intrenchments with inconfiderable Lofs, on the 7th Day of *July*, 1705. He
defeated a great Part of the Army which defended
them. The Reft efcaped by a precipitate Retreat.
If Advantages proportionable to this Succefs were
not immediately obtained, let the Failure be afcribed
to that Misfortune which attends moft Confede-
racies, a Divifion of Opinions, where one alone
fhould judge ; a Divifion of Power, where one
alone fhould command. The Difappointment itfelf did Honour to the Duke. It became the
Wonder of Mankind, how he could do fo much
under thofe Reftraints, which had hindered him
from doing more.

Powers more abfolute were given him afterwards.
The Increafe of his Powers multiplied his Victories.
At the Opening of the next Campaign, when all
his Army was not yet affembled, when it was
hardly known that he had taken the Field, the
Noife of his Triumphs was heard over *Europe*.
On the 12th of *May*, 1706, he attacked the
French at *Ramillies*. In the Space of two Hours,
the whole Army was put to Flight. The Vigour
and Conduct with which he improved this Suc-
cefs, were equal to thofe with which he gained it.
*Louvain, Bruffels, Malines, Liere, Ghent, Oudenard,
Antwerp, Damme, Bruges, Courtray,* furrendered.
Oftend, Men, Dendermond, and *Aeth,* were taken.
Brabant and *Flanders* were recovered. Places
which had refifted the greateft Generals for
Months, for Years ; Provinces difputed for Ages;
were the Conquefts of a Summer. Nor was the
Duke content to triumph alone. Solicitous for
the general Intereft, his Care extended to the
remoteft Scenes of the War. He chofe to leffen
his own Army, that he might enable the Leaders
of other Armies to conquer. To this it muft be
afcribed, that *Turin* was relieved ; the Duke of
Savoy reinftated , the *French* driven with Confufion out of *Italy*.

Thefe Victories gave the Confederates an Opportunity of carrying the War, on every Side, into
the Dominions of *France*. But fhe continued to
enjoy

enjoy a Kind of peaceful Neutrality in *Germany.* From *Italy* she was once alarmed, and had no more to fear. The entire Reduction of his Power, whose Ambition had caused, whose Strength supported the War; seemed reserved for him a-lone, who had so triumphantly begun the glorious Work.

The Barrier of *France,* on the Side of the *Low Countries,* had been forming for more than half a Century. What Art, Power, and Expence could do, had been done to render it impenetrable. Yet there she was most exposed; for here the Duke of *Marlborough* threatened to attack her.

To cover what they had gained by Surprize, or had been yielded to them by Treachery, the *French* marched to the Banks of the *Schelde:* At their Head were the Princes of the Blood, and their most fortunate General, the Duke of *Vendosme.* Thus commanded, thus posted, they hoped to check the Victor in his Course. Vain were their Hopes. The Duke of MARLBOROUGH passed the River in their Sight. He defeated their whole Army. The Approach of Night concealed, the Proximity of *Ghent* favoured their Flight. They neglected nothing to repair their Loss, to defend their Frontier. New Generals, new Armies, appeared in the *Netherlauds:* All contributed to inhance the Glory, none were able to retard the Progress, of the confederate Army.

Lisle, the Bulwark of this Barrier, was besieged. A numerous Garrison, and a Marshal of *France,* defended the Place. Prince EUGENE of *Savoy* commanded, the Duke of MARLBOROUGH covered and sustained the Siege. The Rivers were seized, and the Communication with *Holland* interrupted. The Duke opened new Communications with great Labour, and much greater Art. Through Countries over-run by the Enemy, the necessary Convoys arrived in Safety. One alone was attacked. The Troops which attacked it were beat. The Defence of *Lisle* was animated by Assurances of Relief.

The

The *French* aſſembled all their Force. They marched towards the Town. The Duke of MARLBOROUGH offered them Battle, without ſuſpending the Siege. They abandoned the Enterprize. They came to ſave the Town. They were Spectators of its Fall.

From this Conqueſt, the Duke haſtened to others. The Poſts taken by the Enemy on the *Schelde* were ſurpriſed. That River was paſſed the ſecond Time, and, notwithſtanding the great Preparations made to prevent it, without Oppoſition.

Bruſſels, beſieged by the Elector of *Bavaria,* was relieved. *Ghent* ſurrendered to the Duke, in the Middle of a Winter remarkably ſevere. An Army, little inferior to his own, marched out of the Place.

As ſoon as the Seaſon of the Year permitted him t° open another Campaign, the Duke beſieged and took *Tournay.* He inveſted *Mons.* Near this City, the *French* Army, covered by thick Woods, defended by noble Intrenchments, waited to moleſt, nor preſumed to offer Battle. Even this was not attempted by them with Impunity. On the laſt Day of *Auguſt,* 1709, the Duke attacked them in their Camp. All was employed; nothing availed againſt the Reſolution of ſuch a General, againſt the Fury of ſuch Troops. The Battle was bloody. The Event deciſive. The Woods were pierced. The Fortifications trampled down; The Enemy fled. The Town was taken. *Doway, Bethune, St. Venant, Bouchain,* underwent the ſame Fate in two ſucceeding Years. Their vigorous Reſiſtance could not ſave them. The Army of *France* durſt not attempt to relieve them. It ſeemed preſerved to defend the Capital of the Monarchy.

The Proſpect of this extreme Diſtreſs was neither diſtant nor dubious. The *French* acknowledged their Conqueror, and ſued for Peace.

These are the Actions of the Duke of MARLBOROUGH,
Performed in the Compass of few Years,
Sufficient to adorn the Annals of Ages.
The Admiration of other Nations
Will be conveyed to latest Posterity,
In the Histories even of the Enemies of *Britain*.
The Sense which the *British* Nation had
Of his transcendent Merit,
Was expressed
In the most solemn, most effectual, most durable Manner.
The Acts of Parliament * inscribed on this Pillar
Shall stand,
As long as the *British* Name and Language last,
Illustrious Monuments
Of MARLBOROUGH's Glory,
And
Of BRITAIN's Gratitude.

We returned in the Cool of the Evening, and
my Fellow-Traveller entertained me with many
Particulars relating to this Country, which I may
hereafter communicate to you.

We arrived before Night, and in the Morning
mounted our Horses ; for he was resolved to take
another Ride with me.

A little beyond *Blechington*, we crossed the
River *Charwell*, which here creeps (if the Expression may be suffered) through a deep Bottom, and seems almost a standing Water. The
Bridge is a good one, but the Place where it
stands is gloomy enough. The high Road soon
brought us to a small River, very different
from the last, being a gentle Stream in a lovely
Vale.

From this Place we came to *Glimpton*, or *Glim-
ton*, upon the River *Glim*, which runs through
the Duke of *Marlborough*'s Park at *Woodstock* beforementioned, and then falls into the *Evenlode*,
which

* On this noble Pillar are engraven several Recitals of
Clauses of Acts of Parliament, which were made to do Honour
to this invincible Commander.

which difembogues itfelf into the *Thames* near *Yarnton*. At *Glimpton* lived Mr. *Thomas Tifdale,* who, in the Year 1610, by his Will, gave Five thoufand Pounds to purchafe Eftates, for the Maintenance of Fellows and Scholars, to be chofen from the Free-School at *Abingdon* in *Berkfhire*, into any College in the Univerfity of *Oxford*. They are now fettled in that of *Pembroke*. In this Village, where is a fine Seat and Park belonging to the Heir of the late Sir *Thomas Wheat*, are two or three indifferent Inns.

The next Place is *Enfton*; a large Village, fituate on the Side of a fteep Hill, at the Bottom of which is Part of the laft Stream that I paffed. This Place has been famous for its Mineral Waters. Between this Village and *Chipping-Norton*, is a good View of *Heathrope*, a Seat of the Earl of *Shrewfbury*. It is a fine Stone Building, to which Avenues are cut through the Woods.

I was now conducted by my hofpitable and very obliging Friend, through fome fequeftered, though delightful Lanes, to *Ditchley*, the Seat of the Earl of *Litchfield*. This Houfe is fituate between three and four Miles to the North Weft of *Blenheim*, which noble Palace, from this Seat, has a moft magnificent Appearance. *Ditchley* is built with hewn Stone, according to the true Rules of Architecture, and in an elegant Tafte. The South Front is extreamly beautiful, which, with the two correfpending Wings, command moft pleafing and extenfive Profpects. In the Center of the Front is the *great Hall*, a Room of excellent Proportion, and beautifully decorated. The Sides and Cieling are Stucco, in which there is an admirable Boldnefs. The Cieling was painted by the ingenious *Kent*, and reprefents an *Affembly of the Gods*. Two of the Compartments contain Pieces taken from the Story of the *Æneid*. The one is

Æneas

Æneas and his Mother, *Venus*, meeting in the Wood near *Carthage*; and in the other she prefents him with new Armour. The Sciences and Bufts of the Poets are here introduced as Ornaments, and in this Room is a good Statue of the *Venus de Medicis*. Over the Chimney-Piece, which is noble and lofty, is a good Portrait of the late Earl, painted by *Akerman*. We were next led into the *Mufic-Room*. This is a very elegant Apartment, and finely adapted to its Purpose. Here is a Picture of the Grandfather and Grandmother of the prefent Earl, and alfo thefe following; the prefent Earl of *Litchfield*; the two late Dukes of *Beaufort*; the late Sir *Watkin Williams Wynne*, and the Hon. Mr. *Lee*, both in Crayons, by *Hoare*. *Rubens* and Family, hunting; two Courtezans of *Venice*; a Landfcape, in which the prefent Earl and the Hon. Mr. *Lee* are introduced as Shooters; and three Hunting-Pieces. Thefe four laft were done by *Wootton*. In the *Dining-Room*, which has fimple Elegance in its Furniture, are the capital Portraits of *Henry* the Eighth, and Prince *Edward*. This Piece was produced by the Pencil of that high Finifher, *Hans Holben*, and is done with a Strength and Freedom not common in his Performances. In this Room is a Family-Piece of King *Charles* the Firft, with a Child (afterwards *Charles* the Second) at his Knee: This was done by *Vandyke*. Here is a Picture of Prince *Arthur*, and, in another Piece, Sir *Henry Lee*, with a Maftiff who faved his Life, both by *Johnfon*: The late Lord and prefent Dowager, in their Coronation Robes, by *Richardfon*, and *Vanderbank*: The Pictures of the Duke of *Monmouth* and his Mother: Sir *Charles Rich*, Sir *Chriftopher Hatton*, and four Portraits of the Brothers of Sir *Henry Lee*. The *Damafk Bed-Chamber* is ornamented with fine Tapeftry,

try, reprefenting Boys engaged in fqueezing Grapes, and other Sports, in which is great Juftnefs of Defign, and ftriking Expreffion. Here is a fine Piece of Admiral *Lee*, by *Vandyke*; the Queen of *Bohemia*, by *Johnfon*; and the Portraits of Lord *Teynham* and his Lady. The Furniture of the Bed, *&c.* is rich Crimfon Damafk. In the Hangings of the *Tapeftry Drawing-Room* are *Apollo* and the *Mufes*, finging and playing on their various Inftruments ; a Vintage, and Bacchanalian Scenes. The Paintings are the Countefles of *Rochefter* and *Lindefay*, by Sir *Peter Lely* , Sir *Francis Harry Lee*, by *Vandyke*; and Sir *Harry Lee* at full Length, in his Robes as Knight of the Gàrter, by *Johnfon*. From the Windows of this Room is a delightful Profpect, confifting of a fweet winding Valley, with a ferpentine Canal, over which is a beautiful Bridge in the *Chinefe* Tafte. The Profpect is terminated with a charming extended Declivity, decorated with Groupes of Trees. The Roof of the *Saloon* is ftuccoed in a rich, as well as elegant Tafte. The middle Compartment is *Flora*, with the Zephyrs. The Walls, which are painted with an Olive Colour, are alfo ftuccoed. In this Room is a fine antique of the Goddefs *Health* : It is about thirty Inches in Height, and was purchafed from the late Dr. *Mead's* Collection. On the Pedeftal is a Bas-Relief of the Head of *Æfculapius*, boldly cut. We were here fhewn a Medallion of a *fleeping Cupid*, about nine Inches in Diameter. In the *Green Damafk Drawing-Room* is a Chimney-Piece, done by the mafterly Hand of *Skeemaker*, and furnifhed with two fmall *Corinthian* Columns. In the Middle is a moft charming Landfcape, by *Wootton*. Here is a Table of *Italian Marble*, which is looked upon as a great Curiofity, having a greenifh Ground, interfperfed with white Veins. Over

Over the Doors are two expreffive Pieces, brought
from *Italy* : They reprefent Ruins, Rocks, and
Cafcades. In the *White Dining-Room* is a Portrait
at full Length of *Charles* the Second, and of the
Dutchefs of *Cleveland*, by *Lely*; the prefent Duke
of *Grafton*'s Great Grandfather, and Lady *Char-
lotte Fitzroy*, both by Sir *Godfrey Kneller*. Here are
two Tables of curious *Egyptian Marble*. The Cieling is ftuccoed in a correfpondent Tafte, and the
Decorations of the Wainfcot are gilt. In the *Velvet
Bed-chamber*, where the Bed and Hangings are of
rich figured *Genoa Velvet*, is another elegant
Chimney-Piece, by *Skeemaker*, and the Profpect
of a Ruin, by an *Italian*. The Dreffing-Table
here is much admired ; it was made in *France*,
of a dark-coloured Wood, inlaid with the Repre-
fentations of Boughs and Branches, in Brafs-
Work. The laft Apartment we were fhewn was
the *Tapeftry-Room* ; it is prettily ornamented in
the *Chinefe* Tafte. Here is a ftriking Piece of
Tapeftry, reprefenting the *Cyclops* forging the
Armour of *Æneas*. The other is *Neptune*, properly attended, delivering his Directions about
refitting a Ship, which has juft been wrecked.
Here is much fpirited Expreffion in the *Dolphins
Heads*, and the Sea Scape is extreamly delightful,
being finely fancied, and judicioufly finifhed. The
Chimney-Piece in this Room is of white Marble,
and highly finifhed. Over it is a capital Picture
of the Duke and Dutchefs of *York*, and their
Daughters, *Mary* and *Anne*. This was done by
Sir *Peter Lely*. The two fine Landfcapes over the
Doors were the Work of an *Italian*. Here is a
curious fmall Fire-Screen, done in beautiful Nee-
dle work, by the late Lady *Litchfield*. On the
Tapeftry which cover the Chairs, are Stories from
the Fables of *Æfop*. Confiftent with the Tafte
of this Apartment, here are two good *Chinefe* Figures,

gures, the one is a *Lady*, the other a *Porter* with a *Cheſt*.

Having thus viſited this elegant Seat, where Taſte rather than Splendor, Simplicity rather than Oſtentation, abound, I parted from my very obliging Companion, and directed my Courſe to *Chipping-Norton*, intending to ſee the inconſiderable Town of *Charlbury* at another Time.

Chipping-Norton is a large ſtraggling Town, ſituated upon the Brow of a Hill, looking towards the *Weſt*. Truth would be offended ſhould one ſay, that this Town hath any Thing agreeable as to itſelf : But I muſt obſerve to you, that here are many very pretty Women. It is a Corporation, governed by two Bailiffs, and other Officers : But has not ſent Burgeſſes to Parliament ſince the Reign of *Edward* the Third. The Market here is on *Wedneſdays*, and the Fairs on the 7th of *March*, the 6th of *May*, the laſt *Friday* in the ſame Month, the 18th of *July*, the 5th of *September*, the 8th of *November*, and the laſt *Friday* in the ſame Month. The chief Commodities are Horſes, Cows, Sheep, and Swine.

King *James* the Firſt erected a Free-School here, and two Almſhouſes have been built for the Uſe of the Indigent.

That wonderful Piece of Antiquity, called *Rollrich*, or *Rollwright*, near *Long Compton*, is not far from hence. I was conducted thither by Mr. *James*. It conſiſts of conſiderable large Stones, placed in a circular Manner, with one higher than the Reſt, which ſtands a little to the *Eaſtward* of the Circle. Theſe Stones are all ſingle, and without Architraves or Epiſtyles ; and there are only two of them that are more than four Feet high. Their Situation is upon an Eminence, and afford an Appearance that ſtrikes the Mind with Reflection. Some of our Antiquaries ſuppoſe it to be the Place where *Rollo*, the *Dane*, was inaugurated,

rated, after his Succeſs againſt the *Saxons:* And as the Word *Reich* ſignifies a *Kingdom,* their Suppoſition ſeems reaſonable; for it was a Cuſtom among the Kings of the North, to have as many Circles as Kingdoms. 'Tis conjectured, that the Electors ſtood upon the circular Stones to give their Votes; and that which ſtands out of the Circle, was the *King's Stolen,* or Seat, where their Monarch was crowned.

The People here have a Tradition, that when *Rollo* was met upon the neighbouring Heath by a Witch, ſhe told him,

> When *Long-Compton* thou ſhalt ſee,
> King of *England* thou ſhalt be.

On our Return to *Chipping Norton,* we paſſed to *Hoke-Norton,* or, as it is generally pronounced, *Hogs-Norton,* on account of the Inhabitants being a very churliſh and clowniſh ſet of People *.

This Place is famous for a furious Battle between the *Engliſh* and *Danes,* about the Year (according to *Florence* of *Worceſter*) 914, though other Writers fix it in 911, and 917. However, the *Engliſh* were terribly ſlaughtered. In this Neighbourhood are Barrows, which probably were caſt up on this Occaſion. The Manor here was given by the Conqueror to *Robert de Oily,* as a Reward for his Services in that Expedition. Of this Family I ſhall hereafter ſay more.

Mr. *James* is a judicious Perſon. His Knowledge of the World is conſiderable, and his Search after Antiquities laudable. He is a good Scholar, and a worthy Man. His Grandfather, who lived at *Burford,* was very intimate with Mr. *William Lenthal,* Speaker of the Long Parliament. He died,

---

* Inſomuch that a Proverb aroſe, and is ſtill applied to a rude, ill-bred Fellow, " He was born at *Hogs-Norton,* where " the Pigs play on the Organ."

West View of CANTERBURY CATHEDRAL.

died, and was buried in that Town. From this Gentleman Mr. *James*'s Anceſtor had the following Liſt of the Speakers of that Honourable Houſe, which he has preſented to me as a Curioſity.

SPEAKERS *of the* HOUSE *of* COMMONS,

In the particular Year of each King's Reign till the Uſurpation.

HENRY the Third.

Petrus de Mountfort 44

EDWARD the Third.

Scroope	6
William Treſſel	13
Sir Peter de la Mare	49
Sir Tho. Hungerford	51

RICHARD the Second.

Sir Pierce de la Mare	1
Sir James Pickering	2
Sir Joh. Goldeſborough	3
Sir Joh. Goldeſborough	4
Sir Richard Walgrave	5
Sir James Pickering	6
Sir John Buſhey	17
Sir John Buſhey	20
Sir John Buſhey	21

HENRY the Fourth.

Sir John Cheney	1
John Dorewood, *Eſq*;	1
Sir Arnold Savage	2
Sir H. de Rodeford	4
Sir Arnold Savage	5

Sir Will. Sturmy	6
Sir John Cheney	6
Sir John Tiptoft	7
Tho. Chaucer, *Eſq*;	9
Tho. Chaucer, *Eſq*;	10
Tho. Chaucer, *Eſq*;	13

HENRY the Fifth.

Will. Sturton, *Eſq*;	1
John Dorewood, *Eſq*;	1
Tho. Chaucer, *Eſq*;	2
Wal. Hungerford, *Eſq*;	3
Rich. Redman, *Eſq*;	3
Sir Wal. Beauchamo	3
Roger Flower, *Eſq*	4
Roger Flower, *Eſq*;	5
Roger Flower, *Eſq*;	7
Rich. Baynard, *Eſq*;	9

HENRY the Sixth.

Roger Flower, *Eſq*;	1
John Ruſſel, *Eſq*;	2
Sir Tho. Wanton	3
Rich. Vernon, *Eſq*;	4
John Tirell, *Eſq*,	6
Will. Allington, *Eſq*;	8
John Tirell, *Eſq*,	9
John Ruſſel, *Eſq*,	10

Roger

Roger Hurſt, *Eſq*; 11
John Bowes, *Eſq*; 14
Sir John Tirell 15
Sir John Tirrel 17
Will. Boerly, *Eſq*; 17
Will. Treſham, *Eſq*; 18
Will. Burley, *Eſq*; 23
Will. Treſham, *Eſq*; 25
John Day, *Eſq*; 27
Sir John Popham 28
Will. Treſham, *Eſq*; 28
Sir Will. Oldham 29
Tho. Thorp, *Eſq*; 31
Tho. Thorp, *Eſq*; 31
Sir Tho. Charlton 31
Sir John Wenlock 33
Tho. Treſham, *Eſq*; 38
John Green, *Eſq*; 39

EDWARD the Fourth.

Sir Ja. Strangwaies 1
John Say, *Eſq*; 7
Will. Allington, *Eſq*; 12
Will. Allington, *Eſq*; 17
John Wood, *Eſq*; 22

RICHARD the Third.

Will. Cateſby, *Eſq*; 1

HENRY the Seventh.

Tho. Lovel, *Eſq*, 1
John Mordant, *Eſq*; 3
Sir Tho. Fitzwilliams 4
Rich. Empſon, *Eſq*, 7
Sir Reginald Bray 11

Robert Drury, *Eſq*; 11
Tho. Inglefield, *Eſq*; 12
Edmond Dudley, *Eſq*; 19

HENRY the Eighth.

Sir Tho. Inglefield 1
Sir Robert Sheffield 3
Sir Thomas Nevil 6
Sir Tho. More 14/15
Thomas Audley 21
Richard Rich 28
Sir Nich. Hare 31
Tho. Moyle, *Eſq*; 34

EDWARD the Sixth.

Sir John Baker 1/1
Sir Ja. Dyer Knight 7

MARY.

John Pollard, *Eſq*; 1
Clem. Higham, *Eſq*; 1/1
William Cordal, *Eſq*; ib.
John Pollard, *Eſq*; 2/1

ELIZABETH.

Sir Tho. Gargrave 1
Tho. Williams, *Eſq*; 5
Rich. Onſlow, *Eſq*; 8
Chriſt. Wray, *Eſq*, 13
Robert Bell, *Eſq*; 14
John Popham, *Eſq*; 23
Puckering 27
Snag 31
Edward Cook, *Eſq*; 35
Yelverton

Yelverton 39

Crook 43

JAMES the Firſt.

Phelips 1

Sir Ranulph Crew 12

Sir Tho Richardſon 18

Sir Tho. Crew 21

CHARLES the Firſt.

Sir Tho. Carew 1

Sir John Finch

Sir Heneage Finch 1

John Glanvile, *Eſq*;

Will. Lenthall, *Eſq*, cho-

ſen *Nov.* 13, 1640, and

continued to be Speaker

during the Long Parliament.

This Mr. *Lenthall* is well known in the Hiſtories of thoſe Times , his Manſion-Houſe, as before obſerved, was at *Burford*. This noble Fabric, together with the Rectory and Demeſne of the Town, he bought of *Lucius*, Lord *Falkland*, for 7000 l. and there reſided till his Death, which happened on the 5th of *September*, 1662, when this, together with another large Eſtate, became the Property of his Son, *John*.

Although Mr. *Lenthall* did ſome Matters prejudicial to the Royal Intereſt, he was, in ſome Degree, inſtrumental in its Service ; particularly in carrying the Point for the Treaty in the *Iſle of Wight*, when it depended on his ſingle Vote. He broke the Abjuration, and endeavoured to procure the Reſtoration of *Charles* the Second, for which he obtained his Pardon, and was a Witneſs againſt *Thomas Scot*, a Regicide. He built a pretty Chapel at *Burford*, and was buried in the Church there, near his Wife, and her Father, *Sir Lawrence Tanfield*, Lord Chief Baron of the Exchequer.

The Names of the Speakers till the preſent Time, I ſhall hereafter mention, when I come to treat of *Lincolnſhire*.

L E T-

LETTER XXIV.

From *Perſhore*, in *Worceſterſhire*.

S I R,

THE Church at *Chipping Norton* is built below the Town, and is a good Fabric. On
many of the old Braſſes over Monuments here
many Perſons are called Merchants. Near this
Building I croſſed a Stream which falls into the
Evenlode ; and paſſed thro' a good Country, where
a ſquare Building is erected, to ſhew that the four
Counties of *Worceſter*, *Warwick*, *Oxford*, and
Glouceſter meet in that Place ; being near to one
of the firſt Springs of the *Evenlode* River. I now
entered the laſt mentioned County, and ſoon came
to *Morton-in-Marſh*, or, as vulgarly called, *Morton
Hindmoſt*. This Place had formerly a Market,
which is now diſuſed. 'Tis a large ſtraggling
Village, whoſe Situation is low, and in its Neighbourhood are many excellent Paſtures. The *Roman* Foſſway paſſes from *Leamington* through this
Place to *Stow* in the *Would*. Here is no Church,
but a Chapel belong to the Pariſh of *Beurton*, in
which this Village lies. In this Chapel are ſome
Inſcriptions regarding the *Creſwick* Family.

This Manor, in the Time of the Conqueror,
was held by one *Auſfred* of *Corneille*, in whoſe
Family it continued long ; but in the Reign of
Henry the Third, it came to the Abbey of *Weſt-
miniſter*, and is now enjoyed by the Dean and
Chapter of that Collegiate Church.

From hence there is a continued Aſcent to a
Village called *Morton-on-the-Hill* ; this Place is
very pleaſant, having a fine View towards the Eaſt.

I had

I had scarce left this Village, when I found myself on the Top of *Broadway Downs*, a large Tract of Land, that feeds a great Number of Sheep, whose Wool, I am informed, is not inferior to that of *Cotswould*. At some Distance, on my Right-Hand, I had the Town of *Campden*, and, on my Left, *Toddington*, a Seat of the *Traceys*.

These Downs have been very troublesome to Travellers in the Winter-Season; but that Grievance is now about to be redressed, many Hands being employed here in making a Turnpike Road. After travelling about seven Miles upon these Downs, I came to an Inn, where is a neat Bowling-Green, and one of the finest Prospects perhaps in the Universe; for in the Bottom lies the famous Vale of *Evesham*, which both for Beauty and Fruitfulness, by far excels even the excelling Vale of *Aylesbury*.

The late Mr. *Somervile* has thus described this Spot;

> In that rich Vale, where with *Dobunian* Fields
> *Cornavian* Borders meet, far fam'd of old
> For *Montfort*'s hapless Fate, undaunted Earl!
> Where, from her fruitful Urn, *Avona* pours
> Her kindly Torrent on the thirsty Glebe,
> And pillages the Hills t' enrich the Plains
> On whose luxuriant Banks, Flow'rs of all Hues
> Start up spontaneous; and the teeming Soil,
> With hasty Shoots, prevents its Owner's Pray'r:
> The pamper'd, wanton Steer, of the sharp Axe
> Regardless, that o'er his devoted Head
> Hangs menacing, crops his delicious Bane,
> Nor knows the Price is Life; with envious Eye,
> His lab'ring Yoke-Fellow beholds his Plight,
> And deems him blest, while, on his languid Neck,
> In solemn Sloth, he tugs the ling'ring Plough.
> So blind are Mortals, of each other's State
> Mis-judging, self-deceiv'd!

Those

Thofe who have never feen the fine Counties of *Worcefter* and *Warwick*, can have but faint Ideas of this Profpeƈt ; efpecially when one comes a little nearer to the Declivity of *Broadway Hill*.

The Hills of *Breodun* and *Malvern* on the Right, and thofe of *Woodberry* and *Abberly* (all in *Worcefterfhire*) in the Front; and beyond the latter, the *Clee Hills*, in the South of *Shropfhire*; together with *Clent* and *Baffet Hills*, in the firft of thefe Counties ; I fay, all thefe ftupendous Mounts not only ferve to enhance the Appearance of *Evefham Vale* in *Worcefterfhire*, and that in *Warwick-fhire*, called the *Vale of Red Horfe*; but alfo to add, if it were poffible, additional Charms to the Waters of the ftately *Severn*, and the gentle Stream of the delicious *Avon*. The numerous Towns, Villages and Farms here prefented to the View, are both beyond Conception, and out of the Power of all Defcription.

After defcending this Hill, which is very fteep, and at whofe Bottom is a fine Spring of Water, I came to the large Village of *Broadway*, a Place of trifling Note : At the Eaft End of this Village the *Vale of Evefham* begins. Formerly the *London* Road acrofs this luxuriant Spot, was fo extreamly bad, that twenty Horfes were frequently infufficient to draw a common loaded Waggon ; whereas now, owing to the Turnpike Scheme, there is fcarce a more excellent Road in *England*.

The prodigious Crops of Grain now waving in this delicious Vale muft give Exultation to the Heart, even of the moft town-bred Traveller. Joyous, buxom *Mirth* here trips o'er the jocund Field ! and fweet, all-pleafing *Contentment* fmiles at the Farmer's Door ! The rofy Face of *Health* confronts the meridian Sun, and plain, unaffeƈted *Friendfhip* dances in the beechen Bowl. *Induftry* rifes with the melodious Lark, and Life-preferving *Temperance* attends at their Evening Regale. *Frugality,*

gality adorns the Manſion of the Huſbandman, while thrice-beauteous *Honeſty* holds forth the compenſating Crown. *Drayton* ſays,

> Great *Ev'ſham*'s fertile Glebe what Tongue hath not extoll'd ?

Having travelled about three Miles in this incomparable *Vale*, I entered the County of *Worceſter* : And ſoon after came to *Bengſworth*, a large Village on the Southern Bank of the River *Avon*; from whence a Stone Bridge leads to the Town of *Eveſham*. This River by the *Romans* has been called *Avona*, *Aufona*, and *Antona* : It riſes in the County of *Northampton*, and runs almoſt through the Middle of that of *Warwick*, where it is augmented by many conſiderable Streams ; and leaving *Stratford*, falls gently down by *Bitford*, to this Place. The Navigation on this beautiful Stream is of great Benefit to this luxuriant Country, by cheaply carrying off the great Produce of its fertile Fields. The Town of *Eveſham*, by the *Latins* called *Eoveſum*, ſtands on its Northern Bank, and to which there is a pleaſing Aſcent from the Bridge. About the Year 702, or, according to *Dugdale*, in 692, *Egwin*, third Biſhop of *Worceſter*, who was of the Blood-Royal, having been driven from his See, went to *Rome* : Where he obtained a Grant of this Place, built a Monaſtery upon it, and was the Cauſe of its being, by *Kenredus*, King of the *Mercians*, and *Offa*, Governor of the *Eaſt Angles*, endowed with many extraordinary Privileges : In 708, was held the Synod of *Alne*, which was principally convened to confirm the Grants of Lands made to this Monaſtery. Theſe Endowments, beſides other Poſſeſſions, conſiſted of twenty-two Towns. To this Monaſtery belonged ſixty-ſeven Monks, five Nuns, three poor People, three Clerks, who had the

ſame

fame Allowance as the Monks, and here were fixty Servants. The Under-Offiers of this Houfe, fuch as Prior, Sub-Prior, Third-Prior, Precentor, Sachriftan, Celarer, &c. were appointed by the Abbot, with the Advice and Confent of the major Part of the Convent, in Chapter. All which Officers had their feveral Rents arifing from diftinct and feveral Places appropriated to their feveral Offices. This Houfe was dedicated to the Virgin *Mary*, and *Egwin*, fince called St. *Egwin*, became the firft Abbot : After whofe Death, fucceeded eighteen Abbots, till the Year 941, when the Monks were difperfed, and fecular Canons fubftituted in their room.

In the Time of King *Edgar*, A. D. 960, the Monks were again reftored, but two Years after his Death, in 977, they were expelled again. This Houfe and Eftate were afterwards given to a potent Man, whofe Name was *Godwin*, and fucceffively came into feveral Hands, till King *Ethelred*, in the Year 1014, made *Alfwardus*, a Monk of *Ramfey*, Abbot of *Evefham*, who was at the fame Time Bifhop of *London*. The Abbey, under this Abbot and his Succeffors, greatly flourifhed. In the Year 1174, *Waldemarus*, King of *Denmark*, gave and confirmed the Priory of *Othenefia*, in that Kingdom, as a Cell to this Abbey of *Evefham*.

The Monks were of the Order of St. *Benedict*, and the Abbots were mitred. That they fat in Parliament may appear from the Teftimonial of a Licence of Abfence in the Parliamentary Records*.

This

---

* " 25 H. VIII 7th *Jan* Literæ Procurat, in quibus Abbas de
" Evefham fub Reg grat abfens, atteftante Thoma Cromwel
" Arm. conftituit procur &c " Among the valuable Manufcripts burnt in the *Cotton* Library, were the following ; " *Ca-*
" lendarium;

This Religious Houſe, at the Diſſolution, was valued at One thouſand one hundred and eighty-three Pounds twelve Shillings and Nine Pence *per Annum**.

In *Auguſt*, 1265, here was fought a bloody Battle, between the Army commanded by Prince *Edward*, Son of King *Henry* the Third, and that headed by old *Simon de Montfort*, Earl of *Leiceſter*; in which the latter, with his Son *Henry*, was killed, and his Son *Guy* taken Priſoner, when the King, who had been a Priſoner, and carried from Place to Place, like a *Bajazet*, was delivered. Our Hiſtorians are circumſtantial in this Affair.

Near the two Churches which are in this Town, one of which is dedicated to *All Saints*, the other to St. *Lawrence*, ſtands an old Tower that belonged to the Monaſtery, from whence is a fine View of the Vale. On the other Side of the River is another Church, and formerly there ſtood a Caſtle, which, in 1157, the Abbot de *Audeville* recovered from *William de Beauchamp*. Owing to an Overſight of Prince *Rupert*, *Eveſham* was ſurpriſed by the Parliament's Forces in the Year 1645.

This Town, which is large and populous, is a very ancient Borough. It was governed by Bailiffs till the third Year of King *James* the Firſt, who, at the Requeſt of his eldeſt Son, Prince *Henry*, by a Charter, incorporated it, and alſo *Bengſworth*,

" *lendarium ; in quo benefaſtorum monaſterii Eveſhamenſis qui diebus*
" *illic ſignatis commemorantur, nomina oponuntur.*" " *Culendarium,*
" *in quo Obitus Abbatum Priorum, Fratrum & Benefaſtorum, iſtius*
" *Monaſterii adnotantur.*" "And *Nomina Benefaſtorum, Fratrum*
" *& Sororum viventium monaſterii Eveſhamenſis, ſcripta anno* 1444,
" *& anno* 1450."

* There is among the *Harleian* MSS in the *Britiſh Muſeum*, the Tranſlation of a Charter, whereby *Rodbert de Stadford* (or *Stafford*) gave *Worteſley* to the Monaſtery of *Eveſham*, A D. 1072, with Croſſes before the Names of the Witneſſes, after the *Anglo-Saxon* Manner 'Tis a very curious Thing.

with the Title of Mayor, Recorder, feven Aldermen, twelve capital Burgeffes, and a Chamberlain, who are all of the Common-Council; and
twenty-four other Burgeffes, who are called Affift-
ants. The Mayor for the Time being, and four
Aldermen, are Juftices of the Peace, and alfo of
Oyer and Terminer, and Gaol-Delivery, having
the Power even of trying and executing Felons,
and punifhing every Offence committed in the
Corporation, excepting that of High-Treafon.
In this Town is a large Manufactory of Woollen
Stockings. It hath a large Market on *Mondays,*
and will doubtlefs be a more thriving Place when
the great Road from *London* to *Worcefter* (for
which an Act is paffed) is carried through it,
which will be nearer than that through *Perfhore*
by at leaft three Miles.

The Fairs of this Town are held on *Candlemas-
Day, February* the 2d, the firft *Monday* after *Eafter,
Whit-Monday,* and *September* the 21ft, for Horfes
and Cattle.

Here is a Charity-School, being the Produce
of a Legacy of One thoufand Pounds, and another at *Bengfworth* (where thirty Boys are taught,
cloathed, and maintained) of twice that Sum;
which were both left by one Mr. *Deacle,* late of
St. *Paul's Church-Yard, London,* who was a Member of Parliament for this Borough.

This Town has had the Honour of giving the
Title of Baron to that great Perfonage, the Lord
Chancellor *Somers.*

Nothing can be more delightful than the Country appeared from *Evefham* to *Perfhore.* On the
Right-Hand, the gently-flowing *Avon* meandered
through the beautiful Meadows, and the Orchards of
Charlton, Fladbury, and *Piddle;* and, on the Left,
were the richeft Lands of this richeft Vale, teeming
with the pregnant Grain. Still farther on the
Left,

Left, arofe the lofty Hills of *Breodon*; where innumerable Flocks were grazing, and the Meads
on the River's Side decorated with an Immenfity of
Flowers. The Writer of a Poem in Honour of
this delicious River, has thefe Lines;

> Mild *Avon* drains her frugal Urn to feed
> The fwelling Bud, or cool the fmiling Mead,
> To lave the fleecy Flock, or kindly yield
> Her genial Moifture to the gen'rous Field;
> But fees gay *Plenty* follow where fhe flows,
> Pay the Swain's Toil, and fweeten his Repofe;
> Sees her green Banks the bleating Nations throng,
> Or tunes her Murmurs to the Fair One's Song,
> Who carrols, while fhe fills the balmy Pail,
> In feign'd Indifference to her Lover's Tale.

On my Way to *Perfhore*, I met with a Gentle-
man-Farmer, who would have quarrelled with
me, if I had not allowed with him, that Mr. *Samuel Foote*, who had a good Eftate hereabouts,
was the Battle Conjurer: Be the Schemift who he
may, it certainly was a fine Piece of Ridicule.
You remember *Trincalo*'s Words to *Caliban**.

Having parted from my Country Companion, I
travelled flowly through this *Britifh* Paradife, to
the Neighbourhood of *Perfhore*, which, together
with the Hundred, took its Name from the Abundance of *Pear-Trees* that fo greatly flourifhed here;
and at this Time of my Vifitation, they are loaded
with fuch Quantities of that Fruit, that without
the utmoft Care in the Owners, a vaft Number of

I i 2   Trees

---

* *Shakefpear*, in his *Tempeft*, when *Trincalo* finds *Caliban*,
makes the former cry out, " What have we here, a Man or a
" Fifh? Dead or alive? A Fifh; he fmells like a Fifh: A very
" ancient and fifh-like Smell. A Kind of, not of the neweft,
" *Poor John*; a 'ftrange Fifh! Were I in *England* now, as
" once I was, and had but this Fifh painted, not an Holiday
" Fool there, but would give a Piece of Silver. There would
" this Monfter make a Man; any ftrange Beaft there makes a
" Man. When they will not give a Doit to relieve a lame
" *Beggar*, they will lay out ten to fee a dead *Indian*."

Trees muſt be deprived of their Branches. Such a Sight as this to ſome *real Cockneys* would be almoſt as ſurpriſing as a *Bottle-Conjurer.* The ſweet, deſcriptive *Drayton* hath thus written;

The cheerful Nymphs,that haunt the Valley rank and low,
(Where full *Pomona* ſeems moſt plenteouſly to flow,
And with her Fruitery ſwells by *Perſhore* in her Pride)
Amongſt the charming Meads on *Severn's* either Side;
To theſe their confluent Floods full Bowls of *Perry*
    brought,
Where to each other's Health paſs'd many a deep-fetch'd
    Draught,
And many a ſound Carouſe from Friend to Friend doth go.

The Town of *Perſhore* alſo ſtands upon the North Side of the River *Avon,* over which is a good Bridge. The Town is not very large, but clean, and ſome of it well-built, and, as 'tis at preſent a great Thorough-Fare between *Worceſter* and *London,* it hath ſeveral good Inns. They have here alſo a Manufactory of Woollen Stockings. By the *Romans* it was called *Perſora,* or *Perſcora.* In the Reign of *Edgar,* a conſiderable Monaſtery was built here by Duke *Egelwardus.* But the greateſt Part of its Eſtate was afterwards transferred by King *Edward* and King *William* to *Weſtminſter.* Others will have it, that this Houſe was founded about the Year 604, by *Oſwald,* Nephew to King *Ethelred*; that *Oſwald* at firſt placed ſecular Canons here, which were afterwards changed to Monks ; then Canons reſtored, and then Monks again were introduced by *Edgar.* In the Year 1223, here happened a terrible Fire, in which all the Deeds and Charters of their Liberties were conſumed; and the Monks having for ſome Time left the Place, their Eſtate was uſurped by the Monks of *Weſtminſter.* This Houſe, at the Diſſolution, was valued at Six hundred and fortythree Pounds four Shillings and five Pence *per Annum.* Among

Among the Manuscripts burnt in Sir *Robert Cotton*'s Library, was one bearing this Title, " Li-
" tera certificatoria, missa ad *Willielmum*, Abba-
" tem Monasterii de *Perschore* in Diocesi *Wigo-*
" *mienssi*, de futura istius Monasterii Visitatione."
Here are two Churches almost contiguous to each
other, which formerly belonged to the Monastery,
but now are different Parish Churches, and are
dedicated to St. *Andrew* and *Holy Cross*. In one
of them is an Inscription to the Memory of one
Mr. *Haslewood*, and another to that of his Wife,
which is much to her Honour. The Market here
is on *Tuesdays*, and the Fairs on *Easter Tuesday*,
June the 26th, *Tuesday* before *All Saints*, and *No-*
vember the 1st, for Horses and Cattle.

About three Miles below this Town, the *Avon*
glides by the Village of *Strentham*, which is rendered famous by being the native Place of the inimitable *Butler*, Author of *Hudibras*. I am, Sir,
Yours, *&c.*

L E T T E R XXV.

From *Worcester*.

S I R,

HAVING passed the little River *Bow*, which
falls into the *Avon* below *Pershore*, I had
the Hills of *Malvern* at some Distance on my
Left, which have a pleasing Aspect from this flat
Country. In a short Time, I came within Sight
of the noble River *Severn*, and the delightful City
of *Worcester*.

This City is supposed to have been built by the
Romans, who called it *Branovium*; the *Britons*,
whom it was intended to curb, gave it the Appellation of *Caer-Wrangon*. In the Year 679 or
680,

680, King *Ethelred* erected it into an *Episcopal See*, and *Boselus* was the first Bishop. The Church was filled with the secular Clergy, till *Dunstan*, Archbishop of *Canterbury*, discharged them, and put Monks of the *Benedictine* Order in their Stead. *Offa*, *Edgar*, and other *Saxons*, had been great *Benefactors* to this Church. It continued long in a flourishing Condition, and at the Dissolution was valued at One thousand two hundred and twenty-nine Pounds twelve Shillings and eight Pence *per Annum* *.

In the Year 1041, King *Hardicanute* greatly distressed this City of *Worcester*, the Particulars of which are well related by *Guthrie*. Part of it was burnt down, and, in the Reign of *William* the Second, it was in some Degree subjected to the same Fate by the *Welch*. In the Wars between King *Stephen* and *Maud*, the Empress, it suffered extreamly; notwithstanding, in the Year 1139, that King, in his March to the Siege of *Ludlow Castle* (to which Place, as an Hostage, he was attended by the Prince Royal of *Scotland*) stopped at *Worcester*, and offered his Ring at the High Altar, by Way of a votive Present. In the Year 1159, King *Henry* the Second, upon his Return from *Normandy*, together with his Queen, took a Progress to this City; where, being solemnly crowned, they came to the Oblation, and offered their Crowns at the High Altar, with a Vow never to wear those Crowns again.

In the Year 1651 was the last military Affair which affected this City of *Worcester* : For then was fought the definitive Battle between the

Royalists,

---

* In the Library at *Westminster* this Manuscript was burnt, " Literæ Alexandri Regis Scotorum ad Priorem & Conventum " Coenobii Wigorniensis ; in quibus gratias agit pro munere " quodam, .h. e. si conjecturam facere licet, quod admissus " fuisset in fraternitatis illius consortium."

Royalifts, commanded by *Charles* the Second, and the famous *Oliver Cromwell*; in which the latter gained a complete Victory, and from which the King with much Difficulty efcaped through St. *Martin*'s Gate, but *Cromwell* ftaid to fee the Walls laid level with the Ground.

The City of *Worcefter*, which is fituate upon the Eaftern Banks of the noble River *Severn*, is one of the beft built, genteel, and agreeable Places in the whole Kingdom. From the Cathedral, the High-Street, which is extreamly handfome, and in which ftands the *Guildhall* (a very large, modern Building, though the Statues are wretched) runs Northward to the End of the *Forgate-ftreet*, which is large, fpacious, and elegant : So that in a ftrait Line, I have not met with any Thing like it out of *London*. The Shops in thefe, as in the *Broad-Street*, and many others, are large, and furnifhed like thofe in *Cheapfide*, or the *Strand*; and here is a great Deal of Bufinefs done in the wholefale Way.

This City is a County of itfelf, divided into feven Wards, and is governed by a Mayor, fix Aldermen (who are Juftices of the Peace) two Sheriffs, a Common-Council of forty-eight, two Chamberlains, a Recorder (at prefent *John*, Lord *Ward*) a Town-Clerk, two Coroners, a Sword-Bearer, thirteen Conftables, and four Serjeants at Mace. The chief Manufactories of this Place are Gloves and burying Crapes. It had formerly a good one of Woollen Cloths, but that is gone to the Southward, where Labour is cheaper*.

How-

---

* The Compiler of the *Tour* has the following Words, which manifeftly demonftrate that he is perfonally a Stranger to *Worcefter*. "The Inhabitants are generally efteemed rich, being "full of Bufinefs, occafioned chiefly by the Cloathing Trade, " of which the City and the Country round carry on a great "Share,

However, owing to its Situation on the *Severn*, and other Advantages, *Worcester* is a brilliant City. The Markets, which are on *Wednesdays, Fridays,* and *Saturdays*, are most plentifully supplied. The latter is a great one for Hops, which is the general Standard for the Price of that Commodity in the neighbouring Counties.

The Fairs are on the *Saturday* before *Palm-Sunday*, and *Saturday* in the *Easter* Week, both for Horned Cattle, Horses, and Linen Cloth ; and two others for Horses, Horned Cattle, Lambs, Cheese, Hops, and Linen Cloth, on *August* the 15th, and *September* the 19th.

The Cathedral here is after the Model of that which you have seen at *Brussels.* The Nave of this Church is very light, being lately edified, and the Choir of the Chapel on the South Side exhibits very curious Workmanship. Here was buried the turbulent King *John*, a Countess of *Surry* of the *Warren* Family *, and Prince *Arthur :* Upon the Monument of the last is this engraven ;

Here lyeth buried
Prince *Arthure*,
The first-bogotten Sonne of the Renowned
King *Henry* the Seaventhe.
Which noble Prince
Departed out of this transitory Life at the
Castell of *Ludlowe*,
In the seaventeenthe Yeere of his Father's
Raygne ;
And in the Yeere of our Lord God 1502.

In

" Share, as well for the *Turky* as the Home Trade. The
" Number of Hands which it employs in this Town, and ad-
" joining Villages, in Spinning, Carding, Rowing, Fulling,
" Weaving, &c. is *almost incredible.* One Part of this Town
" is wholly possessed by *Welch* People, who speak their own
" Language, and are employed in this Manufacture."

* The Writer of the *Tour* erroneously calls this the Countess of *Salisbury*, who dropped her Garter at *Windsor*, when she was dancing before King *Edward* the Third.

Both the Church and Cloyfters are well arched
with Stone, and in very good Repair; the former
of which was done about the Year 1320, by *Thomas Cobham*, then Bifhop thereof. The outward
Walls being of a foft, reddifh Stone, of which
this Country abounds, were much mouldered,
when, about forty Years fince, the Chapter new-
cafed them, and rebuilt the four Pinnacles on the
Top of the Tower, which is One hundred and
fixty-two Feet high. This Tower, in which are
eight Bells, is fituate in the Section or Middle of
the Cathedral, which is built in Form of a Crofs.
The Length of this Church from Eaft to Weft is
Three hundred and ninety-four Feet, of which the
Choir takes up an hundred and twenty : The Body and Side Ifles are feventy-four Feet. The
Height of the Vaulting from the Area of the
Floor to the Roof within-fide eighty-feven Feet.

The Cloyfters open through two Doors into the
South Ifle of the Church; the Square of them is
One hundred and twenty-four Feet, and they are
in Breadth fixteen Feet.

The Chapter-Houfe is on the Eaft Side : 'Tis a
large circular Room, whofe Diameter is fixty
Feet : It is arched at the Top, and the Arches
center on a Pillar in the Middle, which fupports
them all. 'Tis now ufed as a Library, and well
furnifhed with valuable Books.

The Refectory, or Monks Hall, joins to the
South Cloyfter, and is One hundred and twenty
Feet in Length, and fixty-four Feet broad. It is
now ufed for a Free-School.

In this Church, among thofe already mentioned,
is buried the Body of *Thomas de Lyttelton*, Lord of
Frankley, the famous Author of the *Tenures*, with
this Infcription;

Hic jacet Corpus *Thomæ Lyttelton de Frankley*, Militis de Balneo, et unius Jufticiarorum de Communi Banco, qui obiit 23 *Augufti*, A. D. 1481.

Here the learned Bifhop *Stillingfleet* was alfo interred, with a Character of him, written by Dr. *Richard Bentley* : And here alfo were depofited the Remains of the illuftrious Dr. *Hough*, tranflated to this See in 1717, with a very juft hiftoric Character.

This all-accomplifhed Bifhop was the ninety-ninth of this See.

This Church has a Dean, ten Prebendaries or Major Canons, ten Minor Canons, or Priefts Vicars, ten Singing Men, and as many Choirifters, a Mafter and Ufher of the Grammar-School, and forty Scholars, twelve Beadfmen, a Mafter of the Choirifters, who is alfo Organift, two Vergers, two Sextons, two Porters, two Cooks, a Manciple, and Caterer : In all One hundred and three.

Henry the Eighth, who founded this Bifhopric, in the thirty-third Year of his Reign, appointed the Prior's Houfe for the Dean, and other good Houfes to be made out of the conventual Apartments, for the Prebends. The Statutes of this Cathedral are fimilar to thofe of *Gloucefter*, which I purpofe to mention hereafter.

The pious and refolute Dr. *Hugh Latimer*, who was burnt in Queen *Mary*'s Time, Anno 1555, was Bifhop of this See ; as has been his Fellow-Sufferer, Dr. *John Hooper*, then Bifhop of *Gloucefter*.

Befides the Cathedral (which hath a difagreeable modern Building of Brick againft the North Side of it, and an offenfive old Gate, which hides it from the City) are eleven Churches at *Worcefter*, but three of them are without the City.

They are dedicated to *All Saints*, St. *Alban*, St. *Andrew*, St. *Clement*, St. *Helen*, St. *John Baptift*, St.

St. *Martin*, St. *Michael*, St. *Nicholas*, St. *Peter* and St. *Swithin*.

The Spire of St. *Nicholas* is very pretty. The King's School here was founded by *Henry* the Eighth, and has fent many good Scholars to the Univerfity. Here are many others for poor Children; and, among other Hofpitals, that erected by Mr. *Robert Berkley*, of *Spetchley* (which was a Donation of Six thoufand Pounds) is a noble Endowment. The County Hofpital here, called the *Infirmary*, is under a good Regulation, attended by able Phyficians and Surgeons, and is of great Utility to the City, and alfo to all *Worcesterfhire*.

This City has (among other Perfons) given Title of Earl to *Thomas*, Lord *Piercy*, Brother to the Earl of *Northumberland*; fo created by King *Richard* the Second, in the Year 1397. He was beheaded by *Henry* the Fourth, after the Battle of *Shrewfbury*.

To *John Tiptoft*, who had been Speaker of the Houfe of Commons: He was a Perfon of Abilities, and a great Favourite of *Henry* the Fifth, as may be feen in *Hollingfhead*; but was both created and beheaded in the Reign of his Son, *Henry* the Sixth.

To Sir *Charles Somerfet*, fo created in 1514, by King *Henry* the Eighth: It now gives the Title of Marquis to the Duke of *Beaufort*, whofe Anceftor was fo created by King *Charles* the Second.

Worcester is famous for *Florence*, a Monk here, who compofed a Chronicle of the World to the Year 1118, and died in the Year following: This Work is valued for its Correctnefs. And here was born the illuftrious *John*, Lord *Somers*, Baron of *Evefham*.

The City of *Worcester* is fituated in 2 Degrees 15 Min. of Weft Longitude from *London*, and its Latitude is 52 Deg. 15 Min. from the Equator.

I pur-

I purpofe croffing the *Severn* in the Morning, after which you may expect fome Account of that noble River, from, Sir, Yours, &c.

LETTER XXIV.

From the *Hundred Houfe*, in *Worcefterfhire*.

S I R,

HAVING paffed the Bridge at *Worcefter*, which is a very good one, built of Stone, and in fome Sort fupported by a Peninfula*, and turning to the Right, I found my Road very pleafant, having on my Left a pretty Rife, on which are many neat Houfes ; and on the other Hand, the beautiful *Severn*, flowing through a Variety of charming Meadows. On its Bofom were many Veffels paffing againft the Stream, to attain which, the Cuftom of drawing by Horfes, as in *Cambridgefhire*, *Effex*, and other Counties, is not ufed here, that Labour being performed by Men ; and, as like Chairmen or Soldiers, they ftep exactly together, it hath a very confiderable Power. Here I had the Pleafure to fee twelve or fourteen of thefe amphibious Fellows at a Diftance, in their Shirts, and a Veffel of perhaps eighty or an hundred Tons following them, laden with various Sorts of foreign Merchandize. Having paffed about a Mile, at a fmall Diftance from this noble River, I took a View of the City, which is vaftly fine. *Malvern Hills* had here an aerial Appearance ; and thofe of *Abberly* and *Woodberry* to the North, feem almoft as lofty. Among the former of thefe ftupendous Mounts, in the 18th Year of *William* the Fuft, one *Ald wine*,

---

* The Author of the *Tour* erroneoufly fays, it has a Tower upon it, faid to be built by the *Romans*.

wine, a Hermit, and his Brethren, began to erect a Monastery for *Benedictines*; to which House that King gave many Lands and Revenues. And *Henry* the First, by his Charter, in the Year 1127, granted and confirmed to them many Lands, Liberties, and Immunities. This House was a Cell to *Westminster*, and that of *Aucot* in *Warwickshire* was a Cell to this; which, at the Diffolution, was valued at ninety-eight Pounds ten Shillings and nine Pence *per Annum*.

One cannot think on the Confusion made by *Henry* the Eighth in this his Desolation of Monasteries, without wondering at the Passiveness of the People! Indeed it must be owned, that the reproachful and dissolute Lives then led in Religious Houses called loudly for Reformation, though perhaps not for the Diffolution of the Houses. Nothing surely could equal the Sloth and Debauchery of Monks and Friars in those Days, excepting their Illiterateness. Old *Robert Longland*, of *Shropshire*, in his Description of Sloth, makes his *Pierce Plowman* to speak satyrically in his Vision upon these Hills, which doubtless was levelled at all the Brethren of this Monastery at least. Such wretched Ignorance as he has depicted is scarcely to be equalled. The ingenious Mr. *Giles Fletcher* tells us of a *Russian* Bishop, whom out of Curiosity he examined, when he was there in the Service of Queen *Elizabeth*, anno 1588*.

These

---

* I think these are his Words. " What Learning there is " among their *Friars* may be known by their *Bishops*, that are " the choice Men out of all their Monasteries. I talked with " one of them at the City of *Vologda*, where, to try his Skill, " I offered him a *Russe* Testament, and turned him to the first " Chapter of St *Mathew*'s Gospel, where he began to read in " very good Order, I asked him first, what Part of Scripture " it was that he had read? He answered, that he could not

" well

These Hills of *Malvern*, which take their Name from two Villages built there, were formerly famous for Game : For I find in the Reign of *Edward* the Third, that the Bishop of *Hereford* excommunicated every Man who should hunt in his Woods, Parks, Chaces, or Warrens, in *Malvern*; and catch Hares, Pheasants, or Rabbits there. These Hills are now remarkable for an antiscorbutic Spring, which causes much Company to visit them. The ingenious and learned Doctor *Wall*, of *Worcester*, has wrote much in favour of these Wells, but his Account of their Operations on a Boy from *Leicestershire*, is so extraordinary, that, I must confess, it borders on the Marvellous. I shall now take my Leave of these lofty Mounts, with *Michael Drayton*'s Description ;

—— *Malvern* (*King of Hills*) fair *Severn* overlooks,
Attendant on his State, with tributary Brooks :
And how the fertile Fields of *Hereford* do lye,
And from his many Heads, with many an amorous Eye,
Beholds his goodly Site, how tow'rds the pleasant Rise,
Abounding in Excess, the Vale of *Ev'sham* lies.

My Road was now vastly pleasing through small Hamlets, embowered with Fruit-Trees, as Apples, Pears, Plumbs, Cherries, Walnuts, and also Hop-Gardens : Insomuch, that, I think, with great Propriety, this Country is termed the *Garden*
of

" well tell. How many *Evangelists* there were in the New
" Testament ? He said, he knew not. How many *Apostles*
" there were ? He thought there were twelve. How he should
" be saved ? Whereunto he answered me, with a Piece of
" *Russe* Doctrine, that he know not whether he should be
" saved or no ; but if God would *Poshallovate*, or gratify him
" so much as to save him, so it was, he would be glad of it ;
" if not, what Remedy ? I asked him, why he shore himself
" like a *Friar* ? He answered, because he would eat his Bread
" in Peace. This (continues Mr. *Fletcher*) is the Learning
" of the *Friars* of *Russia*, which, though it be not measured by
" one, yet partly it may be guessed by the Ignorance of this
" Man, what is in the Rest."

of England. Having travelled a few Miles, I came to a wide Tract, planted with many Walks of venerable Trees; near which is *Holt-Caſtle*, the Seat of the late Dowager Counteſs of *Coventry*. From hence I came to *Whitley*, the Seat of *Thomas*, Lord *Foley*, Baron of *Kidderminſter*, in this County, whoſe Father was ſo created in the memorable Year 1711. This Nobleman's Great Grandfather, from a very ſmall Beginning, acquired an immenſe Fortune by Iron Works ; inſomuch, that to be called *as rich as Old Foley*, became an Adage of this Country. He built and endowed a School at *Stourbridge*, in the County of *Worceſter*, which I ſhall ſhortly viſit.

The Houſe at *Whitley* is a ſmall Diſtance from the Road ; it is large, but rather inelegant : Yet cloſe to it is erected one of the moſt elegant Churches I have ſeen. This was done at the Expence of the late Lady *Foley*, who was alſo the firſt Perſon interred therein. Here are ſome Family Monuments, and the Paintings of the Church are extreamly fine.

About a Mile farther I came to the large and good Inn from whence this is dated. Here the Courts for the Hundred, Leet, and Baron are held, and behind it is a delightful Bowling-Green, to which there is an handſome Subſcription by the neighbouring Gentlemen. As this Houſe is ſituate under that lofty Mount, called *Abberley Hill*, it is much defended in Winter from the North Wind. Standing in the Bowling-Green, the higheſt Part of the Hill ſeems to hang almoſt over one's Head, and a little to the Left of it, in the Receſs of a lower Part thereof, embowered with various and lofty Trees, ſtands *Abberley-Lodge*, late the Seat of that Stateſman, Poet, Philoſopher, and accompliſhed Gentleman, *William Walſh*, Eſq; It

was

was here that he wrote his Poem, call the *Retire-ment*, which has this Beginning;

> All hail, ye Fields, where conſtant Peace attends!
> All hail, ye ſacred, ſolitary Groves!
> All hail, ye Books, my true, my real Friends,
> Whoſe Converſation pleaſes and improves!
>
> Cou'd one who ſtudy'd your ſublimer Rules,
> Become ſo mad to ſearch for Joys abroad?
> To run to Towns, to herd with Knaves and Fools,
> And undiſtinguiſh'd paſs among the Crowd?

Mr. *Walſh* was frequently viſited here by the Earl of *Oxford*, Lord *Bolingbroke*, and others his learned Friends: For at that Time *Abberley-Lodge* was one of the moſt delightful Seats in the Kingdom, and to which its Owner, in another Place, hath this Alluſion;

> *Sicilian* Muſe, begin a loftier Flight;
> Not all in Trees and lowly Shrubs delight:
> Or, if your rural Shades you ſtill purſue,
> *Make your Shades fit for able Stateſmen's View.*

But this *Olympus*, this Seat of the Muſes, is now greatly fallen. 'Tis inhabited by one *Dixon*, a Farmer, and nothing but a few Atchievements of Arms, a large Houſe in indifferent Repair, and the obſcure Traces of Gardens, with ſome Groves of Trees, remain to ſay, " Here lived *Walſh* !" A Perſon, whom Mr. *Pope*, in his Eſſay on Criticiſm, after Encomiums on the Duke of *Buckingham*, and Lord *Roſcommon*, thus juſtly celebrates ;

> Such late was *Walſh*—the Muſe's Judge and Friend;
> Who juſtly knew to blame, and to commend :
> To Failings mild, but zealous for deſert,
> The cleareſt Head, and the ſincereſt Heart.
> This humble Praiſe, lamented Shade, receive,
> This Praiſe at leaſt, a grateful Muſe may give.

Mr.

Mr. *Smart*'s *Latin* Verſion of this Paſſage is extreamly fine.

I have now both Inclination to Reſpite, and an Opportunity of ſending this directly; therefore ſhall end- it with my beſt Wiſhes ; and am, Sir, Yours, *&c.*

L E T T E R   XXVII.

‑From *Ludlow*, in *Shropſhire*.

S I R,

MY laſt, dated from the *Hundred - Houſe* in *Worceſterſhire*, ended with *Pope*'s Character of Mr. *Walſh* : From whoſe once Dwelling-Houſe, I followed a double Row of Trees, which leads to the Village of *Abberley* ; but turning to the Right, I attempted an arduous Taſk, I mean, that of aſcending to the higheſt Point of theſe lofty Hills, and, having attained it, had a moſt amazing Proſpect ; of which I ſhall ſet down a true, though imperfect Sketch. A little to the South-Weſt I had *Woodberry-Hill*, which is very high. Of this ſings *Drayton* ;

—— *Woodberry* ſo nigh, and neighbourly doth live
With *Abberley*, his Friend. ———
—— Both of good Account are reckon'd in the Shire,
And highly grac'd of *Teme*, in his proud paſſing by.

On the Weſt Side of theſe Hills flows the River *Teme*, which riſes in *Radnorſhire*, and having paſſed through the Towns of *Knighton*, *Ludlow*, and *Temebury*, or corruptly *Tenbury*, runs through a fine Country, called *Temeſide*, and falls into the *Severn* about three Miles below the City of *Worceſter*. Towards the South I had *Malvern Hills*, already ſpoken of, and alſo a fine View (over long and

L l   beautiful

beautiful Reaches of the laft-mentioned River) of the City of *Worcefter*: And beyond that to *Breodon Hills*, already noted, near *Tewkefbury* in *Gloucefter-fhire*. To the South Eaft I faw *Omberfley-Court*, the Seat of the Lord *Sandys*, near the Village of that Name, which gives to him the Title of Ba-ion. This Seat was built by his Lordfhip, and hath a fine Effect from *Abberley-Hill.*

This Nobleman is now Chief Juftice in Eyre North of *Trent*: And his eldeft Son (a Gentleman of an amiable Character) Member of Parliament for *Boffiney* in *Cornwall*. To the Eaft ftands *Hartlebury Caftle*, the ancient Seat of the Bifhops of *Worcefter*. In the Year 1645, it was a Garrifon for King *Charles* the Firft : But what has done the greateft Honour to this Place was, its being the Refidence of the venerable Dr. *Hough*, whofe monumental Character I have already mentioned: Notwithstanding which, I cannot forbear a Quotation from the prefent Lord *Lyttelton*'s Letter to Dr. *Ayfcough*, written before the Death of that illuftrious Prelate.

> Good *Wor'fter* thus fupports his drooping Age,
> Far from Court Flatt'ry, far from Party Rage ;
> He, who in Youth a Tyrant's Frown defy'd,
> Firm and intrepid on his Country's Side,
> Her boldeft Champion then, and now her mildeft Guide.

The confummate Goodnefs of this Prelate was tranfcendent : His Hofpitality and Benevolence were fuch, that he expended the Profits of his Bifhopric, but his Œconomy would not fuffer him to be in Debt. Beyond, or rather to the North-Eaft of *Hartlebury-Caftle*, I had a full View of *Clent Hills*, at whofe Bafe the new Houfe of Lord *Lyttelton* was very confpicuous. On the North, at a great Diftance, appeared that celebrated Hill, the *Wrekin* in *Shropfhire* ; and to the North-Weft, thofe called the *Clee Hills*, looked

very

very lofty. The Mountains of *Wales* terminate the Weſtern View. I thus have ſlightly touched the moſt ſtriking Objects; but were I to deſcend to the numerous Towns, Villages, Hamlets, Seats, Rivers, Plantations, and amazing Varieties which are to be beheld from this Spot, ſuch an Attempt might infringe upon my Time, and I fear would alſo greatly fail to ſatisfy your Mind.

The Village from whence theſe Hills take their Name ſtands on the Eaſtern Side, looking towards the *Severn*, and its copious and fertile Valley. The Situation is quite romantic.

Deſcending from my Height, near a Turnpike, I aſcended another of theſe ſtupendous Hills, which ſtands to the S. W. or rather W. S. W. From this Hill I had a fine View of the River *Teme*, and the ſweet Valley through which it flows, as alſo of the Hills and Woods which appear on its South-Weſtern Side, and beyond theſe the fertile Fields and Orchards of the matchleſs County of *Hereford*. On the Banks of this River is a charming Seat, called *Standford's Court*, the Dwelling of Sir *Edward Winnington*, Bart. Heir of the late Paymaſter of the Forces, and Son in-Law to the ingenious *John Ingram*, of *Bewdley*, in this County, Eſq; This Houſe is handſome, but the Situation is in a dirty, though plentiful Country

From hence I entered the Road which leads to *Tenbury*, and paſſing to the Village of *Stockton*, found the Country almoſt covered with Orchards, and Hop-Gardens, all in the moſt promiſing Condition. The Inhabitants tell me, that they expect the largeſt Crops from the former, they have known for many Years.

At this Village I was informed, there lately lived one Dr. *Walſh*, or, as the People pronounce it, *Welch* (perhaps of ſome Conſangui-

nity

nity with Mr. *Walſh* juſt mentioned) who left by Will an handſome Fortune to the well known Mr. *Gordon*, merely on the Suppoſition that he was the Author of a Work, called the *Independent Whig*; and ordered his Body to be buried in his own Garden, which was performed accordingly. From hence I purſued one of the worſt Turnpike Roads in *England*, through this fine Country, called *Temeſide* (that River being on my Left) to *Lindridge*; where, if poſſible, the Face of a general Garden was more obvious. At *Newnham-Bridge* I croſſed the River *Rea*, which comes from the *Clee Hills*, and, having paſſed by *Cleobury*, here diſembogues itſelf into the *Teme*.

This Country is not only famous for Hops and Cyder, for feeding fine Cattle, and the upper Lands for their Produce of excellent Wheat; but perhaps no Country can equal the Openheartedneſs of the Farmers, the Cleanlineſs and good Houſewifry of their Dames, the frank and friendly Behaviour of their Sons, or the natural Beauty, Simplicity, and Modeſty of their Daughters. Such have I found the Vale and Inhabitants of *Temeſide*.

Having rode a few Miles farther, I turned to the Left-Hand, by a large Wooden-Bridge, over the River *Teme*, into the Town of *Tenbury*, The Bottom of this River is here very rocky, which, though it has a ſtrong Current of Water, muſt cauſe the making of it navigable to be very expenſive. This Town, which the *Latins* call *Tenburia*, is but ſmall, though they have a Market on *Tueſdays*, and Fairs on the 26th of *April*, the 18th of *July*, and the 26th of *September*, for Horſes, Horned Cattle and Sheep.

The Situation is low, but very healthy; and Proviſions of almoſt all Kinds plentiful. Here is no Manufactory, or any Thing very remarkable: It

ſtands

ftands in the County of *Worcefter*, but the other End of the Bridge is joined to that of *Salop*. The River produces various Sorts of Fifh, efpecially Trout and Grayling, which are very fine.

Leaving this Place, I came to the Village of *Burford*, the ancient Dwelling of the *Cornwalls*, Barons thereof, who were defcended from the famous Prince *Richard de Cornwall* : But I do not find, that they ever fat in Parliament as Peers, till King *Henry* the Eighth at *Calais*, in the Year 1513, is faid to have conferred that Honour on Sir *Thomas Cornwall*, for his Bravery in the Expedition againft *Tournay*; but the Honour and Title are now extinct ; and, if he did fit in the Houfe, he was perhaps the only Perfon of this Branch of the Family who enjoyed that Privilege *.

The Country People here tell many Stories of the laft *Cornwall*, who was called Baron of *Burford*; whom they reprefent as a more athletic Perfon than the famous Wreftler, Sir *Thomas Parkyns*.

In the Church here, are feveral Monuments of this Family, particularly of the Lady of the aforefaid illuftrious *Richard de Cornwall*. The Manfion-Houfe, which is a modern and handfome Building, ftands on too low Ground to be agreeable in the Winter; but the Gardens are good, and at the Bottom of them runs the River *Teme*, which renders it a pleafing Refidence in the Summer Seafon. It now is the Property of *Humphry Bowles*, Efq; a Gentleman much concerned in the Glafs Manufactories in *London*.

From

* In *Spelman*'s Gloffary are thefe Words. " Sed villa Bur-" ford in comitat. Salop. reperitur per inquifitionem capt. anno " 40 Edw 3tii. tenere de rege ad inveniend. quinque homines " pro exercitu Walliæ & per fervitium Baroniæ, dicunturque inde " Domini ejus Barones de Burford . fed tamen in parliamenta " non proderunt."

From *Burford* the Road is extreamly pleafant to the Bridge of *Little Hereford*, where I again croffed this River: And continuing to a fine Seat, called the *Moore*, belonging to one Mr. *Salway:* (which is fweetly fituated, and is a charming Retirement) in a fhort Time I came to *Ludford*, the Seat of Sir *Francis Charlton*, Bart. who is Receiver-General of the Poft-Office. There is nothing very material here. From *Ludford* I next paffed upon the Bridge of that Name, once more over the *Teme*, and then entered the Town from whence this Letter is dated.

Ludlow, called by the *Welch Dinan*, and *Lystwyfoc*, i. e. the Prince's Palace, is fituate on a Hill, at the Conflux of the Rivers *Teme* and *Corve**, and is one of the moft agreeable Towns I have feen. The Streets are well laid out, and the Buildings very handfome, efpecially the *Broad-Street*, *Caftle-Street*, *Mill-Street*, and *Corve-Street*; the laft of which is very long. The Church (for though the Town is large, there is but one) is very beautiful. The Tower is lofty, and well built, in which is a pleafant Ring of Bells. In the Church are fome Monuments of thofe who were *Lords Prefidents* of the *Welch* Marches, and though the Body of Prince *Arthur*, as I have before faid, was buried at *Worcefter*, his Bowels were depofited here, where is an Infcription relating to his.

* Such a Geographer as the Author of the *Tour*, I have never yet met with. In the 333d Page of his fecond Volume are thefe Words. " The *Clun* meets the *Teme* at *Ludlow*, and both " united run to *Clebury*, a fmall Town on the Borders of *Worcefterfhire*; where it falls, as I mentioned before, into the Se- " vern." Every Word of which is void of all Truth For the *Clun* falls into the *Teme* at *Lantwerdine*, eight Miles to the Weft of *Ludlow* The *Teme* runs no nearer to *Clebury* than at *Newnham Bridge*, before fpoken of, which is diftant about fix Miles, and fo far from its falling into the *Severn* at that Place, that *Powick*, where it actually does difembogue itfelf, is at leaft twenty Miles from *Clebury*.

his Death. From a Walk in the Church-Yard, is a moſt charming View of the neighbouring Valley, called *Corve Dale*, through which the River of that Name having ſweetly ſtrayed, falls into the *Teme* beyond the Caſtle; the Courſe of which laſt Stream is thus deſcribed by *Drayton*;

—————— *Teme* they mightier make,
Which in her lively Courſe to *Ludlow* comes at laſt,
Where *Corve* into her Stream herſelf doth headlong caſt;
With due Attendance next comes *Ledwich* and the *Rhea*;
When ſpeeding as though ſent Poſt unto the Sea,
Her native *Shropſhire* leaves, and bids thoſe Towns adieu,
Her only ſovereign Queen, proud *Severn*, to purſue.

In the laſt Line but one this Poet was miſtaken, for the *Teme* riſes in the County of *Radnor*, as I have ſaid before.

Near to the Church, and fronting down the *Broad-Street*, is a neat Market-Croſs of modern Conſtruction; and, in the *Caſtle-Street*, a long Market-Houſe for Corn, over which are held the Courts of Juſtice; and there is alſo a very good Ball-Room. At the End of this Building is a Conduit or Reſervoir for ſupplying the Town with Water, which is thrown up by a Wheel after the Manner of the Works at *London-Bridge*. From hence is a bold Approach to the outer Gate of the Caſtle; which having entered, I was ſtruck with much Awe at the venerable Ruins of this princely Seat. It was built all of hewn Stone, and of a large Extent. Some of the Apartments are yet covered: The great Hall is a large Room, and here are ſome decayed Armoury, Hangings, &c. &c. of no Value; the reſt was taken away, *temp. Will.* III. and indeed the whole furniſhes one with a ſtrong Idea of its former Grandeur. From the Battlements is a fine Proſpect of the Rivers and adjacent Country; and from *Whitcliff*, an Hill on the oppoſite Side of the *Teme*, i the beautifulleſt Proſpect of the Town. The Caſtle was built by the famous

mous *Róger de Montgomery*; and has been confidered as a Place of great Strength ; witnefs the fruitlefs Siege of it by King *Stephen*. After the Birth of *Edward* of *Caernarvon*, it was generally the Refidence of the *Englifh* Princes of *Wales* ; efpecially of *Edward*, the eldeft Son of King *Edward* the Fourth ; and *Arthur*, the eldeft Son of King *Henry* the Seventh. The former of whom was, by the Contrivances of *Richard*, the wicked Duke of *Gloucefter*, hurried from hence to his Cataftrophe, and the other died on the Spot. *Henry* the Eighth eftablifhed here the *Court* or *Council of the Marches of Wales*, which had a fimilar Jurifdiction with the *Parliaments* of *France*. Thefe Courts had fubfifted perhaps from the Times of the *Saxons*, and by the Noblemen who had the Title of *Barones Marchiæ* was exercifed, within their refpective Liberties, a Sort of Palatine Jurifdiction. Our Hiftorians further tell us, that they had held Courts of Juftice to determine Controverfies among Neighbours, and pleaded Prefcription for feveral Privileges and Immunities ; among which this was one, that the King's Writ fhould not take Place in fome Caufes, but, if Difputes arofe between themfelves touching the Rights of their Baronies or Extents, they fhould be ended only in the King's Courts of Juftice. At the Coronation of *Eleanor*, Queen to King *Henry* the Third, the *Lords Marchers* claimed, and were allowed, their Right of providing Silver Spears, and fupporting the Canopy at that Solemnity. Thus they had long held thefe Courts in their refpective Jurifdictions : But when King *Henry* fixed them at *Ludlow*, he appointed a *Lord-Prefident*, *Counfellors*, a *Secretary*, an *Attorney*, and *Solicitor*, who, together with the four Juftices of *Wales*, were to adminifter Juftice to all the Inhabitants of the *Marches*. Among the Number of *Prefidents* in this Court (which fubfifted till

the

the Reign of *William* the Third) was the famous
Statefman, and Friend to his Country, Sir *Henry
Sydney* (Father to the illuftrious Sir *Philip*) a Perfon, whofe benevolent Heart was remarkable for
compromifing the Difputes between the People,
at his own Houfe in this County, and when he
had reconciled two Parties without Expence to
themfelves, would fay, " *Now is not this better*
" *than going to* Ludlow *or* London?" *John Egerton*, Earl of *Bridgewater*, was alfo Lord Prefident
here. At whofe Command, the incomparable
Milton wrote his *Comus*, which, for the firft Time,
was performed in this Caftle by three of the Lord
Prefident's Offspring, i. e. *John*, Vifcount *Brackley*,
the Hon. Mr. *Thomas Egerton*, and Lady *Alice Egerton*, and other Perfons of Diftinction. This was, I
think, in the Year 1734. And now I muft be ex-
cufed ten Lines from Mr. *Smart's* Prologue to the
Reprefentation of the Tragedy of *Othello*, exhibited about twelve Years ago, by Perfons of Diftinction, at one of the Theatres, for their Amufement.

When *Britain*, with tranfcendent Glory crown'd,
For high Atchievements, as for Wit renown'd,
Cull'd from each growing Grace the pureft Part,
And cropt the Flowers from ev'ry blooming Art,
Our nobleft Youth would then embrace the Tafk
Of *Comic Humour*, and the *Myftic Mafque*.
'Twas theirs t' encourage *Worth*, and give to *Bards*
What now is fpent in *Boxing* and in *Cards*.
Good Senfe their Pleafure—*Virtue* ftill their Guide,
And *Englifh Magnanimity*—*their Pride*.

This illuftrious Prefident died in the Year 1649,
and was buried at *Gadefden* in *Hertfordfhire*.

This Town, which is governed by two Bailiffs,
a Recorder (at prefent Mr. *Knight*, Son of the remarkable Mr. *Knight*, of *Bringwood)* * twelve Al-
M m der-

* A Perfon, who, from a low Beginning, by treading in the
Paths of Honefty and Induftry, acquired an immenfe Fortune,
which

dermen, twenty-four Common-Council-Men, and other Officers. They have a Power, diftinct from the County, of judging, condemning, and executing Criminals by Hanging, and, in Cafes of Treafon, that of Drawing and Quartering. *Ludlow* gives the Title of Vifcount to the Earl of *Powis*, and fends two Members to Parliament.

It is fo excellently fituated, that, like * St. *Edmundſbury*, it cannot be dirty; and though the former is not fo much vifited by Perfons of the firft Diftinction, yet as it hath more People of independent Fortunes in it, who are behind none for Tafte and Politenefs, I muft be allowed to give the Preference to *Ludlow*.

The Family of the famous Lieutenant General *Ludlow* were originally of this Place, which gave Birth to that able Artift, and accomplifhed Gentleman, Mr. *Cæfar Hawkins*, one of the Serjeant Surgeons to the prefent King.

The Market is on *Mondays*, where Provifions are very cheap, efpecially Fowls. The Fairs are on the *Tuefday* before *Eafter*, and *Wednefday* in *Whitfun-Week*, both for Horned Cattle, Horfes, Woollen and Linen Cloth, and Swine; and three others for the fame Commodities, and alfo Hops, on the 21ft of *Auguft*, the 28th of *September*, and the 8th of *December*.

On the whole, it is one of the moft elegant and genteel Towns in *England*, and perhaps the moft agreeable Place for Perfons of middling Fortunes. I am, Sir, Yours, &c.

L E T-

which he left among his Family. His Sons are very accomplifhed and worthy Gentlemen.
* The Writer of the *Tour* ufes thefe Words " It will be " no Wonder, that this noble Caftle (of *Ludlow*) is in the " very Perfection of Decay, when *we* acquaint our Readers, " that the prefent Inhabitants live upon the Sale of the ancient " Materials." This, I take upon me to fay, is falfe and ridiculous.

L E T T E R XXVIII.

From *Acton-Burnel*, in *Shropshire*.

S I R,

LORD *Orrery* obferves, that " Abfence is the
" Touchftone of Friendfhip. A Man of an
" unfteady Difpofition, fays he, flights and for-
" gets thofe when abfent, who were his darling
" Favourites when prefent ; but the Heart of a
" *firm and faithful Friend* is not to be altered by
" Time, Place, or other feparating Circumftan-
" ces." The Obfervation, Sir, was fully verified
in your laft Difpatches.

Ludlow is fo pretty a Town, that I left it with
fome Degree of Reluctancy. I had fcarce paffed the
Gate, called *Gawford's Tower*, which is ufed as a Prifon, when I faw before me the large Mountain,
called *Titterftone-Clee*, which I purpofed to afcend.
The firft Place of Note that I arrived at was the Hamlet of *Henley*, or *Henlegh*, fituate on the Banks of
the fmall River *Ledwich*. This Hamlet was formerly honoured with the Refidence of Sir *Edward
Lyttelton*, Knt. Chief Juftice of *North Wales*, and
Father to the famous Sir *Edward Lyttelton*, Lord
Lyttelton, Baron of *Mounflow*, and Keeper of the
Great Seal, in the Reign of *Charles* the Firft.
Thefe *Lytteltons* of *Henley* were lineally defcended
from *Thomas de Lyttelton*, the younger Son of the
famous Author of the *Tenures*, whofe Burial-
Place I have mentioned.

The Seat, which is large, and has good Gardens, became the Property of the *Powys's*, and
Sir *Thomas Powys*, who made himfelf remarkable
at the Trial of the *feven Bifhops*, in the Reign of
James the Second (being then Attorney-General)

fpent

spent his retired Hours here. He afterwards was a Juſtice of the Court of King's Bench, and is buried in the Pariſh Church of *Bitterley*, to which this Hamlet belongs. The Houſe, and a large improved Eſtate, now belongs to his Nephew, Mr. *Powys* of *Hardwick*, in *Oxfordſhire*. From *Henley*, the Road gradually riſes till the Entrance upon the aforeſaid Mountain, which the Inhabitants modeſtly call one of the *Clee Hills*. A new-made Road led me partly to the Right, and paſſing between the Heights on the Left, and a beautiful Valley on the South Side of the Mountain, I came to the Houſe of my reverend Friend, the Elegance of whoſe Entertainment could be equalled only by the Sincerity of his Friendſhip.

Upon my Departure, I aſcended to the Summit of the Mountain, where are the viſible Remains of a large *Roman* Encampment, capable of incloſing Fifty thouſand Men. On the Brow of this Mountain's Weſtern Side are large Stones, where the Country People ſhew you what they call the *Giant's Chair*; and add many fabulous Stories, too ridiculous to mention.

Looking towards the North, the Sight is intercepted by another Mountain, called the *Brown Clee*; which, by an Experiment of the Barometer, has been found to be about twenty-four Feet higher than this of *Titterſtone*. On the North-Eaſt I again ſaw the *Wrekin*, and my Proſpects to the Eaſt and South-Eaſt, in which appeared *Mawley*, a Seat of Sir *Edward Blount*, Bart. were vaſtly fine to *Clent Hills*, and thoſe of *Abberley* and *Malvern* before mentioned. To the South my View was bounded only by the Horizon: but that towards the Weſt I ſhall more particularly deſcribe. Under the Summit of the Hill lies the Village of *Bitterley* already noted; and beyond it, a little to the South, the Town of *Ludlow* had a pleaſant Appearance,

pearance. Facing me was *Stipperstone* or *Stitterstone Hill*, at a confiderable Diftance : 'Tis very lofty, and beyond it rife the Mountains of many Counties in *Wales*, *Pelion* on *Offa* piled.

The Author of *Poly-Olbion* thus mentions thefe Hills ;

The *Clees*, like loving Twins, and *Stitterstone* that ftands,
Tranfevered, behold fair *England* tow'rds the Rife,
And on their fetting Side, how ancient *Cambria* lies.

Towards the North-Weft, I could eafily difcern a Hill, which the *Britons* called *Kaer Caradoc*, now vulgarly called the *Quordock*. This, by fome of our Antiquaries, is fuppofed to be the Spot on which *Caradoc* or *Caractacus*, the famous *Silurian* Commander of the *Britons*, was attacked by *Oftorius Publius*, which unfortunate Defence put a Period to the *Britifh Liberty*. Though others fix it at the Conflux of the Rivers *Clun* and *Teme*, which is at *Lanterdine*, upon the Borders of *Radnorfhire* : This Place alfo is within Ken of the *Clee Hills*. Be the Engagement on which Spot it may, this is fairly owned by the *Roman* Writers themfelves, that the Behaviour of *Caractacus*, both in the Field with his Sword, and at *Rome* in Chains, was brave, intrepid, noble, and every Way worthy a General, who fought for the Blefling of Liberty ; and thus is he celebrated by *Drayton*,

Her *Caradock* (with Caufe) fo *Britain* may prefer,
Than whom a braver Spirit was ne'er brought forth by her.

This brave Commander, whofe *Britifh* Name fignifies in *Englifh*, *Beft-beloved*, was, you well remember, betrayed by the perfidious *Brigantian* Queen : And being fent to *Rome*, in the Year 51, addreffed himfelf to *Claudius*, (if our Hiftorians are to be credited,) in the following Manner, which gained him his Liberty ;

" Had

" Had my Moderation in Prosperity been ade-
" quate to my Family and Fortune, then had I
" entered this City rather as a Friend than a Cap-
" tive : Nor would you, Sir, have disdained an
" Alliance with a Prince descended from illustrious
" Ancestors, and the Chief of many Nations.
" My present Condition, to me dishonourable, to
" you is glorious ! I was Master of Horses, Men,
" Arms, and Riches : *No Wonder then I was un-*
" *willing to lose them.* For, though your Ambi-
" tion is universal, does it follow that all Man-
" kind is to submit to the Yoke ? Had I been
" sooner betrayed, I had neither been distinguished
" by Misfortune, nor you by Glory. And had I
" fallen, Oblivion had been the immediate Conse-
" quence of my Fate. But, if you now preserve
" me, I shall be an eternal Monument of your
" Clemency."

Speaking of the *Bards*, who conveyed down the
Descents of the *British* Heroes, *Drayton* has these
Lines :

O memorable *Bards* ! of unmix'd Blood, which still
Posterity * shall praise, for your so wondrous Skill,
That in your noble Songs the long Descents have kept,

From Hills I shall now lead you down to the Valley, which those on the Western Part encompass,
and this *Corve-Dale*; which I have mentioned in my
Account of *Ludlow*. In this Bottom, which is very
large, and consists of exceeding rich Land, are a
great Number of Gentlemens Seats, and agreeable
Villages, affording the most gratifying View imaginable. Among the Number of the latter is *Moun-*
slow,

---

* There is, among the *Harleian* Manuscripts of the late Earl
of *Oxford*, an Account of the Descendants from *Cradock*, or
Caradoc Vraith vras, with Arms. 'Tis in Number 1412, but
whether of Affinity to this Prince I know not.

ſlow, which gave both Birth and Title to Sir *Edward Lyttelton*, Lord Keeper, already ſpoken of.

He was born in the Year 1589, and, having received good School Inſtruction, was ſent to *Chriſt-Church* in *Oxford*, where he became *Batchelor of Arts*. From thence he removed to the *Inner Temple*, where he became ſo eminent in his Profeſſion, that in a ſhort Time he was choſen Recorder of the City of *London*. In the eighth Year of King *Charles* the Firſt he was Autumn Reader to his own Society ; and on the 17th of *October*, two Years after, he was by the King made Sollicitor-General, and knighted the 6th of *June* following. On the 27th of *January*, in the fifteenth Year of the ſame King, he was made Chief Juſtice of the Common Pleas ; and on the 23d of *January*, in the ſucceeding Year, his Sovereign conferred on him the high Honour of Keeper of the Great Seal ; and on the 18th of *January* following, created him Lord *Lyttelton*, Baron of *Mounſlow*. As the civil War broke out ſoon after, this Nobleman eſcaped to the King, then at *York*, in *June*, 1642, having firſt conveyed thither the *Great Seal :* And afterwards conſtantly, till the Time of his Death, attended his Royal Maſter. In *Auguſt*, 1645, he ended his Life at *Oxford*, where he had been Colonel of a Regiment of Foot, in which were liſted all the Judges, Lawyers, and Officers belonging to the ſeveral Courts of Juſtice. He was attended to his Grave at *Chriſtchurch* by all the Nobility then at *Oxford*, and alſo in a ſolemn Manner by his own Regiment : After which, a Funeral Oration was made over him, by the incomparable Dr. *Hammond*, then Orator of the Univerſity, and ſince the Lady *Anne Lyttelton*, his Daughter and Heir, has, in the ſame Church, erected an handſome Monument to his Memory. He was firſt married to *Anne*, Daughter of *John Lyttelton* of *Frank-*
ley,

ley, in the County of *Worcester*, Esq; by whom he had Children, who died young. His second Wife was the Lady *Sydney Calverly*, Widow of Sir *George Calverly*, of *Calverly*, in *Chesbire*, and eldest Daughter to Sir *William Jones*, a learned Justice of the King's Bench : By this Lady, he left one Child, whom I have mentioned. She was married to Sir *Thomas Lyttelton*, of *North Okenden*, in the County of *Essex*, Bart. The following Character is given of the Lord-Keeper by a good Writer :

" In the Year 1628, being a Member of Par-
" liament, he had the Management of the Charge
" against the Duke of *Buckingham*, concerning
" the Death of King *James*; in which Busi-
" ness he behaved himself with admirable Dif-
" cretion. His Name carried hereditary Credit,
" his Virtue authorifed his Nobility. His Ex-
" traction was great, his Parts greater! His Judg-
" ment was clear and piercing, his Learning va-
" rious and ufeful. His Skill in the Maxims of
" Government, and the fundamental Laws of his
" Country, fingular. His Experience long and
" obferving. His Integrity unblemifhed and un-
" biafed. His Eloquence powerful and majeftic,
" and of his Loyalty the World is a Witnefs."

After delighting my Eyes with this Valley, I alighted, reclined on the Turf for near an Hour, often repeating from *Dyer*'s *Grongar Hill*,

> Now, even now, my Joy runs high,
> As on the Mountain's Turf I lie;
> While the wanton Zephyr fings,
> And in the Vale perfumes his Wings;
> While the Waters murmur deep,
> While the Shepherd charms the Sheep,
> While the Birds unbounded fly,
> And with Mufic fill the Sky,
> Now, ev'n now, my Joy runs high!

This

This Mountain produces much Grafs for Sheep, and greatly abounds with Lime-Stone, Iron-Ore, and Pit-Coal: But how Mr. *Camden* came to reprefent it as producing excellent *Barley*, I cannot conceive: For the Soil is vaftly unfit for that Sort of Tillage, and indeed for almoft any other. His Continuator has, with much Judgment, changed that Word for Pit-Coal.

I now directed my Courfe due South, over the flat Part of this Mountain, which is pleafant enough in Summer, but, owing to the many Sloughs, muft be very difagreeable in the Winter Seafon. I foon entered a Lane at an Hamlet called *Hince*, which, together with the neighbouring one of *Dutton*, was the Eftate of the *Baldwins*, an ancient Family, but now belongs to the Lord *Craven*. From hence I came to *Coreley*, a fmall Village, where are many fine Plantations of Fruit-Trees and Hops; as are alfo at *Milfon*. I next came to *Neen-Sollers*, this Church-Living is in the Gift of the Heireffes of the late Lord *Coningfby*, of *Hampton-Court*, in *Herefordfhire*, whofe Anceftor, *John Coningfby*, Son and Heir of *Roger de Coningsby*, Lord and Baron of *Coningsby*, who lived in the Reign of King *John*, married *Margery*, Daughter and Heir of *Roger de Solers*, of this Village of *Neen Solers*, where formerly was a fine Family Seat, of which there are not now the leaft Veftigia. Probably where this Manfion ftood is now an Orchard or Hop-Garden, with which this Village abounds, and they are at prefent fo delighting to the Eye, that I left them with fome Unwillingnefs. Having croffed the River *Rea*, I rode to *Chekenhurft*, or, as now fpelt, *Shakenkurft*, and more erroneoufly called *Shakeminfter*, the ancient Seat of the *Meyfeys*. This is one of the worft Houfes, ftanding on fo fweet a Spot, that can be found. It is about a Quarter of a Mile from the River juft mentioned, upon a fine Elevation, commanding a Profpect more beautiful than can be imagined. The Woods, Lawns, and Plantations near it are wonderfully delightful, and the diftant Hills afford a moft charming Contraft. It belongs, together with an Eftate of about Fifteen hundred Pounds *per Annum*, to Mr *John Meyfey*, a Clergyman, who is Vicar of *Rock*, a Parifh at fome Diftance. In the Houfe are feveral good Family-Pictures, done by *Worlidge*. The Gardens might be rendered pleafing, were a filthy Moat, which almoft furrounds them, drained, and levelled. From this rude, uncultivated Place (where indeed fome winding Walks though the adjacent Woods were attempted, but with no great Tafte) I paffed to *Soddington*, the ancient Seat of the ancient Family of the *Blounts*, fo named, according to *Camden*, on account of their *Yellow-Locks*. One of the Anceftors of this Family, having married the Daughter and Heir of *William*, or rather *Ralph de Soddington*, became poffeffed of this Eftate and Manor. The Situation of *Sodaington-Houfe* is vaftly delightful, commanding moft extenfive Profpects over a charming Country, into the Principality of *Wales*. The Houfe ftands in a Garden, enclofed by a deep dry Ditch (over which are three Bridges) which formerly they could fill with Water. Indeed that which now is called *Soddington-Houfe* is no more than what was formerly called the *Dairy*, the reft having been blown up, or burnt down, by the Negligence or Unfkilfulnefs of fome of the Family, who were preparing Cartridges, or other Combuftible Matters, for its Defence. The Trees which grow on the Margin of the Ditch are venerably pleafing. In the Church of *Mamble* (in which Parifh this Houfe ftands) by the Side of the Communion-Rails, lies the Effigies of a Man at full Length, which the Inhabitants call *Ralph*

of

of Mamble ; but I am inclined to think it reprefents the aforefaid *Ralph de Soddington*, or fome other of that Family. Here, in a Chapel, or rather Burial-Place, are many of the *Blounts* interred, and Infcriptions to their Memories, but nothing expreffive of their Virtues or heroic Acts, though 'tis a very illuftrious Family. It is about a Mile from this Seat of *Soddington*, to *Bayton*, where is a fmall Church, dedicated to St. *Bartholomew*, and in this Parifh (where a worthy Clergyman, whom I fhall hereafter mention, was late Vicar, a Perfon whofe Memory I fhall ever revere) are many pretty Orchards and Hop-Gardens, that fweetly amufe the Traveller.

From hence I rode to an Iron-Forge, upon the River *Rea :* 'Tis a very good Work, and produces excellent Iron. Here is a good Brick Houfe, romantically fituated, with Gardens cut out of the neighbouring Woods, but now they are going to Ruin. Above this Forge, on the Eminence, is a large modern Brick Building, erected by the late Sir *Edward Blount*, Bart. which I have mentioned before. This Houfe is extreamly neat ; though 'tis not built according to the exact Rules of Architecture. The Spot on which it ftands commands Profpects into many Weftern Counties ; but the grand Front of the Houfe, before which is a Bafon, looks only to an Avenue or Vifta, through a Wood, towards the Foreft of *Wyre*. On the Left Hand, at a proper Diftance from the Front, is an handfome Pile of Offices, with a Cupola and Clock, but, for Want of another on the Right, has a very ununiform Appearance. On the Weft Side of the Houfe is a pleafant Bowling-Green, from whence is a Profpect of the River, which rolls fwiftly by the Side of the fweet Meads, underneath a fine Bridge confifting of one Arch. Beyond this appears the little Town of *Cleebury* or *Cleobury*, which ftands in a

Valley

Valley at some Diftance, having a lofty, though crooked, wooden Spire, and fix mufical Bells. And ftill farther the numerous Cottages upon the *Clee Hill*, which rife one above another, in a pleafing Manner, and are, at the Expence of the Owner of this Seat, wafhed white. I fay, the whole is fo exquifitely pleafing, that can fcarcely be fancied. On the Outfide of the Gardens and Bowling-Green, was enclofed a delightful Walk, with gentle Declivities, the Contrivance of one *Phipps*, an ingenious Perfon in thefe Matters. This has been thought one of the moft agreeable Walks imaginable ; but now, fince the prefent Owner's Deer have been removed from *Gawdy-Wood* near *Soddington*, a Paddock is formed here for them, and this fweet Walk is laid open to the Grazing of the Deer. The Grand Hall of this Houfe is large and handfome ; and the Staircafe is very noble. The Saloon alfo is a good Room, but the Furniture, Paintings, &c. anfwer not the Expectation of a curious Eye.

The Town of *Cleebury*, or *Cleobury-Mortimer*, is about a Mile from *Mawley* ; it confifts of one Street, Part of which is pretty well built, but the Market-Houfe is tumbling down. Here is indeed a Market on *Wednefdays*, but 'tis very fmall, and a Fair on the 2d of *May*, *Trinity-Eve*, *Monday* and *Tuefday*, and the 27th of *October*.

The Church here, which was dedicated to St. *Mary*, and before the Diffolution belonged to the Priory of *Wigmore*, is a Vicarage, in the Gift of Mr. *Baldwin*, of *Aqualate* in *Staffordfhire*. The Building is large, but very inelegant. In the Chancel, on a flat *Englifh* Marble, are the following Words, written by Mr. *Robert Edwards*, Rector of *Hopton*.

The Rev. Mr. *William Edwards*,
Late Vicar of this Church,
Departed this Life
Feb. 16, 1738, aged 77.   The

The Ritual Stone thy Son doth lay
O'er thy refpected Duft,
Only proclaims the-mournful Day
When he a Parent loft.

Fame will convey thy Virtues down,
Through Ages yet to come ;
'Tis needlefs, fince fo well they're known,
To croud them on thy Tomb.

Deep to engrave them on my Heart,
Rather demands my Care ,
Ah ! could I ftamp in ev'ry Part
The fair Impreffion there.

In Life to copy thee I'll ftrive,
And when I that refign,
May fome good-natur'd Friend furvive
To lay my Bones by thine.

In this Church a Lay-Deacon reads the firft Lef-
fon, both Morning and Evening, and officiates as
a Parifh-Clerk, notwithftanding there is one of
that Profeffion. The Tythes gathered by this
Deacon amount to about twenty-two Pounds a
Year. It is in the Gift of the Crown.

On the North Side of this Church is the entire
Form of a fmall *Danifh* Encampment; and near it
an handfome School, and Dwelling-Houfe for a Mafter. It is built of Stone, at the Expence of the late
Sir *Lacon William Childe*, who had been a Mafter in
Chancery, and died in the Year 1719, leaving
Three thoufand five hundred Pounds for this Purpofe, and fettling a yearly Salary of thirty Pounds
upon a Mafter, who teaches *Englifh*, Writing, and
Arithmetic to all the Children of this Town who
are fent to him. Over the Door of the Houfe is
this Infcription * ; Sir

* The Writer of this Work takes the prefent Opporunity of
returning his beft Thanks to that ingenious Mathematician, and
truly worthy Man, Mr *William Brown*, late Mafter of this
School (but now happily enjoying the Fruits of his Labours)
for his obliging him with the Copy of this Infcription, in the
room of another which is miflaid.

Sir *Lacon William Childe*,
Of *Kinlett*, Knight,
By his Will endowed this School.
The Building was erected 1740.

Below this School is a copious Spring, which the Inhabitants call *Burrall*, or rather *Burwell*. It is not indeed so large as that of *Holywell* in *Flintshire*, but it is so powerful, that, after it has served the whole Town, it, even in the Summer, turns a Corn-Mill by the Strength of its own Stream. In this Town stands a Grammar-School, built by the voluntary Subscription of the neighbouring Gentry, but without Endowment; and, on the Promotion of a Gentleman (whom I shall hereafter mention) to the School of *Kidderminster*, in *Worcestershire*, this began to decline, and is now disused.

This Town, in the Reign of *Edward* the Third, gave Birth to *Robert Longland*, or *de Langland*, who was bred a Priest, but being a Person of Wit and Learning, exploded some pious Frauds of his Brethren, and became a Follower of the ever-famous *Wickliffe*, the first Reformer, about the Year 1369. He then wrote the Vision of *Piers* or *Pierce*, the *Ploughman*, beforementioned. " Which " Discovery of the infecting Corruptions of those " Times (says Mr. *Selden*) I prefer before many of " the more seemingly serious Invectives, as well " for Invention as Judgment."

About half a Mile to the Eastward of this Town, *Hugh de Mortimer*, a considerable Baron in the Reign of *Henry* the Second, built on the Brow of an Hill, which hangs over the River *Rea*, a small Castle with hewn Stone, and round it, excepting towards the River (where there was no Necessity for it) cut a deep Ditch, which is yet conspicuous. Before me lies the Ichnography of this Building, which is called *Castle-Tcut*; it was taken under the
Direction

Direction of the late Master of *Cleobury-School*, by
which it appears to have been only fifty-four Feet
in Length, and forty-eight in Breadth ; though
the Walls were twelve Feet thick. The Remains
of this Fabric (which were very curious, being
built somewhat in a pyramidic Form) were lately
taken away by *William Lacon Childe*, Esq; then Lord
of the Manor, and Owner of the Spot, in order to
repair his Farmers Houses and Barns.

From this Place 'tis about four Miles to the Village of *Kinlet*, where stood an ancient Seat of the
Blounts, afterwards possessed by the *Lacons* and
Childes ; but the Gentleman who spoiled the Remains of *Castle-Tout* dying without Issue, it is become the occasional Seat of Mr. *Baldwin* of *Aqualate* beforementioned, who married his eldest
Daughter. The House is modern and handsome ;
'twas built about thirty-five Years ago. The Park
behind it is fine, the Top of which commands an
extensive Prospect. The Gardens have nothing
very pleasing, for Mr. *Childe*'s Taste was turned towards Regularity. The Church here is very neat,
especially within ; it is extremely well pewed, and,
in the North Isle, is a beautiful Alabaster Monument, raised to the Memory of the famous Sir
George Blount, who died in 1581. Here is another for Sir *John Blount* and his Lady, somewhat
defaced ; and a mural one for Sir *William Childe*
and Lady. In the Chancel is one to the Memory
of Sir *Lacon William Childe*, who endowed the
School at *Cleobury* ; and one for his Brother, *Thomas Childe*, with a good Character of him, which
he deserved. That on *William Lacon Childe*, Son
to Mr. *Thomas Childe*, tells us, that he was Lord of
the Manor, and died in 1735, and, modest as it is,
it says enough.

From hence I rode to *Sidbury*, the old Seat of the
Cresswells. It is now much on the Decline, and
stands

ſtands in a woody, though plentiful Country. In one Room here are ſome Family Pictures, among which is one of Mr. *Gervaſe Scroop*, of *Lincoln*. It was in this Room, that his Siſter had at Prayers the *Love Qualm*, which drew on a Paper-War between that Lady and her Kinſman, Mr. *Creſwell*, of which the Reading Part of the Public are not unacquainted.

I now bent my Courſe to *Aldenham*, or, as the Country People pronounce it, *Audnam*, the Seat of Sir *Richard Acton*, Bart. the Heir of a very ancient Family in this County, as is manifeſt from the many Places which bear their Name, as *Round-Acton, Acton on the Hill, Acton-Burnel, Acton Scot, &c.* This Gentleman is married to a moſt accompliſhed Wife, the Lady *Mary Grey*, eldeſt Siſter to the Earl of *Stamford*, by whom he has two Daughters.

The Houſe is large and handſome ; in it are many Family Pictures, and the Gardens are neat : But the prettieſt Improvements here are the Plantations at a Place, which is callad *Mount-Pleaſant*. Near *Aldenham* is *Morvile*, a Seat belonginging to the Family of *Weaver*, but 'tis not elegant.

From hence 'tis about three Miles, on a Turnpike Road, to *Great Wenlock*, or, as the Country People call it, *Much-Wenlock*, by Way of Diſtinction from *Little-Wenlock*, a neighbouring Village. In this Town of *Great-Wenlock*, *Milburga*, a Niece to *Wulpher*, King of *Mercia*, lived and died an Abbeſs. But neither *Camden* nor *Dugdale* tell us by whom it was founded. However, this Houſe came to Decay, when *Roger de Montgomery* rebuilt it for Cluniac Monks. The Church here was dedicated to St. *Mildred*. *Iſabel de Say*, Wife of *William Fitz-Alan*, was a great Benefactreſs, and the Priory was made *indegena* in the 18th Year of King *Richard* the Second, which, at the Diſſolution,

A View of Hagley Park from Thomson's Seat

tion, was valued at Four hundred and one Pounds and feven Pence *per Annum*. There are now much Remains of this Religious Houfe. *Camden* fays, that *Wenlock*, in the Reign of *Richard* the Second, was famous for a Copper-Mine, but 'tis now re-markable only for the neighbouring Quarries of Lime-Stone. This Town, which is dirty and in-differently built, fends two Member to Parliament, has a weekly Market on *Mondays*, and Fairs on *May* the 12th, *July* the 5th, *October* the 17th, and *December* the 4th.

From *Wenlock* I came to the Brow of an Hill, called *Wenlock-Edge*, this is a high Ridge of Land that is fimilar to *Chiltern-Hill* in *Buckinghamfhire*, and affords an extenfive View.

Having defcended, I left the direct Road to *Shrewfbury*, and rode through a rough Country to *Langley*, formerly the Seat of the *Leas*, an ancient and noble Family, when I had but a Mile more to that Village, which was rendered famous by a Par-liament held there by King *Edward* the Firft, on his Return from *Wales*, in the 13th of his Reign, I mean, *Acton-Burnel*. The Walls of the Building in which this Parliament fat are in Part ftanding, near the Houfe of Sir *Edward Smith*, Bart. Here the Laity granted a Thirtieth Part of all their moveable Goods, and the Clergy a Twentieth Part, by Way of an Indemnification to the King for his Expences in the late War. In this Parliament, fome of the *Welch* were pardoned, and reftored to their Eftates; while the King, to remunerate the Bounty of his Subjects, paffed the Law, which is ftill called the Statute of *Acton-Burnel*; and or-dained the *Statute-Merchant*, by which a Remedy was provided for the Recovery of Merchants Debts by Recognizances, in the three capital Ci-ties of *London*, *York*, and *Briftol*; that is, the

Debtor fhould come before the Mayor of either of the faid Cities, or before the Mayor and Clerk which the King fhall appoint, to acknowledge the Debt, and the Day of Payment, and the Recognizance fhould be entered in a Roll by the Clerk, who was alfo to make a Bill obligatory, whereunto the Seal of the Debtor fhould be put, with the King's Seal for that Purpofe provided : And if the Debtor did not pay at the Day, then the Creditor might come before the faid Mayor, with his Bill obligatory, and it fhould be levied of the Debtor's Goods ; and, if he had no Goods, his Body fhould be taken. The faid Statute further enacted, " that, if thofe who praifed, i. e. priced them, did it too high, they fhould be compelled to take them at their own Appraifement." It alfo further ordained, " that there fhould be a double Roll, one to remain with the Mayor, the other with the Clerk ; the Seal to be of two Pieces, whereof the greater Piece was to remain alfo in the Cuftody of the Mayor, and the other in that of the Clerk, and on Failure of Payment, the Mayor to commit to Prifon, on fhewing the Obligation ; and if the Debtor fold not enough to fatisfy in half a Year's Time, all his Lands and Goods were to be delivered to the Creditor by reafonable Extent, to hold them till his Debt was levied, and yet the Body to remain in Prifon."

Acton-Burnel (through which the *Roman* confular or prætorian Highway, called *Watling-Street*, paffes from *Roxeter* to *Cardigan* in *Wales*) is a large Village, where the Family of the *Burnels* lived ; from which Place I fubfcribe myfelf, Sir, Yours, *&c.*

LETTER XXIX.

From *Shewsbury*.

SIR,

THE ingenious Author of the *Rambler* has obferved, that *Curiofity* is one of the permanent
and certain Characteriftics of a *vigorous Intellect*; to
which every Advance to Knowledge opens new
Profpects, and produces new Incitements to farther
Progrefs. To apply this Obfervation to one's felf,
would favour much of one of the moft ridiculous
Paffions, that of Vanity. However, be the Source
of my *Curiofity* whence it may, I believe the Stream
of it will remain with my Life.

The Road from *Acton-Burnel* is tolerably good
to *Pitchford*, where there is a remarkable Well of
bituminous Water, from which the Place took its
Name. Here is a delightful Seat of one Mr. *Ot-
tley :* Leaving that Village, I paffed through a fine
Country to this charmingly fituated Town.

The firft Thing of Note on my entering *Shrewfbury* was the Church of St. *Giles*, which Parifh anciently was no Part of the Borough of *Shrewsbury*.
I next entered a broad indifferent Street, called the
Abbey-Foregate, that brought me to the Walls of
the Abbey, which was built by *Roger de Montgomery ;* who alfo erected the Walls round the
Town, and fortified it with the Caftle. This great
Norman (on whom the Conqueror, his Uncle, conferred the Honour of Earl of *Shrewfbury)* after
having built many Caftles, and enjoyed the greateft
Employments under the Crown, was at laft fhorn,
and lived and died a Monk in this Abbey, to whofe
Memory a Monument was erected in the Church,
which falling to Decay, is now repaired.

This

This Abbey was founded in the Year 1081 of the Order of the Canons of St. *Augustine* in *Canterbury**, and at the Diffolution was valued at Six hundred and fifteen Pounds four Shillings and three Pence †.

There are fome confiderable Remains of this Religious Houfe.

Leaving the *Abbey*, I paffed over the *Severn* upon the great Bridge (the other is called the *Welch* Bridge)· and entered into the Body of the Place : The Situation is extreamly delightful, being on a rifing Ground, encompaffed by the *Severn* on all Sides, excepting the North, where the Caftle ftands: So that the River forms a Peninfula in the Shape of an Horfefhoe. The Town is generally well built, though far from being regular. The Market Houfe is a ftrong Stone Fabric, where, and at the Green-Market, Provifions of all Kinds are very reafonable : And here alfo is a Market for the Woollen Manufactures of *Wales*. The Fairs are on *Saturday* after *March* 15, *Wednefday* after *Eafter* Week, *Wednefday* before *Whitfuntide*, *July* 5, *Auguft* 12, *October* 2, and *December* 12.

Not far from the Caftle formerly ftood a good School, which had been built by the Townfmen, and maintained long by their own Contributions, for which, fays *Camden*, *Thomas Afton*, the firft Schoolmafter, a Peifon of great Worth and Integrity, provided, by his own Induftry, a competent Salary : But Queen *Elizabeth* caufed it to be taken down, and built that fine Fabric as it now ftands. She alfo endowed it with a genteel Maintence for a

Head-

---

* *Dugdale* fays, 'twas that of St. *Bened.Ct.*

† That the Abbots fat Lords of Parliament, and occafionally by Proxy, may be feen by the following Words, taken from the Parliament Regifter. " An 3 H VIII 20 Die Parliamenti " Relat. eft quod Abbas Salop. gravi gravi infirmitate detinetur " quod hic intereffe requeat, & ideo conftituit procuratores " fuos Epifc. Covent. & Lichfield, & conirem Salop conjunc· tim & divifim."

Head-Mafter, and three Under-Mafters or Ufhers, who have handfome Dwelling - Houfes. The Buildings are large, efpecially the Library, in which is a good Collection of Books ; on the whole, it hath much the Appearance of a College *. The Mafters of this School (which has been the moft confiderable in this Part of *England*) have qualified a great Number of Gentlemen for the Univerfities ; for which the late Mr. *Hotchkis* was much efteemed.

From the Scite of the Caftle of *Shrewfbury*, which Building is ruinous, is a fine Profpect, having the *Severn* on the Eaft, Weft, and South, and a fine champaign Country towards the North. Not far from hence is the *County Infirmary*, which Fabric was erected for a Manfion-Houfe by the late Mr. *Corbett Kynafton*, a Gentleman of fpecial Note, defcended from the two ancient Families of thofe Names. This Hofpital is extreamly well managed, and confequently of great Utility to the whole County. The greateft Ornament of *Shrewfbury* is that beautiful Track called the *Quarry*. It lies on the South and South-Weft Sides of the Town, betwixt its Walls and the *Severn*, which here forms the Point of the Peninfula. This Spot is about twenty-two Acres of Ground, which fome Years fince (the late Mr *Jenks* being Mayor) was laid out in the delightful Manner as it now appears. In other Words, the whole, but efpecially the grand Walk fhaded with Rows of delicious Lime-Trees, that are planted next the *Severn*, which here glides with a Tranfparency beyond Defcription, is perhaps fuperior to any Thing in *England*.

Mr.

---

* At *Greenfhill* is another School-Houfe, built of the fame Sort of Stone, to which Place, in cafe of any contagious Diftemper, or other Caufe, the Mafter and Scholars may repair.

Mr. *Ambrofe Philips*, the beft Paftoral-Writer of our Times, who was born in this Town, hath this beautiful Lamentation ;

> Ah me, the While ! Ah me, the lucklefs Day !
> Ah lucklefs Lad ! befits me more to fay.
> Unhappy Hour ! when frefh in youthful Bud,
> I left, *Sabrina* fair, thy filv'ry Flood.
> Ah filly I ! more filly than my Sheep,
> Which on thy flow'ry Banks I wont to keep.
> Sweet are thy Banks, oh when fhall I, once more,
> With ravifh'd Eyes review thy amell'd Shore ?
> When, in the Cryftal of thy Water, fcan
> Each Feature faded, and my Colour wan ?
> When fhall I fee my Hut, the fmall Abode
> Myfelf did raife, and cover'd o'er with Sod ?
> Small though it be, a mean and humble Cell,
> Yet there is Room for Peace and Me to dwell.

Mr. *Philips* was of a good Family, and went early to *London*. The Excellency of his Genius was foon diftinguifhed by the Earl of *Dorfet*, at whofe Command he wrote his Paftorals. Mr. *Addifon*'s Character of his Works and Abilities is warm and friendly ; and Mr. *Walfh* thus mentions him,

> With *Philips* fhall the peaceful Vallies ring,
> And *Britain* hear a fecond *Spencer* fing.

Mr. *Pope* difliked him : He excelled in two Species of Writing which the former was not happy in, namely, *Paftoral* and *Tragedy*. His *Diftrefs'd Mother* is a Mafter-Piece. Like *Spencer*, he excelled in Paftoral ; like him alfo was fent to *Ireland* by the Government, where Mr. *Philips* had a very genteel Place in the Prerogative Office, which was continued to him till his Death : This happened when he had attained to a good old Age His two Sifters are now alive, as I am informed, and much refpected Ladies in this Town.

I now return to the *Severn*, which is by far the fineft River in *Britain :* For, though it is navigable
upwards

upwards of One hundred and fifty Miles, there is not one Lock or Flood-Gate from its Rise to the Sea. The first Spring is in a large Mountain, between *Machuntleth* and *Llanidlos*, in *Montgomeryshire*, called *Plinillimon Hill*: On this Spot also rises the River *Wye*, which, after running through *Radnorshire*, *Brecknockshire*, *Herefordshire*, and *Monmouthshire*, falls into the *Severn* Sea a little below *Chepstow*. The *Ridoll* likewise has its Source on the same Hill, and passing through the County of *Cardigan*, disembogues itself into St. *George's* Channel a little to the North of *Aberistwith*. Of this Hill *Drayton* thus sings;

> Next proud *Plynillimon* she plies,
> Where *Severn*, *Wye*, and *Rydoll* rise:
> With *Severn* she along doth go,
> Her Metamorphosis to show.

A little to the North of *Plynillimon Hill* stands that called *Moylvadian*, of which the same Poet adds;

> For though *Moylvadian* bear his craggy Top so high,
> As scorning all that come in Compass of his Eye;
> Yet greatly is he pleas'd *Plynillimon* will grace
> Him with a chearful Look; and fawning in his Face,
> His Love to *Severn* shews, as though his own she were,
> Thus comforting the Flood, O ever-during Heir
> Of *Sabrine*, *Locrine's* Child (who of her Life bereft)
> Her ever-living Name to the fair River left.

From this Mountain the *Severn* runs Eastward to *Llanidlos*, where it takes in the *Carno* or *Clewedog*. It then turns to the North-East, and leaving *Newtown* and *Montgomery* on the Right, receives the Rivers *Rue* and *Camlet*; then runs almost North to *Welch* Pool, having *Powis Castle*, a Seat of Earl *Powis*, on its Western Side. It soon after turns to the North-East, and a little below the Village of *Llandrenio* receives the rapid River, called *Vurn-*

way,

way, or *Vunwey* ; which being augmented by the *Wutway*, *Tanot*, and *Raider*, fometimes pours into the *Severn* with fuch Impetuofity, that it overflows the oppofite Banks, to the great Detriment of the Farmers. The *Severn* now running almoft due Eaft, and having entered the County of *Salop*, receives the *Mord*, a River from *Ofweftry*; and gliding through a fine Country, betwixt *Rowton Caftle*, the Seat of Mr. *Lyfter* (one of the Reprefentatives for the County) and *Melverley*, and paffing *Shawarden*, forms a larger Peninfula than that of *Shrewfbury*, called the Ifle (of which fine Track of Meadow one Mr. *Sanford* is the Owner) and after fome more Windings, receives the *Mele* at *Salop*, by which Account it will appear, that *Drayton* was a little miftaken, for thus fings he ;

Firft *Camlet* cometh in, a *Montgomerian* Maid,
Her Source in *Severn*'s Banks that fafely having laid,
Mele her great Miftrefs next at *Shrewfbury* doth meet,
To fee with what a Grace fhe that fair Town doth greet ;
Into what fundry gyres her wondered felf fhe throws,
And oft in iles the Shore as wantonly fhe flows.
Of it oft taking Leave, oft turns it to embrace,
As though fhe only were enamoured of that Place !
Her fore-intended Courfe determined to leave,
And to that moft lov'd Town eternally to cleave.
With much ado, at length, yet bidding it adieu,
Her Journey tow'rds the Sea doth ferioufly purfue.

There is fomething exceffively beautiful in this poetic Defcription of the Winding of the River : Perhaps few *Laureats* have equalled it.

The Excurfion that I have been guilty of, in tracing the *Severn* from its Rife to this Place, is now over. The Walls of *Shrewfbury* towards the *Quarry* are in Part remaining, near which are many pretty Houfes with Views of that charming Place, which in Summer Afternoons is almoft crowded with as genteel, and in general *better* Company

than

than is to be seen in the *Mall*. I have compared *Ludlow* to St. *Edmondsbury*; but *Shrewsbury*, which is larger than both these Towns, is also more abundant in Gentry. The People are indeed charged with Pride, even to an Adage; for a Report prevails, that King *Charles* the Second, for their Loyalty to his Father, offered to raise it to the Dignity of a City, which the Townsmen refusing, on the Consideration that 'twas the largest, best, and most polite Town in *England*, they received the Appellation of *Proud Salopians*. For my Part, I have found no other Cause for such a Charge, nor have ever, in any Place, met with more affable and accomplished Ladies or Gentlemen. The Assemblies are indeed of two Sorts, for no Person in Trade is suffered to belong to that which is composed of Persons of independent Fortunes, of whom there are a prodigious Number in the Town and its Neighbourhood.

Shrewsbury, which is in 2 Deg. 46 Min. of West Longitude from *London*, and in the Latitude of 52 Deg. 46 Min. is a Corporation, governed by a Mayor, twenty-four Aldermen, sixty-eight Common-Council-Men, a Recorder (at present the Earl *Powis*) Steward, Town-Clerk, and other Officers. They have the Power of trying capital Causes within themselves, provided they are not for High-Treason. The senior Alderman below the Chair is generally chosen Mayor. Here are twelve incorporated trading Companies; who, on the *Monday* Fortnight after *Whitsuntide*, at *Kingsland*, a Place on the opposite Side of the *Severn* from the *Quarry*, have the Honour of entertaining the Mayor and Corporation at their particular Bowers, for that Purpose erected, and distinguished by Mottoes or Devices suitable to their Arts or Trades. This I have seen managed with much Pomp and Decorum, and it is commonly called *Shrewsbury Shew*.

Vol. I.   P p   The

The Trade of this Town is very confiderable, owing to the Navigation on the *Severn*, the Conflux of Gentry, and its Vicinity to the manufacturing Parts of *Wales*. The Markets are held on *Wednefdays*, *Thurfdays*, and *Saturdays*; and the Fairs on *Saturday* next after the 15th of *March*, *Wednefday* after *Eafter* Week, *Wednefday* before *Whitfunday*, all for Horfes, Horned Cattle, Sheep, Cheefe, and Linen-Cloth; and on the 3d of *July*, and the 12th of *Auguft*, for the fame, together with Swine, Sheep, and Lambs Wool; and on *October* the 2d, and *December* the 12th, for the fame, and alfo for Butter and Cheefe *.

Befides

---

* In St. *Chad*'s Church, which is in the Middle of the Town, is a Monument bearing this Infcription;

Richardo Onfloweo Salopienfe Armigero generofa orto Familia; libere educato: ab incurabilis bonarum literarum Studiofiffimo. Juris domeftici legumque orarum peritiffimo. Academiæ Templariæ facile Principi. Scribæ cancel. Duc Lancaftr. pro civitate Londinenfi oratori publico ac Judici quam Recordatorem ipfi dicunt equiffimo dein Regio in regni fore Supremo Oratori. Sereniffimæ ma Regiæ admonitori. In curia Parliamenti de rebus arduis primum loquuto. Majoris amplitudinis pertæfo. ma. Regiæ Tutelarum procuratori. Tandem febri correpto peftilenti. in patria Hernegia in villa quintum poft diem mortuo Summo cum Dolore. Imperiis maximis Katherina Hardinga Suaviffimo conjugi pofuit. MDCIIII. Kal. Aprilis Secundo, natus a redempto genere humano MDXXVIII anno mortuus anno MDCXXI. vixit annos xlvi. Fuit Statura procera fronte gratiff voce gravi, lingua facunda veritatis Studiofiff. virtutum omnium thefaurus. Sincerus, liberalis, incorruptus.

Repaired 1742, by the Right Hon. *Arthur Onflow*, Efq, Speaker of the Houfe of Commons, lineally defcended from this Mr. *Onflow*, who was Speaker of the Houfe of Commons in the 8th of Queen *Elizabeth*, and was lineal Anceftor alfo to the Right Hon. Sir *Richard Onflow*, Bart Speaker of the Houfe of Commons in the 8th of Queen *Anne*, afterwards Lord *Onflow*.

Befides St: *Chad*'s, here are thefe five Churches, St *Mary*'s, which hath a fine and lofty Steeple ; St. *Alkman*'s, St. *Julian*'s, *Holy-Crofs* or *Abbey-Forgate*, and St. *Giles*.

From the Top of St. *Mary*'s Steeple, one *Cadman* fome Years fince, attempting to fly down a Rope, which was fixed on the other Side of the *Severn*, was killed : In which Church is the following Epitaph, written on him by Mr. *Meredith*, a School-Mafter of no mean Repute in the mathematic Way.

Let this fmall Monument record the Name
Of *Cadman*; and to future Times proclaim,
How by an Attempt to fly from this high Spire,
Acrofs the *Sabrine* Stream, he did acquire
His fatal End. 'Twas not for Want of Skill,
Or Courage to perform the Tafk, he fell :
No, no; a faulty Cord b'ing drawn too tight,
Hurry'd his Soul from high to take her Flight,
Which bid the Body from this lofty Spire good Night.

How do you like this figurative Poetry ? I remember one of a Taylor's Wife, which hath a fimilar Ending. It runs thus ;

From *Abraham*'s Bofom, full of Lice,
To *Abraham*'s Bofom, in *Paradife*,
The Soul of *Sarah* took its Flight,
And bid the loufy Rogue good Night.

St. *Mary*'s is a Peculiar, the reft are in the Diocefe of *Litchfield* and *Coventry*. I am, Sir, Yours, &c.

L E T T E R XXX.

From *Atcham* upon the *Severn*, in *Shropfhire*.

S I R,

THE Reign of his prefent Majefty has been found fo mild, that Party Diftinctions have fubfided, even at *Shrewfbury*; of the Hiftory of

which

which Town I shall say a little. It takes its Appellation from the *Saxon* Word *Scrobbefrig*, which signifies a Town built upon a woody Hill. When *Doomsday-Book* was made, it appeared, that in the Reign of *Edward* the Confessor, it paid *Gelt* according to Two hundred Hides of Land. It was then a populous and well built Town *.

In the Reign of *Stephen*, the Governor of this Town, *William Fitz-Alan* (who was also Sheriff of the County,) held out the Castle for the Empress *Maud*, till the King took it by Assault.

This Town had indeed been partly burnt by *Llewellyn*, and *Richard Marshal*, Earl of *Pembroke*, in the preceding Reign, the Consequence of which was the Peace in the Year 1267. In 1398 a Parliament sat here, in which King *Richard* the Second had all the Allowance of arbitrary Power, and

---

* There was burnt at the Fire in the *Cottonian* Library a MSS. containing twenty Pages, bearing this Title. " Compo- " sitio Pacis & Concordiæ inter Henricum, Regem Angliæ, & " Lewellinum, Filium Griffini, Principem Walliæ, facta per " Cardinalem Ottobonum, Salopiæ, 7 Kal. Octob. A.D. " 1267." But in the Year 1283, that King's Son and Successor, *Edward* the First, summoned a Parliament here on the Trial of *David*, Brother to the brave, but unfortunate *Llewellyn*. The Sentence and Execution on him was savagely severe. It drew a general Odium on the King.

Llewellyn was induced to take up Arms by the Ambition of his Brother, *David*. They surprized the Lord *Clifford* on the Frontiers, and defeated the Earl of *Surry*, upon which *Edward* marched against them with a numerous Army, and the Princes took Refuge in the Mountains of *Snowdon*. But *Edward* so blockaded them in their Retreat, that they descended into the Plain, when an Engagement ensued near the Town of *Reult*, in the County of *Brecknock*, in which they were defeated, the brave *Llewellyn* being slain His Head was afterwards struck off from his Body, crowned with a Paper Diadem, pitched on a Stake, carried triumphantly through the City to the *Tower* of *London*, and exposed to View on the Walls *David* was taken Prisoner, sent to *Ruthin*, and tried at *Shrewsbury*; where he was condemned, and executed as a Traitor, with all the Circumstances

and the parliamentary Proceedings that had paſſed againſt the wicked *Treſilian* were made null and void.

The Battle of *Shrewſbury*, fought in 1403, I have often heard you mention, as an Event favourable to ſucceſſive Kings. The Affair was on a Spot about two Miles North of the Town, from thence called *Battle-Field*, where is annually a Fair for Cattle.

The Character of *Hotſpur*, as a Soldier, is finely depicted by the inimitable *Shakeſpeare*, when he is told of the King's Approach.

> I thank him, that he cuts me from my Tale,
> For I profeſs not talking : Only this,
> Let each Man do his beſt : And here draw I
> A Sword, whoſe Temper I intend to ſtain
> With the beſt Blood that I can meet withal,
> In the Adventure of this perilous Day.
> Now, *Eſperance !* *Piercy !* and ſo ſet on :
> Sound all the lofty Inſtruments of War,
> And by that Muſic let us all embrace,
> For (Heaven to Earth) ſome of us never ſhall
> A ſecond Time do ſuch a Courteſy *.

King *Henry* the Fourth, in the eleventh Year of his Reign, granted to *Roger Ive*, Rector of the Chapel of St. *John Baptiſt*, of *Adbrighton*, or *Albrighton-Huſee*, two Acres of Ground in that Lordſhip, adjoining to *Shrewſbury*, at *Battle-Field*, where he overcame *Henry Piercy* and his Army, for the Building thereon a Chapel, in Honour of

Mary

cumſtances attending that infamous Puniſhment, his Head being fixed near that of his Brother, and his four Quarters ſent to *York*, *Briſtol*, *Winton*, and *Northampton*. This was the fiiſt Example of puniſhing Treaſon in *England* with ſuch Severity ; and with theſe Princes expired the Liberty of *Wales*.

Upon one of the Bridges in *Shrewſbury* is a noble **Gate**, and over the Arch the Statue of this *Llewellyn*.

* In the Battle of *Shrewſbury*, which was fought on the 22d of *July*, 1403, was by *Henry* ſought to be avoided, having
em

Mary Magdalen, for the Mafter and five Chaplains;
of which Chapel and five Chaplains he appointed
the faid *Roger*, and his Succeffors, Rectors of the
faid Chapel of St. *John Baptift*, to be Mafters or
Wardens: and *Richard Huffee*, Lord of *Albrighton*,
and his Heirs, to be Patrons of the fame : Incor-
porating the faid Foundation, and freeing them
from Tenths, Subfidies, and all Taxes; with the
Grant of a Fair to the faid *Roger*, and his Succeffors, to be held there yearly on the Feaft of St.
Mary Magdalen; which *Roger Ive*, by Will, in the
Year 1444, gave to this College three Chalices,
Silver and gilt ; one *Paxbrede*, Silver gilt; two
Phials, Silver ; three Bells in the Steeple; three
Croffes gilt ; with feveral Veftments and Books for
Church-Service, various houfhold Goods, &c.
and encreafed the Stipend of each of the Chaplains
from eight to ten Marks *per Annum*, on Condition
that they pray in a more efpecial Manner for the
Souls of King *Henry* the Fourth and King *Henry*
the Fifth, *Richard Huffee*, firft Patron of the College, and for the Souls of all the Faithful flain in
the Fight of *Battle-Field*, and there buried. All
the reft of his Goods and Chattels he gave to the
Fabric

employed the Clerk of his Privy-Seal, and the Abbot of *Salop*,
to treat with the Earl of *Worcefter*, who was employed by his
Nephew, *Piercy*; but, owing to the Treachery of the Uncle,
Hotfpur was deceived, and this brought on the Battle, in which
Hotfpur was killed, together with 5000 of his Followers ; the
Earl of *Worcefter*, the Baron *Kinderton*, and Sir *Richard Vernon*,
were taken, and executed. The Body of *Hotfpur* was firft bu-
ried, afterwards dug up, his Head fet upon *London-Bridge*, and
his Quarters fent into different Parts of the Kingdom, but the
Earl *Douglas* had his Liberty. In the King's Army were flain
the Earl of *Stafford*, Sir *Hugh Shelly*, Sir *John Clifton*, Sir *John
Cockayne*, Sir *Nicholas Cauffel*, Sir *Walter Blount*, Sir *John Cal-
verley*, Sir *John Maffey*, of *Podrington*, Sir *Hugh Mortimer*, and
Sir *John Cauffel*. Sir *John Wendefley* died afterwards. The
King had 1600 killed, and 4000 wounded. The Prince of
Wales was wounded in the Face.

Fabric of the faid College, and to the Relief of the Poor, in the Hofpital of the fame. He alfo appointed a new Seal to be made for the College, with this Circumfcription. *S. commune Domini Rogeri Ive, primi Magiftri & Succefforum fuorum Collegii beatæ Mariæ Magdalenæ juxta Salop.*

This Houfe, at the Diffolution, was valued at fifty-four Pounds one Shilling and ten Pence *per Annum.*

That *Edward* the Fourth kept his Court fometimes at *Shrewfbury*, may be fairly fuppofed, for he had two Sons born there, *Richard*, Duke of *York*, and *George Plantagenet*, who died before the Murder of his Brothers.

Some of our Hiftorians have told us, that the Sweating-Sickhefs began here in 1483, but *Camden* fays it was in 1551.

Shrewsbury was the firft Place where the People's Loyalty gave King *Charles* the Firft any Hopes of Succefs from Arms ; but in 1645 it was taken fiom the Royalifts by the Colonels *Langher a* and *Mitton*, for the Parliament.

When *Charles* the Second marched, with his *Scottifh* Army, towards *Wercefter*, he caufed Colonel *Mackworth*, then Governor of the Garrifon here, to be fummoned to furrender ; which he thought proper to refufe. Yet, when that King was abroad, the Lord *Newport* attempted to feize *Shrewsbury*, in order to favour the Reftoration ; but the Scheme being difcovered to Sir *Richard Willis*, many of his Adherents were apprehended and punifhed.

This Town hath given the Title of Earl to many Perfonages, befides *Roger de Montgomery*, a few of whom I fhall juft mention.

To *Hugh Montgomery*, who joined the Earl of *Hereford* againft *William Rufus*. He invaded *Wales*,
but

but was ſhot by *Magnus*, King of *Norway*, in the Year 1099.

In 1101, *Robert de Beleſme*, called the *Reſtleſs Earl*, ſucceeded: He was rich, enterprizing, and arrogant; and gave *Henry* the Firſt a vaſt Deal of Trouble, both in *England* and *Normandy*; but at length he fell into that King's Hands, who confined him in *Warham-Caſtle* for Life.

The next I ſhall mention is, the famous *John*, Lord *Talbot*, called the *Engliſh Achilles*, who was ſo greatly renowned in *France*. I have here been favoured with a curious Account of his Exploits, which I ſhall do myſelf the Pleaſure of delivering into your own Hands. *Drayton* thus ſpeaks of him;

Our *Talbot*, to the *French* ſo terrible in War,
That with his very Name, their Babes they us'd to ſcare.

At *Whitchurch*, in this County, is a Cenotaph erected to his Memory, on which are engraven theſe Words;

Orate pro Anima prænobilis Domini,
Domini *Joannis Talbott*,
Quondam Comitis *Salopiæ*;
Domini *Talbott*, Domini *Furnivall*,
Domini *Verdon*,
Domini *Strange* de *Black Mere*,
Et Mareſcalli *Franciæ*,
Qui obiit in Bello apud *Burdews*,
vii *Julii*, MCCCCLIII.

But this great Soldier was buried at *Roan* in *Normandy*, on whoſe Monument there was written,

Here lyeth the right noble Knight
John Talbot, Earle of *Shrewsbury*, *Weſhford*, *Water-ford*, and *Valence*; Lord *Talbot*, of *Goodrich* and *Orchenfield*; Lord *Strange*, of *Blackmere*; Lord *Verdun*, of *Acton*; Lord *Cromwell*, of *Wingfield*; Lord *Lovetoft*, of *Worſop*; Lord *Furnivall*, of *Sheffield*, Lord *Fauconbridge*, Knight of the noble Orders of Saint *George*, and Saint *Michael*, and the *Golden Fleece*. Great Marſhall to King *Henry* the Sixth, of his Realme of *France*.

It

It may be noted, that three Earls of *Shrewsbury* suffered in the Quarrel between the Houses of *York* and *Lancaster*.

At the Trial of the Duke of *Norfolk*, in the Reign of *Elizabeth*, *George Talbot*, Earl of *Shrewsbury*, sat as Lord High-Steward. In the Year 1596, she sent him to invest *Henry* the Fourth, King of *France*, with the Order of the Garter. He was magnificently received in that Kingdom, where great Honours were paid him, and he maintained his Dignity with great Splendor and Applause.

Charles Talbot, Earl of *Shrewsbury*, Lord Chamberlain to King *James* the Second, mortgaged his Estate for Forty thousand Pounds, and went over to the Prince of *Orange*; with whom he returned, and was created Marquis and Duke of *Shrewsbury*. But dying without Male Issue, his Titles ceased. However, the Earldom reverted to a Descendant of his Uncle, *George Talbot*, now Earl of *Shrewsbury*, of *Heathorpe*, in *Oxfordshire*, beforementioned.

The Lord Lieutenant and Custos Rotulorum of the County is the Earl of *Bath*. I am, Sir, Yours, &c.

LETTER XXXI.

From *Bridgenorth*, in *Shropshire*.

S I R,

THOUGH, as *Drayton* observes, the *Severn* runs South-West at *Shrewsbury*, yet, having formed the Peninsula of that Town, its Course becomes due East to the Remains of *Hamon* or *Haghmond* Abbey. This Religious House was founded in the Year 1100, by *William Fitz-Allen*. The

Monks were of the Order of St. *Augustine of Canterbury*; and King *Henry*, at the Desire of *Alured*, Abbot of this Monastery, granted the Custody of it, in Times of Vacation, to the said *Fitz-Allen*, and his Heirs.

King *Edward*, in the thirteenth Year of his Reign, confirmed to the Church of St. *John the Evangelist*, and to the Canons here, all the Lands and Revenues given by the several Benefactors, among whom were some of the Princes of *Wales*.

In the third Year of King *Henry* the Fifth, *Ralph*, then Abbot of this House, and his Convent, at the Instance of *Thomas*, Earl of *Arundel* and *Surry*, granted to *Robert Lee*, one Corrody for his Life, he being with the said Abbot as his Squire, with a Boy and two Horses, as others of the Abbots Squires for the Times past used to have, during such Time as the said *Robert* shall please to abide in the said Monastery, so also for Apparel. *Richard*, Bishop of *Coventry*, granted to this Abbey of *Haghman*, that the Sachristan, under the Abbot, might baptize *Jews* as well as *Christians* in the Monastery, and might use parochial Rights within the same. *Nicholas*, Abbot of this House, in the Year 1332, allotted certain Revenues for the Maintenance of the Kitchen, and for twenty Hogs a Year for the Bacon of the House, &c. *Richard Burnell*, Abbot in the Year 1459, made Ordinances relating to the Offices of the Prior and Sub-Prior, wherein he settles their Precedencies, &c. Pope *Alexander* the Third granted to the Canons of this House many Privileges, particularly an Exemption from paying Tythes of the Lands and Cattle of their own Possession; to have a free Burial-Place; to present Clerks to the parochial Churches which they hold, who shall account to the House for the Profits; to celebrate the divine Offices privately in the Time

of

of a general Interdict; and to pay no Tythes of their Mills and Meadows, unless the Usage hath been otherwise, &c. Pope *Boniface* IX. granted Indulgencies to those who should visit this Church on certain Days yearly, being truly penitent, and having been confessed.

At the Dissolution, the Rents of this House were valued at Two hundred and fifty-nine Pounds thirteen Shillings and seven Pence.

Nothing can be more charming than the Beauties afforded to the Eye, in a Passage upon the *Severn*, from *Shrewsbury* to this Place; where it turns to the South-West, until one comes to the pretty Village of *Atcham*.

In this Neighbourhood lived the perfidious *Humphry Bannister*, who, in the Reign of *Richard* the Third, betrayed his Friend and Patron, the unfortunate Duke of *Buckingham*, to *John Mitton*, High-Sheriff of *Shropshire*, who conveyed him to *Shrewsbury*, from whence the Tyrant *Richard* ordered him to *Salisbury*, as before related *.

From

---

* When the Duke of *Buckingham*, anno 1483, arrived on the Banks of the *Severn*, in his Way to *Gloucester*, with the Army which he had raised against the Tyrant, *Richard* the Third, he found that River so swollen, as if Nature had broken up her Depths: The Waters covered even Woods and Mountains. The Fruits of Industry, and the means of Subsistence, were swept away by the dreadful Deluge; nor did the Waters much subside for ten Days. *Buckingham*, not foreseeing this Calamity, had advanced without Provisions for his Army; expecting to find Magazines on the *English* Side, but not being able to pass the River, he found it equally impracticable to keep his Men in a Body. His Difficulties were increased by a Distaste which the Soldiers in general had for his Person, and, in short, his Army mouldered away to one single Servant, who was faithful enough to attend his Master in his Distress. In this dismal Condition, he fled to the House of one *Bannister*, a Creature who had subsisted on his Bounty, and who had been raised by him to a comfortable Estate near *Shrewsbury*. By this Wretch he was betrayed to *John Mitton*, the Sheriff of *Shropshire*, who sur-

rounding

From *Atcham*, 'tis about a Mile to the Disemboguing of the fine River *Theme* into that of the *Severn*, near the Spot where anciently stood the *Roman* Station, called *Uriconium*, by the *Saxons*, *Wroxceter*, which latter Name the Village still bears ; and in its Neighbourhood not only great Numbers of *Roman* Coins have been found, but many very curious Pavements, and other Vestigia of its Greatnss. The *Watling-Street* Road here crossed the *Severn* from *Wellington*, or *Wattlington*, to *Acton-Burnel* already spoken of. Between this Highway and the *Severn*, rises that famous Hill, called the *Wrekin* ; to all Friends round which stupendous Mount, is the common Toast of this County ; and to whom that excellent dramatic Writer, *Farquhar*, has dedicated his *Recruiting Officer*.

From the Brow of this celebrated Hill, we had a most amazing Prospect all around, to which the *Severn* affords a happy Assistance. As this Hill is not rivalled, by any Neighbour, 'tis singular in its Views, which are terminated only by the Horizon, if we except the Mountains of *Wales*, which rise towards the West. In the *Poli-Olbion* we find these Lines ;

> The Muse that Part of *England* plies,
> Which on the East of *Severn* lies,
> Where mighty *Wrekin*, from his Height
> In the proud *Cambrian* Mountain's Spight,
> Sings those great *Saxons* ruling here,
> Which the most famous Warriors were.

He then recounts the Actions of our great *Saxon* Commanders, and afterwards, in the twelfth Song

rounding the House, seized the Duke, who was in the Habit of a Peasant, and carried him to *Salisbury*. *Guthrie*.

Richard punctually fulfilled the Terms of the Proclamation which he had issued for the Taking of *Buckingham*, by giving to *Bannister* the Manor and Lordship of *Yielding* in *Kent*, then lately belonging to the Duke of *Buckingham*.

Song, thus oppofes this *Olympus*, or rather *Parnaf-fus* (for *Wycherley* and *Philips* were born under it's Shadow) to the diftant Hills of *Wales*. The *Wre-kin* is higher than the *Brown Clee* before noted. Thefe Lines are poetically picturefque;

When *Wrekin*, as a Hill his proper Worth that knew,
And underftood from whence their Infolency grew,
For all that they appear'd fo terrible in Sight,
Yet would not once forego a Jot that was his Right;
And when they ftar'd on him, to them the like he gave,
And anfwered Glance for Glance, and Brave again for Brave.

Then, after afferting his Eminence in Contra-diftinction to them, he caufes the Mountain thus to addrefs the *filvery Sabrine Stream*;

Therefore, quoth he, " Brave Flood, though forth by
          Cambria brought,
" Yet, as fair *England*'s Friend, or mine thou wouldft
          " be thought,
" O *Severn*, let thine Ear my juft Defence partake !"

From *Wroxceter*, the River runs in a pleafing Meander through charming Meadows to *Cund*, where is a very beautiful Houfe and Gardens, late the Seat of Dr. *Creffet*, Bifhop of *Llandaff*, who died in the Year 1555 *. In this Village of *Cund* now live fome Perfons of the Name and Family of the celebrated Poet *Wycherley*. He was the eldeft Son of *Daniel Wycherley*, of *Clive*, or *Cleeve*, in this County. It appears, by a Defcent in MS. now in the *Britifh Mufeum* (Numb. 1174) that this Family took their Name from the Place of their Abode, namely, *Wycherley*, of *Wycherley*, in the County of *Salop*. However, one Gentleman, Mr. *Daniel Wycherley*, afforded this his Son a good Share of School-Learning in this Country, from whence, at
                                        the

---

* There is, among the *Harleian* MSS in the *Britifh Mufeum*, Numb. 1465, the Pedigree of the ancient Family of *Creffet*, of *Upton-Creffet*, from whence this Gentleman was defcended.

the Age of fifteen, he was sent to *France*. He was afterwards a Fellow-Commoner of *Queen's College* in *Oxford*, but never matriculated, nor had he any Degree. From the Univerſity he went to the *Middle-Temple*, and ſoon became famous for his Wit, in the witty Days of *Charles* the Second. Few People lived with more Gaiety than he, none excelled him as a Poet. His *Plain-Dealer*, and *Country Wife*, are dramatic Pieces, which will render him famous to Poſterity. In deſcribing a Feaſt of Blockheads, he has theſe biting Lines ;

> A huge Calf's Head, as oft it comes to paſs,
> At the Board's upper End Demands its Place ;
> Who, that he had his *Brains about him* ſhew'd;
> And that was more than *ſome about him* cou'd.

From *Cund*, the *Severn* glides North-Eaſt, between the ſweet Villages of *Creſſedge* and *Eaton*; at which latter Place is a Seat of the Earl of *Bradford*. We next left *Shenton* on our Right, and here the Banks of the River were interſperſed with ſuch Variety that cannot be expreſſed.

The ſingular Practice of Fiſhing here, in what they call a Coracle, is very pleaſing to the Eye of a Stranger. This Veſſel is formed with ſplit Sort of Lath, in the Shape of a large Cloaths-Baſket, the Outſide is the Hide of a Horſe. Acroſs it is laid a Board, upon which the Fiſherman ſits, with his Rod and Lines, and with a Paddle guides himſelf to the different Parts of the River: But his Situation is ſo ticklish, that a Novice in the Buſineſs would not, without Difficulty, keep it from overſetting. When it has drove down the River as far as the Fiſherman chuſes to go, he paddles to the Shore, and taking both his Fiſh and Boat upon his Back (excepting his Sport has been extraordinaiy good) with Eaſe carries them home.

The

The Stream now beginning to turn towards the South, became swifter, and we soon arrived at *Buildwas*, or *Bildewas*. Here a wooden Bridge crosses the River, where we landed again, and visited the Remains of *Buildwas* Abbey.

This Abbey was founded in the Year 1135, and King *Stephen*, four Years after, gave and confirmed to God and the Church of St. *Ceadde*, and to the Abbot and Monks here, their Estate, in the same Manner as *Roger*, Bishop of *Chester*, had given it; and also granted them several Immunities. *Walter de Dunstanville*, *Robert Corbet*, and others, were great Benefactors to this House. Their Estate was confirmed to them by *Richard* the First, in the first Year of his Year. King *Henry* the Second confirmed to the White Monks of St. *Mary*, near *Dublin*, in *Ireland*, all their Lands and Possessions, and by another Deed, subjected the said Monks to the Abbot of *Bildewas*; which Abbey, at the Dissolution, was valued at One hundred and ten Pounds nineteen Shillings and three Pence *per Annum*.

The next Village on the Right-Hand Side was *Bental*, and here the Banks became very high, and were covered with Woods; the *Severn* here is a swift Stream. We landed on the opposite Shore, and walked up to see the Iron and other Works, at a Place called *Coalbrook-Dale*. Here is a Furnace for casting Cannon, Cannon-Balls, Cylinders, and various other Vessels; at this Place is also a Plate-Iron Forge, Machines for boring Cannon, and an House for the melting of Lead-Ore, which is brought down the *Severn*, from the Mines in *Wales*, the effluvia or Smoke of which is very poisonous, both to the Workmen, and the Cattle, Hogs, and Poultry near it. I never saw such wan-looking People as the Workers in this Building, or any Ore so heavy as that which they were

about

about to melt. At this Place, which in the Night is called *Little Hell*, the *British Oil* is extracted, from a particular Sort of Stone; 'tis a Medicine of most salutary Qualities. Somewhat lower is *Madeley*, a Place where much Pit-Coal is dug, and put on board Vessels on the *Severn*. At this Place King *Charles* the Second lay in a Barn, accompanied only by *Richard Pendroll*, who is buried in the Church-Yard of St *Giles in the Fields*, *London*. They had come on Foot by Night from *Boscobel*, which is about six Miles off, with an Intent to pass the *Severn*: But this River was so strictly watched, by the Command of *Cromwell*, that, in the ensuing Night, they were obliged to return from whence they came. On the opposite Side of the *Severn* is *Broseley*, where are also many great Coal-Works, and the Coals are conducted to the River somewhat after the manner of those near *Newcastle*. Here are a great Number of Vessels weekly laden with that useful Commodity, which carry it to *Shrewsbury, Bridgenorth, Bewdley, Worcester, Upton, Tewkesbury, Gloucester,* and many other Places on the *Severn*; and also to *Pershore, Evesham,* and *Stratford on the Avon,* from which last Place they are sent into the inland Parts of the Country, even to the City of *Oxford*. At *Broseley* is a large Manufactory of earthen Ware, and another of the best Tobacco-pipes in *England*. About fifty Years ago a Well here sent forth a strong Vapour or Steam, over which some Persons having laid an Iron Cover with a semicircular Hole in it, through which the Vapour being forced to exhale, they put a Candle, or any other Flame over the Hole, when it instantly took Fire, and burnt with such Violence, that in less than two Hours it would boil a large Piece of Beef; and, though they lighted Tobacco, or broiled Beef at the Flame, it afforded no fulphureous Tafte or Smell. It would not ceafe burning till the Cover was taken off, but that being done, the Flame was alfo inftantaneoufly extinguifhed, and the Water became as cold as any other Spring. But this Well, by the Drains made for the Ufe of the Coal-Works, is now deftroyed.

Having left *Brofeley*, where the *Severn* runs pretty fwift, fhe turns her Courfe almoft due South; and foon after, the Valley through which it flows becomes wider, and is furnifhed with more Variety, having many Rivulets falling into its Bofom, as thus fingeth the fecond Poet of *Warwick-fhire*.

> The goodly *Severn* bravely fings
> The nobleft of her *Britifh* Kings;
> At *Cæfar's* Landing what we were,
> And of the *Roman* Conqueft here.
> Then fhews, to her dear *Britons* Fame,
> How quickly chriften'd we became,
> And of their Conftancy doth boaft,
> In fundry Fortunes ftrangely toft.
> Then doth the *Saxons* Landing tell,
> And how by them the *Britons* fell.
> Chears the *Salopian* Mountains high
> That on the Weft of *Severn* lie,
> Calls down each Riv'let from her Spring,
> Their Queen upon her Way to bring;
> Whom down to *Bruge* the Mufe attends.

Having fallen down the River about two Miles, our Eyes were fuddenly ftruck with the Appearance of a neat Obelifk on the Weftern Bank, where one Mr. *Stevens* has laid out fome delightful Walks in a Wood, fomewhat after the Manner of thofe at *Gobions* before treated of; but this Place, as to Situation, hath vaftly the Preference: For this fweet Retirement has delicious Views both up and down the *Severn*, whofe oppofite Shore is bold, and in fome Parts covered with venerable Woods. In a Word, I am of Opinion, that 'tis

owing only to the prefent Obfcurity of the charming Spots upon the gently-rifing Banks of this
noble River, that fo many of the Citizens of *London*, who have acquired ample Fortunes, lay out
thoufands, and end their Days in fuch crowded
Villages, that they never know what the fweet
Pleafures of true Retirement are ; and form but
faint Ideas of the life-prolonging Air of this delightful, this very plentiful Country.

A little lower, and on the oppofite Bank, ftands
Apley, a fine old Seat of the ancient and honourable Family of *Whitmore*. The prefent Sir *Thomas
Whitmore*, Knight of the *Bath*, lives entirely at
this venerable Manfion, which, in the Year 1645,
was a Garrifon for King *Charles*. The Houfe is
chiefly of Brick , before it is a fpacious Court,
and, on the Weftern Side, charming hanging
Gardens towards the *Severn*. On the North is a
Garden laid out with good Tafte, in which is a
fine Terrace, from whence is a fweet Profpect,
though fomewhat confined. That Part of the
Houfe next the Park, which lies on the Eaft Side,
is modern built ; and within the Manfion are many good Family Pictures. The Park is large,
very pleafant, and well ftocked with excellent
Deer. Sir *Thomas* has no Son, therefore his fine
Eftate may defcend to his Brother, General *William Whitmore*, of *Slaughter* in *Gloucefterfhire*.

From *Apley* we drove gently down the River, and,
on the Left-Hand, had an high, rocky Bank,
partly covered with Wood, called the *Red-Deer Park*.
I think fome Goats here would have a pleafing Effect from the *Severn*. On our Right was an high
Track of Land, called *Dunhilly-Common*; below
which the Weftern Side of the River is ornamented with charming fertile Meadows ; but the Left
continues to form an hilly Variety almoft to *Bridgenorth*, within half a Mile of which Town, at the
Difemboguing of the River *Wor* or *Worf*, is a
fine

fine Set of Mills, belonging to the Corporation of
the the laſt mentioned Town : And a little lower,
almoſt upon the Brink of the River, ſtands what
is very properly called the *High Rock* ; it is of a
red Sort of ſoft Stone, and overhangs the *Severn* in
an affecting Manner. On the oppoſite Shore are
fine and large Meads, being Part of a Farm, called
Hord's Park, which, though not above Two hundred and fifty Pounds a Year, is perhaps the moſt
compact and complete one in *England.* 'Tis the Property of the aforementioned Sir *Thomas Whitmore*.

On the ſame Side of the River is *Stanley*, a delightful, though ſequeſter'd Seat, formerly belonging to the Family of *Huxley*, but now the
Property of Mr. *Jones*, of *Windſor*, who married
the Heireſs of this Family.

We now glided ſoftly down to the Town of
Bridgenorth, which had been in our View for
about a Mile and half, and, having paſſed through
an Arch of the Bridge, landed at Mr. *Aſhbury's*
Key there. I am, Sir, Yours, *&c.*

L E T T E R   XXXII.

From *Upper Areley*, upon the *Severn*, in
Staffordſhire.

S I R,

FROM the *Severn* Side we advanced by a ſteep,
hollow Way, which is cut through the ſolid
Rock, up to the *High-Town*, and took up our
Inn at the *Crown* in the *High-Street*, which Street
is broad, ſtrait, and well built; in the Middle of
it ſtands the Town-Hall, where the County Aſ-
fizes were held about thirty Years ago, on account
of ſome Indignities offered to the Judges by the
People of *Shrewſbury* Under the Town-Hall is
the Market-Place, which is plentifully ſupplied
on *Saturdays :* There is alſo generally to the

North

North of it a very large Quantity of Grain expofed to Sale on thofe Days ; for the Farmers here do not, as in many other Parts of *England*, difpofe of their Grain by Sample. At the upper End of this Street is a handfome modern Gate, and at the lower End, one which leads to the Caftle. Before I proceed to any farther Defcription of the prefent State of this Town, I fhall crave your Patience a little. *Brugenorth, Bruges,* or *Bridgenorth,* according to the Opinion of fome Writers, was called *Burgh,* and *Morfe,* from the Foreft on the oppofite Shore of the *Severn :* But *Leland* and the late Bifhop *Gibfon* fay, that *Bridgenorth* is a Name only of late Ufe, it being anciently called only *Brugge* or *Bridge* ; and that the Word *North* was added to it, on account of the building fome Bridge over the *Severn,* to the South of it.

This Town was built by *Elfleda,* or *Ethelfleda,* the famous Queen of the *Mercians.* She was an *Amazonian* Sort of a Lady, the Widow of *Etherod,* Prince or King of *Mercia,* and Sifter to King *Edward* the Elder.

Some have fuppofed the Caftle to be a Work of the *Danes,* but the Lines of *Simon de Lowfeld,* a Monk of *Lillyfhal* Abbey, who wrote in the Year 1120, puts it out of Difpute *.

In the Year 1101, *Robert de Belefme* built the Walls of the Town, rebuilt the Caftle, and put therein a ftrong Garrifon of *Welchmen* ; and having engaged them to hold out to the laft Extremity,

* And ther a Ladie, *Elfleda* that hight,
  By lerned Clerkys ycliped *Mercian* Quene ;
  Whoe famos for hir galant Dedes and Witte
  Throu al the Lend I wis had fothely bene,
  A Caftil bilte, al on a lofty Roke ;
  Wyth mony a Toure and Battelment of Ston ;
  On oon more faire the Eye mote feldom lok,
  Below her Wals did *Severn* fteal elong,
  And Winding here and there, the plefaunt Medes emong.

mity, fet out for *Shrewfbury*. Soon after which, King *Henry* the Firft befieged it, and preffed it with much Vigour, but being greatly harraffed and ftraitened by *de Belefme*'s Army, he attempted to corrupt the Garrifon with Money, which fucceeded to his Wifhes, and the *Welch*, after a Defence of three Weeks, furrendered the Place.

At another Siege of this Caftle, King *Henry* the Second had been killed by an Arrow, which was levelled at him, had it not been voluntarily intercepted by *Hubert de St. Clere*, whofe Loyalty, or rather Affection, for the King, loft him his own Life.

In 1322, the Earl of *Hereford*, the two *Mortimers*, and other Lords of their Party, furprized and burnt this Town. At the Breaking out of the civil War, King *Charles*, having marched his Army from *Shrewfbury*, reviewed it here for the firft Time. In that fatal Quarrel this Town fuffered greatly ; and in the *High*, or St. *Leonard*'s Church-Yard, was a fharp Engagement, in which Colonel *Billingfby*, a worthy Gentleman of this County, was killed, the King's Party was routed, and the Church burnt to the Ground. The Caftle here ftood on the Top of a perpendicular Rock, fo that before the Ufe of Cannon, it was impregnable: But the Parliament's Forces having erected a Battery on an Eminence to the Southward, levelled moft of it with the Ground ; the prefent Veftigia are Part of one of its lofty Towers ; which curious Piece of Ruins is much higher than the Tower of St. *Mary Magdalen's*, or the *Lower Church*, and is the ftrongeft Building I have ever feen. There is a large Crack or Fracture almoft through it, which would feem to endanger its falling; but, according to the Laws of Gravity, if 'tis never taken down (which cannot eafily be effected, the Mortar being harder

than

than the Stone) it muſt fall the Way from whence it has declined. The laſt mentioned Church is neat, in which is an Inſcription to the Memory of the learned Mr. *Davis*, of *Kingſland*, in *Herefordſhire* : and another to that of the worthy Clergyman, Mr. *Hugh Stackhouſe*, late Incumbent of this Church, which Building having been within the Walls of the Caſtle, was in ancient Records, ſtiled *Libera Regia Capella* ; it was exempted from epiſcopal Juriſdiction, and *Bridgenorth* to this Day is a Peculiar in eccleſiaſtic Affairs, whoſe Superior is Sir *Thomas Whitmore*.

The Church-Yard of St. *Mary* is extreamly pleaſant, having a moſt charming View of the *Lower Town*, and the *Severn* ; but as I ſhall preſently attempt the Deſcription of what is called the *Caſtle-Hill*, which includes this View, I may be ſuppoſed to lead you through an handſome Street, where Part of the Caſtle ſtood, which Place ſtill retains the Name. The Houſes on the Eaſt Side have Gardens behind them, which alſo participate of this pleaſant View. Upon the higheſt Part of the Rock on which the Upper Town is erected, ſtands the Church dedicated to St. *Leonard* ; 'tis built of a red, ſoft Stone, of which this Neighbourhood abounds, and is a tolerable good Fabric. Of this Church *Francis Wheeler*, A. M. was Miniſter, and alſo Archdeacon of *Salop*. He gave by his Will ten Pounds *per Annum*, to be diſtributed to the Poor of this Town in Bread, and was buried in this Church, with a *Latin* Inſcription *.

Near

---

* Juxta chariſſimam ſuam Uxorem depoſuit Exuvias *Franciſ. Wheeler*, Archid *Salopiæ*, & hujus Oppidi Miniſter deſideratiſſimus Vir Exquiſitimis animi dotibus imbutus exemplari Pietate et Candore prædituserga pauperas obliviis non gruerda ſpectabilis hic poſtquam vitam ſummâ cum Laude feliciter

Near this Church ſtands a Free-School for the Sons of the Burgeſſes ; it was founded in the Reign of Queen *Elizabeth*, and has ſent ſome Scholars to the Univerſity of *Oxford*. The Church-Yard is adorned with handſome Walks; planted with double Rows of Trees ; and from that called the *Old Walk*, are delightful Proſpects both up and down the *Severn*, over the *Low Town*, and the adjacent Country. This Place would be much more pleaſing, were it not for a large Building (erected by one of the Weavers of *Morvil* beforementioned for a Grainery) which ſtands before the very Center of the Walk.

On the ſame Side of the Church-Yard are ſeveral good Houſes, eſpecially that belonging to Mr. *White*, an Attorney, from whoſe Garden is a fine View, though a little interrupted by a Summer-Houſe belonging to Colonel *John Littlehales*, a Gentleman who has bravely diſtinguiſhed himſelf in *North-America*, but was taken Priſoner at *Oſwego*, and ſent to *Old France*.

In this Church-Yard is a neat Building, intended as a Library for the Uſe of the neighbouring Clergy, towards which Mr. *Stackhouſe*, juſt mentioned, left his valuable Collection of Books; And between the Church and Mr. *White*'s Houſe ſtands an handſome Dial, drawn by, and erected at the Expence of, Mr. *Brown*, of *Cleobury*, before ſpoken of, formerly a Teacher of the Mathematics here.

Here is an Hoſpital erected and endowed for poor Widows, by one Mr. *Palmer*, and, in the Church-Lane, are ſeveral Almſhouſes for poor Widows alſo.

Beſides

feliciter exegiſſet diuturna Corporis intemperie Confectus inter Amicorum amplexus & Bonorum omnium deſiderio animam Deo placide redd'dit An 1686, Ætatis 49.

Befides thofe Parts of the *Upper Town* already mentioned, are the *Raven, Hungary*, and *Lefley* Streets, which run parallel with each other, and continue from the *High-Street*, to the Road which leads towards *Shrewfbury*. From the Bottom of the *High-Street*, and near the Entrance into the Caftle, the Way for Carriages begins, which, with many Windings down the fteep Hill, or rather Rock, leads to the Bridge over the *Severn*, and thence into the *Lower Town* (or, according to the common Appellation, the *Low Town*); this is called the *Cartway*; near the Top of which I entered the Walk, called the *Caftle-Hill*, where are the Profpects which I have intended to defcribe.

This Walk, which is about eight or ten Feet wide, has the Gardens beforementioned on the Right-Hand, and, on the Left, the *Severn*. After I had gone about an hundred Yards, and looking towards the Eaft, I had thefe Views: Directly before me lay the *Low Town*, fituate in the Midft of moft charming Meadows; and almoft in a Line leading to it, the large Stone Bridge, on which, befides the Gatehoufe, now a Prifon for Debtors, are many Dwelling-Houfes. As the *Low Town* is well built, having Gardens and Groves beyond it, which run gradually up the Sides of the Hill, called *Morfe*, the Sight is wonderfully fine.

Here is a beautiful Ifland in the *Severn*, of an oval Form, and confiderably large, on which are feveral Trees. From the Banks of the River to the Spot where I ftood, the Rock is near One hundred Feet perpendicular. Towards the North, I had the *Severn* gently meandering through delightful Meadows, the ftupenduous high Rock which hangs over it, and Part of the Foreft of *Morfe*. Underneath, a little to the Right-Hand, and oppofite to the South End of the Ifland beforementioned, are the Water-Works,

which

which throw the *Severn* Water up the Rock to
a large Refervoir, erected near the Spot where
I ftood. They too were contrived by the fame
Perfons who made thofe at *London-Bridge*. Farther on my Right, the *Severn* gently glided between the Meads, through a moft beautiful Valley, and here the Profpect is vaftly extenfive
and various. On the other Side of the *Severn*,
in a pretty Inclofure of Trees, ftands an Houfe
and Farm, called St. *James*'s. Towards the Eaft,
the large Common of *Morfe* rifes to a great Height,
and terminates the View that Way. Having
feafted my Eyes with thefe Views, I walked
on, under the Refervoir beforementioned (the
South View ftill being exceffive fine) to St. *Mary*'s
Church-Yard, where are pretty Walks and pleafant Seats, and rifing a little, I came to a moft neat
Bowling Green, over one Side of which hangs the
awful Ruin already fpoken of; on the other Side
was Part of the Profpect before noted; and towards the South another, over a deep Valley, through
which runs a Stream of Water, to the Village of
Oldbury, fituate on a gently-rifing Hill, around
which Village are excellently cultivated Fields and
Gardens. The unhappy King *Charles* the Firft,
who was here three Times during his Troubles,
ufed to fay, that this Bowling-Green was the pleafanteft Place in all his Dominions. Mr. *Dyer*, in his
Poem called *Grongar-Hill*, hath thefe Lines, which
are in a great Degree picturefque of this Place.

> Ever charming, ever new,
> When will the Landfcape tire the View?
> The Fountain's Fall, the River's Flow,
> The woody Vallies, warm and low,
> The windy Summit, wild and high,
> Roughly rufhing on the Sky,
> The pleafing Seat, the ruin'd Tow'r,
> The naked Rock, the fhady Bow'r,

The Town and Village, Dome and Farm,
Each give each a noble Charm,
As Pearls upon an *Æthiop's* Arm.

From this Bowling-Green, the *Caſtle-Hill* Walk
continues Southward ſome Way, and then turns
ſhort to the Weſt; at this Turning is a Summer-
Houſe, from whence the Proſpect is exceedingly
fine. The Walk now continues upon the Edge of
a Rock (below which is the deep Valley juſt mentioned) to a very neat Houſe, which fronts the Eaſt;
it was built by one Mr. *Bradfield*, and has a charming Situation. As the Rock on which this Town
ſtands is of a ſoft Nature, here are very many Dwellings cut out of the ſame *, eſpecially at the North
End near the River-Side, where ſtand the Remains
of a ſmall Religious Houſe, or Hoſpital, for Infirm of the Order of St. *Auguſtine*. This Hoſpital was founded and endowed in Honour of the
Trinity, the Virgin *Mary*, and St. *John Baptiſt*,
by *Radulph*, or *Ralph de Strange*, from whom
lineally deſcended the famous *John Talbot*, Earl of
Shrewſbury, before noted. By an Inquiſition made
in the fourteenth of *Edward* the Fourth, it appears
that the Name of Cuſtos of this Hoſpital was in
Proceſs of Time changed to that of Prior. *Dugdale* ſays, it was, at the Diſſolution, valued at four
Pounds *per Annum.*

Here are many Yards for building and repairing
Trows, Barges, and Boats, a great Number of which
are uſed upon this River. There is not perhaps in
Europe a more pure Air, or delightful Place, than
the *High-Town* of *Bridgenorth*; but very few Gentry
live here, which is ſomewhat extraordinary. The
People are well enough behaved in their Way, but
whoever

* The Compiler of the *Tour through Great-Britain*, ſays,
" Part of the *Cow-gate-Street* is a Rock riſing perpendicular,
" where are ſeveral Tenements." I lived more than five Years
in this Town, and know of no Street of that Name in it.

whoever expects high Politeness here, will probably meet with a Disappointment.

It is governed by two Bailiffs, twenty-four Aldermen, a Recorder, Town-Clerk, and other inferior Officers, and sends two Members to Parliament.

The Fairs here are on *Thursday* before *Shrovetide*, *June* the 30th, *August* the 2d, and the 29th of *October*; the first and last of which are very large, for Horses, Horned Cattle, Sheep, Bacon, Butter, Cheese, Hops, Linen-Cloth, Wick-Yarn, and Wool.

From this Town we made a short Excursion to *Worvile*, where is a beautiful modern Seat, the Residence of *Sherington Davenport*, Esq. The Gardens are prettily laid out, and every Thing within and without Doors has the Appearance of Elegance, though not of Profusion.

We also rode to *Willey*, on the other Side of the *Severn*. *Camden* calls it *Willely*, and says, 'twas formerly the Seat of the *Warners*, from whose Posterity, by the *Harleys* and *Peshals*, it came to the famous Family of the *Lacons*, who were much enriched by Marriage with the Heir of *Passelew*, and afterwards improved by the Possessions of Sir *John Blount*, of *Kinlet*, Knight, already mention'd. It was lately the Seat of Mr. *Wild*, a Gentleman of Honour and Integrity, who, as an active and upright Magistrate, was greatly respected. But now it belongs to *Brooke Forester*, Esq; who married his only Child, a Lady of exemplary Virtue, and other amiable Accomplishments. The present Owner has lately built a very handsome House in the Park, and made many fine Improvements.

Our Entertainment at the *Crown* was very good and reasonable. Here are many agreeable Lasses, and the Gaiety of the Inhabitants (though they

S s 2   and

and all in *Bridgenorth* are in Trade) is pleafing enough. Their Dialeƈt is a Mixture of Words founded both too broad and to fine. And now, Sir, as our Boat is ready, I take my leave of you and *Bridgenorth* together, being Yours, &c.

L E T T E R XXXIII.

From *Kidderminfter*, in *Worcefterfhire*.

S I R,

HAVING put off from the Key at *Bridgenorth*, we were rowed gently down between the Ifland (which the Inhabitants call the *Bannut Tree Bylot*) and the Water-Works ; and were carried on the Bofom of this noble Stream through the Meadows,

> Where the Milk-Maid fingeth blithe,
> And the Mower whets his Scythe,
> And the Shepherd tells his Tale,
> Under the Hawthorn in the Dale.

When we had gone about half a Mile, the View of the Town appeared vaftly romantic, the Trees and Shrubs with which the Rocks and Hill abound, being intermixed with Caves and Buildings, gave it an Afpeƈt very different from that of any other Town I have feen. From a rifing Ground on our Right-Hand, my Friend Mr. *Buck* took his Profpeƈt of that Place.

A little lower we came to *Quatford*, a Place famous for Intrenchments thrown up there by the *Danes*, in the Year 897. It is a fmall Place on a fandy Soil, *Eardington*, an Hamlet, and the principal Part of the Parifh, being on the oppofite Side of the *Severn*. The Church ftands upon a

Rock,

Rock, and the old Incumbent, Mr. *Higgs*, is fo
fingularly thrifty, as to have his Bands made of
Paper inftead of Cambrick; fo that he cannot
be faid to be an Encourager of this Branch of
French Manufactory.

On our Right, the Meads belonging to a Farm,
called the *Hay*, were extreamly pleafing; and
here the *Marbrook*, a confiderable Stream, falls
into the *Severn*, where *Drayton* ends his Defcip-
tion of this River.

—— As along the Shores fhe profp'roufly doth fweep,
Small *Marbrook* maketh in to her enticing Deep;
And as fhe lends her Eye to *Bruges*' lofty Sight,
That Foreft Nymph, mild *Morf*, doth kindly her invite
To fee within her fhade what Paftime fhe could make:
Where fhe of *Shropfhire*, I my Leave of *Severn* take.

Although at that Time the *Morfe*, which is now
an open Heath, might have Woods upon it, yet
Mafter *Drayton* is miftaken here; for the *Severn*
does not leave *Shropfhire* till it comes almoft to
Over-Areley, feveral Miles below. On the other
Side the River from *Marbrook*, is *Dudmarfton*, or
Dodmarfton, the ancient Seat of the Family of *Wolryche*. There is among the *Harleian* MSS, Numb.
1174, two Defcents of this honourable Family,
whofe Title of Baronet is extinct, by the Death
of the late Sir *John Wolryche*, who was drowned in
the *Severn*, on his Return from an Horfe-Race.
His Mother, the old Lady *Wolryche*, is yet alive,
though near an hundred Years of Age. I don't
know whom to compare to her for true Goodnefs,
except the celebrated Lady *Parkington*, of whom
hereafter, who was the fuppofed Authorefs of the
Whole Duty of Man. The River here is extreamly
pleafant; nothing can excel the beautiful Exhibitions of her charming Banks. Nature is luxuriant,
Art is almoft unknown. Health is a Reveller on
the Hills, and Contentment fits fmiling in the
Vale;

Vale: Liberty sings through the Woods, and
Labour is chearful in the Meadow : Mirth dances
around the sweet Cocks of new Hay, and Jollity
urges the Can of old *English* Beer. *Milton*, you
remember, in his *Comus*, thus delivers the History
and Character of the Goddess of this River :

> There is a gentle Nymph, not far from hence,
> That with moist curb sways the smooth *Severn* Stream,
> *Sabrina* is her Name, a Virgin pure ;
> Whilom she was the Daughter of *Locrine*,
> That had the Sceptre from his Father *Brute* ;
> She, guiltless Damsel, flying the mad Persuit
> Of her enraged Stepdame *Guendolen*,
> Commended her fair Innocence to the Flood,
> That stay'd her Flight with his cross-flowing Course ;
> The *Water-Nymphs*, that at the Bottom play'd,
> Held up their pearled Wrists, and took her in,
> Bearing her strait to aged *Nereus'* Hall ;
> Who, piteous of her Woes, rear'd her lank Head,
> And gave her to his Daughters to embathe
> In nectar'd Lavers, strew'd with Asphodil ;
> And through the Porch and Inlet of each Sense,
> Dropt in ambrosial Oils, till she reviv'd,
> And underwent a quick immortal Change ;
> Made Goddess of the River, still she retains
> Her Maiden-Gentleness, and oft at Eve
> Visits the Herds along the twilight Meadows,
> Helping all Urchin Blasts, and Ill-luck Signs,
> That the shrewd meddling Elf delights to make,
> Which she with precious viol'd Liquors heals.
> For which the Shepherds, at their Festivals,
> Carrol her Goodness loud in rustic Lays,
> And throw sweet Garland Wreaths into her Stream,
> Of Pancies, Pinks, and gaudy Daffodils.

And after she has relieved the Lady from the
Enchantment, the Spirit is supposed thus to address her,

> Virgin Daughter of *Locrine*,
> Sprung of old *Anchises'* Line,
> May thy brimmed Waves for this
> Their full Tribute never miss,

From

From a thoufand pretty Rills,
That tumble down the fnowy Hills:
Summer Drought or finged Air
Never fcorch thy Treffes fair;
Nor wet *October*'s torrent Flood
Thy molten Cryftal fill with Mud;
May thy Billows roll afhore
The Beryl and the golden Ore;
May thy lofty Head be crown'd
With many a Tow'r and Terrace round;
And here and there, thy Banks upon,
With Groves of Myrrh and Cinnamon.

We gently fell down by the *Rea*, a pretty Seat belonging to Mr. *Bernard Holland*, to *Hawry-Lodge*, where there is a Horfe-ferry, and here alfo the Views continued to be very beautiful. *Over-Areley* beforementioned foon after came into our Sight. This Village is pleafantly fituated on the Eaftern Bank. Here the County of *Stafford* runs out into a fmall Point, and croffes the *Severn*. In half an Hour we entered *Worcefterfhire*. At *Over-Areley* the elegant Lord *Lyttelton* has a Seat, and he is alfo Patron of the Church, where an handfome Monument is erected, with this Infcription *;

* In the Vault beneath is interred the Body of Sir *Henry Lyttelton*, Baronet, of *Frankley*, in the County of *Worcefter*, who died the 24th of *June*, 1693, aged 69 Years. He was firft married to Mrs. *Philadelphia Cary*, one of the Daughters and Coheireffes of Mr. *Thomas Cary*, Son of the Earl of *Monmouth*, and, after her Death, to the Hon. Mrs. *Elizabeth Newport*, Daughter of *Francis*, Lord Vifcount *Newport*, of *Bradford*, in *Shropfhire*, to whofe Memory this Monument is erected by his Brother and Heir, Sir *Charles Lyttelton*, Knt. and Baronet.

In the Chancel of this Church lies alfo buried his Brother, Captain *William Lyttelton*, and his beloved Nephew, *Henry Lyttelton*, eldeft Son of Sir *Charles Lyttelton*.

This

This Sir *Charles Lyttelton*, Grandfather to the Lord *Lyttelton*, was formerly attached to the *Stuart* Family. He was in Garrison when *Colchester* furrendered, and then went to *France* till Sir *George Booth*'s Rising, and was afterwards very serviceable to King *Charles* the Second. He was knighted in 1662, and became Governor of *Jamaica*; was at the Sea-Fight in *Solebay*, and a Commander at the Siege of *Maestricht*. He had other Employments till the Revolution, when he retired, and died at *Hagley*, from whence his Body was removed to this Church; to whose Memory a plain black Marble Stone is erected, and thus inscribed;

In Memory of Sir *Charles Lyttelton*, Knt. and Bart.
Who departed
This Life the 2d of *May*, 1716, in the 87th Year of his Age,
This humble Monument was set up by his particular and
Exprefs Direction, in his laft Will.

From *Areley* to *Bewdley*, this River and its Banks are (if poffible) more charming than before; in a Word, I own myfelf incapable of defcribing their Beauties, perhaps there are none in the Univerfe that can excel them.

The Town of *Bewdley*, or *Beau-lieu*, is overlooked by an ancient Royal Seat, ftanding upon an Eminence, called *Ticen-Hill*, or *Ticken-Hill*, i. e. *Goats-Hill*. This Houfe was built by King *Henry* the Seventh, for the Retirement of his Son, Prince *Arthur*, and hath a fweet Situation on the Weftern Side of the *Severn*. The greater Part of the Houfe at *Ticken-Hill*, together with a fine Park, was deftroyed in the civil Wars. That Part of the former which remains, is inhabited by the Families of Mr. *John Ingram* beforementioned (an honeft Lawyer). The other Inhabitant is Mr. *Beft*, a great Virtufo. Above this Houfe formerly ftood the extenfive Foreft of *Wyre*, in which about a thoufand

Trees were blown down in a Tempeſt, which happened about an hundred and ſeventy Years ago; and ſoon after the Remainder were cut down, ſo that, though this Foreſt continues to the Weſtward about ſix Miles, there are now no lofty Trees, the Practice of the Owners being that of cutting them down at fourteen Years Growth, for the Uſe of Furnaces and Forges. *Drayton* thus laments this Practice;

—— Soon the goodly *Wyre*, that wonted was ſo high
Her ſtately Top to rear, aſhamed to behold
Her ſtrait and goodly Woods unto the Furnace ſold,
(And looking on herſelf, by her Decay doth ſee
The Miſery wherein her Siſter-Foreſts be)
Of *Erſicthon*'s End begins her to bethink,
And of his cruel Plagues doth wiſh they all might drink,
That thus have them deſpoil'd, then of her own Deſpight
That ſhe in whom her Town, fair *Beaudley*, took Delight,
And, from her goodly Seat, conceived ſo high a Pride
In *Severn* on her Eaſt, *Wyre* on the ſetting Side,
So naked left of Woods, of Pleaſure, and forlorn,
As ſhe that lov'd her moſt, her now the moſt doth ſcorn.

Mr. *Tomkins*, Prebendary of *Worceſter*, in the Reign of Queen *Elizabeth*, a Gentleman of good Credit, who perſonally knew Sir *John Pakington*, of this County, Knight, and has left MS. Memoirs of his Life, affirms, that he had it from Sir *John* himſelf, that he, the ſaid Knight, bought at one Time ſo much Timber of the Earl of *Leiceſter*, out of this Foreſt of *Wyre*, that the very marking of them at four Pence *per* Tree, one with another, amounted to forty eight Pounds.

The Town of *Bewdley*, though not large, is remarkable for the Extenſiveneſs of its Trade, eſpecially in all Sorts of Groceries, Oils, Colours for dying, Cyder, Hops, and Clover-Seed. The Situation of it upon the *Severn* is ſuch, that to its oppoſite Shore arrive daily inconceivable Num-

Vol. I.   T t   bers

bers of Waggons from *Birmingham*, *Wolverhamp-ton*, *Walfal*, *Bilfon*, *Wednefbury*, *Halefowen*, and other Places, with innumerable Articles of Hard-Ware, which here are put on board Veffels upon the *Severn*, in order for Exportation. Befides thefe, come many laden with Glafs from *Stour-bridge*, and great Numbers of Packhorfes from *Manchefter* and *Wiggan* ; fo that back Carriage of Goods of all Kinds is very cheap from *Bewdley*, which enables the People of thofe diftant Places to have almoft all foreign Commodities cheapeft from this Town, more efpecially fo, as the Tradefmen here have generally large Stocks of Goods, and fell for a very low Profit The Town is very well built, but the lower Part of it is fometimes overflown by the fudden Rifes of the *Severn*. They have a neat Market-Houfe, and a new Chapel (for the whole Town is in the Parifh of *Ribbesford*) which is very elegant ; in which is a Ring of unharmonious Bells. The poorer Peo-ple, who inhabit in that Part called the *Wyre-Hill*, that leads towards *Cleobury* beforementioned, are chiefly employed in knitting what is called *Mon-mouth* Caps, for the Ufe of *Dutch* Sailors, and they are fuch very Vixens, that even the Damfels and Matrons of *Billingfgate*, or St. *Giles's*, cannot go beyond them.

The Town of *Bewdley* fent Burgeffes to Parlia-ment fo early as the Reign of *Edward* the Firft, and *Edward* the Fourth granted them a Charter of Incorporation ; but it has undergone many Inter-ruptions and Alterations : However, on the 19th of *December*, 1710, the Commons refolved, that the Charter, dated the 20th of *April*, 1708, at-tempted to be impofed on the Borough of *Bewd-ley*, againft the Confent of that antient Corpora-tion, was void, illegal, and deftructive of the Conftitution of Parliaments ; upon which Occa-sion,

fion, Sir *John Packington*, of this County, delivered himfelf very eloquently-bold, and the Queen
directed her Attorney and Sollicitor-General to
take the moft proper and effectual Meafures for
repealing the faid Charter. The Town is now
governed by a Bailiff, twelve Aldermen, a Recorder, Steward, Town-Clerk, twelve Capital Burgeffes, and two Serjeants at Mace. The Bailiff is
Juftice of Peace and Quorum, and Juftice for the
next Year; the Recorder is alfo a Juftice. The
Corporation elect only one Member to Parliament.
On the oppofite Side of the *Severn* ftands the
Hamlet of *Ribbefhall*, or *Rubbenhall*. Here it is
that the Waggons which I have mentioned unload. At the North End of this Hamlet is a fine
Houfe, fituate delightfully in the Meads, with
the *Severn* and Town of *Bewdley* in Front; it was
built by a Grocer in that Town, who ferved the
Office of High Sheriff for the County; but 'tis
now let out to different Families. To the Eaft of
it, upon an Hill, is a moft charming little Seat,
erected by a Quaker, which commands a moft delightful Profpect. The Bridge over the *Severn*
here is incommoded (like that at *Bedford)* with
what they call the *Bridge-Houfe*, and a large Hollow on the *Ribbenhall* Side is a great Inconve-
nience when the River is high. This Hollow, I
am told, is about to be filled up by one *Newton*,
who is the clevereft Fellow in forming and executing Turnpike Roads perhaps in *England*. On
the whole, *Bewdley* and its Neighbourhood is fo
inviting a Place, that I could like to fpend the
Remainder of my Days there. The Market is
on *Saturdays*, and the Fairs on *May* the 4th, for
Horfes, Horned Cattle, Cheefe, Linen and Woollen Cloth; another on *December* the 10th, for
Hogs only; the following Day, for Horned Cattle, Horfes, Cheefe, Linen and Woollen Cloth.

Richard

Richard Willis, D.D. Prebendary of *Weſtmin-ſter*, Biſhop of *Gloucefter*, and, in 1721, tranſ-lated to the See of *Saliſbury*, was a Native of *Bewdley*.

From *Rubbenhall*, which is in the Pariſh of *Kid-derminſter*, I ſet out for that Town, being at the Diſtance of two Miles: The Way to it is over a large Common, called *Kidderminſter-Heath*. On my Left Hand, I had a fine Hill, covered with Woods, where the late Lord *Herbert of Cher-bury* had a hunting Seat, fince occupied for the ſame Purpoſe by one Mr. *Ballard*, an Attorney in *Lincoln*'s *Inn*, or *Chancery-Lane*. My Road was fandy to *Kidderminſter*, which Town I entered by an hollow Way, and have not much to ſay of the Beauty of the whole Place. Its Situation is upon the Banks of the River *Stour*, which appears as dead a Water as the *Charwell* at *Oxford*. How-ever, it is of vaſt Service in the Buſineſs of Dy-ing: For this Town having an extraordinary good Manufactory of plain and figured Stuffs, and what is called *Linfey-Woolfeys*, and alſo having lately ſtruck into the making of Carpets, has much Occaſion for good Water. So happily are the Weavers here fallen into this latter Branch, that they equal thoſe of *Wilton*, and the Maſters can afford them much cheaper; and I am informed the Quantities of this Commodity made here, both for home Conſumption and foreign Trade, is incredible. One Quality in which their Carpets excel thoſe of *Wilton*, is, that they are much thicker. *Kidderminſter* is ſuppoſed to contain about Four thouſand Inhabitants, and that near Three thouſand are employed in the Manufac-tories.

They have a good Market on *Thurſdays*, and three Fairs, that is, on *Holy Thurſday*, three Weeks after that Day, and on the 4th of *September*, for

Horſes,

Horses, Horned Cattle, Cheese, Linen and Woollen Cloth.

Here is but one Church, the Incumbent is **Dr. Charlton**, Brother to Sir *Francis* already mentioned, and the Living (though half the Town are Diffenters) is worth Three hundred Pounds a Year.

In the Church are some Monuments of the *Cookseys* and *Blounts*, and one, with a Knight crosslegged, for Sir *Thomas Afton*.

The famous *Richard Baxter*, so ill used by Judge *Jefferies*, was a diffenting Minister of this Town*.

The Church, which is a good one, stands upon an Hill; and from it is a tolerable Prospect over the *Stour*. This River is capable of being made navigable for Barges. At the End of the Church is a Free-School, of which the late reverend, learned, eloquent, ingenious, and truly worthy Clergyman, Mr. *Thomas Cooke*, Rector of *Bayton*, in this County, was Sur-Master, whose Character is thus drawn, by a Gentleman who knew him well;

He had an excellent Genius, and a good Education,
Both which he improved so as to become
A Man of sound and solid Learning.
His Poems on the Divine Attributes
Are greatly admired,
And the Doctrine, which he delivered from the Pulpit,
Gained him general Applause,

Both

---

* Mr *Richard Baxter*, an eminent Presbyterian Divine, who had refused the Bishopric of *Hereford* soon after the Restoration, and who was equally remarkable for his Learning and Piety, was tried in the Year 1685, before *Jefferies*, at the King's Bench Bar, on a Charge of Sedition, for reflecting on the Prelates of the Church of *England*, in his Paraphrase on the *New Testament* The Jury were packed, and *Jefferies* treated the venerable old Gentleman with unparalleled Brutality, who was found guilty, and sentenced to pay a Fine of Five hundred Marks, to be in Prison till he paid it, and to be bound to his good Behaviour for seven Years; which Usage and Sentence were generally thought cruel.

Both as a Divine and Orator.
He was not cramped with the Stiffnefs of the Prieſt,
Yet ſuffered nothing that favour'd Immoralıty.
His Wıt was ſharp,
But ſhot from the Bow of Candour ;
His Sprıts were uncommon,
And hıs Company the moſt deſirable.
His Profeſſions were few, hıs Friendſhips laſting ;
His Heart honeſt, hıs Afflictions many;
His Conſtitution ſtrong, his Patience great ;
And his Submiſſion to the Will of Heaven
The moſt exemplary !

His Son, the Rev. Mr. *James Cooke*, ſucceeded
his Father in the School, but died ſoon afterwards;
the Place is now filled by the Rev. Mr. *Martyn*:
The Salary ıs ſixty Pounds a Year. In this Town
are two or three Almſhouſes. *Kidderminſter* formerly ſent Members to Parliament. It is now governed by a Bailiff, who is a Juſtice of Peace ;
twelve Capital Burgeſſes, twenty-five Common-
Council-Men, and other Officers, and, on the
whole, is a very flouriſhing Place, though partly
ſurrounded with Heaths and barren Sands. Such
are the Effects of Induſtry.

In the eleventh Year of *Richard* the Second,
Lord *John Beauchamp*, of *Holt*, was by Patent
created Baron of *Kidderminſter*, or, as then called,
Kiddermoſter, ın taıl to hıs Heir Male. This Nobleman had been before created by Inveſtiture of
Robes, and ſome Antiquaries affirm this to be the
fiıſt Patent of the Creation, or rather Confirmation, of a Baron*.

This Nobleman was afterwards beheaded by the
Barons.

Kid-

* The Words are " (Ipſum Johannem in unum Parium & Ba-
" ronum Regni noſtri Angliæ preficimus) volentes quod ıdem
" Johannes, & hæred maſculi de corpore ſuo exeuntes, ſtatum
" Baronis obtineant, ac domini de Beauchamp & Barones de
" Kiddermaſter nuncupenter In cujus reı Teſtimonium, &ç.
" Teſte Rege apud Weſtmonaſt. 10 die Octob."

Kidderminfter, as before obferved, gives at pre-fent the Title of Baron to the Lord *Foley*. I have now a few Miles to *Droitwich*, where I purpofe to take up my Evening Quarters, and am, Sir, Yours, *&c.*

L E T T E R XXXIV.

From *Hagley*, in *Worcefterfhire*.

S I R,

FROM *Kidderminfter*, the *Stour* runs to *Mitton*, a Place where are many Iron Forges belong-ing to the Knights already fpoken of. I rode to this Village, and leaving *Hertlebury Caftle* on the Right Hand, directed my Courfe to *Weftwood*, the Seat of the ancient Family of *Pakington*, or *Packington*. According to Sir *William Dugdale*, *Ofbert Fitz-Hugh*, and *Euftachia de Say*, his Mo-ther, erected here a Convent of Nuns, which was a Cell to *Font Ebrand*, or rather *Font-Evrand*.

The Family of *Packington* may be traced up to the Reign of *Henry* the Third. *William de Pa-kington* was Secretary and Treafure to *Edward*, the Black Prince, in *Gafcoigne*, and wrote a Chro-nicle in *French*, from the ninth Year of King *John*, to his own Time. One Sir *John Pakington* was Chirographer of the Court of Common-Pleas to King *Henry* the Eighth, from whom he had this memorable Grant, " That he, the faid *John Pa-* " *kington*, for the Time to come, fhall have full " Liberty, during his Life, to wear his Hat in " his [the King's] Prefence, and his Succeffors, " or of any other Perfon whatfoever," *&c.* His Grandfon, Sir *John Packington*, whom I have men-tioned in my laft Letter, was called *Lufty Pa-kington*. He was a noble Gentleman, and in great

Favour

Favour with Queen *Elizabeth*. The Timber which he bought of the Earl of *Leicefter* out of *Wyre* Foreft, was partly intended to keep out the frefh Springs from the Brine-Pits at *Droitwich*, which I fhall foon treat of, and partly for the building of his magnificent Houfe at *Weftwood*, which hath a moft delightful Situation, in the Center of a fine Wood, which, at confiderable Diftances, he cut into twelve large Ridings, with one Ring-Riding through all of them, and encompaffed the whole with a Park of fix or feven Miles in Campafs ; at the farther End of which, and facing the Houfe, he formed a grand Pond or Canal, which covered 122 Acres of Ground ; to this Piece of Water the bordering Woods afford a fine Contraft.

Sir *John Pakington*, the Grandfon of this Gentleman, was alfo a Perfon of Merit, and a great Sufferer for his Adherence to King *Charles* the Firft. His Lady, the Daughter of the Lord-Keeper *Coventry*, was, without Difpute, the Authorefs of that univerfal Book, *The Whole Duty of Man*, and the moft accomplifhed Lady of her Time. She had the Efteem and Affiftance of the incomparable Dr. *Hammond* (who was comfortably entertained, and highly honoured, in the Family many Years, and at length repofed his Bones in their Chapel at *Hampton-Lovit*). She was alfo highly honoured by the Bifhops *Morley*, *Fell*, *Pearfon*, *Henchman*, and *Gunning*. Mr. *Lloyd* (who lived at this Time) in his Lives of the Statefmen and Favourites of *England*, has drawn a Comparifon between thefe two Sir *John Pakingtons**.

During

---

* " Sir *John Pakington*, in Queen *Elizabeth*'s Time, was " virtuous and modeft ; and Sir *John Pakington*, in King " *Charles*'s Time, loyal and valiant , the one did well, the " other

During the Life of that Sir *John Packington* (the Grandson of the latter of these) who died in 1727, *Westwood* continued in its ancient Splendor and Magnificence, but, alas! 'tis now shamefully neglected, and suffered to fall into Ruin and Decay.

Near this House is the Church of *Hampton-Lovet*, where is the Burial-Place of this illustrious Family, from whence I could not forbear to copy the two monumental Inscriptions following;

Henricus Hammondus,
Ad cujus nomen assurgit quicquid
Est gentis literatâ
(Dignum nomen, quod auro,
Non atramento,
Nec in marmore perituro,
Sed adamante potius exaretur)
Musagetes celeberrimus,
Vir plane summus,
Theologus omnium consummatissimus,
Eruditæ pietatis decus simul & exemplar,
Sacri codicis Interpres
Facile omnium oculatissimus,
Errorm malleus post homines natos
Felicissimus,
Veritatis hyperaspystes
Supra quam dici potest nervosus;
In cujus scriptis elucescunt
Ingenii gravitas & acumen,
Judicii sublimitas & 'Ακρίβεια,
Sententiarum ογκ@ & Δεινότης,
Docendi methodus utilissima,
Nusquam dormitans diligentia.

" other suffered to. *Greenham* was his Favourite; *Hammond* his.
" The one had a competent Estate, and was contented; the
" other hath a large one, and is noble. This suppresseth Fac-
" tions in the Kingdom; the other composed them in the Court,
" and was called by Queen *Elizabeth,* her *Temperance;* by the
" Earl of *Leicester,* his *Modesty;* and by the other Courtiers,
" *Moderation. Westmoreland* tempted his Fidelity, and *Norfolk*
" his Steadfastness. But he died in his Bed, an honest and an-
" happy Man,"

Hammondus
(Inquam)
Ὁ πᾶν, in ipfa mortis vicinia pofitus,
Immortalitati quafi contiguus,
Exuvias mortis venerandas
Præter quas nihil mortale habuit
Sub obfcuro hoc marmore latere
Voluit vii. Cal. Majas, Ann. Ætat. LV,
MDCLX.

Here lies Sir *John Pakington*, Knt. and Bart. aged 65 Years ; an indulgent Father to his Children, a kind Mafter to his Servants ; charitable to the Poor, loyal to the King, and faithful to his Country : Who ferved in many Parliaments for the County of *Worcefter*, fpeaking his Mind there without Referve, neither fearing nor flattering thofe in Power, but defpifing all their Offers of Title and Preferment upon bafe and difhonourable Terms of Compliance : He was chofen Recorder for the City of *Worcefter* the 21ft of *February*, 1725, in the room of the Earl of *Plymouth*, deceafed, an Honour few ever enjoyed, under the Degree and Dignity of a Peer of the Realm. He died the 13th of *Auguft*, 1727.

Here alfo lie Sir *John Pakington*, Knt. and Bart, and his Lady, Grandfather and Grandmother to Sir *John*: The firft was try'd for his Life, and fpent the greateft Part of his Fortune in adhering to King *Charles* the Firft, and the latter, juftly reputed the Authorefs of *The Whole Duty of Man*, who was exemplary for her great Piety and Goodnefs.

Near *Weftwood*, upon the Banks of the River *Salwarp*, lies the Town of *Droitwich*, or rather *Dirtwich*, which Name *Camden* fuppofes to have been given to it (as *Hyetus* in *Bœotia*) on Account of its dirty Soil. By Grants of the *Saxon* Kings, *Kenulph*, *Edwin*, *Edgar*, and *Athelftan*, to the Church of *Worcefter*, and the Convent of *Perfhore*, it appears, that this Place was famous for its

Brine-

Brine-Pits, and that Salt was made here long before the Conqueſt, and is ſo mentioned in *Doomſday-Book*. There are now many Salt-Springs about this Town: Where they are ſalteſt, there grow no Herbs or Flowers; but in the adjoining Ditches may be found the *After Atticus*, with a pale Flower. Thoſe Springs which riſe to the Surface of the Earth, are not ſo ſalt as others, and there is great Variety in the Strength of the other Brines. That the whole Spot where theſe Waters riſe was a Bog, is generally allowed. They form their Pits of ſquare Elms, which continue long in moiſt Earth. The Soil on the lower Side of the Town is a black rich Earth, under which is a ſtiff, gravelly Clay, and below that is a Marle: If Springs are found in the Marle, the Waters are generally freſh, but if they ſink through the Marle, they come to a whitiſh Clay, mixed with Gravel, in which the Springs are brackiſh. The *Brines* at *Droitwich* are called *Firſt Man*, *Middle Man*, and *Laſt Man*. Four Tuns of the *Firſt Man*, or ſtrongeſt Brine, make upwards of a Tun of pure Salt; but the Produce of the others is leſs. That every Perſon may know his own Proportion, the *Brine* is divided into *Phats Wallings*. A *Phat Walling* is divided into twelve *Weaker Brines*, and every *Weaker Brine* into eight *Burdens*, every *Burden* being a Veſſel that contains about thirty-two Gallons; of this, every one has ſix Burdens of *Firſt Man*, ſix of *Middle Man*, and ſix of *Laſt Man*; ſo that every Perſon has not only his juſt Proportion in Quantity, but in Quality alſo. The *Brine* is carried to every Perſon's *Seal*, or *Boiling-Houſe*, by eight ſworn Men, who are called *Piaſters* of the *Beachin*, and four *Middle Men*, and there put into Veſſels, as ready for Uſe.

The Fuel formerly uſed for fixing the Salt here, was Wood from the Foreſt of *Feckenham* and *Nor-*

ton

ton Woods. But now they ufe Coals, which are brought from *Dudley* and its Neighbourhood, from whence this Place is diftant about thirteen Miles. The *Phats*, which the *Brine* is boiled in, are made of Lead, caft into flat Plates of a confiderable Length and Breadth, the Sides and Ends of which are beaten up, and they are a little raifed in the Middle. Thefe are fet upon Brick-Work, and have the Appellation of *Ovens*, in which is a Grate for the Fire, and an Hole for the Afhes, called a *Trunk.*

Three Pecks of white Salt are called a *Lade*, and is taken out of the Pan with a *Loot*, and put into *Barrows*, which are fet into *Baftals*, over Veffels denominated *Leachcombs*, that the *Brine* may run from the *Salt*. This *Brine* is called *Leach*, with which they drefs their *Phats*, when the cold *Brine* they are filled with is fomewhat boiled away. In thefe *Baftals* the Salt ftands till it is pretty dry, which is generally in about four Hours, and then is carried into *Cribs*, which are Houfes boarded on the Bottom and Sides, or into *Stoves*, to dry it for more immediate Sale.

It is to be obferved, that the *Brine* is clarified with nothing but the Whites of *Eggs*. A Quarter of one White, being put into a Gallon or two of *Brine*, and beaten with the Hand, lathers as though it were Soap. A fmall Quantity of which Froth thrown into each *Phat*, raifes all the Scum ; fo that the White of one Egg will clarify twenty Bufhels of Salt, by which means the Salt is extreamly white, and has not that ill Savour with that which is clarified with Blood.

Nothing is ufed to granulate the *Brine* here ; for is naturally fo ftrong, that unlefs it be often ftirred, the Grain will be as large as that of *Bay-Salt.*

You

You may boil this Brine to the Height of a *Candy*, when it will produce Clods of Salt as tranf-parent as the cleareft Allum, like the Salt of the Ifle of *May*: So that the People of *Droitwich* are obliged to put a fmall Quantity of Rofin into the *Brine*, that the Grain of the Salt may be fmall.

They have another Sort, which is called *Clot-Salt*, which adheres to the Bottom of the *Phats*, and after the *White Salt* is laded out, they dig up with a *Picker*, which is an Inftrument fimilar to a Mafon's Trowel, pointed with Steel, and fixed upon a fhort Staff. This *Salt* is exceflive ftrong, and is chiefly ufed for falting of Bacon and Neats Tongues. It is remarkable for making the Ba-con redder than any other Salt, and for confidera-bly hardening the Fat. The Dairy-Women like it beft of any in their *Rennet Pots*, and allow it to be the beft for their Cheefe ; but this Sort of Salt is held to be too ftrong for the falting of Beef, as 'tis known to carry off too much of its Sweetnefs and rich Juices.

Here is a third Sort, called *Knockings*, which candies on the *Barrow*, as the *Brine* runs from the *Salt*, after it is laded out of the *Phats*. This is bought by the lower Clafs of People to falt their Meat, Butter, &c.

A fourth Sort is called *Pidgeon Salt*. This is nothing but *Brine* hardened, after it has run through the Crack of a *Phat*, and hangs on the Outfide, over the Fire.

The *Salt-Loaves* made here are perhaps the fineft in the World: for by a fmall Addition of *Rofin*, the Salt wonderfully adheres together, and the Grain, which is extreamly fmall, is as clear and white as the driven Snow.

In a Word, the Salt made here hath thefe Quali-ties beyond any other: It is whiter, and confequently freer

freer from Drofs. It is heavier, and therefore better. It is ftronger, and therefore more profitable. And it preferves Flefh longer, efpecialiy in hot Climates, for which, without doubt, it is more valuable to a maritime Country.

Mr. *Wheeler*, formerly High Sheriff for *Worcefterfhire*, and a confiderable Propiietor in thefe Salt-Works, has often affured me, that he has made many Experiments of the Power of *Droitwich Salt*, and thofe of *Chefhire*, and that which is called *Salt upon Salt*, which is a Diffolution and Clarification of *Bay Salt*) and proved, that the former does not fo foon diffolve in damp Weather, moift Rooms, &c. as any of the o'hers.

The Town of *Droitwich* is large and populous; but cannot be fet down as an agreeable Place, for the Smoke of the Salt-Works is very offenfive.

By their Charter, granted by King *John*, which is now in the Poffeffion of the Corporation, this Town was allowed many fingular Privileges. King *Henry* the Third, and other Kings, have greatly favoured it. In the Reigns of *Edward* the Firft and Second, it returned Members eight Times to Parliament; but this was afterwards difcontinued, till the firft Year of Queen *Mary*, when new Privileges were added to the former; and *James* the Firft afterwards granted them a new Charter. It now fends two Reprefentatives to that honourable Houfe.

The Proprietors of the Salt-Springs are a Corporation, and no Perfon can be a Burgefs of this Town, without having fome Property in the Salt-Springs.

It is governed by a Bailiff, Burgeffes, &c. The former is a Juftice of the Quorum, and a Juftice of the Peace the Year afterwards. The Recorder is alfo a Juftice by his Office.

In

In the Year 1290, St. *Andrew's* Church, together with the greateſt Part of the Town, was burnt down, but 'tis now in a flouriſhing Condition. Here are a great Number of Salt-Officers, who are obliged to do Duty alternately both Night and Day. This Town has been rendered remarkable by its violently conteſted Elections, and for the *Woods* (Father and Son) who acquired conſiderable Fortunes by caſting the Water of the credulous People around. But this profitable Trade ſeems now to be fallen into the Hands of an Apothecary in the next Market-Town, which I intend to viſit. The Market here is held on *Fridays*, and Fairs on *Good-Friday*, *October* 28th, and *December* 21ſt, for Linen-Cloth, and Hats.

A little to the South of *Droitwich* is *Henlip*, a Place remarkable for the taking of *Garnet* and *Oldcorn*, two Jeſuits, concerned in the Powder-Plot, who were diſcovered in the Cavity of a Wall, over a Chimney. In this Houſe alſo was written by Mrs. *Abingdon*, Siſter to the Lord *Monteagle*, that well-known Letter, which gave Light into that moſt horrid Deſign.

From *Droitwich*, it is about ſeven Miles to the Town of *Bromſgrave*, or *Broomſgrave*. 'Tis ſituated on the ſmall River *Salwarp* beforementioned. This Town, which does ſome conſiderable Buſineſs in the Linen Manufactory (the Article is called *Bromſgrave Flaxen*) is pretty well built, and formerly ſent Members to Parliament : But, notwithſtanding this Privilege is loſt, it is ſtill governed by a Bailiff, Recorder, Aldermen, and other Officers. Here is a Charity-School for Teaching, Cloathing, and Putting out twelve Boys Apprentices annually. In this Town lives Mr. *Woodcock*, an Apothecary, who gets much pecuniary Advantage, and conſiderable Applauſe, from the *Woods* Myſtery of Water caſting beforementioned.

mentioned. The Market here is on *Tuesday*, and
Fairs on *June* the 24th, and *October* the 1st, for
Linen Cloth, Cheefe, and Horfes.

About Six o'clock on *Sunday* in the Afternoon,
I arrived at a large Inn, whofe Sign is the Arms
of the Family of *Lyttelton*. As this Houfe is
fituate at the End of *Hagley* Park, where four
Roads meet, it is fo much frequented by People
from the neighbouring, and even diftant Towns
and Villages, that, though it is a large Building,
they are making confiderable Additions. The
People of the Houfe are well behaved; they
fhewed me their Garden, which is pleafantly
fituated, and well laid out; but the moft remarkable Thing here is the Well, from whence they
draw their Water, after the Manner of the old one
in *Dover-Caftle*, that is, by Men in a large Wheel,
it being Two hundred and ten Feet deep.

The Chirping of domeftic Birds difturbed me
at Six o'Clock, and the fragrant Breath of the
Morning invited me abroad. Having croffed the
Road, I entered a broad and venerable Walk of
Trees, which leads to a fweet-fmelling Shrubbery.
On your Entrance into the Park is a Board fixed,
defiring that Vifitors would keep in the Paths,
and forbear fcribbling on the Buildings. From
this Place the Eye meets the Front of the
Manfion-Houfe, which Lord *Lyttelton* has juft
completed. The Situation is on a bold rifing
Ground in the Park, from whence the Profpect is
very extenfive. It is built with a fine-grained
Stone, of a dark brown Colour, and is a noble
Fabric. The Afcent to the Hall is by a Flight of
Steps, fomewhat like thofe of the Lord-Mayor's
Manfion-Houfe in *London*. What is very uncommon, here are no Offices, or any Buildings or Gardens whatfoever, adjoining to, or near the Houfe,
a broad Gravel Walk only furrounding the Whole.

The

The House is an elegant Building of One hundred and twenty Feet by sixty, with a ruftic Bafement, and four fquare Towers at the Corners. A Portico would perhaps afford a better Air to that large Flight of Steps in Front, as well as furnifh that Degree of Lightnefs and of Ornament, which has been thought wanting by fome Obfervers. From thefe Steps you enter an Hall twenty-eight Feet fquare, adorned with handfome Cafts of the *Dancing Faun*, of *Bacchus*, *Apollo*, and *Venus*, in four Niches. The Walls alfo are embellifhed with *Cupids*, and other Decorations in Plaifter, by *Verfalles*. Particularly, over the Chimney-Piece, is a *Pan*, as big as Life, offering up the Fleece to *Diana*.

Fronting this Hall is the Saloon ; to which you pafs betwixt two handfome Staircafes, that are each lighted from the Roof.

From the Hall you are led, firft to a Library on the Left, of thirty-two Feet by twenty-five ; where, over the Chimney, is an Half-Length of Mr. *Pope* ; and, over the two Doors, the Heads of Mr. *James Thomfon* and Mr. *Gilbert Weft*. The Cieling of this (as are thofe of all the chief Rooms) is agreeably ornamented with Stucco.

From hence you are conducted through two elegant Apartments, confifting of two Bed-Chambers, with double Dreffing-Rooms to each. The Dreffing-Room you enter from the Library, has its Walls almoft covered with Paintings, many of them by the moft famous Mafters.

You now enter a noble Saloon, of twenty-five Feet by twenty-eight, and nineteen high, the Walls whereof are enriched with large capital Pictures by *Vandyke*, *Rubens*, *Baffan*, *Titian*, &c. The Spaces betwixt the Pictures, as well as the Cieling, and the Cornice, are highly decorated with Stucco Ornaments. The Chimney-Piece is extreamly beautiful, as is alſo that in the Drawing-Room, to which you paſs from the Saloon.

The Walls of the Drawing-Room are covered with beautiful modern Tapeſtry, and the Cieling painted by a young *Italian*, lately arrived in *England*, with a Figure of *Flora*, within a large Oval, and four Boys, repreſenting the Seaſons, in four Compartments at the Corners. Over the Doors are the Heads of Lord *Hardwick*, Lord *Cheſterfield*, Lord *Cobham*, and Mr. *Pelham*. The Carving, Furniture, &c. in this Room is very elegant and well imagined.

You now enter the Gallery, which extends the Depth of the whole Houſe, a Square of its own Breadth being cut off at each End by two elegant fluted Columns. This Gallery is genteelly furniſhed, and adorned with many admirable Paintings.

From hence you paſs into the Dining-Room, of the ſame Dimenſions with the Library, the Walls of Stucco, with Embelliſhments : The Pictures are thoſe of Admiral *Smith*, Commodore *Weſt*, and Judge *Lyttelton*, Governor *Lyttelton*, and Miſs *Lyttelton*, at full Length. From hence you return into the Hall again.

The Views from the Windows of this Front are very extenſive, including *Malvern Hills*, &c. towards your Left, the *Black Mountains* in *Wales*, and other diſtant Hills towards the Right: As thoſe from the back Front afford agreeable home Scenes of Retirement and Tranquillity.

There are ſome good antique and modern Buſts in the Apartments of this Houſe, which demonſtrate the elegant Taſte of its Owner.

Leaving the Houſe, I was ſoon led by a gravelly Path into the Church-Yard, which, together with the Church, is ſo embowered in Trees, that you would not gueſs what Place it is till you enter

by

by a little Wicket. Advancing farther, it ftrikes
you juft as fuch a Church-Yard as Mr. *Gray* drew
his Picture from. At one End of it is an Infcription, which for its Simplicity I enclofe to you.

Here lies the Body of Mrs.
Cath. Lyttelton, who lived free from
The Cares of this World,
And died happily in the 68th
Year of her Age, in the Year of
Our Lord 1742.

In this Church is a Monument to the Memory
of Lord *Lyttelton*'s firft Lady. The Epitaph was
written by his Lordfhip, and of which I know you
have a Copy.

From the Church I gradually afcended an Hill,
the Top of which prefents to you the moft amazing View you ever beheld. It looks towards the
Weft, having the Houfe at fome Diftance below,
which from hence affords a grand Appearance.
Over this, the Eye is enticed to a prodigious Variety of Lawns, Towns, and Villages, quite to
the *Clee-Hills* already mentioned, and beyond them
to the Mountains in many Counties of *Wales*. On
the Right, beyond the Village of *Hagley*, the View
continues to the *Wrekin*, and then over a fine
Country to the Mountains of *Denbigh* and *Montgomery* Shires. On the South is a Wood, and beyond
that the lofty Hill of *Clent* (on Part of which this
Park is formed) obftructs the View that Way. In
order to feaft the Minds of Beholders, on this Spot
is placed a Seat, on which are painted thefe Words:

Thefe are thy glorious Works, Parent of Good!
Almighty! thine this univerfal Frame,
Thus wond'rous fair, Thyfelf how wond'rous then!
Unfpeakable! who, Firft above thefe Heavens,
To us invifible, or dimly feen,
In thefe thy loweft Works, yet thefe declare
Thy Goodnefs beyond Thought, and Pow'r divine.

X x 2

From

From this celestial Spot (if I may use the Expression) I followed my Path, which brought me to the finest Contrast, as to Situation, that can be conceived. After turning down a Steep, embowered with Trees, I came to the most charming Retirement in the World. Here is a fine Piece of crystal Water, where Art and Nature, Taste and Judgment, seem to be Candidates for the Preference. On one Side of this Water is a most affecting Cave or Grotto, so nicely lined and covered with Mofs, that can fcarcely be imagined, and within it, on a fmall Tablet, is written,

—— Ego laudo Ruris amæni,
Rives & Mufco circumlita Saxa nemufque.

At the Head of this Water is a pretty Seat, from whence the View to an Ifland, a Cafcade, and a Vifta through the Trees, is beyond Defcription. From hence, rifing up a fmall Bank, I came to an Hermitage, which is built with Roots of Trees, covered and lined with Mofs. At the Entrance is a plain, homely Bench, and a ruftic Wicket. The Infide is furrounded with a Seat, covered with Matting, and againft the further End hangs a Tablet, with thefe Lines, from *Milton*'s *Il Penferofo* ;

> May at laft my weary Age
> Find out the peaceful Hermitage,
> The hairy Gown, and mofly Cell,
> Where I may fit, and rightly fpell
> Of ev'ry Star that Heav'n doth fhew,
> And ev'ry Herb that fips the Dew ,
> Till old Experience do attain
> To fomething like prophetic Strain.
> Thefe Pleafures, Melancholly, give,
> And I with thee will choofe to live.

This Building hath a much more natural Appearance than the Hermitage at *Stowe* ; and the Place is fo inviting, being cool and reclufe, though
full

full of the airy Songsters, that I could willingly
have given myself a longer Indulgence. From
hence I pursued my Path to a pretty Alcove, which
faces the thick Part of a Wood; and here the
Eye is much confined. Overhead is a large Star,
done with Shells of various Colours, and on the
Back of the Building, these Letters of the same
Materials;

Cut
281.

Sedes Contemplationis.

Omnia Vanitas.

' From hence, following the Path, some Steps
lead you out of the Park to the lofty Summit of
Clent-Hill. Here Lord *Lyttelton* has planted several
Clumps of Fir-Trees, which Clumps might perhaps be caused to have similar Effects as that called
Nelson's Seat at *Stowe.* From this lofty Mountain
the Prospect is more extensive than that in the Park,
but not so exquisite. *Drayton,* speaking of *Clent-
Hills,* says,

—— By his swelling Soil set in so high a Place,
That *Malvern*'s mighty self he seemeth to out-face.

Malvern-Hills I have before mentioned. On the
South of *Clent-Hill* formerly stood the great Forest
of *Feckenham,* the Fall of which the same Author
thus makes him lament;

Now back again I turn, the Land with me to take
From the *Staffordian* Heaths, as *Stour* her Course doth
    make,
Which *Clent* from his proud Top contentedly doth view:
But yet the aged Hill immoderately doth rue
Her loved *Feck'nam*'s Fall, and doth her State bemoan,
To please his am'rous Eye, whose like the World had none.

I returned into the Park by the Way I left it,
and then had before me, in Appearance, the Remains of an ancient Castle, which had one Tower
standing; the others, which were three in Number,

ber, feemed to have been demolifhed by Hoftilities, or the devouring Tooth of Time. The Remains of a *Gothic* Window, the Ivy, and other Vegetables, creeping on the decayed Walls, and the Peacocks and Turkeys ftanding upon the fame, all together formed a tolerable good Deception ; but what betrays it much, is the Whitenefs and Smoothnefs of the Mortar which cements the whole : For I am to inform you, Sir, that 'tis all a modern Building, done by Mr. *Miller*, of *Radway* in *Warwickfhire* (the Architect of the Manfion-Houfe here) who has been famous for this Sort of Impofition upon the Underftandings of his Majefty's liege Subjects.

From this Place I directed my Courfe to the Eaft, where the Land became more open, and here is one of the prettieft *Gothic* Alcoves imaginable, fupported by four neat fluted Pillars.

I purfued my Walk to an Houfe, called, I think, the *Dairy* ; here is a good Garden, and two or three fmall Images. Near this Garden is a Well, with a Machine and Buckets of a fingular Conftruction. From hence I came to a beautiful Summer-Houfe, or Temple, delightfully fituated (and facing another, which is erected in the Midft of a Wood). This Place, before which is a fine Lawn, and beyond that the moft veneiable Affemblage of Foreft-Trees, over which, towaids the Left-Hand, the Mock Ruin before mentioned, and a Tuft of Trees upon *Clent Hill*, appeared to fine Advantage, and, on the Right, as it were enclofed in a Wood, a Lawn full of Deer, and another Seat, render the whole quite charming, and make one think of nothing but the Plains of *Arcadia*. Over the Seat in the Building where I ftood, is this Infcription ;

Ingenio

Ingenio immortali
Jacobi Thomfon,
Poetæ fublimis,
Viri boni,
Ædiculum hanc, in Seceffu quem vivus dilexit,
Poft Mortem ejus conftructam,
Dicat, dedicatque
Georgius Lyttelton.

Thence, towards the Weft, you come to a Wood, and then to a lofty Obelifk, on which are the Arms and Motto of the late Prince of *Wales,* to whom it was dedicated. It ftands on a fine rifing Lawn, with hanging Woods; and from whence to the Weft, is a full View of the Eaft Side of the Manfion-Houfe already mentioned. Turning to the Left, you come to a moft pleafing cryftal Stream, that gurgles over Pebbles, in which there are little Falls, through a fweet graffy Margin, to the Side of the Church-Yard, where it difappears. From this Place, purfuing the Side of the Stream, you are led into another fweet Recefs, where alfo is another Piece of Water; upon the Dam of which is a whimfical Brick Building, with wicker Chairs in it, and on the Wall thefe Words,

—— Viridantia Tempe,
Tempe, quæ fylvæ circunt fuper-impendentes.

What Pity is it, that neither Gratitude or Good-Manners can prevail with fome People; for here and elfewhere, notwithftanding his Lordfhip's Requeft to the contrary, are many Scribblings on the Wall, which give Offence to Decency. From this Fabric, over the Piece of Water (where occafion-ally is a Cafcade) is a fine Vifta through the Woods, to an elegant Temple upon a rifing Ground: 'Tis built fomewhat like the Rotunda at
Stowe,

Stowe, but much neater: That at Lord *Temple*'s is supported by ten Columns, with a *Venus* in the Center, but this stands only upon eight, without any Statue within, and therefore hath a more airy and unclouded Appearance.

Not far off, in the Wood, stands the Building, which I have before observed to face *Thomson*'s Temple; and here the Woods were vastly cool and agreeable. I now returned partly by the Way I came, and, ascending an easy Path, was led to a Seat, close by which the murmuring Water gushes out from beneath the grassy Surface. Here I sat me down, and contemplated the Happiness of this desirable Retreat, and the unrivalled Bliss which this illustrious Person must have enjoyed, during the matrimonial Days of his beloved *Lucy*, whom he so finely laments in that Poem, from which (as it touches so much on the Beauties of this incomparable Spot) I must be indulged a Quotation.

> Ye tufted Groves, ye gently-falling Rills,
>   Ye high o'er-shadowing Hills,
> Ye Lawns, gay-smiling with eternal Green,
>   Oft have you my *Lucy* seen!
> But never shall you now behold her more:
>   Nor will she now, with fond Delight,
> And Taste refin'd, your rural Charms explore.
>   Clos'd are those beauteous Eyes in endless Night,
> Those beauteous Eyes, where, beaming, us'd to shine
> Reason's pure Light, and Virtue's Spark divine.
>
> Oft would the *Dryads* of these Woods rejoice
>   To hear her heavenly Voice,
> For her despising, when she deign'd to sing,
>   The sweetest Songsters of the Spring.
> The Woodlark and the Linet pleas'd no more;
>   The Nightingale was mute,
>   And ev'ry Shepherd's Flute,
>   Was cast in silent Scorn away,
>   While all attended to her sweeter Lay.

Ye

Ye Larks and Linnets now resume your Song,
　　And thou, melodious *Philomel*,
　　Again thy plaintiff Story tell,
For Death has stopt that tuneful Tongue,
Whose Music could alone your warbling Notes excel.

　　In vain I look around,
　　Oe'r all the well-known Ground,
My *Lucy*'s wonted Footsteps to descry ;
　　Where oft we us'd to walk,
　　Where, in soft, tender Talk,
We saw the Summer Sun go down the Sky ;
　　Nor by yon Fountain's Side,
　　Nor where the Waters glide
Along the Valley, can she now be found :
In all the wide-stretch'd Prospects ample Bound,
　　No more my mournful Eye
　　Can aught of her espy,
But the sad sacred Earth where her dear Relics lie.

　　O Shades of *Hagley* ! where is now your Boast ?
　　Your bright Inhabitant is lost.
You she prefer'd to all the gay Resorts,
　　Where female Vanity might wish to shine,
The Pomp of Cities, and the Pride of Courts.
Her modest Beauties shun'd the public Eye.
　　To your sequester'd Dales,
　　And flow'r-embroider'd Vales,
From an admiring World she chose to fly ;
With Nature there retir'd, and Nature's God,
　　The silent Paths of Wisdom trod,
And banish'd ev'ry Passion from her Breast,
　　But those, the gentlest, and the best,
Whose holy Flames, with Energy divine,
The virtuous Heart enliven and improve,
The conjugal and the maternal Love.

I shall end my Letter with a few Lines from the
excellent Mr. *Thomson*'s Description of *Hagley*
Park (though written before the above Poem).
He thus addresses his Patron ;

Courting the Muse, through *Hagley* Park thou strayest ;
Thy *British Tempe* ! There along the Dale,
With Woods o'erhung, and shagg'd with mossy Rocks,

Whence on each Hand the gushing Waters play,
And down the rough Cascade white-dashing fall,
Or gleam in lengthen'd Vista through the Trees,
You silent steal ; or sit beneath the Shade
Of solemn Oaks, that tuft the swelling Mounts,
Thrown graceful round by Nature's careless Hand,
And pensive listen to the various Voice
Of rural Peace : The Herds, the Flocks, the Birds,
The hollow-whisp'ring Breeze, the Plaint of Rills,
That, purling down, amid the twisted Roots
Which creep around, their dewy Murmurs shake
On the sooth'd Ear.

Again,

——You gain the Height, from whose fair Brow
The bursting Prospect gains immense around :
And snatch'd o'er Hill and Dale, and Wood and Lawn,
And verdant Field, and dark'ning Heath between,
And Villages embosom'd soft in Trees,
And spiry Towns, by surging Columns mark'd
Of houshold Smoke, your Eye excursive roams :
Wide-stretching from the Hall, in whose kind Haunt
The hospitable Genius lingers still,
To where the broken Landscape, by Degrees,
Ascending, roughens into rigid Hills ;
O'er which the *Cambrian* Mountains, like far Clouds,
That skirt the blue Horizon, dusky rise.

It is well known, that *Thomson* had not much
Reason to repine at the Happiness of *Horace.* The
Roman had his *Mecænas* ; the *Briton,* his *Lyttelton.*
I am, Sir, Yours, &c.

L E T T E R XXXV.

From *Hales-Owen*, in *Shropſhire*.

S I R,

FROM *Hagley* to *Hales-Owen* is about two Miles and a half; the Road is good, and the Country pleaſant, but I found nothing material.

Hales-Owen is a tolerably large Town, though the Market there is not conſiderable. It is encloſed by the Counties of *Stafford* and *Worceſter*, but belongs to that of *Salop.*

The Manor and Advowſon of the Church of *Hales-Owen* was by King *John*, in the 16th Year of his Reign, given to *Peter de Rupibus*, Biſhop of *Wincheſter*, with a View to his erecting a Religious Houſe here, which he founded accordingly; and endowed with this Eſtate, which was confirmed by King *Henry* the Third. In the Year 1248, *Roger*, Biſhop of *Litchfield* and *Coventry*, appropriated the Church of *Waleſhale*, to this Abbey, after the Death of *Vincent*, then Rector of the ſaid Church, reſerving out of it thirteen Marks, to be aſſigned to a Vicar, with all Obventions, *&c.* In the Year 1270, *Godfrey*, Biſhop of *Worceſter*, made a Settlement between the Abbot of *Hales-Owen* and the perpetual Vicar of the Pariſh Church there; the ſaid Vicar to have and receive from the Abbot, ten Marks yearly, an Houſe, with Outhouſes, Orchard, Garden, and the Veſture of the Church-Yard: The Canons to find another Prieſt to be under the Vicar, and to bear all ordinary and extraordinary Charges. *Emma*, the Daughter of *Thomas de Lyttelton*, was a great Benefactreſs to this Abbey · She died in 1298. *John de Hampton*,

Joan

Joan Botecourt, and *John*, her Son, conditioning for Chantries, gave several Manors and Advowsons to this Abbey. *Wolstan*, Bishop of *Worcester*, appropriated to it the Church of *Clent*, and Chapel of *Rowley*, reserving to the perpetual Vicar, who had the Cure of Souls there, a Revenue of ten Pounds, i. e. a Messuage and Curtelage on the South Side of the Church-Yard, with Tythe of Calves, Lambs, &c. and all Small Tythes (except of the Monasteries proper Lands) Mortuaries, and the Herbage and Trees of the Church Yard, and all the Altarage.

This House, whose Monks were of the Order of *Premonstratenses*, was, at the Dissolution, valued at Two hundred and eighty Pounds thirteen Shillings and two Pence *per Annum* *.

There are yet some Remains of this Abbey. The Church (which has a Miniature Appearance of *Salisbury* Cathedral) hath a very beautiful Spire, and the Roof the Church is supported by four curious *Gothic* Arches.

The Manufactures of this Place are Nails, and various Sorts of Hardware. Their nearest considerable Market is that of *Stourbridge*. There is at *Hales-Owen*, a Pleasure-Fair held on *Easter-Monday*, and one for Horses, Horned Cattle, and Sheep, on the 22d of *June*. I am, Sir, Yours, &c.

---

* In the Will of Sir *Thomas de Lyttelton*, the celebrated Author of the *Tenures*, are these Words :

" I will and bequeth to the Abbot and Covent of *Hales*
" *Oweyn*, a Boke of myn, called *Catholicon*, to theyr own
" Use for ever, and another Boke of myn, wherein is con-
" taigned, the Constitutions Provincial, and *De Gestis Romano-*
" *rum*, and other Treatis therein, which I will to be laid and
" bounded with an Yron Chain, in som convenient Parte with
" in the said Church, at my Costs, so that all Preests and others
" may se and rede it whenne it pleasith them "

LETTER XXXVI.

From Stratford upon Avon, in Warwickſhire.

S I R,

FROM the Seat of Mr. *Shenſtone*, near this Town (which I ſhall hereafter deſcribe) the Road to *Birmingham* is good, and the Country pleaſant. I entered this Town on the Side where ſtands St. *Philip's*, or, as 'tis commonly called, the *New Church*. This is a very beautiful modern Building of Free-Stone; 'tis ſomewhat like that of St. *Mary's* in the *Strand*. There are but few in *London* ſo elegant. It ſtands in the Middle of a large Church-Yard, around which is a beautiful Walk, adorned with Trees like thoſe in *Lincolns-Inn* Gardens. On one Side of this Church-Yard the Buildings are as lofty, elegant, and uniform as thoſe of *Bedford-Row*, and are inhabited by People of Fortune, who are great wholeſale Dealers in the Manufactures of this Town (particularly Mr. *Thomas Tipping*, whoſe Father, Mr. *Walter Tipping*, has been known to ſend away a Waggon-Load of what are called *Jews-Harps* at a Time). Theſe Buildings have the Appellation of *Tory-Row*; and this is the higheſt and genteeleſt Part of the Town of *Birmingham*. The other Church is dedicated to St. *Martin*, and is called, by Way of Diſtinction, the *Old Church*; which hath a lofty Spire, and a new Set of tuneable Bells, caſt by Mr. *Leſter* of *Whitechapel*. Theſe are all the Churches in this prodigious Town, excepting that of *Deritend*, which is on the other Side of the River *Tame* (this Stream, after having flowed by *Tamworth*, falls into the *Trent* a little below *Litchfield*). Indeed at

'the

the Weſt End of the Town of *Birmingham* is lately
erected a very large and handſome Chapel, ſomething like the Church of *Bethnall-Green*. Thus
this amazing Place, which is near as large as *Briſtol*, hath but two Churches and a Chapel. The
ſuperior Officer at *Birmingham* (excepting Gentle-
tlemen in the Commiſſion of the Peace) is a Con-
ſtable. It is owing, in a great Meaſure, to its
being a free Place, that 'tis ſo wonderfully populous and thriving ; for which Reaſon, I look upon
the Incorporations of almoſt all Towns to be, in
many Reſpects, greatly to their own Detriment.

Bremingham, *Bermincham*, or, as 'tis modernly
called, *Birmingham*, is in general well built; it has
a very wholeſome Air, and the Markets are well
ſupplied. Coals are cheap here, otherwiſe the
Place muſt be ruined ; for the Conſumption of
that Commodity is prodigious. In a Word, ſo
large are the Manufactures of this Town, that I
am well informed, they amount to more than Five
millions *per Annum*. This might ſeems ſtrange to
one who has not been in *Birmingham* ; but one Vi-
ſitation of it would ſoon remove ſuch Surprize.
The lower Part of the Place is watery and dirty,
but all the new Streets (of which there are Abundance) are very dry and clean. This Town gives
the Title of Baron, to *John*, Lord *Ward*.

The Lord Lieutenant and Cuſtos Rotulorum of
this County of *Warwick* is the Earl of *Hertford*.

In St. *Philip*'s Pariſh is a Charity-School for
fifty Boys and Girls, and in what is called the *New
Street*, though there are above fifty newer, is a
large handſome Free-School, rebuilt, and over the
Gate this Inſcription ;

Edvardus Sextus
Scholam hanc fundavit,
Anno Regni Quinto.

In this Town, in the Time of the late Rebellion, the whole Army of his Royal Highness the Duke of *Cumberland* was quartered. To which Place, by forced Marches from *Stonefield*, he got that Advantage over the Rebels, which made them return from *Derby*, and was, in a great Measure, the Crushing of that bold Attempt, and the unhappy Adventurer's leaving this Kingdom.

The Market at *Birmingham* is held on *Thursdays*, and the Fairs on *Thursday* in *Whitsun-Week*, and the 10th of *October*, for Hardware, Horses, Cattle, and Sheep.

Near this Town is *Afton* or *Birmingham-Afton*; Sir *William Dugdale* calls it *Afton-Stocklands*, the Seat of the ancient and loyal Family of *Holte*. The House is noble, and adorned with many good Paintings; and the Park is enclosed by a strong Wall of Brick. The present Baronet, Sir *Lifter Holte*, who married the Lady *Anne Legge*, Daughter of *William*, Earl of *Dartmouth*, resides at this Seat, where King *Charles* the First lay two Nights just before the Battle of *Edgehill*. Sir *Thomas Holte*, the Possessor of this House and Estate, was then about seventy Years old, and therefore uncapable of joining the King's Forces; but his Son being actually in the Royal Service, the Troops of the Parliament plundered this House, imprisoned him, decimated his Estate, and forced such Contributions, that he sustained upwards of Twenty thousand Pounds Damages. This good old Gentleman left by Will Three hundred Pounds for the building an Hospital in this Village, for five Men and five Women, and appointed a Rent-Charge of eighty-eight Pounds, out of the Manor of *Eraington*, for their Support. Over the Door of this Almshouse are the Arms of *Holte*, together with this Inscription;

This

This Almshouse was,
By the Charity of Sir *Thomas Holte*, late of this Town and
County, Knight and Baronet, deceased,
Provided for
And appointed to be built, and was in order thereto
Accordingly erected by his Grandson and Heir, Sir *Robert
Holte*, Baronet,
In the Year of our Lord God 1655 and 1656.
Laus Deo.

In the Church of this Village, this Sir *Thomas
Holte* was interred, where, on a large Marble Mo-
nument, on the East Wall of the North Ile, these
Words are inscribed;

H. S. E.
Thomas Holte, Eques & Baronettus,
Quibus Titulis a Jacobo I°.
Ob Patriæ Amorem, Vitæ Integritatem,
Morum Candorem, erga Principem Fidem,
Erga Pauperes Liberalitatem, erga omnes Justitiam,
Insignitus est
Flagrante Bello Civili,
E re sua familaribis confiscata & decima parte semel proscripta
Quicquid reliquit Fanatica Rabies
Caroli I^{mi}, (cui *Edwardus* filius a Cubiculus fuit)
Incarceratus licet in Subsidium contulit
Tandem vero Ædes *Astonianas* nobili Magnificentia extruxit
Nec tamen Egenis defuit
Quibus Hospitium pari Munificentia Vicinum condidit,
Eximia ingentis Animi Monumenta,
Cujus Memoriæ alterum hoc Monumentum
Non Supervacaneum censuit
Carolus Holte, Baronettus, Pronepos.
Duas habuit Uxores, Gratiam, *Gul. Brad-
Bourne*, & de *Hough*, in Agro *Derbiensi*, Arm.
Filiam & Cohæredem; ex qua Quindenam
Suscepit Sobolem,
Sed nullam Superstitem præter Gratiam, *Rich.
Shukburgh* de *Shukburgh*, in Agro
Warwicensi Militis Uxorem;
Anna *Edv. Lyttleton*, de *Pillaton*,
In Agro *Staffordiensi*, Baronetti, Filiam,

Quam

Quam fine prole reliquit Viduam

Obiit Anno $\left\{\begin{array}{l}\text{Ætatis fuæ 83,} \\ \text{Sal. Hum. MDCLIV.}\end{array}\right.$

About a Mile from this Seat, and near to *Bir-mingham*, is *Dudfton*, or *Duddleftone*, formerly a Gentleman's Seat, but now converted into a Place for Mufic and other Entertainments, after the Manner of *Vauxhall*.

From *Birmingham* to *Stratford upon Avon*, the Road was good, and chiefly through that Part of *Warwickfhire*, which was formerly the Foreft of *Arden*, but 'tis now well cultivated by the Plough. *Drayton*'s Argument to his thirteenth Song is very pretty ;

His Song our Shire of *Warwick* founds ;
Revives old *Arden*'s ancient Bounds.
Through many Shapes the Mufe here roves,
Now fporting in thefe fhady Groves,
The Tunes of Birds oft ftays to hear ;
Then finding Herds of lufty Deer,
She, Huntrefs-like, the Hart purfues,
And, like a Hermit, walks to chufe
The Simples every where that grow.

He then difcovers himfelf to be the Country-man of his Cotemporary, *William Shakefpeare* ;

My native Country then, which fo brave Spirits has bred:
If there be Virtue yet remaining in this Earth,
Or any good of thine thou breath'dft into my Birth,
Accept it as thine own : Whilft now I fing of thee,
Of all thy later Brood, th' unworthieft though I be.

I rode to *Henley*, which is a pretty Town, near which ftood *Bell-Defert*, a Caftle belonging to the *Montfords*, now in Ruins ; and foon after arrived at the *White-Lion* in *Stratford upon Avon*. This is one of the beft Inns, and has perhaps the moft fenfible, obliging Landlord in *England* ; his Name is *Peyton* Over the Gateway in the Yard is a good Half-Length of *Shakefpeare*. This Houfe, which

VOL. I.   Z z   has

has large Bow-Windows on each Side of this Picture, is one of the neateſt and beſt managed of any Thing I have ſeen of the Kind. In a Word, every Thing was ſo quiet and well conducted, that I fancied myſelf under your Roof in the Iſle of *Wight.* The Town of *Stratford* ſtands upon the ſame Side of the *Avon* with *Eveſham* and *Perſhore;* but is as large as both thoſe Towns ; the Streets are ſpacious, and the Buildings good. It is very full of Inhabitants, and remaikable for the Buſi-neſs of Malt-making. The River *Avon* is of great Benefit to it, for the carrying off their Malt, Corn, Cheeſe, and other Commodities, and the Importation (if it may be ſo termed) of Groceries, Iron, Lead, Coals, &c. The Bridge over this River is a very good one, having fourteen Arches, and was built by Sir *Hugh Cloſton,* Lord Mayor of *London.* The Lordſhip of *Stratford,* for many Years before the Conqueſt, has belonged to the Biſhops of *Worceſter.* King *Edward* the Sixth in-corporated this Town by a Bailiff, Burgeſſes, and other Officers, and allowed them a Common Seal. He alſo granted to the Inhabitants Lands and Poſ-feſſions, which had belonged to that called the *Gild of the Holy Croſs,* for the Maintenance of a Gram-mar-School and Almſhouſes. *Stratford* is now go-verned by a Mayor, Recorder, High-Steward (the Duke of *Dorſet*) twelve Aldermen, of whom two are Juſtices of the Peace, and twelve Capital Bur-geſſes. The Market is on *Thurſdays,* and the Fairs on *May* the 14th, *September* the 25th, and *Thurſday* ſe'nnight after, for Cheeſe, Hops, and Cattle

The Church, dedicated to the *Holy Trinity,* is ſituate by the Side of the *Avon,* at the Weſt End of the Town : The Church-Yard is beautifully planted with Trees, and commands a delicious

View,

View, both up and down that gently-gliding River, whofe Courfe *Drayton* thus defcribes;

> ——— *Avon's* winding Streame'
> By *Warwick*, entertains the high-complexion'd *Leame*:
> And as fhe thence along to *Stratford* on doth ftrain,
> Receiveth little *Heile*, the next into her Train.
> Then taketh in the *Stour*, the Brook of all the reft
> Which that moft goodly *Vale* of *Red-Horfe* loveth beft ,
> A Valley that enjoys a very great Eftate.

In this Town a Nunnery, dedicated to St. *Leo-
pard*, was founded and endowed by *Chriftiana de
Sameri*, and her Son, which was confirmed by
King *Stephen*. *Galienea*, and her Son, *Bartholomeus
de Daumartin*, Patrons of the House, alfo gave
Lands to it, which were confirmed by King *Richard* the Firft.

The Church (Part of which was built before
the Conqueft) is very handfome, and in good Repair. The prefent South Ifle was erected at the
Expence of *John de Stratford*, Archbifhop of *Canterbury*; the Choir, by *Thomas Balfhal*; both Na-
tives of this Town. And the North and South
Crofs, by the Executors of Sir *Hugh Clifton* be- Clopton
forementioned. But what renders it moft remarkable is, its having the Honour of enclofing the
Bones of the immortal *Shakefpeare*. They lie under a flat Stone, on the North Side of the Chancel, near thofe of his Daughter *Hall*, and Mr.
John Coombe His Monument is placed on the
Wall, with his Buft in the Habit of the Times,
and under it the Arms of his Family : But the Infcriptions are too mean to deferve copying, fave
this,

Obiit An. Dom. 1616. Ætat. 53. Die. 23. Apri.

That the Father of this inimitable Man was a
Dealer in Wool, and of a good Family, Mr. *Rowe*
and Mr. *Anftis* have clearly made appear : There-

fore

fore what Mr. *Aubrey* fays, that he had been told he was a Butcher, is of no Weight. However, though I made what Enquiry I could, I do not find that there is now one Perfon of the Name of *Shakefpeare* in the whole Town of *Stratford*. His Monument, the Sexton's Wife told me, had been very much neglected, and had a lamentable Appearance till about four or five Years fince, when *Ward's Company of Comedians* repaired and beautified it, from the Produce of a Benefit Play, exhibited tor that Purpofe. I fhall now juft trouble you with a few fhort Quotations regarding this great Genius.

The firft is the Lines of *Ben Johnfon.*

Sweet Swan of *Avon !* what a Sight it were
To fee thee in our Water yet appear,
And make thofe Flights upon the Banks of *Thames,*
That fo did take *Eliza* and our *James.*
But ftay, I fee thee in the Hemifphere
Advanc'd, and made a Conftellation there.
Shine forth, thou *Starre of Poets,* and with Rage,
Or Influence, chide, or cheer the drooping Stage,
Which, fince thy Flight from hence, hath mourn'd like
     Night,
And defpairs Day, but for thy Volumes Light.

The fecond is from Mr. *Smart's* Prologue to *Othello.*

Methinks I fee, with Fancy's magic Eye,
The Shade of *Shakefpeare* in yon azure Sky !
On yon high Cloud, behold the Bard advance,
Piercing all Nature with a fingle Glance !
In various Attitudes, around him ftand
The Paffions, waiting for his dread Command.
Firft, kneeling *Love* before his Feet appears,
And mufically-fighing melts in Tears
Near him fell *Jealoufy* with Fury burns,
And into Storms the am'rous Breathings turns.
Then *Hope,* with heav'n-ward Look, and *Joy,* draw near,
While palfied *Terror* trembles in the Rear.

Mr.

Mr. *Gray*'s are very pretty.

Far from the Sun and Summer's Gale,
In thy green Lap was Nature's darling laid,
What Time, where lucid *Avon* ſtray'd,
To him the mighty Mother did unveil
Her awful Face : The dauntleſs Child
Stretch'd forth his little Arms, and ſmil'd.
This Pencil take (ſhe ſaid) whoſe Colours clear,
Richly paint the vernal Year :
Thine too theſe golden Keys, immortal Boy !
This can unlock the Gates of Joy ;
Of Horror that, and thrilling Fears,
Or ope the ſacred Source of ſympathetic Tears.

These laſt were written by, and ſhewn to me in
MS. by the ingenious Mr. *Charles Churchill*.

In the firſt Seat, in Robe of various Dyes,
A noble Wildneſs flaſhing from his Eyes,
Sat *Shakeſpeare* :—In one Hand a Wand he bore,
For mighty Wonders fam'd in Days of Yore;
The other held a Globe, which to his Will
Obedient bow'd, and own'd the Maſter's Skill :
Things of the nobleſt Kind his Genius drew,
And look'd through *Nature* at a ſingle View :
A Looſe he gave to his unbounded Soul,
And taught new Lands to riſe, new Seas to roll ;
Call'd into Being Things unknown before,
And, paſſing Nature's Bounds, was ſomething more.

I am, Sir, Yours, &c.

LETTER XXXVII.

From *Warwick*. 329

SIR,

ABOUT three Miles above *Stratford*, on the
Eaſtern Bank of the *Avon*, is *Charlecote* ;
where the ancient and knightly Family of the *Lucies* have long reſided. Upon a Monument in the
Church

Church here, is the following Infcription to the
Memory of that Lady, whofe eldeft Son, Sir *Thomas Lucy*, fo feverely profecuted *William Shakefpeare*,
for being concerned, with others, in purloining
his Deer, that he was obliged to leave the Country : And to this Event perhaps 'twas owing, that
this amazing Genius burft forth, which, beyond
all others, has moved, aftonifhed, and delighted
Mankind.

Here emtombed lyeth
The Lady *Joyce Lucy*,
Wife of Sir *Thomas Lucy*, of *Charlecote*,
In the County of *Warwick*, Knt.
Daughter and Heir of
Thomas Acton, of *Sutton*,
In the County of *Worcefter*, Efq;
Who departed out of this wretched World,
To her heavenly Kingdome,
The 10th Day of *Feb.* Anno Dom. 1593, aged 63,
All the Time of her Life
A true and faithful Servant of her good God.
Never detected of any Crime or Vice.
In Religion moft found.
In Love to her Hufband, moft faithful and true.
In Friendfhip moft conftant.
To what in Truft was committed to her, moft fecret,
In Wifdome excelling.
In governing of her Houfe, and bringing up of Youth
In the Fear of God, that did converfe with her,
Moft rare and fingular.
A great Maintainer of Hofpitality,
Greatly efteemed of her Betters,
Mifliked of none, unleffe of the Envious.
When all is fpoken that can be faid,
A Woman fo furnifh'd and garnifh'd with Vertue,
As not to be bettered,
And hardly to be equalled by any.
As fhe lived moft vertuoufly,
So fhe died moft Godly.
Set down by him,
That did beft know what hath been written to be true.
THOMAS LUCY.

The

The *Avon*, which here glides between *Charlecote* and *Bishops-Hampton*, affords a most beautiful Reach almost up to the Village of *Burford*, or *Borford*, where, in the Year 1647, one *Samuel Fairfax* was born, who, when twelve Years old, lived under the same Roof, and eat at the same Table, with his Father and Mother, Grandfather and Grandmother, Great Grandfather and Great Grandmother. They all lived very happily toge-gether, and none of the three Generations of either Sex had been twice married.

Betwixt the River and the great Road to *Warwick*, is *Clopton-Park*, which formerly gave the Title of Baron to that celebrated Antiquary, Sir *George Carew*. From hence, after riding about five Miles, we came to *Warwick*, a Town well famed in Story.

This Town is delightfully situated upon a rocky Ascent, on the Western Bank of the River *Avon*, about half a Mile after that River hath received a considerable Brook, called the *Leame*, which rises in the County of *Northampton*.

After promising to treat of the Antiquity of this Town in a future Letter, I now proceed to inform you, that, on the 5th Day of *December*, 1694, it was almost entirely destroyed by an accidental Fire; the Damage of which was modestly computed to be near One hundred thousand Pounds. But, in pursuance of an Act of Parliament, the liberal Contributions of the Kingdom enabled the Inhabitants to rebuild it in the regular and beautiful Manner, in which it now appears. The Free-Stone for the Superstructure was dug from the Quarries of the Rock, on which the whole is founded.

The Entrances to this Town are answerable to the four Cardinal Points, and all meet in the Center of the Place; and, owing to the Descents from it, the whole Town is extreamly clean. The Cel-

·lars,

lars, and indeed Wells, are made in the Rock, but
Warwick is chiefly supplied with Water by Pipes,
laid from Springs at the Distance of half a Mile.
The Bridge over the *Avon* consists of twelve Arches, and is a noble Structure. The County-Hall is
an elegant new Building. Here are also a Court-
House, and an Hospital for twelve decayed Gentlemen, with an Allowance of twenty Pounds *per
Annum* to each, and fifty Pounds to a Chaplain.

In this Town are three Charity-Schools, in
which are taught and cloathed sixty-two Boys, and
forty-two Girls.

Notwithstanding the fine Situation and Popu-
lousness of this Town, it has but two Churches,
and a very small Portion of Trade. A modern
Poet gives it this Description ;

Where *Avon* wider flows, and gathers Fame,
A Town there stands, and *Warwick* is its Name:
For useful Arts entitled once to share
The *Mercian* Dame, *Elfleda*'s guardian Care.
Nor less for Feats of Chivalry renown'd,
When her own *Guy* was with her Laurels crown'd:
Now Indolence subjects the drowzy Place,
And binds in silken Bonds her feeble Race ;
No busy Artizans their Fellows greet,
No loaded Carriages obstruct the Street,
Scarce here and there a saunt'ring Band is seen,
And Pavements dread the Turf's encroaching Green.

The Church of St. *Mary* is a very beautiful Edifice, the greatest Part of it, together with its fine
lofty Tower, is new built. The East End of
this Fabric is old; but extream good Work; within it is a fine old Monument for *Richard Beauchamp*, Earl of *Warwick*, Lord *Despenser* of *Ber-
gavenny*, Lieutenant General of *France* and *Normandy*. The Inscription you will find in my Collections. Here are also Monuments to the Memories of the famous *Robert Dudley*, Earl of *Leicester*,

cefter, and *Ambrofe Dudley*, his Brother, Earl of
Warwick; and one for the celebrated Countefs of
Leicefter, whofe Epitaph, written by Sir *Gervas*
Clifton, is as follows;

Upon the Death of
The excellent and pious Lady,
Lettice, Counteffe of *Leycefter*;
Who dyed upon *Chriftmas-Day* in the Morning, 1634.

Look in this Vault, and fearch it well,
Much Treafure in it lately fell.
Wee all are rob'd, and all do fay,
Our Wealth was carryed this-away,
And that the Theft might ne'er be found,
'Tis buried clofely under Ground.
Yet if you gently ftir the Mould,
There all our Loffe you may behold;
There may you fee that Face, that Hand,
Which once was faireft in the Land.
She, that in her younger Yeares
Match'd with two great *Englifh* Peeres;
She, that did fupply the Warrs
With Thunder, and the Court with Starrs.
She, that in her Youth had bene
Darling to the Maiden Quene.
'Till fhe was content to quitt
Her Favour for her Favoritt.

Whofe Gould Thread when fhe faw fpunn,
And the Death of her brave Son,
Thought it fafeft to retire,
From all Care and vain Defire
To a private Countrie Cell;
Where fhe fpent her Days fo well,
That to her the better Sort
Came as to an holy Court;
And the Poore that lived near
Dearth or Famine could not fear.
While fhe liv'd, fhe lived thus!
'Till that God, difpleas'd with us,
Suffer'd her at laft to fall,
Not from Him, but from us all.
And becaufe fhe took Delight
Chrift's poor Members to invite,

He fully now requites her Love,
And fends his Angels from above,
That did to Heaven her Soul convey,
To folemnife his own Birth-Day.

GERVAS CLIFTON.

On the Monument of the accomplifhed *Fulk
Greville*, Lord *Brooke*, is the following *Laconic*
Character;

Fulk Grevil,
Servant to Queen *Elizabeth,*
Councellor to King *James,*
And
Friend to Sir *Philip Sidney.*

Trophœum Peccati.

This famous Nobleman, who (to ufe Mr.
Lloyd's Words) " was liberal to *William Camden,*
" Mafter to *William Shakefpeare,* and *Ben Johnfon*;
" Patron to Chancellor *Egerton*; Lord to Bifhop
" *Overall*; and Friend to Sir *Philip Sydney*;" was
a great Scholar, and a moft accomplifhed Gentleman, greatly in Favour with Queen *Elizabeth,*
created a Baron by King *James,* the Admiration
and Darling of Courts, the Friend and Favourite
of his Country, and yet fo unfortunate as to be
murdered in the 75th Year of his Age, by a cruel
and ungrateful Domeftic, who had afterwards
Hardinefs enough to deftroy himfelf.

The Caftle of *Warwick* has been accounted the
moft princely Seat in this Part of *England.* Nothing can exceed the Beauty of its Situation. The
Profpect from its Terrace in the Gardens is extream fine; for below the perpendicular Rock, on
which it is made, glides the River *Avon,* from
whofe Margin this Walk is upwards of fifty Feet
high. You here fee the Park, which is neatly diverfified with Woods, Lawns, &c. and a moft
charming Country extends beyond it.

The

The Caftle ftands upon a Spot, which is more than forty Feet higher than the River, but on the North Side it is even with the Town. Its Appearance is grand, and exhibits a Specimen of the ancient Power and Magnificence of the Nobility of *England*. The Height of the Apartments in the Caftle, which are elevated above the Court, is five Feet fix Inches. Towards the River, this Building is ninety-nine Feet; towards the Court, thirty-nine Feet fix Inches. The firft Floor in the North, or *Guy's* Tower, viz. the Evidence-Room, is nineteen Feet fix Inches. The Tower above the Court, ninety-fix Feet fix Inches. The firft Floor in *Cæfar's* Tower, above the Court, is ninety-three Feet four Inches, and, on the Side next the River, one hundred and forty-feven Feet.

This Caftle is now the Seat of *Francis*, Lord *Brooke*, Earl of *Warwick*, an immediate Defcendant from *Robert Grevile*, of *Thorp-Latimer*, in the County of *Lincoln*, fecond Brother to *Fulk Grevile*, Lord *Brooke*, beforementioned.

The Apartments are extreamly well contrived, and adorned with many original Pictures by *Vandyke*, and other celebrated Mafters. The Great Hall is very magnificent, and, with the Galleries, preferves fuch a Communication with the remoteft Parts of the Building, that, notwithftanding its ancient Plan, as being intended a Caftle for Strength, and not a Palace for Pleafure, no Irregularity is to be found.

The Tales of the famous *Guy*, who is reported to have killed the Giant *Colebrand*, the *Dun-Cow*, and other fabulous Creatures, are too ridiculous to fet down. Yet certain it is, that many of the ancient Earls of *Warwick* paid great Veneration to his Memory. *William Beauchamp*, Earl of *Warwick*, in the Reign of *Edward* the Firft, called his eldeft Son after him, *Guy*. *Thomas Beauchamp*,

Earl

Earl of *Warwick*, by his laſt Will, gave the
Sword and Coat of Mail of this *Guy*, to his Son,
who built the remarkable Tower at the North-Eaſt
Corner of the Caſtle, and called it *Guy's* Tower;
and left to his Son, *Richard*, the Sword and Coat
of Mail of that Champion, which himſelf had received as an Heirlome from his Father. They
ſhew you the enormous Pot of this Warrior, and
other wonderful Matters, which are explained by
as wonderful Tales. Mr. *Somerville*, in his *Rural
Games*, ironically makes young *Hobbinol* ſay;

—————— That mighty *Guy*,
So fam'd in antique Song, *Warwick's* great Earl,
Who ſlew the Giant *Colbrand* in fierce Fight,
Maintain'd a Summer's Day, and freed this Realm
From *Daniſh* Vaſſalage; his pond'rous Sword,
And maſſy Spear, atteſt the glorious Deed:
Nor leſs his hoſpitable Soul is ſeen
In that capacious Cauldron, whoſe large Freight
Might feaſt a Province.

I ſhall ſay more of this Caſtle, when I come to
mention the Antiquity of the Town, and at preſent
ſhall obſerve, that about the Time when the *Chriſ-
tians* had taken the *Holy Land*, *Henry*, Earl of
Warwick, gave many Lands to the Church of St.
Mary beforementioned, which were not only confirmed, but augmented, by Earl *Roger*, his Son;
who alſo granted to the Canons of this Church,
the Privileges of having a Dean and Chapter, in
like Manner as the Canons of *London*, *Lincoln*,
Sarum, and *York*. In the Year 1123, he tranſ-
lated the College, which was in the Caſtle of *Warwick*, to the Church of St. *Mary* and *All Saints*;
and, by and with the Authority of *Simon*, Biſhop of
Worceſter, the Canons and Clerks were transferred
thither. To this Collegiate Church the ſaid *Roger*, Earl of *Warwick*, gave ſeveral Churches, particularly that of the *Holy Sepulchre* at *Warwick*, and
the

the Parish Church of *Greetham* in *Rutlandshire*, which Churches being alienated from this College (that of St. *Sepulchre* being made a Priory of Canons Regular, and *Greetham* appropriated to the same) these two could not possibly be restored, but the other Churches, which had been alienated (seven in Number) were restored, and re-united to this of St. *Mary*, by the Decree of *William*, Bishop of *Worcester*: And all the Parishioners of the Churches in *Warwick*, were ordered to repair to the said Church of St. *Mary*, for Sacraments and Sacramentals, and not to bury elsewhere than in the Church-Yard of the same. The said *William*, Bishop of *Worcester*, decreed, that the Dean, who is bound by his Place to reside, receive forty Pounds; every residing Canon, twenty Marks; every other Prebend, who does not reside, forty Shillings only; and every Vicar, ten Marks a Year. It was valued, at the Dissolution, at Two hundred forty-seven Pounds thirteen Shillings *per Annum*.

The same *Henry*, Earl of *Warwick*, who settled the Dean and Chapter at St. *Mary's*, erected the Priory of the *Holy Sepulchre*, in the Suburbs of this Town. The Canons here wore the same Habit with other Canons Regular, without any Distinction besides a double Cross of Red in the Breast of their upper Garment. This House was the first and superior of this Order in *England*, *Wales*, *Scotland*, and *Ireland*, till the Loss of *Jerusalem*, when this Order decayed almost to nothing, their Profits and Privileges being transferred to the *Trinitarians*. *Simon*, Bishop of *Worcester*, dedicated the Altar and Cemetery here, with express Provision, that the Parish Churches of *All Saints* and St. *Mary*, should not suffer any Diminution or Detriment in their Tythes, Buryings, Oblations, Confessions, Visiting the Sick, or any other accustomed Benefits belonging to the said Church, and that

these

thefe Canons fhould pay to the faid Parifh, or Mother Church of *All Saints*, an Acknowledgement of thirty Pence yearly, at the Feaft of *All Saints*.

This Priory, at the Diffolution, was valued at forty-one Pounds ten Shillings and two Pence.

This Town was by the *Britons* called *Caer-Guaric*, and *Caer-Leon* ; and *Camden* thinks thefe Names are derived from the *Britifh* Word *Guarth*, whichfignifies *Præfidium*, and that this was the Town, which the *Romans* called *Præfidium*, where the Præfect of the *Dalmatian* Horfe was pofted, by the Appointment of the Governor of *Britain*. It will not, he obferves, feem ftrange, that the *Romans* fhould have a Fortrefs or military Station in this Place, if we confider its Situation, on a fteep and rocky Eminence, over the River *Avon* ; and that the Ways on every Side leading up to it, are cut through the Rock.

John *Rous* derives it Name from *Gwayr*, a *Britifh* Prince ; and *Matt. Paris* calls it *Warre-wyk*, from *Warfmund*, Father of the firft *Offa*, King of the *Mercians* ; and fome Writers have fuppofed it to have been built by *Cymbeline*, a King of *Britain*, about the Time of the Birth of *Chrift*. But be its Origin when it may, certainly *Warwick* is a very ancient Town, and fuffered much during the various Quarrels of the *Britifh* Princes, and alfo after the *Roman* Invafion. It was almoft demolifhed by the *Saxons*, and fhared the Fury of the ravaging *Danes* ; fo that it remained in a defolate State till *Ethelfleda*, that famous *Mercian* Lady beforementioned, rebuilt it, about the Year 911, or, according to fome Accounts, in 914, and reftored it to that flourifhing Condition in which it was found by the *Normans* At this Time it had many Burgeffes, of whom twelve were, by Tenure, to accompany the King in his Wars. It appears by *Doomf- day-Book*, that " He, who, upon Warning given, " did not go, was fined one hundred Shillings to " the King. But if the King croffed the Seas a- " gainft

" gainſt an Enemy, then they were either to ſend
" him four *Boatſwains*, or, in lieu of them, four
" Pounds in Deniers. In this Burgh, the King
" hath in Demeſne One hundred and thirteen
" Burgeſſes; and the Barons of the King, One
" hundred and twelve."

The Corporation of *Warwick* is now governed
by a Mayor, and Recorder, twelve Aldemen, and
twelve Aſſiſtant Burgeſſes. The firſt Mayor mentioned on their Records was, in the ſeventh Year
of King *Edward* the Firſt, but it ſent Members to
Parliament as ſoon as any Place whatſoever. In the
firſt Year of Queen *Mary*, it was incorporated
anew, by the Name of Bailiff and Burgeſſes, with
a perpetual Succeſſion, Common Seal, and twelve
Aſſiſtants to the Bailiff, called principal Burgeſſes;
who ſhould have Power to regulate the Borough,
and to chuſe a Bailiff, Recorder, Serjeant at Mace,
and Clerk of the Markets, of whom the Bailiff
and Recorder ſhould be ſole Juſtices of the Peace
within the Borough.

To this Charter *James* the Firſt, by his Letters
Patent, in the 10th Year of his Reign, added, that
the two ancient Burgeſſes, for the Time being,
ſhould, after it, be Juſtices of the Peace within the
Precincts thereof, together with the Bailiff and Recorder, and that the ſaid Bailiff, and one of the Senior Burgeſſes, ſhould always be of the Quorum.
This Borough was laſtly reincorporated by King
Charles the Second.

As this is the County-Town, the Aſſizes and
Seſſions are held here, and it ſends two Members to the Houſe of Commons. The Markets
are on *Wedneſdays* and *Saturdays*, and the Fairs on
May the 12th, and *July* the 5th, for Horſes, Cows,
and Sheep; *September* the 4th, for ditto, and
Cheeſe; and *November* the 8th, for Horſes, Cows,
and Sheep.

It

It is fituate in 1 Deg. 32 Min. Weft Longitude, and in the Latitude of 52 Deg. 20 Min.

I fhall now fay fomewhat of the illuftrious Perfons, to whom this Town has given the Titles of Earl and Duke.

Henry de Newburgh, who was born in the Caftle of that Name, in the Dutchy of *Normandy,* was, by *William* the Firft (after that Monarch had fortified this Town with a Ditch and Gates, and enlarged and ftrengthened the Caftle) appointed Governor of *Warwick* ; and towards the End of that King's Reign, was advanced to the Dignity of Earl of *Warwick,* and to the Earldom was annexed the Caftle and Manor of *Warwick,* which latter was then in the Hands of the King, and included the Royalty of the Borough. After the Death of the Conqueror, *William Rufus* enriched this Earl with the whole Inheritance of *Turchil de Warwick,* who, before the Conqueft, bore the Title of Earl of *Warwick,* though he was only a Deputy to the Earl of *Mercia* *. This *Henry de Newburgh,* on the Grant of this Inheritance, affumed the *Bear and ragged Staff,* as the Enfign of his Family (it having been that of *Turchil*'s from before the Time of his Anceftor, the famous *Guy)* and hence it became the Badge of the fucceffive Earls of *Warwick,* through the Lines of *Newburgh, Beauchamp, Nevil, Plantagenet,* and *Dudley.* This *Henry* was a Perfon of Honour, Prowefs, Fortitude, Fidelity, and Piety. I have already mentioned his religious Foundations.

Roger, his Son, was a Witnefs to the Laws of King *Stephen,* but adhered to the Emprefs *Maud.* He built the beautiful Church of St. *Mary* beforemen-

---

* By which Inftance, fays Sir *William Dugdale,* we may partly fee how hardly the *native Englifh* were dealt with; i. e. not to enjoy their Inheritances, though they did not at all oppofe the Conqueror's Title.

mentioned, and perfected the religious Works which his Father had begun.

On Failure of Male-Issue in the *Newbury* Family, the Title and Estate became vested in the *Beauchamps*, an illustrious Stock, *William de Beauchamp*, having married *Isabel*, the Heiress of that Family; she was Countess of *Warwick* in her own Right. Her Son, *William de Beauchamp*, was, in Right of his Mother, Earl of *Warwick*, Baron of *Hanslape*, and Chamberlain to the King in his Exchequer; and, in Right of his Father, Baron of *Elmley*, Hereditary Constable of the Castle of *Worcester*, and Hereditary Sheriff of that County. This Nobleman eminently distinguished himself by his great Services to the Crown, having been employed, either in civil or military Affairs, during twenty-six Years of the Reign of *Edward* the First.

Guy de Beauchamp, his Son, had a brave and noble Spirit, and so sensible a Feeling of his Country's Wrongs, that he joined the Barons in the Reign of *Edward* the Second, and became one of the Chiefs of that celebrated Confederacy. He was bred to Arms, and had an early Aversion to all Favourites (particularly to *Pierce Gaveston*, as I shall soon observe). Nothing could damp his Resolutions; no one could charge his Honour with a Stain. He loved his Country heartily, but perhaps had too little Regard for kingly Power. He died in the fortieth Year of his Age, not without strong Suspicions of Poison.

Thomas Beauchamp, his Son, after distinguishing himself in many great Acts, was made Admiral in Chief to King *Edward* the Third, who placed so much Confidence in him, that he ordered him particularly to take Care of the Person of his Son, the illustrious *Black Prince*, at the famous Battle of *Cressy*. He defeated the *French* Fleet before *Ca-*

lais, and behaved with the utmoſt Bravery at the Battle of *Poictiers*. He was one of the firſt Knights of the Garter. He rebuilt the Walls, added ſtrong Gates, and embattled Towers, to the Gateways of *Warwick-Caſtle*. He alſo built a Booth-Hall in the Market-Place, and made the Town toll-free.

Thomas, his Son, was Governor to *Richard* the Second, but being diſguſted at the Court Favourites, was diſmiſſed the Court, and retired to his Caſtle here; where he continued ſome Time in Quiet, and amuſed himſelf with Building, and other Occupations, agreeable to his noble Fortune and Spirit. I have mentioned his Building of *Guy*'s Tower at the North-Eaſt Corner of the Caſtle; he alſo built the Body of St. *Mary*'s Church, both which were finiſhed in the Year 1394. But joining the Duke of *Glouceſter* againſt the King's Favourites, he was confined in the *Tower* of *London*, impeached, and, according to *Rapin*, baniſhed to the *Iſle of Man*. He died in the Year 1401, being the ſecond of King *Henry* the Fourth.

Richard, his Son, whoſe Monument I have ſpoken of, was perhaps the moſt eminent of the truly eminent Line of *Beauchamp*. In his early Years he acquired immortal Fame by his Chivalry and Feats of Arms, having travelled over *Europe* in Search of Exploits. He was not only a moſt accompliſhed Soldier, but generally allowed to be the fineſt Gentleman of his Time. He was employed in almoſt all the Courts of *Europe*, and all of them were ſurprized at his Addreſs and amiable Politeneſs. By the magnanimous King *Henry* the Fifth, he was appointed Tutor to his Son, afterwards King *Henry* the Sixth. He had few or no Enemies, and his prodigious Eſtate, his numerous Relations (all of which were Perſons of conſiderable Degree) joined to the Strength of his Alliances,

liances, gave him a greater natural Intereſt in *England* than perhaps any other Subject, not of the Royal Blood, then enjoyed. His Progreſſes in *France*, during the Abſence of the Duke of *Bedford*, are, to his immortal Honour, recorded in the Annals of both Nations. I have before noted, that he died at *Roan*, in 1440, being then Lieutenant-General of *France*. His Riches were then ſo immenſe, that one would ſcarce believe, for, according to S.r *William Dugdale*, the annual Income of his Eſtate amounted to Eight thouſand three hundred and ſix Merks eleven Shillings and eleven Pence Halfpenny, when Barley was no more than four Shillings and two Pence *per* Quarter, Oats at two Shillings and a Penny, Capons at three Pence a-piece, Hens at a Penny, and all other Neceſſaries of Life in Proportion. *Margaret*, his eldeſt Daughter, was married to the famous *John Talbot*, Earl of *Shrewſbury*.

Henry, his Son, the laſt of that illuſtrious Family in the Male Line, was about fourteen Years old when his Father died: But by King *Henry* the Sixth, he was created Premier Earl of *England*, Duke of *Warwick*, and crowned King of the *Iſle of Wight*, by the King's own Hand. He died in the 23d Year of *Henry* the Sixth, aged twenty-two, and was ſucceeded by

Richard Nevil, Son and Heir to *Richard*, Earl of *Saliſbury*. This Nobleman was commonly ſtiled the *King-Maker*, and alſo the *Great Earl of Warwick*. He attained to this Earldom by marrying *Anne*, the Siſter of the ſaid *Henry*. He was a factious, turbulent, and ambitious Man. His common Phraſe was, *That he had rather be able to ſet up or pull down a King, than be a King*. He conſpired with the Duke of *York* againſt King *Henry* the Sixth. He behaved bravely at the Battle of St. *Alban's*, was made Governor of *Calais*, and diſtinguiſhed him-

ſelf

felf at the Battle of *Towton*; was made Lord
Chamberlain, Lord High Admiral, and Lord
Warden of the Marches towards *Scotland*, and of
the Cinque Ports, *&c.* He was fent to *France*, to
demand *Bona* of *Savoy*, for the King (*Edward* the
Fourth) who, in the mean Time, married *Elizabeth Woodville*, at which *Warwick* was affronted,
and retired from Court, where his Popularity was
great. He had an Interview with *Lewis* of *France*,
married one of his Daughters to the Duke of *Clarence*, took King *Edward* Prifoner, reftored *Henry*,
and got the Crown fettled on his Son-in-Law, the
Duke of *Clarence*. He was at laft killed at the
Battle of *Barnet*, as I have formerly mentioned *.

George,

* " After the Death of this Earl (fays *Dugdale*) his Coun-
" tefs underwent no little Diftrefs, being conftrained to take
" Sanctuary in the Abbey of *Beaulieu*, in *Hampfhire*, where fhe
" continued for a long Time in a mean Condition, but thence
" privately got into the North, where alfo fhe abode in great
" Streights, all her vaft Inheritance, by Authority of Parlia-
" ment, being taken from her, and fettled upon *Ifabell* and
" *Anne*, her two Daughters and Heirs. The firft of them
" Wife to *George*, Duke of *Clarence*, and the fecond to *Richard*,
" Duke of *Gloucefter*, as if fhe, the faid *Anne*, had been natu-
" rally dead. Which was witheld from her till the third of
" King *Henry* the Seventh, that the King (having a Mind
" thereto, her faid Daughters being being both dead) by a
" new Act of Parliament, anulled the former, *as againft all
" Reafon, Confcience, and Courfe of Nature, and contrary to the
" Laws of God and Man* (as the Words thereof import) ; and,
" in Confideration of the true and faithful Service and Alle-
" giance by her born to King *Henry* the Sixth, as alfo that fhe
" never gave Caufe for fuch Difherifon, reftored unto her the
" Poffeffion of the Premifes, with Power to alien the fame, or
" any Part thereof. But with little Purpofe that fhe fhould
" enjoy it, as it feems ; for it appears, that the fame Year, by
" a fpecial Feoffement, bearing Date 13 *Dec.* and a Fine there-
" upon, fhe conveyed it wholly to the King ; entailing it upon
" the Iffue Male of his Body, with Remainder to herfelf, and
" her Heirs. The particular Lordfhips in which Grant, foraf-
much

George, Duke of *Clarence*, succeeded to the Title of Earl of *Warwick*, but was murdered in the Tower of *London*; and to him succeeded

Edward Plantagenet, his Son, who was most barbarously and unjustly beheaded on *Tower-Hill*.

The famous *John Dudley*, Viscount *Lisle*, was created Earl of *Warwick* in 1574, and afterwards Earl of *Northumberland*, under which last Title I shall

" much as the Magnificence of our preceding Earls may there-
" by be the better illustrated, I have here set down, *viz.*
" The Mannours of *Warrewyk, Tomworth, Lightborne, Mor-*
" *ton, Berkswell, Brayles, Claverdon, Sutton, Winterton, Bud-*
" *broke, Haseley, Snitterfield,* and *Pipeball,* in this County; *Ab-*
" *botley, Shraweley, Elmley-Lovet, Salwarpe, Hull-Place, Wyche,*
" *Elmley-Castle, Chadsley, Hervington, Shrieve-Lench, Yardley,*
" *Cromb-Simonds, Warpdell, Hanley, Busheley, Ridmerley, Upton*
" *super Sabrinam,* with the City of *Worcester,* all in *Worcester-*
" *shire ; Tewksbury, Stoke-Archer, Whittington, Fairford, Sobbury,*
" *Tredington, Panyngton, Fydington, Northey, Muth, Berton-*
" *s Regis juxta Bristoll, Barton-Hundred, Kenmerton, Chedworth,*
" and *Lydney;* in *Gloucestershire ; Burford, Shypton, Spellsbury,*
" *Chadlington-Hundred,* and *Langley,* in *Oxfordshire, Kaversham,*
" and *Stanford,* in *Berkshire ; Chyrtel, Sherston,* and *Brodton,* in
" *Wiltshire ; Dertford, Willington,* and *Hendon,* in *Kent ; Wal-*
" *thamstow,* and *Fraunceys,* in *Essex ; Flampsted,* in *Hertford-*
" *shire, Potters Pirye, Asherugge-Hundred, Querendon, Aylesbury,*
" *Buckland, Agmondesham, Kingesbury, Hanslape, Olney,* and
" *Merlaw,* in com *Bucks ; Buckby, Multon, Conesgrave,* and
" *Yelvertoff,* in com. *Northampton , Walshale, Perry Bar, Pat-*
" *tingham,* and *Shenston,* in com *Staff Barnard Castle,* in the Bi-
" shoprick of *Durham ; Kibworth,* in com *Leicest Kymbworth,*
" *Bautre,* and *Hotham,* in com *Ebor. Essingdon, Shellingthorp,*
" *Gretham, Barowden, Preston,* and *Uppingbam,* in com. *Rut-*
" land ; *Stilingthorp,* in com *Lincoln ; Kertling,* in com. *Can-*
" *tabr.' Snodell,* and *Faunhope,* in com *Hereford , Saham-Toney,*
" *Outsckyn, Neckton, Pannesworshall,* and *Gressingham-Parva,* in
" com *Norf Carnaunton, Hofton-Toney, Blyston,* and *Lantran,* in
" *Cornwall , Glarmorgan, Burgavenny, Elvell, Snodbyll, Llang-*
" *tre, Llangero,* and *Wale-Bykyneour,* in *Wales,* and the Marches
" thereof , *South-Tanton,* and *Sele,* with the Hundred of *South-*
" *Tanton,* in com *Devon.* the Isles of *Jersey, Guernsey, Serke,*
" and *Aurenev,* with the Castles therein, and certain Houses in
" *South-Sarke.*"

ſhall write of him. He was ſucceeded; as Earl of
Warwick, by his Son,

Ambroſe Dudley, a worthy Nobleman : He died
a Batchelor.

In the Year 1618, King *James* created *Robert*,
Lord *Rich*, Earl of *Warwick*, whoſe Poſterity is
extinct by the Death of the laſt Earl of *Warwick*,
when his late Majeſty revived the Title in Favour of *Francis*, Earl *Brooke*, a Nobleman of Merit, and an Encourager of the Meritorious.

I am juſt ſetting out towards *Kenilworth*, and
am, Sir, Yours, &c.

L E T T E R XXXVIII.

From *Daventry*, in *Northamptonſhire*.

S I R,

AT about a Mile and Half Diſtance from
Warwick, we came to *Guyſcliff*, or *Gib-Cliff*,
which is ſituate on the Weſtern Bank of the River
Avon. *Dugdale* ſays, that St. *Dubritius*, who, in
the Time of the *Britons*, had an epiſcopal Seat at
Warwick, choſe this for a Place of Devotion, built
an Oratory here, and dedicated it to St. *Mary
Magdalen*. He alſo ſays, that, in the *Saxons* Time,
an Hermit lived here; and that the celebrated *Guy*,
after his notable Atchievements, likewiſe retired
here, and continued to receive ghoſtly Comfort
from the ſaid Hermit, till his Death; and that
from this *Guy*, the Place took its Name. But
Camden, who tells us it was the Seat of *Thomas de
Bellofago*, or *Beaufoe*, thinks the Place took its
Name from *Guy de Beauchamp*, who lived much
later than the other *Guy*, and ſays, it is certain,
that *Richard de Beauchamp*, Earl of *Warwick*, built
here,

here, and dedicated a Chapel to St. *Margaret*, and fet up in it the giant-like Statue of the famous *Guy*.

Drayton hath left us thefe Lines concerning this Place.

Towards *Warwick*, with her Train, as *Avon* trips along,
To *Guy-Cliffe* being come, her Nymphs thus bravely fong,
To thee, renowned Knight, continual Praife we owe,
And at thy hallow'd Tomb thy yearly Objts fhew.

To this Place alfo retired that great and learned Antiquary, *John Rous*, or *Roffe*, who was the Son of *Geffrey Rous*, of *Warwick*, defcended from the *Roufes*, of *Brinklow*, in this County. He was a Perfon of Genius, and fingular Induftry. He was bred at *Oxford*, and travelled over the greateft Part of *England*; and having made large Collections out of the Libraries where he came, relating to the Hiftory and Antiquities of this Kingdom, he became a Chauntry-Prieft in this Chapel, and compiled his *Chron. de Regibus*, which *Dugdale* often quotes. This Place, during his being an Inhabitant of it (according to his Words) was the Seat of Pleafure, having a fhady Grove, cryftal Springs, moffy Caves, Meadows ever green, a foft and murmuring Fall of Waters under the Rocks; and to crown all, Solitude and Quiet, the great Delight of the Mufes. (He died in the Year 1491) and *Leland* and *Dugdale* have obferved, that this, in their Times, was a Place of fo great Delight, in refpeft of the River gliding below the Rock, the dry and wholefome Situation of the Houfe, and the fine Grove of lofty Elms overfhadowing it, that to one who defired a retired Life, either for his Devotions or Study, the like was hardly to be found [a].

This

* The former of thefe Antiquaries obferves, that it is a Houfe of Pleafure, a Place meet for the Mufes; here is Silence,

This Place is now the delightful Seat of *Samuel Greatheed*, Eſq; a Gentleman whom I have mentioned in *Hampſhire*, who has ſo finely improved it, that *Nature*, which here is wonderfully laviſh in her beautiful Exhibitions, is ſo rivalled by *Art*, that 'tis not eaſy to diſtinguiſh to which the Preference belongs.

From *Guycliff*, we came to *Blacklow-Hill*, a Place rendered famous by the Execution of *Pierce de Gaveſton*, the arrogant Favourite of King *Edward* the Second. The Matter was of this Sort. In the Year 1312, the King, having left his Favourite in the Caſtle of *Scarborough*, the Earls of *Pembroke* and *Warren* laid Siege to it, and the Garriſon being ill-provided, *Gaveſton* was ſoon obliged to capitulate.

In this Capitulation, ſays *Rapin*, " was promiſed " him, that he ſhould ſpeak with the King, and " be tried by his Peers, according to the uſual " Form." As ſoon as *Edward* heard of his Favourite's being thus taken, he earneſtly ſollicited that he might ſee and ſpeak to him, according to the ſaid Promiſe, aſſuring them, that, on ſuch Condition, he would give them entire Satisfaction concerning their Grievances. Moſt of the Barons were againſt this Requeſt; but, upon the Earl of *Pembroke*'s repreſenting to them, that he had given his Word, in the Name of all the Confederates, they were obliged in Honour to perform it.

Pembroke engaged to convey him to the King, and to reſtore him to them at the Day and Place appointed. He intended to conduct his Priſoner to *Wallingford-Caſtle* (where the King was to come, and ſpeak with him) and therefore carried him to

Ded-

---

lence, a pretty Wood, *antra in vivo ſaxo*, the River rolling over the Stones, with a pretty Noiſe, *nemuſculum ibidem opacum, fontes liquidæ & gemmei ; prata florida, antra muſcoſa, rivi levis & per ſaxa diſcurſus, necnon ſolitudo & quies, muſis amiciſſima.*

North West View of LUDLOW CASTLE.

Deddington, about four Miles from *Banbury*, in *Oxfordshire*; where, committing him to the Care of his Servants (fays *Walfingham*) he went, and lodged with his Lady at a neighbouring Place. As the King had no Troops hereabouts, more Precaution was by *Pembroke* thought unneceffary; but he found himfelf greatly miftaken; For *Guy*, Earl of *Warwick*, in the Midft of the Night, fuddenly took him out of their Hands, and carried him to *Warwick-Caftle*, where the Earls of *Lancafter*, *Hereford*, and *Arundel* were affembled; who having now their capital Enemy in their Power, deliberated whether they fhould obferve the Capitulation of *Scarborough*, or put him to immediate Death. The latter Opinion was preferred; and, after a fham Trial, the unfortunate Criminal was condemned to lofe his Head, which was put in immediate Execution upon the Side of this Hill, called *Blacklow*, in a Place where, fince that Time, ftood a Crofs, called *Gavefton's Crofs*.

That *Gaveftone* had rendered himfelf odious to the Nobility, the Words of *Robert of Gloucefter* manifeft*.

* " *Perys* (meaning *Pierce de Gavefton*) went into the King's
" Treafury, in the Abbey of *Weftminfter*, and yer tooke away
" a Table of Gold, wyth the Weffel, and other riche Jewels,
" the whyche were fum Time King *Arthury*'s. And hem he
" toke to a Merchant yat het *Aymery* of *Fifcomband*, and bare
" them over the See into *Gafcoigne*, and yay were never brought
" agen, yat was grete Harm to the Reme. And this fiure *Perys* gretly defpifed the Lords of the Land; and at yat Time
" fiure *Perys* clupyd (called) *Robard*, of *Clare*, the Erle of
" *Gloucetre*, HORE SON. And the Erle of *Penbrok*, JOSEPH
" THE JEW. And the Erle *Nycol* (*Lincoln*) Siure HENRY
" DE LACY, BROKBELLY. And *Gowy* (*Guy*) of *Warwike*,
" BLAKEHOUND OF ANTERN. And alfo he clupyd ye nobil
" and gentil Erle of *Lancafter*, THERLE. (Carle or Churle)
" and over many Defpytes, he fayd to ye Lords of *Englonde*,
" wherefor yay wer yn fore agrevy'd."

The Views from this Hill are very fine, especially that which looks towards the Town and Castle of *Warwick*. We now directed our Course to the Remains of the ancient Castle of *Kenelworth*. This prodigious Building was first begun by *Gelfrey de Clinton*, Chamberlain and Treasurer to King *Henry* the First. As it is situate near a considerable Piece of Water, formed by several little Streams into a Chanel, or Kennel, *Camden* thinks the Village from thence had its Name, vulgarly *Kenelworda*, and now corruptly *Killingworth*.

This *Gelfrey de Clinton* also founded the Church here for Canons Regular of the Order of St. *Augustine*, to the Honour of St. *Mary*, and gave to it all his Lands in *Kenelworth* (except what he had retained to his Castle, and for making a Park) with many other Lands and Liberties; all which he enjoined his Heir to observe, and not to violate on Pain of his Curse, and God's Wrath. *Geffrey*, his Son, not only confirmed his Father's Gifts, but granted them Tythes of all Provisions whatsoever, that came to his Castle of *Kenelworth*.

Henry, his Son, confirmed these Gifts, and granted it farther Advantages. King *Henry* the First recited and confirmed all former Benefactions, and granted the Canons here great Liberties and Immunities; and the like Confirmation was made by King *Henry* the Second. This House, at the Dissolution, was valued at Five hundred and thirty-eight Pounds nineteen Shillings *per Annum*.

The Castle of *Kenelworth* was not long enjoyed by the *Clintons*; for in the 19th of King *Henry* the Second, it was garrisoned by the Crown *.

Henry

---

* At which Time, says Sir *William Dugdale*, there were laid in an hundred Quarters of Bread Corn, eight Pounds eight Shillings and two Pence Charge (not much more than two Pence a Bushel) twenty Quarters of Barley, thirty-three Shillings and
four

Henry the Third granted this Caſtle to *Simon de Mountfort,* Earl of *Leiceſter,* as a Portion with his Siſter *Eleanor,* ſhe being married to that turbulent and ambitious Lord, who was killed at the Battle of *Eveſham,* as I have before noted. After the Death of his Father, *Simon Mountfort,* the younger, fortified, and garriſoned this his Caſtle, and leaving the Command of it to *Henry de Haſtings,* went privately to *France,* when the Caſtle underwent a Siege of ſix Months; but having ſurrendered to King *Henry* the Third, he made it Part of the Inheritance of the *Lancaſtrian* Family. At the Time of this Siege was made and publiſhed that Act, which, in our Law-Books, is ſtiled *Dictum de Kenelworth :* Whereby it was enacted, that all who had taken up Arms againſt the King, ſhould pay five Years Value of their Lands. This was conſidered as a wholeſome and prudent Piece of Severity.

I have already obſerved that *Pierce de Gaveſton,* Earl of *Cornwall,* was hurried to *Warwick-Caſtle,* which was a Prelude to his Murder : So fourteen Years afterwards was his Royal Maſter, *Edward* the Second, brought by Force to this of *Kenelworth;* when, having reſigned the Crown to his Son, he was hurried about from Place to Place, till his Murder was compleated in the Caſtle of *Berkley,* in the County of *Glouceſter.*

In this Caſtle of *Kenelworth* was alſo confined, *Eleanor,* Dutcheſs of *Glouceſter,* the Wife of the Good Duke *Humphry,* after ſhe had been ſhamefully convicted of Sorcery, by the Artifices of her Enemies. This Caſtle was a State Priſon for ma-

four Pence ; an hundred Hogs, ſeven Pounds ten Shillings; forty Cows, ſalted, four Pounds ; one hundred and twenty Cheeſes, forty Shillings ; twenty-five Quarters of Salt, thirty Shillings, at which Time an hundred Shillings were allowed for making a Gaol there.

ny

by others, and continued in the Crown till Queen *Elizabeth*, in the fifth Year of her Reign, granted it to *Robert*, Lord *Dudley*, afterwards Earl of *Leicester*, who spared no Expence in enlarging, adorning, and beautifying this noble Seat. He built a magnificent Gate-House towards the North, where (formerly the Backside of the Castle) he made the Front, filling up a great Part of the wide and deep double Ditch, wherein the Water of the Pond came. He erected a stately Piece on the South-East Part, called *Leicester's Buildings*, and raised from the Ground the *Gallery Tower*, standing at one End of the *Tilt-Yard*, in which was a grand Room for Ladies to see the Exercises of *Tilting* and *Barriers*: And at the other End, that called *Mortimer's Tower*, whereon the Arms of *Mortimer* were cut in Stone. He also enlarged the Chase and Park, besides other Improvements to the Amount, in the whole, of Sixty thousand Pounds; a prodigious Sum then !

Here, in *July*, 1575, he entertained Queen *Elizabeth*, and her Court, for seventeen Days, at an immense Expence, when Varieties of Shews and other Amusements were very extraordinary, the Particulars of which were soon after printed, and called *The Princely Pleasures of Kenelworth-Castle*, from which Sir *William Dugdale* took an Extract*.

This

---

* On the first Entrance of the *Queen*, was a floating Island upon the Pool, bright blazing with Torches, upon which were clad in Silks the *Lady of the Lake*, and two Nymphs waiting on her, who made a Speech to the Queen in Meeter, of the Antiquity and Owners of that Castle, which was closed with Coronets, and other loud Music. Within the Base-Court was there a very goodly Bridge set up, of twenty Foot wide, and seventy Foot long, over which the *Queen* did pass; on each Side whereof were Posts erected, with Presents upon them unto her, by the Gods, *viz.* a Cage of Wild Fowl, by *Silvanus*; sundry Sorts of rare Fruits, by *Pomona*; of Corn, by *Ceres*; of Wine,

by

This Caftle, upon the Demife of *Ambrofe Dudley*, Earl of *Warwick*, became the Property of Sir
Robert Dudley, Son to the Earl of *Leicefter* ; who,
going to *Italy*, was fummoned to return by a Special Privy-Seal, which he not obeying, King *James*
feized this Caftle, and all his Lands. Soon after
Sir *Robert* fold both to Prince *Henry*, for Fourteen
thoufand five hundred Pounds ; but the Prince dying, there was not above Three thoufand Pouhds
of it ever paid, and that too to a Merchant, who
failed ; notwithftanding which, Prince *Charles*, as
Heir to his Brother, held the Poffeffion of *Kenelworth*, and obtained a Special Act, to enable the
Lady of Sir *Robert*, who had a Jointure therein,
to alien her Right to him ; which fhe did for Four
thoufand Pounds. Prince *Charles* then committed
the Cuftody of the Caftle to *Robert*, Earl of *Monmouth*, and his two Sons ; the Inheritance whereof

was

by *Bacchus* ; of Sea-Fifh, by *Neptune* ; of all Habiliments of
War, by *Mars* ; and of Mufical Inftruments, by *Phœbus*.
And, for the feveral Days of her Stay, various and rare Shews
and Sports were there exercifed, *viz.* in the *Chafe*, a *Savage-
Man*, with *Satyrs*, Bear-baitings, Fire-Works, *Italian* Tum-
blers ; a Country Bride-Ale, with running at the *Quintin*, and
Morrice-dancing. And, that there might be nothing wanting,
that thefe Parts could afford, hither came the *Coventree-Men*,
and acted the ancient Play, long fince ufed in that City, called
Hocks-Tuefday ; fetting forth the Deftruction of the *Danes* in
Ethelred's Time, with which the Queen was fo pleafed, that fhe
gave them a Brace of Bucks, and five Marks in Money, to bear
the Charges of a Feaft.

Befides all this, he had upon the Pool, a *Triton*, riding upon
a Mermaid eighteen Foot long ; as alfo *Arion*, on a Dolphin,
with rare Mufick. And, to honour this Entertainment the
more, there were then knighted here, Sir *Thomas Cecill*, Son
and Heir to the Lord Treafurer ; Sir *Henry Cobham*, Brother to
the Lord *Cobham* ; Sir *Francis Stanhope*, and Sir *Thomas Trefham*.
The Cofts and Expence whereof may be guefs'd at, by the
Quantity of Beer then drank ; which amounted to Three hundred and twenty Hogfheads of the ordinary Sort, as I have cre-
dibly heard.   *Dugdale*

was granted to *Lawrence*, Vifcount *Hyde*, of this Place, Earl of *Rochefter*.

This noble Caftle, in the late civil Wars, was demolifhed by thofe who purchafed it of the Parliament, with Defign to make Sale of the Materials. It now is in a very ruinous State, though the Veftigia of its ancient Grandeur are very confpicuous. By the Views of it publifhed by Sir *William Dugdale*, which were engraved by the famous and excellent *Hollar*, fome high Ideas may be formed of its matchlefs Magnificence.

From *Kenelworth*, in which Village is nothing very material, I went to *Stoneley*, intending to take *Southam* in my Way to *Daventry*.

Stoneley, or *Stoneleigh*, was anciently a Royal Demefne, and it is to be obferved, that *Maud*, the Emprefs, firft founded the Priory of *Radmere*, in the Foreft of *Canock*, or *Cank*, in the County of *Stafford*; which was confirmed by King *Stephen*. This is fomewhat odd, for in every Thing elfe they difagreed. This Priory was afterwards advanced to be an Abbey of *Ciftercian* Monks, by *Henry Fitz Emprefs*, then Duke of *Normandy*; and in the Year 1154 (thirteen Years after the Monks had remained at *Radmere*) when the faid *Henry* became King of *England*, with his Confent, they changed their Habitation of *Radmere*, or *Radmore*, for that of *Stoneley*, and the Lordfhip of the fame; the firft Stone of the Abbey-Church here being laid in *April*, 1154, and the faid King *Henry* the Firft endowed this Houfe with many other Lands and Revenues. Its Value at the Diffolution was One hundred and fifty-one Pounds and three Pence *per Annum*. After this, it was purchafed, in the Reign of Queen *Elizabeth*, by Sir *Thomas Leigh*, in whofe Family it continued long; one of whom, *Alice Leigh*, Widow of Sir *Robert Dudley*, endowed an Hofpital here, for ten unmarried Perfons. In the

the Reign of *Charles* the Firſt, Sir *Thomas Leigh* was advanced to the Dignity of a Baron, by the Title of Lord *Leigh*, of *Stoneley*, or *Stoneleigh*. His Deſcendant, *Edward*, Eord *Leigh*, who is a Minor, has a Seat here, called *Stoneleigh-Abbey*.

The Road from *Stoneley* to *Southam* lies through a very fine Country, Part of which is called the *Cornavy*; through this Diviſion paſſes the great *Roman* Way, called the *Foſſe*, which joins the *Watling-Street* at *High-Croſs*, upon the Borders of *Leiceſterſhire*.

Southam is a tolerable good Town, ſituate on a Stream that falls into the *Leame*. This Town, before the *Norman* Conqueſt, was given to the Monks of *Coventry*, and continued in their Poſſeſſion till the Diſſolution of Religious Houſes. The Market is held on *Mondays*, and the Fair on *July* the 10th, for Horſes, Cows, and Sheep.

From hence, in the Morning, I came to the two Villages, called *Upper* and *Nether Shuckborough*. Here the *Aſtroites*, or *Star-Stones*, are found, which being put into a Glaſs of Vinegar, keep themſelves in Motion.

In the Church of *Upper Shuckborough* are Monuments for the Family of *Shuckborough*, who have long been Lords of this Manor. My Road now was good to this Town, called *Daventry*, which is ſituate upon a little Hill, in the fine open County of *Northampton*. *Daventry* is chiefly built with Stone, but 'tis far from being an elegant, though a clean Place; and, notwithſtanding there does not appear much Taſte in their Buildings, the Ladies and Gentlemen are very polite. Here are many Perſons of independent Fortunes, and that the Town is rather rich than otherwiſe, may be reaſonably concluded, from their having lately built their Church, at a great Expence, without the Aſſiſtance of a Brief, or any other Foreign Contribu-

tion;

tion. This Church is alfo of Stone, after a pretty Model, and the Tower, or rather Steeple, is vaftly whimfical. In the Church-Yard is a Monument, bearing this remarkable Infcription ;

Here lies
John Farrer, Gent.
Who died the 23ᵈ of *October*, 1730.
He was inferior to few in his Knowledge
Of his Profeffion, the Law ;
And fecond to none in the Practice of it.
A good Friend, a kind Relation,
And a pious Benefactor to this Church ;
In providing for Prayers to be read
Four Days of the Week in it.

Daventry is a Place of confiderable Antiquity, being built on the *Roman* Way, now called *Watling-Street*, and near it, at *Borough-Hill*, are the Veftigia of a large *Roman* Fortification, which enclofed near Two hundred Acres of Ground. At the Eaft Side of it was a Mount, afterwards called *Spelwell*, when the *Saxons* made ufe of this Camp.

The Priory of *Daventry* was firft founded at *Prefton*, by *Hugh de Leyceftre* (called the Vifcount) for *Cluniac* Monks. But that Place being found inconvenient, they were, by the Licence of *Simon de Seynliz*, the elder, Earl of *Northampton*, removed to *Daventry*, where he built a Monaftery in Honour of St. *Auguftine*, the Apoftle of the *English*. King *Henry* the Firft granted to them and St. *Mary of Charity* (the capital Houfe of this Order abroad) many Liberties and Franchifes, which were confirmed by King *Henry* the Second. *Matilda de Seynliz*, *Richard de Foxton*, *Stephen de Welton*, *Henry de Braybrooke*, and others, were Benefactors to this Houfe, of which there are yet fome Remains.

In this Town was born the infamous Sir *Richard Empfon*, who, together with *Edmund Dudley* (Father

ther to *John*, Duke of *Northumberland*) were, in the Reign of the avaricious *Henry* the Seventh, called the *King's Horse-Leeches*. *Empson's* Father was a Sieve-Maker, who bred his Son to the Law. Of this Person I shall say somewhat more, when I come to *Coventry*, of which City he was Recorder.

In the Year 1645, King *Charles* lay five Days, with his Army, at *Daventry*, where they were plentifully furnished with Provision and Forage.

This Town is governed by a Mayor, Aldermen, Steward, and twelve Freemen : but does not send Members to Parliament. The Market is held on *Wednesdays*, and the Fairs on *Easter-Tuesday*, for Horses and Horned Cattle ; *June* the 6th, for Swine, and all Sorts of Goods ; *August* the 3d, for Horned Cattle, Horses, and Sheep ; *October* the 2d, for Cattle, Cheese, Onions, *&c.* and *October* the 27th (called *Ram-Fair*) for Sheep chiefly.

It is furnished with some good Inns, where Firing is dear enough. According to your Desire, I shall now proceed to *Coventry* and *Meriden* ; from whence you may expect another Letter from, Sir, Yours, *&c.*

L E T E R XXXIX.

From *Meriden*, in *Warwickshire*.

S I R,

THE Road from *Daventry* was very pleasant. After riding about two Miles, the Village of *Braunston*, on my Right, had a pretty Appearance among Woods, surrounded by extensive open Fields, with which this Country abounds. Perhaps few Counties in *England* employ the Plough more, or to better Advantage, than this of *Northampton* : For here Persons of high Character and

Fortune vie with each other in producing the moſt excellent Grain, which is much to their Honour. *Tully*, in his *Offices*, obſerves, that of all the Methods of Gain, there is no one better, no on e more profitable, no one more agreeable, no one more woithy of a Man and a Gentleman, than *Agriculture*.

Having met with a Companion, a Perſon of Corpulency, but of infinite Humour, and genteel Behaviour ; and it being hot, we rode on ſlowly to a Brook, and, on the other Side of the Hedge, enjoyed ſuch a Scene as this, which was painted by *Smart* and *Worlidge*.

> By the Rivulet, on the Ruſhes,
> Beneath a Canopy of Buſhes,
> Where the ever-faithful *Tray*
> Guards the Dumplings and the Whey,
> *Collin Clout* and *Yorkſhire Will*
> From the Leathern Bottle ſwill.
>
> Their Scythes, upon the adverſe Bank,
> Glitter 'mongſt th' entangled Trees,
> Where the Hazles form a Rank,
> And court'ſy to the courting Breeze.

After my Fellow-Traveller had crack'd his Jokes with theſe Clowns, in which each Paity had thrown out Sentences which the other did not undeiſtand, we jogged on to *Dunchurch*, a Village in *Warwickſhire*, wheie are ſeveral good Inns. In *Doomſday-Book* it is written *Donecerce*, and ceitified to contain five Hides of Land, valued at One hundred Shillings : And before the Conqueſt, was the Property of one *Ulmarus* (*Done*, or *Dune*, ſignifying in the old *Engliſh*, an *Hill*, and *Crece*, a *Church*).

The Church here is dedicated to St. *Peter*, and in the Reign of King *Stephen* was, by *Hengelramus Clement*, then Lord of this Place, given to the Monaſtery of *Pipewell*, in *Northamptonſhire* ; and

ſo

fo continued till the Diffolution. In the Church Windows are the Arms of *Clinton*, Earl of *Huntingdon*; *Clinton*, of *Colefhill*; *Beauchamp*, &c. Between this Village and *Riton upon Dunfmore*, is the Sign of a Dun-Cow, which, they tell you, was a Terror to all this Neighbourhood; and that fhe was at laft killed by the famous *Guy*, Earl of *Warwick* : But as to the enormous Breed fhe belonged to, or the Time of her Death, they are quite filent. Yet the Vulgar around give thefe Tales the utmoft Credit.

Riton is a Village, which takes its Name from its producing good Rye (according to *Dugdale*). This Part was formerly an Heath, called *Dunfmore-Heath*, from its Vicinity to the low, flat Land through which the *Avon* flows, which was called *Dunfmere*, or *Dunfmire*; or perhaps from the famous Robber, of whom I fhall fpeak when I come to *Bedfordfhire*. The Bridge over the *Avon* here is of Stone, and at leaft Three hundred Feet long, though the Stream in Summer is but trifling. When we came to a rifing Ground, which afforded us a View of *Coventry*, my merry Companion alighted, and,. with much Compofure of Countenance, and infinite Humour, thus addreffed me *.

This

---

* If I be not afhamed of my Soldiers, I am a fouc'd Gurnet · I have mif-us'd the King's Prefs damnably. I have got, in Exchange of an hundred and fifty Soldiers, three hundred and odd Pounds I prefs me none but good Houfholders, Yeomens Sons; enquire me out contracted Batchelors, fuch as have been ask'd twice on the Banes; fuch a Commodity of warm Slaves, as had as lieve hear the Devil as a Drum; fuch as fear the Report of a Culverin, worfe than a ftruck Deer, or a hurt Wild-fowl. I prefs me none but fuch Toafts and Butter, with Hearts in their Bellies no bigger than Pins Heads, and they have bought out their Services : And now my whole Charge confifts of Ancients, Corporals, Lieutenants, Gentlemen of Companies, Slaves, as ragged as *Lazarus* in the painted Cloth, where the Glutton's Dog licked his Sores , and fuch as

indeed

This, I say, being delivered with such excellent
Humour, and on the Spot where *Falstaff* was supposed to utter it, that I could scarce forbear letting
Imagination get the better of my Senses; while
the neighbouring Women and Children gazed at
him with the utmost Concern, concluding, as the
gravest Matron observed to me, that the poor
Gentleman was out of his Wits, and therefore
they hoped and begged me to take Care of him;
which I having promised to do, we passed a Stone-
Bridge over the small River *Sow*, and soon arrived
at the ancient City of *Coventry*.

The Monastery here, which gave Name to the
Place, was built by *Leofric*, Earl of *Mercia*, and
Godiva, his Wife, in the Year 1040, who plenti-
fully endowed it with Lands and Revenues ; the
Monks were of the *Benedictine* Order, and the
Church was so richly adorned with Gold, Silver,
and precious Stones, that nothing in *England* could
equal it

The Founder, Earl *Leofric*, died in the Year 1057,
and together with his Wife, *Godiva*, was buried in
the

indeed were never Soldiers, but discarded, unjust Servingmen,
younger Sons to younger Brothers, revolted Tapsters, and Ost-
'lers trade-fall'n, the Cankers of a calm World and long Peace ;
ten Times more dishonourably ragged, than an old fac'd Ancient: And such have I to fill up the Rooms of them that have
bought out their Services, that you would think I had a hundred
and fifty tatter'd Prodigals, lately come from Swine-keeping,
from eating Draff and Husks. A mad Fellow met me on the
Way, and told me I had unloaded all the Gibbets, and press'd
the dead Bodies. No Eye hath ever seen such Scare-Crows:
I'll not march through *Coventry* with them, that's flat. Nay,
and the Villains march wide betwixt the Legs, as if they had
Gyves on, for indeed I had most of them out of Prison.
There's but a Shirt and a half in all my Company ; and the
half Shirt is two Napkins tack'd together, and thrown over the
Shoulders like a Herald's Coat, without Sleeves ; and the Shirt,
to say the Truth, stolen from my Host of St. *Alban's*, or the
red-nos'd Innkeeper of *Daintry*. But that's all one, they'll
find Linen enough on every Hedge.

the Church-Porch of this their Foundation ; in which Church was formerly kept a pretended Arm of the great St. *Auguſtine*, incloſed in Silver.

Robert de Limeſey (who was made Biſhop of *Cheſter* A. D. 1088, and died in 1116) obtained of King *Henry* the Firſt the Monaſtery of *Coventry*, and conſtituted it the Capital Cathedral of that Dioceſe. His Succeſſor in that See, *Hugh*, Biſhop of *Coventry*, A. D. 1191, expelled the Monks out of the Cathedral Church here, and placed Secular Canons in their room : But in the Year 1198, *Hubert*, Archbiſhop of *Canterbury*, by Order of Pope *Celeſtine*, reſtored the Monks to the Poſſeſſion of their Church.

By the Charter of Earl *Leofric*'s Foundation, it appears, that he built this Church and Monaſtery to the Honour of *Chriſt*, the Virgin *Mary*, St. *Peter*, St. *Oſburga* the Virgin, and *All Saints*, and gave to the Maintenance of the Monks, ſerving God here, twenty-four Villages, with the Moiety of the Town of *Coventry*, in which it ſtands, with all Liberties and Cuſtoms which he himſelf enjoyed in the ſaid Eſtate, and that the Abbot of the ſaid Houſe ſhould be ſubject to none but the King. All which Grants King *Edward* the Confeſſor confirmed to *Leofwinus*, the firſt Abbot there, and to his Succeſſors : And Pope *Alexander*, by his Bull, directed to the ſaid King *Edward*, bearing Date 1043, confirmed all their Liberties and Exemptions, granting them full Power to chuſe their own Abbots, or Deans, without any Let or Hindrance from the Apoſtolic Authority.

Leofwinus, the firſt Abbot of *Coventry*, being created Biſhop of *Cheſter*, ordained, with the Conſent of the *Monks*, that his Succeſſors, Superiors of that Monaſtery, ſhould be called Priors, and not Abbots.

Lawrence, Prior of *Coventry*, and the Convent there, granted the Scite of the Houfe of St. *John Baptift*, at *Coventry*, and the Appui tenances, in perpetual Alms, for the Receipt of poor and infirm People. This was done at the Petition of *Edmund*, Archdeacon of *Coventry*, and was confirmed by *Richard*, Archbifhop of *Canterbury*, and by a Bull of Pope *Honorius* the Third, dated *Anno* 1221. King *Henry* the Third granted to the Brethren and Sifters of this Hofpital, Liberty and Protection, by themfelves or Meffengers, to afk, gather, and receive Alms abroad, for Relief of their Houfe, for the Space of feven Years.

In the Year 1425, *Richard Crofby* being then Prior of the Cathedral and Regular Church of St. *Mary* of *Coventry*, and *Thomas Everdon*, Mafter or Cuftos of this Hofpital, feveral Orders were made for the Government of this Houfe, *i. e.* that the Prior and Convent aforefaid fhall be accounted Founders of this Hofpital, and *Edmund*, formerly Archdeacon of *Coventry*, Principal Benefactor; that the Mafter of the Hofpital fhould be fubject to the Prior, who was to have the Placing, Creation, and Reception of the faid Mafter, and all the Brethren and Sifters; that the faid Prior, and his Succeffors, may vifit in the faid Hofpital once a Year, attended with eight Perfons only; the Mafter to make Oath of Fidelity to the Prior at his Admiffion; the Brothers and Sifters, a Promife in Writing, figned and fealed; the Mafter to be in Prieft's Orders; the Habit of the Mafter and Brothers to be of a dark Colour, figned with a black Crofs, and on their Mantles alfo a black Crofs; without which Habit they were not to appear abroad: The Mafter to hold Chapter every *Friday*, or at leaft once a Week; the Divine Offices to be devoutly celebrated in the faid Hofpital, at the ufual Hours, *fecundum ufum Sarum*; the Lay-Brothers and Sifters, that were illiterate, to

say,

fay, inftead of Mattins, thirty *Paters*, and as many *Aves*, with the *Creed*, and for every of the other Hours, feven; but thofe Brothers, that have Learning fufficient, to fay the Office of the Bleffed Virgin. The Sifters to be always intent and follicitous about the Care and Service of the infirm in the faid Hofpital; the Common Seal to be kept under three Keys, one to remain with the Mafter, the other two with the Senior Brother and Sifter; that the Mafter fhall pay predial Tythes to the Prior, but not of Cattle nor Wood: That the faid Hofpital fhall have a free *Sepulture*, for thofe who chufe to be buried with them. This Houfe, at the Diffolution, was valued at eighty-three Pounds three Shillings and three Pence.

In the Year 1381, *William*, Lord *de la Zouch*, firft founded the Houfe of St. *Anne*, adjoining to *Coventry*; and fupplied it with three Monks from the *Carthufians* of *London*, and with three others from *Bellevalle*. Befides this Nobleman, they had many other Benefactors, among whom were *Richard Luff*, Mayor of *Coventry*; *John Holmeton*, of *Sleford*; *John Bokington*, Bifhop of *Lincoln*; and *Thomas de Beauchamp*, Earl of *Warwick*, who erected feveral Parts of their Buildings. In the Year 1385, King *Richard* the Second laid the firft Stone in the Foundation of their Church, publicly protefting to be the Founder, and to finifh the Buildings. To this Houfe many Churches were appropriated, and many Lands given; among others, the Manor of *Ediwefton*, in the County of *Rutland*, by the Abbot and Convent of St. *George de Bauquerville*, in *Normandy*.

This Earl *Leofric*, of whom more hereafter, was the moft potent and moft refpected Subject in *England*, excepting the haughty Earl *Godwin*; and indeed the former, in all Matters of State, Arbitration, &c. was confidered as the fuperior Perfon son of the two. He married the Daughter of the Sheriff, or rather Vicount of *Lincolnſhire*, whoſe great Care in her Education (ſhe having a beautiful Perſon, an early Diſpoſition to Virtue, and a Nobleneſs of Soul) rendered her the moſt accompliſhed Lady of that Age. *Brompton*, and almoſt all our Hiſtorians agree, that ſhe rode naked through this City, on the following Account: The Tolls and Taxes here had for ſome Time been exceſſive grievous, of which ſhe was well informed, and being extreamly deſirous that they ſhould be taken off, earneſtly and frequently ſollicited her Huſband to grant that Indulgence. But he, conſidering that they brought great Sums to his Coffers, refuſed. However, ſhe ceaſed not to renew her Requeſt, when, at laſt, he told her jeſtingly, that if ſhe would be content to ride naked through the City, in the Middle of the Day, he would grant her Petition. To this Condition (contrary to his Expectation) ſhe readily conſented, and inſiſted on his keeping his Promiſe. And having commanded all People (at that Time) to keep within Doors, ſhe covered her Body with her own Hair, of which ſhe had ſo great a Quantity, that in this Caſe it ſerved inſtead of a Mantle, and then performed her Taſk. Although it muſt be owned, that this Lady's Zeal is not to be condemned, yet her Huſband's ſuffering her to put it in Practice ſhews, that he had ſomewhat of the Diſpoſition of *Candaules* *, though, in many Reſpects, he was conſidered as a very ſenſible Perſon †.

Michael

---

* *Candaules*, King of *Lydia*, ſhewed his Queen naked to *Gyges*, a *Lydian*, which ſo incenſed her, that ſhe conſpired to kill the King, which being performed by *Gyges*, ſhe afterwards married him

* Earl *Leofric*, who was the moſt reſpected in the Aſſembly on the Trial of Earl *Godwin*, for the Murder of *Alfred* (and of which he was impeached by King *Edward* the Confeſſor, *Alfred*'s

Michael Drayton thus delivers this Matter ;

——— *Coventry* at length
From her fmall meene Regard recovered State and Strength;
By *Leofrick*, her Lord, yet in bafe Bondage held,
The People from her Marts by Tollage who expell'd ;
Whofe *Dutcheffe,* which defir'd this Tribute to releafe,
Their Freedom often begg'd. The Duke to make her
ceafe,
Told her, that if fhe would his Loffe fo farre inforce,
His Will was, fhe fhould ride ftark nak't upon a Horfe,
By Day-Light, through the Street: Which certainly, he
thought,
In her heroick Breaft fo deeply would have wrought,
That in her former Sute fhe would have left to deale ;
But that moft princely Dame, as one devour'd with Zeale,
Went on, and by that meane the Citie cleerly freed,
The firft Part of whofe Name *Godiva* doth forereed.

Leofric performed his Promife, by giving a Charter of Exemptions to the Citizens, to which Charter the Seal of his Lady was alfo affixed. In Memory of this extraordinary Matter, they have at *Coventry* an annual Proceffion, which is the high Holiday for the common People, who tell Abundance of Stuff about this famous Lady. In one Street, againft the Wall of an Houfe, is the Fi-

fred's Brother) on the Queftion being put to him, delivered his Sentiments in the following Manner :

" Earl *Godwin* (faid he) muft be admitted, next to the
" King, to be the Perfon of the higheft Quality in *England,*
" and be cannot deny, that he had a Hand in advifing the
" Murder of *Alfred,* his Majefties Brother. My Opinion there-
" fore is, that he himfelf, his Son, and twelve of us Earls, who
" are all of us his Friends and Kinfmen, fhall humbly come
" before the King, each laden with as much Gold and Silver
" as he can carry between his Arms, and offer the fame for his
" Offence, and moft humbly fupplicate his Pardon, befeeching
" him to lay afide all Ill-will, Rancour, and Malice, towards
" the faid Earl, and peaceably reftore him to his Lands, after
" taking his Homage and Fealty."

This Award, which probably was before concerted, took Place, the Proceffion inftantly fet out, and *Edward* accepted of the Atonement.

Vol. I.   E e e   gure

gure of a Man, in a blue Doublet, with a black
Cap on his Head. This Figure is called *Peeping
Tom*, being the Reprefentation of a *Taylor*, who
(as the Vulgar believe) having more Curiofity than
the reft, popped out his Head as the Lady rode a-
long, but, on the Inftant, was ftruck blind.
They alfo told me, that in the Meadow or Field
(in which, by the faid Charter, all the Citizens
have at one Time of Year the Privilege of putting
their Horfes to feed) no one is fuffered to fend a
Mare, becaufe, fay the common People, it was a
Mare which carried the Lady, and being oppofite
to the Taylor's Door, neighed, which caufed the
faid Curiofity in the poor Taylor.

Sir *William Dugdale* was of Opinion, that the
Immunity then granted was rather a Kind of
Manumiffion from fuch fervile Tenure, whereby
they then held what they had under this great Earl,
than only a Freedom from all Manner of Toll, except Horfes, as is affirmed by *Knighton*.

In the Reign of *Richard* the Second, a Picture
of this Earl, and his Lady, was fet up in a South
Window of *Trinity* Church here, his Right-Hand
holding a Charter, on which thefe Words were
written;

> I, *Luriche*, for Love of thee,
> Doe make *Coventre* Tol-free.

In the thirteenth Year of King *Edward* the Firft,
a Toll was, by Patent, fixed here, in order to the
paving the Streets, which Work was not compleated in twenty Years. In the fecond of *Edward*
the Third, the Monks and Inhabitants of *Coventry*
obtained a Patent for a Toll, in order to their enclofing the Place with a Wall; and in the fixth
Year of the faid King, the Inhabitants had a Licence to erect a common Conduit, twenty Feet
long, and ten Feet broad, in what Street they
thought

thought proper. King *Edward* the Third made it a Corporation, confifting of a Mayor and Bailiffs, and gave it other Privileges and Authorities.

In the Reign of *Henry* the Fourth, a Parliament was held in the great Chamber of the Priory here. This Meeting, to which no Lawyer, or any Perfon fkilled in the Laws, was to come, afforded much Strife betwixt the Clergy and Laity; and is ever fince called *Parliamentum Indoctorum.*

Henry the Sixth, having laid feveral Towns and Villages to *Coventry*, granted by his Charter, that it fhould be an entire County, incorporated by itfelf in Deed and Name, and diftinct from the County of *Warwick*, and that the Bailiffs of the faid City fhould be Sheriffs of the County of the City for ever; yet ftill to continue to officiate as Bailiffs in the City, and fhould hold a monthly Court within their Liberties, like the Sheriffs of other Counties.

In the thirty-eighth Year of this King, another Parliament was held here, which was called *Parliamentum Diabolicum*, becaufe, by an Act paffed then, the Duke of *York*, and the Earls of *Salif-bury*, *Warwick*, and *March* (afterwards King *Edward* the Fourth) and their Adherents, were attainted.

The Inhabitants of this Place having been attached to King *Henry* the Seventh, *Edward* the Fourth, when he had attained the Crown, took the Sword from the Mayor, and disfranchifed the City, which was obliged to pay Five hundred Marks for the Redemption of its Charter: But this King, four Years afterwards, kept St. *George*'s Feaft here, and ftood Godfather to the Mayor's Child.

Sir *William Dugdale*, who takes every Occafion to lament the Diffolution of Religious Houfes, fays, that neither the Luftre of their beautiful Crofs,

nor

nor all the other large and eafy Acquifitions, did in any Sort, balance the Lofs this City fuftained by the Ruin of that great and famous Monaftery (the Priors of which fat in Parliament) and the other Religious Houfes. For, adds he, to fo low an Ebb did their Trading foon after grow, for want of fuch Concourfe of People that numeroufly reforted thither before that fatal Diffolution, when their beautiful Cathedral was pulled to Pieces, that many thoufands of the Inhabitants, to feek better Livelihoods, were conftrained to forfake the City; infomuch as in the third of *Edward* the Sixth, it was reprefented to the Duke of *Somerfet*, then Protector, by *John Hales*, a Perfon of great Note in thofe Days, and whofe Memory is ftill famous here, that there were not, at that Time, above Three thoufand Inhabitants; whereas, within Memory, there had been Fifteen thoufand.

James the Firft granted the Corporation a Charter, by which the Mayor, Recorder, Bailiffs, and other Officers, fhould yearly be elected on their *Leet-Day*, to be held within a Month after *Michaelmas*, by thirty-one Perfons, nominated of thofe who have formerly borne the principal Offices in the City; and likewife that there fhould be ten Aldermen in the ten Wards, as formerly: That the Mayor, Recorder, and thofe ten Aldermen, fhould be Juftices of Peace within the fame City and County thereof; as alfo that the faid thirty-one Perfons fhould have Power to tax themfelves, and all other the Inhabitants, within the Walls of the faid City, to the Charge of repairing the faid Walls; fo as always it difcharge not thofe who of Right or Cuftom are liable thereto.

In 1642, this City fhut its Gates againft King *Charles*, and his Troops; for which Reafon, his Son, *Charles* the Second, after the Reftoration, demolifhed the Walls, with twenty-fix Towers: But

left

left the Gates ftanding, which in general are ftrong and handfome. On that called *Gosford-Gate*, is a vaft Shield-Bone of a Boar, which, fays *Camden*, you may believe, that *Guy*, Earl of *Warwick*, or *Diana of the Groves* (which you pleafe) killed in hunting, after he had, with his Snout, turned up the Pit or Pond, that is now called *Swanfewell-Pool*, but in ancient Charters *Swinefwell*.

Coventry is a tolerably handfome City, if we make Allowances for the Antiquity of the Buildings, which are chiefly of Timber, and indeed in fome Streets project like thofe in *Mary-Port-Street*, at *Briftol*.

The Church of St. *Michael* is a good Fabric, the Architecture is *Gothic*, and the Steeple, which is of Stone, and was twenty-two Years in Building, is Three hundred Feet high. It was begun in 1373, and finifhed in 1395. But *Dugdale* is of Opinion, that the Body of the Church was built in the Reign of *Henry* the Sixth. Here is a new Altar-Piece, the Painting of which is curious, but rather fuperftitious. In this Church, among others, is a Monument for the Lady *Katherine Berkeley*, Daughter to *Thomas*, Duke of *Norfolk*, and another for Sir *Thomas Berkeley*, his Son.

Trinity Church ftands in the fame Yard, is built of the fame Materials, and hath a fimilar Steeple. On the South Wall of the Choir is an Infcription for Dr. *Philemon Holland*, who tranflated *Camden*'s *Britannia*, and in the Windows the Arms of Earl *Leofric*, *Edward* the Confeffor, King *Richard* the Second, and others.

At the South End of this City ftands another tall Spire, but without any Church; though it formerly belonged to that of the *Grey Friars* here. This Houfe being poor (for they had no Endowment of Lands) it was not diffolved till the thirtieth of *Henry* the Eighth, when they were forced

to

to fubfcribe an Inftrument of Surrender, to which
their Common Seal is affixed ; and, as I imagine,
you have not yet met with the Form of fuch Sur-
renders, I have copied it, as fomething curious.

  " For as moche as we, the *Warden* and *Freers*
" of the Houfe of *Saynt Francis*, in *Coventre*, in
" the County of *Warwick*, doo profoundly confi-
" der, that the Perfection of *Chriftian* Livinge
" dothe nott confift in dume Ceremonies, weringe
" of a grey Coot, difgeafinge our felf after ftraunge
" Fafhions, dokynge, noddynge, and beckyng ;
" in gurdyng our felves withe a Gurdle fulle of
" Knotts, and other like papifticall Ceremonies,
" wherein we hade ben mooft principally practifed,
" and miflyd, in Times pafte : But the very tru
" Waye to plefe God, and to live a tru *Chriftian*
" Mon withe out all Ypocrifie and fayned Difcimu-
" lation, is finceerly declared unto us by our Mr.
" *Chrifte*, his Evangelifts, and Apofteles ; being
" myndyd hereaftur to followe the fame, conform-
" yng our felf unto the Will and Plefure of our
" fupreme Hedde under Gode, in Eithe, the
" Kynges Majeftie : And not to folowe henfeforth
" the fuperftitious Traditions of oney forenfecall
" Potentate, or Peere : Withe mutual Affent and
" Confent doo fubmitt our felves unto the Mercy
" of owre feide foveraygn Lord : And wythe like
" mutual Affent and Confent do furrendre and
" yelde up into the Hondes of the fame, all our
" feide Houfe of *Saynt Frances*, in the Citie of *Co-*
" *ventre*, commonly callyd the *Grey-Freers*, in
" *Coventre*, wythe alle the Londs, Tenements,
" Gardens, Medows, Waters, Pondiards, Fed-
" ings, Paftures, Comens, Rents, Reverfions,
" and alle other our Intereft, Ryghtes, or Titles
" appertaining unto the fame. Moofte humbly
" befeechinge his mooft noble Grace to difpofe of
" us and of the fame, as befte fhall ftonde wythe
his

" his mooſt gracious Pleaſure. And further, fre-
" ly to graunte unto every on of us his Licenſe
" under Wretyng and Seealle, to chaunge our
" Habitts into ſecular Faſhion; and to receve
" ſuche Maner of Livinges as other ſecular Prieſts
" commonly be preferred unto. And we all
" faithfully ſhall pray unto Almighty God long
" to preſerve his mooſte noble Grace, wythe In-
" creſe of moche Felicite and Honour. And in
" Witnes of alle and ſinguler the Premiſſes, wee,
" the ſeide *Warden* and Covent of the *Grey-Freers,*
" in *Coventre,* to theſe Preſences have pute our
" Covent Seealle, the 16the Day of *October,* in
" the thertythe Yere of the Raygne of our mooſt
" ſoveraygne Lord King *Henry* the Eyghte.

　　" Par me, *Johannem Stafford,* Gardian. *Tho-*
　　　　mam Maller. Thomam Sanderſon. Jo-
　　　　hannem Abell. Johannem Woode. Ro-
　　　　gerum Lilly. Thomam Aukock. Ma-
　　　　theum Walker. Thomam Bangſit.
　　　　Willielmum Goſnelle."

This Houſe was, by King *Henry* the Eight, in
the thirty-fourth Year of his Reign, among
others, granted to the Mayor, Bailiffs, and Commonalty of this City, and their Succeſſors for ever.

　　Near the Ruins of this Friary is a Building, now
(on Account of its Situation) called *Grey-Friar-
Hoſpital,* upon the Walls of which thus written;

　　　May the 4, An. 1529. Mr. *William Fourd,* of
　　　this City, Merchant of the Staple, founded
　　　this Almehouſe, for five Men and one Woman;
　　　and gave to each of them five Pence a Week,
　　　for their Maintenance. Afterwards Mr. *Wil-
　　　liam Pisford,* his Executor, gave other Lands,
　　　and appointed ſix Men and their Wives to be
　　　placed therein, and each Couple to have ſeaven
　　　Pence Half-penny a Week. But Mr. *William
　　　Wigſton,* having Power from both of them to
　　　alter, adde, or diminiſh their Wills; for the
　　　　　　　　　　　　　　　　　　　　　better

better ordering the faid Houfe, did ordain, that there fhould be but five Men, and their Wives, and a Nurfe, and each Couple to have feven Pence Half-penny a Week, and the Nurfe the fame.

In the feventh Year of King *James*, the Lands given to this Hofpital were queftioned, as concealed from the Crown, and were again purchafed by the City, who have ever fince maintained the charitable Ufes, with a great Addition out of the Chamber of the City.

In the Year 1621, the City added another Man and Woman, at their own Charge, fo that there is now fix Couple, befides the Nurfe, each Couple being allowed two Shillings weekly, and the Nurfe one Shilling a Week, although there be not any Advance of the Rent to the City. Mr. *Simon Norton*, Alderman of this City, gave towards the Maintenance of one Man and Woman in this Hofpital, for which the City doth allow two Shillings a Week alfo, as the reft have ; fo that there is now feaven Couple and a Nurfe in this Hofpital.

The *High-Crofs* at *Coventry* was built by Sir*William Hollies*, Knight, Lord-Mayor of *London*, and Son to *Thomas Hollies*, of *Stoke*, near *Coventry*. It was begun in the Year 1541, and finifhed in 1544. By the Prints publifhed of this Building, it appears to have been very magnificent, but 'tis now in a ruinous Condition *.

It was adorned with the Statues of many Kings of *England*, of which a few only remain ; and indeed the whole appears little better than an Heap of Rubbifh, which ought to be removed.

The Town-Houfe here is old, and the Paintings in the Windows fhew the Figures of fome of the Kings, and other great Perfonages, who have been

Benefactors

---

* The Author of the *Tour* fays, 'tis fixty Feet high, but, fure I am, it does not now meafure above thirty Feet.

Benefactors of this City; in Praise of whom there are some Latin Verses, in which are mentioned the *Henries*, the *Edwards*, the *Black Prince*, Queen *Elizabeth*, the Duke of *Northumberland*, and his Son *Robert Dudley*, Earl of *Leicester*.

In the Year 1734, there being then but two Parish Churches in this City, an Act of Parliament passed for making a Church here, called *Bablack*, Parochial, and for appointing a District or Parish to the same. And also for enabling the Master and Usher of the Free Grammar School, which was founded by *John Hales*, Esq; beforementioned (who gave it the Name of the School of King *Henry* VIII.) to be Rector and Lecturer of the said Parish Church from that Time ; by the Act, it is called " the Church of St. *John Baptist*, in " the City of *Coventry*," where there is no Cathedral or Collegiate Church, as some have imagined.

The Trade of this City is very considerable. There are, perhaps, more Ribbands made here, than in any other Place in the World. It is astonishing to see what Numbers are employed in the Manufacture of this Article, and the Quantities sent weekly to *London*, for the Supply of the Haberdashers and Milliners there, and also for Exportation to all Parts of the World. Tammies, Everlastings, and Plushes, are also made in *Coventry* ; and, as the Water of the *Shireburn*, which runs through it, is peculiar for its blue Dye, their Thread of that Colour surpasses any other ; and is distinguished by the Appellation of *Coventry Blue*.

I should have observed, that after the Time of Earl *Leofric*, this City was in the Possession of the Earls of *Chester*, and afterwards became annexed to the Earldom of *Cornwall*. Besides the Officers already mentioned, this City hath a Steward, a Coroner, two Chamberlains, two Wardens, &c.

Coventry was formerly the only Market Town in the County of *Warwick* ; when the Refort of People was prodigious. The Market is now held on *Fridays,* and the Fairs, May 2, for Horfes, Cows and Sheep ; *Friday* in *Trinity* Week, for Flannels, Linen, and Woollen ; firft Day reprefenting Lady *Godiva* on Horfeback. *November* 1, for Linen, Woollen, and Horfes.

This City, which lies in 1 Deg. 26 Min. of Weft Longitude, and in 52 Deg. 25 Min. Latitude ; fends two Members to the Houfe of Commons.

Here was born that famous Hiftorian, from hence called *Walter de Coventry* ; of whom *Bale* makes honourable Mention. He wrote thefe three Books, *Chron. Britann. Anglo-Sax. Chron.* and *Annales Angl.* *.

I have, when at *Daventry,* mentioned *Empfon,* who, in the Reign of *Henry* VII. was, Speaker of the Houfe of Commons, a Privy Counfellor to the King, and Recorder of the City of *Coventry.* One of the Articles exhibited againft him, by the Council, in the firft of *Henry* the Eighth, was, that whereas a Prifoner being indicted for Theft in this City, to the Value of One Pound, was by the Jury acquitted ; and that the faid *Empfon* conceiving the Evidence to be fufficient, committed the Jury to Prifon, until they entered into a Bond to appear before the King's Council, where the Matter being again confidered, it was ordered they fhould pay Eight Pounds for a Fine, which was thought fo henious, as at a Seffion held afterwards at *Coventry,* a particular Indictment was framed againft him, and he was found guilty. That *Empfon* and *Dudley* were two abominable Perfons, the great Lord *Bacon,* in his Life of *Henry* the

---

* There was burnt in the *Cotton Library,* a Book with this Title, *Gaulteri Coventrienfis* Hiftoria Regum *Angliæ,* à tempore R., *Cadwalladri,* ad tempora R. *Edwardi* I.

Seventh, has clearly demonstrated ; but as all their Extortions and Works of Rapine were abetted by the King, it was thought proper, for the public Peace, to impeach them of Treason (of which they were innocent). *Empson* was tried at *Northampton*, and made an artful ·Defence ; but they were both convicted, and suffered Death *.

In the year 1519, six Men and one Woman were burnt at *Coventry*, for teaching their Children the Lord's Prayer, the Ten Commandments, and the Apostles Creed, in the Vulgar Tongue.

Having dined at the *Bull's-Head*, a good Inn, kept by Mrs. *Terry*, who is a decent well-behaved Land-lady, we set forward towards *Meriden*.

The first Village we came to is *Alesley*, situate upon a pretty rising Hill, at the Bottom of which runs a crystal Stream of Water. On the Right Hand, betwixt the Road and a neat House and Gardens, is a delightful Gravel Walk, which leads to the Church-yard, from whence is a good View of *Coventry*. The Church is small, but very neat, and in the Church-yard is a Monument with this Inscription.

In Memory of the Revd.
Mr. *Benj. Marshall*, A. M.
30 years Rector of *Naunton*,
In *Gloucestershire* ;
9 Years Rector of this Place,
And Prebendary of *Litchfield*.
A Gentleman of a very great Share of Learning,
As is evident from his Works in Print.
An able Divine,
A sincere Christian,

* It so happened, that *Empson* riding through *Warwickshire*, met with an old blind Man, who was esteemed for his Judgment in the Changes of the Weather, whom he asked in a jesting Manner, when the Sun would change. " When (cried the old " Man) such a wicked Lawyer as you goeth to Heaven.

And

And moft dear to his Family.
He died the 22 of Feb. 1748,
Aged 67.

The Church is dedicated to *All-Saints*, and was
formerly a Chapel to the Priory of *Coventry*. I
think this is one of the moft agreeable Villages I
have feen. Through it paffes the great Road from
London to *Shrewsbury*, and *Chefter*, and indeed
through *Carlifle* to *Glafgow*, in *Scotland*.

Leaving this Village, we had on the left Hand
a charming Valley, which running parallel with
the Road, caufed our travelling to be extremely
pleafant. In a fhort Time we came to *Meriden*,
or, as *Dugdale* writes it, *Mireden*. The Church
and great Part of this Village ftand out of the
great Road. It took its Name from *Mire*, and
Dene, that is, a foul or dirty Valley. It was formerly poffeffed by the Lady *Godiva*, beforementioned; and, in the Conqueror's Survey, is written
Ailefpede. In the Body of the Church is a Monument for *John Wyard*, who founded a Chantry
here. He was Efquire to *Thomas de Beauchamp*,
Earl of *Warwick*: and, in the fecond of *Richard*
the Second, one of the Knights for this County,
in the Parliament then held at *Weftminfter*. The
Monument is thus infcribed.

Hic jacet *Johes Wyard* quondam armiger
Comitis de Warewick, fundator iftius
Cantarie, cujus anime propitietur Deus, Amen.

After returning into the great Road, we defcended an eafy Hill, and came to that famous Inn,
the *Bull's Head* at *Meriden*, which, if the Sign
were removed, would have all the Appearance of
the Seat of a Nobleman of Tafte and Spirit. Under this Roof is the prefent Letter written, and
therefore I fhall be the more particular. It is fituate near the Road, on the Side of a fmall but
charming

charming Valley. The Houſe is very large, having two Wings next the Road, and the Apartments are good and well contrived. The Hall is very agreeable in hot Weather. Behind the Houſe the Ground riſes conſiderably, where is a very neat and pleaſant Bowling-green; and above that, towards the Summit of the Hill, is a very beautiful *Chineſe Temple*, which, from the Road, and the oppoſite Side of the Valley, has a charming Effect. The Gardens, which are well laid out and extenſive, are on the Declivity of the Hill, facing the South; and, in the Midſt of them, ſtands a neat modern-built Houſe, which is now uſed only as a Granery. Below this Building are two Canals, and nearer to the Dwelling-houſe is a ſmall Building conſiſting of two Rooms, joined together by an Arch; they ſtand on a riſing Ground overlooking the Road, and are pleaſant. Before the Front of the Houſe, on the oppoſite Side of the Road, and betwixt that and a ſweet verdant Hill, is a fine Piece of Water, upon which is a Pleaſure-boat; and on the Margin of this Water, which is very long, are Walks and Seats for the Amuſement of the Gueſts, who chuſe angling, walking, or ſitting. And for thoſe who like their Fiſh ready caught, here are Lockers, ſtored with various and excellent Sorts. To the Weſtward of the Houſe ſtand the Granaries, Stabling, Yards, &c. which are well contrived; and, having a Deſcent to the Road, are always clean. Between the Road and the Eaſt End of the Piece of Water, ſtands a Bake-houſe, a Brew-houſe, a Slaughter-houſe, a Dairy, and a Blackſmith's Shop; and, on the oppoſite Side, ſomewhat more towards *Coventry*, is a large Malt-houſe, built by the late Landlord, and Father to the preſent, whoſe Name is *Reynolds*. The old Man, who lived to be about Seventy, was a very ingenious Perſon. It was he that brought
the

the whole to the Perfection this Inn is now found to be; which, tho' it is seven Miles from any Market, is well furnished with excellent Provisions: For you are to be informed, that they sow and reap their own Wheat, Barley, and Oats; bake their own Bread, make their own Malt, brew their own Beer, (which is famous for its Strength and Flavour) kill their own Meat, and make their own Butter; so that, with the great Quantity of Poultry they have always fit for killing, they may be said to stand in little or no Need of a Market. The Lord Lieutenants of *Ireland* generally contrive to lie at this House, in their Journies to and from that Kingdom; and there is scarce an *Irish* Gentleman who has come by the Way of *Holyhead*, or *Chester*, to *London*, but remembers the *Bull's-Head* at *Meriden*. I am, Sir, Yours, &c.

L E T T E R XL.

From *Tamworth*, in *Warwickshire*.

S I R,

A Little to the West of the *Bull's-Head*, is *Meriden-Heath*, where the Duke of *Cumberland*'s Army being arrived, after two forced Marches, was the Cause of the Rebels retiring from *Derby*. For, by this Situation, his Royal Highness had it in his Power to attack them before they could have got to *London*. We rode through *Pakington*, formerly the Manor of the *Fishers*, one of whom, *John Fisher*, of the Family of the *Fishers* of *Dothill*, in *Shropshire*, was one of the Pensioners to *Henry* the Eighth, *Edward* the Sixth, and the Queens *Mary* and *Elizabeth*. He was Steward (under *Ambrose Dudley*, Earl of *Warwick*) of the Castle and Town of *Warwick*: And his Son, *Clement*,

-ment, was Treasurer in the *Netherlands*, to the Earl of *Leicester.* They are both buried in the Church here, with Monuments to their Memories.

The next Place of Note is the Town of *Coleshill*, upon the small River *Cole*, between which and *Maxtock Castle*, runs the River *Blithe*. This Town, which is situate upon an Ascent, was sold by King *William* the First, or *William Rufus*, to the Family of *Clinton*; from them it descended to the *Mountforts:* But, upon the Execution and Attainder of Sir *Simon Mountfort*, in the Reign of *Henry* the Seventh, that King gave the Manor to *Simon Digby*, Deputy to *John* Earl of *Oxford*, then Constable of the Tower of *London*. In this Family it still continues.

The Town, though but small, is, in general, pretty well built, and has some very good Inns in it. The Church, dedicated to St. *Peter*, was formerly given to the Nuns of *Merkgate*, in the County of *Bedford*. In the Fourth of *Edward* the Sixth, the beautiful and lofty Steeple here suffered much by Thunder and Lightning; which cracked the West Side of the Tower, and shattered the upper Part of the Spire. The Inhabitants, in order to enable them to repair it, sold one of their Bells, but shortened the Steeple at least fifteen Feet. Notwithstanding which it is seen at a great Distance every Way.

In this Church are many Monuments, particularly of the *Digby* Family; some of whom are in Armour lying cross-legged. I shall only trouble you with one Character, which was drawn by the Pen of Dr. *John Hough*, the good Bishop of *Worcester*, beforementioned.

Mary, Relict of *Kildare* Lord *Digby*,
Departed this Life *December* 23d,
Anno Dom. 1692.

Whom it were unpardonable to lay down in Silence,

And

And of whom 'tis difficult to speak with Justice.
For her just Character will look like Flattery,
And the least Abatement of this, is Injury to her Memory,
In every Condition of Life, she was a Pattern to her Sex ;
Appear'd Mistress of those peculiar Qualities
That were requisite to conduct her through it with Honour,
And never fail'd to exert them in their proper Seasons,
With the utmost Advantage.

She was modest, without Affectation ;
Easy, without Levity ; and reserved, without Pride :
Knew how to stoop without sinking,
And to gain Peoples Affections, without lessening their
Regards.

She was careful, without Anxiety ;
Frugal, without Parsimony.

Not at all fond of the superfluous Trappings of Greatness,
Yet abridg'd herself in nothing that her Quality required.
She was a faithful Member of the Church of *England*.
Her Piety was exemplary, her Charity universal.
She found herself a Widow in the Beginning of her Life,
When the Temptations of Beauty, Honour, Youth,
And Pleasure
Were in their full Strength :
Yet she made them all give way to the Interest of her
Family,
And betook herself entirely to the Matron's Part.
The Education of her Children engrossed all her Cares.
No Charge was spared in the Cultivation of their Minds,
Nor Pains, in the Improvement of their Fortunes.

In a Word,
She was truly Wise, truly Honourable, and truly Good.
More can scarce be said ;
And yet he that says this, knew her well :
And is well assured he has said nothing
Which either Veracity or Modesty should oblige him
To suppress.

Below this Town, in a delightful Valley, is the
Seat and Park of this honourable Family ; and
now possessed by *Henry*, Lord *Digby*, Baron of
Geashill, in the Kingdom of *Ireland*, Great-Grandson,

fon and Heir to *William*, called the *Good Lord Digby*, whom I fhall again mention when I come to *Sherborne*, in *Dorfetfhire*.

The Houfe here is not modern ; and, being on a low Spot, is unpleafing in Winter; but, in the Summer Seafon, the Park is exceffively delightful : The Woods in it are very fine, and the River which ferpentizes through it, affords a moft charming Appearance. This Park, when the neighbouring Fields are almoft burnt up, is cloathed with a moft beautiful Verdure.

The Market at *Colefhill* is held on *Wednefdays*, and the Fairs, *Shrove-Monday*, for Horfes. *May* 6. for *ditto* and Cattle. *October* 2, for all Sorts of Cattle.

I have already obferved, that *Maxtoke Cafile* ftands on the oppofite Side of the River *Blithe*, as do alfo the Remains of a religious Houfe, of which take this Account.

The Priory of *Maxtock*, or *Maxftoke*, was founded by *William Clinton*, Earl of *Huntingdon*, in Honour of the *Holy Trinity*, the *Bleffed Virgin*, St. *Michael*, and all the *Saints*, for Canons-Regular of the Order of St. *Auguftine* ; *viz.* One Prior elective, and a Convent of twelve Canons, in whofe Deed of Foundation, dated *Anno* 1336, he appointed feveral Ordinances relating to their Habit, the Election of the Prior, and that none fhould meddle with the Cuftody of the Houfe in Time of the Vacation, but who the Superior and Convent fhould appoint. Of the Quality of fuch as are to be received for Canons. Of the Number of Canons to be encreafed, as the Revenue encreafes. The Prior and Convent not to fell or grant any Corrodies or Penfions, unlefs compelled by inevitable Neceffity. Of the Account. Of the Founder's Anniverfary. Of the Number of Maffes. That, at the End of every Office of our Lady,

the Prieſt who officiates ſhall ſay the Angelic Salu-
tation, in Manner following, *Ave* Maria *gracia
plena Dominus tecum, Benedicta tu in Mulieribus et
benedictus fructus ventris tui* Jheſus, *Amen, Amen.
Et benedicta ſit venerabilis mater tua* Anna, *ex qua
tua caro virginea et immaculata proceſſit, Amen.* With
ſome other Orders; all which were confirmed by
Roger, Biſhop of *Coventry* and *Litchfield, Anno* 1337.
King *Edward* the Third granted his Licence to
theſe Canons, to exchange their Manor of *Shu-
ſtoke,* for Lands in *Maxtock.* This Priory at the
Diſſolution was valued at Eighty-ſeven Pounds
Twelve Shillings and Three-pence *per Ann.*

The illuſtrious Founder of this Houſe was
Keeper of *Dover Caſtle,* Admiral of the Weſtern
Seas, and Keeper of the King's Foreſts South of
Trent. In the nineteenth Year of *Edward* the
Third, he began the Foundation of a Caſtle here,
in a quadrangular Form, the Remains of which
are curious Ruins; and the following Year he re-
ceived Eight hundred and Twenty-three Pounds
Twelve Shillings and Four Pence, as a Gift from
the King, for his Services in Foreign Wars. This
noble Knight bore for his Arms *Argent, Cruſule fitche,
Sable, upon a Chef, Azure, two Mullets, Or, pierced,
Gules,* and dying in the Year 1354, was buried in
the Priory here.

In the Reign of *Henry* the Sixth, Sir *John Clinton* paſſed away the Inheritance of this Caſtle and
Lordſhip to *Humphry,* Earl of *Stafford,* who plated
the Gates all over with Iron, and adorned them
with his own Coat of Arms. *Edward Stafford,*
Duke of *Buckingham,* his Great-Grandſon, being
executed in the Reign of *Henry* the Eighth, that
King granted it to Sir *William Compton,* Knight,
who held it of the Crown *in Capite,* by Knights
Service. Mr. *Buck* has publiſhed Views both of
this Caſtle and Priory. The Church here is a Vicarage,

carage, which, in the twenty-fixth of *Henry* the Eighth, was valued at One hundred and fix Shillings and Eightpence, *per Annum*; but the Manner of the Vicar's Support was thus; as appears by a Certificate from the Parifhioners to the Vifitors, about the Beginning of the Time of Queen Elizabeth. That he had Meat and Drink for himhimfelf, and a Child to wait upon him; every Year a Gown, every Week three Cafts of Bread; and two Gallons of Ale, his Barber, Launder, Fire and Candle, with Ten Pounds Wages, and all the Cofts of the Houfe.

From *Maxtock* I rode to this Town of *Tamworth*, which is fituate in the two Counties of *Stafford* and *Warwick*. No Country can be more pleafant than this, very few fo plentiful. The *Tame* is here a confiderable River, and waters the neighbouring Meads, which are rich, even to Luxuriancy. This Town has had the Honour of being the Seat of feveral *Mercian* Kings. The King's Ditch, of which there is fome Veftigia, was certainly the Work of fome of thefe Monarchs. It ftretches in a ftrait Line from the River *Anker* (which comes down from *Atherfton*, and here joins the *Tame*) a little below *Bowl-Bridge*, and then making a right Angle, keeps a Courfe parallel to the River for near Four hundred Paces, and then returning by another right Angle, runs into the River *Tame*, juft below what is called *Lady-Bridge:* the Ground within being of a quadrangular Form, and the Ditch about Forty-five Feet broad.

That the *Danes* deftroyed this Place, all our Hiftorians allow; and that it continued in a defolate Condition for fome Time, till (in the Year 914) the renowned Lady *Ethelfleda* reftored it to its antient Strength and Splendor; raifing a ftrong Tower upon an artificial Mount of Earth, called the *Dungeon*, upon which Mount that Building, now

called

called the *Caftle*, has fince, been erected ; for the Body of the Old Caftle ftood confiderably below ; and at this Place this famous Lady died in the Year 918, and was buried at *Gloucefter*.

After the Conqueft, *William* the Firft gave it to *Robert Marmion* ; in whofe Family it long continued. *Baldwin Freville*, who married a *Marmion*, was in great Efteem with *Edward* the *Black Prince* ; and, for his fingular Fidelity and great Services, was, in the Thirty-eighth Year of *Edward* the Third, made by that Prince his Steward of *Xantoigne*, in *France* for Life.

Baldwin, his Son, (a Knight) in the Firft Year of *Richard* the Second, exhibited his Claim to be the King's Champion. on the Day of his Coronation, and to do the Service belonging to that Office, by reafon of the Tenure of this Caftle ; that is, to ride completely armed, upon a barbed Horfe, into *Weftminfter-Hall*, and there to challenge the Combat with any Perfon that fhould be fo bold to oppofe the King's Title to the Crown. Which Service the *Marmions*, antiently Lords thereof, had cuftomarily performed. But Sir *John Dimock* being then his Competitor, carried it from him by Judgment of the Conftable, and Marfhal of *England* ; becaufe he was poffeffed of the Lordfhip of *Scrivelby*, in *Lincolnfhire* ; which, by better Authorities than the faid *Freville* could produce, appeared to have been for many Ages by that Service ; and and that the *Marmions* had the faid Office as Owners thereof, and not in Right of this Caftle ; it being defcended to *Dimock*, which *Scrivelby*, from a female Heir of Sir *Thomas Ludlow*, Knight, Hufband of *Joane*, the youngeft Daughter to Sir *Philip Marmion*.

By Marriage, this Caftle came to the *Ferrers*, many of whom have Monuments in the Church to their Memories. I fhall only fend you the following

lowing Epitaph on Sir *John Ferrers*, who lies buried under an Alabaster Tome-ftone.

> If thou haft a minde to know
> Whofe Corps interred lye below,
> Left thou thinke thefe words in Stone
> Are all that's left of him being gone;]
> Give eafe unto the upright tongue,
> Of whofoere he liv'd among,
> Then freed from doubt, thou wilt confent,
> He left a choicer Monument.
> 1633.

This Borough continued in the Crown from the Reign of *Edward* the Confeffor to that of *Henry* the Third, who granted it to the Inhabitants in Fee-Farm. After this, it confiderably declined, till Queen *Elizabeth*, upon their Petition, incorporated it; appointing two Bailiffs, with Twenty-four principal Burgeffes (one of whom is the Town-Clerk) who, with the Bailiffs, have the Power to call Courts, &c.

The Church in this Town is Collegiate, and a very large Building.

Here is a Grammar School founded by Queen *Elizabeth*, and the Town enjoys Part of the Charity of Mr. *Guy*, who founded and endowed the Hofpital in *Southwark*, which bears his Name.

This Town, which is remarkable for fine Ale, fends two Members to Parliament; its Market is on *Saturdays*; and Fairs, *April* 12, for Cattle; *September* 12, for Cattle and Cheefe.

L E T E R XL.

From *Leominster*, in *Herefordshire*.

S I R,

AFTER riding through a wild and barren
Country, I came to *Sutton-Colefield*, rendered
famous by being the native Place of *John Voisy*,
Bishop of *Exeter*, who, in the Reign of *Henry* the
Eighth, greatly improved and adorned this little
Town, where he erected a Grammar-School. Bishop *Gibson* says, that he died here, in the One
hundred and third Year of his Age. The Air a-
round is extremely wholfome, but the Land is fte-
ril, efpecially that extenfive Common, called the
Coldfield.

I now directed my Courfe towards *Stourbridge*, a
good Town, in the County of *Worcefter*, fituate
upon the River *Stour*, which runs to *Kidderminfter*,
already defcribed. The Glafs-Houfes at, and near,
Stourbridge, are numerous, and almoft conftantly
at Work. They here make various Sorts of
Glafs, but chiefly Bottles and for Windows. And
in this Neighbourhood is found a peculiar Sort of
Clay, of which Crucibles, Pots for melting the
Preparations for Glafs, and other Veffels, which
bear violent Heats, are made. Great Quantities of
this Clay are fent to *Briftol* and *London*; but lately
there is a Pit found in the *Clee Hills*, in *Shropshire*,
whofe Clay, I am told, excels this of *Stourbridge*.
This Town is pretty well built, and of a confiderable Extent, and though it fends no Members to
Parliament, is, as *Birmingham*, *Manchefter*, &c.
of more Confequence than half a Dozen *Cornish* or
Wiltshire Boroughs. Here is a good Manufactory
of Woollen Cloths, which bear the Name of the
Town,

Town, and wear extreamly well. In this Town King *Edward* the Sixth founded and endowed a Grammar-School, and gave an handsome Library; and here, or rather at *Old Swinford*, of which this present Parish was formerly a Member, is a noble Hospital, founded and endowed by *Thomas Foley*, Esq; (Anceftor to Lord *Foley)* for sixty poor Children of this and the neighbouring Parishes, who are taught Reading, Writing, Arithmetic, and Grammar, in order to their being set out to Trades. Their Difcipline and Habit are like those of *Christ's Hospital* in *London*.

In the Year 1726, one Mr. *Biggs*, a Clothier of this Town, gave, by Will, Three hundred Pounds, in Trust, to the Governors of its Free-School, towards building a Church or Chapel, the former of which, with the Affiftance from the Contributions of the neighbouring Nobility and Gentry, has been finifhed at the Expence of about *Two thoufand Pounds* ; and, in the Year 1742, an Act of Parliament paffed for making it a Parifh Church, feparate from that of *Old Swinford.* The Market at *Stourbridge*, which is a very good one, is on *Fridays*; and the Fairs on *March* the 29th, for Horfes, and other Cattle ; and *September* the 8th, for Cattle of all Sorts, and Sheep.

The Town of *Kinfare*, or *Kinver*, lies a little to the Weft of *Stourbridge* ; near it is the Veftigia of an Encampment, but whether it was the Work of the *Danes* or *Saxons*, is uncertain. It is of an oblong Shape, and about Three hundred Yards long, and Two hundred over. This Town is fmall, but fituate in a fine fporting Country. The Church, like that of *Weft Wickham*, is built upon an Hill above the Town, which I left towards the Approach of Evening ; and that Night arrived again at *Bewdley.* The next Morning I went on board a Wherry, from *Bridgencrth*, then bound to the Cities

of

of *Worcester* and *Gloucester*. The Company were very agreeable, and this was one of the moft pleafing Voyages I ever made. Allowances muft be made for the Boatmen, who were vulgar enough, and the moft irregular Rowers I have yet met with.

The beauteous Banks of this excellent River I have mentioned before, but I muft confefs my Admiration of them is vaftly augmented. Surely nothing in Nature can equal the amazing Variety of Woods, Rocks, Meads, Thickets, and promifcuous Buildings which alternately are here exhibited. The firft Village on our Right-Hand was *Ribbesford*, to which Church the Town of *Bewdley* belongs ; and here the late Lord *Herbert* of *Cherbury* had an agreeable Seat. Lower down is *Blackftone*, where was formerly an Hermitage in the Rock. Where the *Stour* falls in, is a Ferry, called *Redftone-Ferry*, and foon after we paffed by the Village of *Aftley* ; and having left *Whitley* on the Right, and *Omberfley* on the Left-Hand, paffed *Holt-Caftle* ; and drove down by the Mouth of the River *Salwarp*, that comes from *Bromfgrove*, as before obferved, and leaving *Gunley*, or *Grimley*, and *Hallow*, on the Right, and *Clains*, on the Left, came to the Side of that delightful Meadow, called *Pitchcraft* ; where the *Severn* fometimes overflows, and fpoils the Horfe-Races of the City of *Worcefter* ; from which delightful Place we put off in the following Morning.

About three Miles below this City, we paffed the Mouth of the River *Teme*, and now the Hills of *Malvern* had moft wonderful Effects ; for at one Place, they had a romantic Appearance directly before us, and from the next Reach of the River feemed to be three or four Miles on our Right-Hand. It is impoffible to fet down thefe ravifhing Scenes.

We

We paſſed *Powick*, a Village remarkable for Cherries of the *Kentiſh* Sort, and leaving *Kemſey*, *Clevelode*, *Severnſtoke*, and *Hanley-Caſtle*, arrived at *Upton upon Severn*, where I left my Fellow-Voyagers.

Upton is a pretty Town, delightfully ſituated on the Weſtern Bank of this famous River, over which is a good Stone Bridge; and on the Eaſtern Bank are moſt charming and extenſive Meads. As the Spot where the Town ſtands is a ſmall Riſe, the Views from it are extreamly fine.

This Place is ſuppoſed to have been a *Roman Station*, on account of Coins of that Nation being formerly found here. The Streets are clean, and well-paved, and here is a Charity-School for ſixteen Girls. The Market is held on *Tueſdays*, and the Fairs on the firſt *Thurſday* after *Midlent*, and *Thurſday* in *Whitſun-Week*, for Horſes, Cattle, and Sheep; *July* the 10th, and *Thurſday* before St. *Matthew*, *September* 21ſt. for ditto, and Leather.

From this agreeable Place, I rode over Part of *Malvern* Hills to *Ledbury*, or *Lidbury*, in the County of *Hereford*. The Proſpects from theſe ſtupendous Mounts were extreme fine.

Hugh Foliot, Biſhop of *Hereford*, founded at *Lebury*, a Religious Houſe, for the Reception of poor People, and Travellers; and dedicated it to the Honour of God, and St. *Katherine* the Virgin. He endowed it with ſeveral Churches, Tenements, &c. all which, with Lands given by others, were confirmed by King *Edward* the Third, in the Second Year of his Reign. This Houſe at the Diſſolution, was valued at Twenty-two Pounds Five Shillings *per Annum*.

King *Henry* the Fourth, in the ſecond Year of his Reign, gave a Licence to *John*, Biſhop of *Hereford*, to found a College in the Pariſh Church here, for Nine Chaplains; of which, one to be Maſter or Cuſtos, allowing them to have a Common Seal, to

VOL. I.　　　　Hhh　　　　be

be capable of purchafing Lands, and of fuing and of being liable to be fued.

The Hofpital here is well endowed, and has generally had fome eminent Perfon as Mafter. The famous Doctor *Thomas Thornton* was Mafter of it in the Reign of *James* I. This learned Perfon, who was Vice-Chancellor of *Oxford*, lies buried in the Chancel of the Parifh Church here. Mr. *Tombs*, a Leader of the Anabaptifts, was alfo Mafter in the Time of the Rump Parliament. The celebrated Dr. *Hofkins* was Minifter of the Church here, and lies interred in it, with an Infcription which begins thus:

Sub Pedibus Doctor jacet hic in Legibus *Hofkins*,
Effe pios docuit, quodque docebat, erat, &c.

Here is a Charity School for Twenty-three poor Children; the Market is held on *Tuefdays*, and Fairs, *Monday* before *Eafter*, *May* 12, for horned Cattle and Cheefe, *June* 22, for ditto and Wool; *October* 2, for Horned Cattle, Hops, Cheefe, and Pigs; *Monday* before St. *Thomas*, *December* 21, for horned Cattle, Cheefe, and fat Hogs.

This Town is fituate in a fine clay Country, and abounds with every Conveniency of Life; Provifions are cheap, and the Air remarkably good. In the Year 1736, the Turnpike Gates here were cut down by a Mob; fome of whom were hanged for it.

In my Way to *Rofs*, I had *Mareley Hill* on my Right Hand *.

* Dr *Fuller*, fays, " that in the Year 1575, this Hill roufed
" itfelf, as it were out of Sleep, or rather, it might be faid to
" be in Labour, for three Days together; fhaking and roaring
" all that Time, to the great Terror of all that heard or beheld
" it. It threw down every Thing that oppofed it, and removed
" itfelf to a higher Place."

From

From *Ledbury* to *Rofs*, I rode through a fine
Country, abounding in Corn Fields, and Plantations of various Apple-Trees, richly laden.

The Town of *Rofs*, is built on the Eaftern Bank
of the delightful River *Wye*, where Peace and
Plenty are Companions. It confifts chiefly of two
Streets, which crofs each other. At the Weft End
is a fine broad Caufeway, made (among the numeous good Things he did for this Town) by the
incomparable Mr. *John Kyrle*, whom Mr. *Pope* fo
finely celebrates, in his Epiftle to the prefent Lord
Bathurft.

But all our Praifes, why fhould Lords engrofs?
Rife honeft Mufe! and fing the MAN OF ROSS:
Pleas'd *Vaga* echoes thro' her winding Bounds,
And rapid *Severn* hoarfe Applaufe refounds.
Who hung with Woods yon Mountains fultry Brow,
From the dry Rock, who bade the Waters flow?
Not to the Skies in ufelefs Columns toft,
Or in proud Falls magnificently loft,
But clear and artlefs, pou'ring thro' the Plain
Health to the Sick, and Solace to the Swain.
Whofe Caufeway parts the Vale with fhady Rows;
Whofe Seats the weary Traveller repofe?
Who taught that Heav'n directed Spire to rife?
The MAN OF ROSS, each lifping Babe replies,
Behold the Market-Place with Poor o'erfpread,
The MAN OF ROSS divides the Weekly Bread.
He feeds yon Alms-Houfe, neat, but void of State,
Where Age and Want fit fmiling at the Gate:
Him portion'd Maids, apprentic'd Orphans bleft,
The Young who labour, and the Old who reft.
Is any fick? the MAN OF ROSS relieves,
Prefcribes, attends, the Medicine makes and gives,
Is there a Variance? enter but his Door,
Balk'd are the Courts, and Conteft is no more.
Defpairing *Quacks* with Curfes fled the Place,
And vile *Attornies*, now an ufelefs Race.
" Thrice happy Man! enabled to perfue,
" What all fo wifh, but want the Pow'r to do,

" Oh

" Oh fay what Sums that gen'rous Hand fupply?
" What Mines to fwell that boundlefs Charity?"
Of Debts and Taxes, Wife and Children clear,
This Man poffeft——Five hundred Pounds a year,
Blufh Grandeur, blufh! proud Courts withdraw your
    Blaze,
Ye *little Stars!* hide your diminifhed Rays.
" And what, no Monument Infcription Stone?
" His Race, his Form, his Name almoft unknown?"
Who builds a Church to God, and not to Fame,
Will never mark the Marble with his Name.
Go fearch it there * where to be born and die,
Of Rich and Poor makes all the Hiftory;
Enough that Virtue fill'd the Space between;
Proved by the Ends of being to have been.

This excellent Perfon died in the Year 1724, at
the Age of Ninety, and is buried in the Chancel
of the Church here.

This Town was made a Free Borough by King
Henry the Third, is pretty well built, and much
frequented, efpecially on *Thurfdays,* when the Market is held, and plentifully furnifhed. The Fairs
are on *Holy Thurfday,* for horned Cattle and Sheep;
Corpus Chrifti, or *June* 13, for horned Cattle and
Cheefe; *July* 20, for horned Cattle, Horfes, Sheep,
and Wool, *October* 10, for horned Cattle, Cheefe,
and Butter; *December* 11, for horned Cattle and
Pigs.

Here are two Charity-Schools, taught and
cloathed by Subfcription.

Having croffed the *Wye,* which here is navigable, and abounds with Fifh of various Sorts; I
directed my Courfe to the City of *Hereford;* which
is pleafantly fituated in a delicious Country. It
ftands on the Northern Bank of the *Wye,* having
the River *Lug* to the Eaftward; which falls into
the *Wye* a little below. The Meadows here are

---

* The Parifh Regifter.

extrem

extreme fine. The *Britons* called this Place *Tre-fawith*, from the *Beech Trees* growing here; and the *Saxons*, *Fern-leg*, from *Fern*. This City was founded under the *Heptarchy*, but, in what Year, our Hiſtorians are not agreed. This is certain, that, after Chriſtianity had made ſome Progreſs, it ſo happened that *Peada*, King of *Mercia*, became a Chriſtian; and, ſoon after, this Place was ſo conſiderable, (when the Church-Government came to be eſtabliſhed in that Kingdom) that it was made an Epiſcopal See; *Putta*, in the Year 680, being ordained the firſt Biſhop thereof.

To the Death of *Ethelbert*, King of the *Eaſt-Angles*, this City owed its great Increaſe and Improvement. For that King, who was learned, ſober, and religious, being invited by *Offa*, King of the *Mercians*, to his Court, then ſeated at *Sutton-Wallis*, in this County, in order to his marrying *Elfryd*, Daughter of the ſaid *Offa*, was, at the Inſtigation of *Quindreda*, Wife to *Offa*, treacherouſly murdered by that King; and buried at *Merden*, near *Sutton* aforeſaid. But, afterwards, his Body was removed, by the Murderer's Order, to *Hereford*. Soon after, a Tomb was built over him, and he gained the Reputation of a Saint; which drew Multitudes to the Place of his Burial, and proved the Cauſe of greatly enriching this Church and City; which, not long afterwards, became ſubject to the *Weſt-Saxon* Kings. *Athelſtan*, one of their Monarchs, forced the Princes of *Wales* to pay him for Tribute, 20 *lib* Weight of Gold, and 300 *lib.* of Silver, annually. But theſe *Antient Britons* bore this Impoſition but a ſhort Time: For *Griffin*, or *Griffith*, Prince of *South-Wales*, aſſiſted by *Algar*, a *Mercian* Lord, rebelled againſt *Edward* the *Confeſſor*; and having beaten the Army of *Ralph*, an Earl that was ſent againſt them, plundered the City, demoliſhed the Cathedral, and
carried

carried *Leofgar* the Bishop away. *Harold* afterwards fortified the City with a broad and high Rampart. At the *Norman* Invasion, this Place was in a low Condition; for, by *Doomsday Book*, it appears to have had but 103 Men, both within and without the Walls: But the *Normans* greatly improved and enlarged it, erecting a Castle near the River *Wye* where the Cathedral had stood, and then walled it.

The End of Vol. I.

ADVERTISEMENT.

THE Proprietors of this Undertaking moſt gratefully acknowledge the Encouragement they have hitherto met with from their kind Subſcribers: And alſo tender their beſt Thanks to thoſe curious and obliging Gentlemen, who have voluntarily favoured them with many excellent Materials towards the carrying it into Execution, which is the principal Reaſon for this Apology. For, theſe Materials being ſo numerous, and affording ſo much Variety, it is found impoſſible to digeſt and incorporate them with the Author's Labours, till towards the Beginning of the enſuing Winter. In the mean time, any thing tending to complete the Work, will be thankfully received by the Author (Poſt-paid) at Mr. *Flexney*'s, near *Grays-Inn-Gate, Holborn*.

Lightning Source UK Ltd.
Milton Keynes UK
UKHW022129060519
342211UK00008B/624/P